Counting the Dead

Counting the Dead

The Culture and Politics
of Human Rights Activism in Colombia

Winifred Tate

UNIVERSITY OF CALIFORNIA PRESS
Berkeley · Los Angeles · London

University of California Press, one of the most distinguished university presses in the United States, enriches lives around the world by advancing scholarship in the humanities, social sciences, and natural sciences. Its activities are supported by the UC Press Foundation and by philanthropic contributions from individuals and institutions. For more information, visit www.ucpress.edu.

University of California Press
Berkeley and Los Angeles, California

University of California Press, Ltd.
London, England

Library of Congress Cataloging-in-Publication Data

Tate, Winifred, 1970–.
  Counting the dead : the culture and politics of human rights activism in Colombia / Winifred Tate.
     p.   cm.   (California series in public anthropology ; 18)
  Includes bibliographical references and index.
  ISBN: 978-0-520-25282-0 (cloth : alk. paper)
  ISBN: 978-0-520-25283-7 (pbk. : alk. paper)
  1. Human rights advocacy—Colombia.   2. Political persecution—Colombia.   3. Colombia—Politics and Government—1974.   4. Colombia—Social conditions—1970.   I. Title.
  JC599.C7T38 2007
  323.09861—dc22   2007015639

Manufactured in the United States of America

16   15   14   13   12   11   10   09   08   07
10   9   8   7   6   5   4   3   2   1

This book is printed on New Leaf EcoBook 50, a 100% recycled fiber of which 50% is de-inked post-consumer waste, processed chlorine-free. EcoBook 50 is acid-free and meets the minimum requirements of ANSI/ASTM D5634-01 (Permanence of Paper).

For the many Colombian human rights defenders and their colleagues around the world who generously shared their reflections, hopes, and fears with me

And for Beatrice

Contents

Acknowledgments   ix

Abbreviations   xiii

Map of Colombia   xvii

Introduction   1

1. Colombia: Mapping the Eternal Crisis   31

2. Solidarity with Our Class Brothers: The First Wave
   of Colombian Human Rights Activism   72

3. The Production of Human Rights Knowledge and
   the Practice of Politics   107

4. The Emotional Politics of Activism in the 1990s   146

5. The Global Imaginaries of Colombian Activists at
   the United Nations and Beyond   175

6. State Activism and the Production of Impunity   215

7. Human Rights and the Colombian Military's War Stories   256

   Conclusion: The Politics of Human Rights Knowledge   290

Notes   307

Selected Bibliography   345

Index   371

Acknowledgments

Many more people than I can name here deserve my thanks and gratitude as they have accompanied me in research, reflection, and activism over the past eighteen years.

First, I could not have written this book without the support and intellectual prodding of the New York University Department of Anthropology, especially my adviser, Tom Abercrombie. Fred Myers, Margaret McLagan, Michael Taussig, and Sally Engle Merry provided critical comments. I was fortunate to find a writing group on my return from the field: many thanks to Jessica Cattelino, Omri Elisha, Ayse Parla, Elizabeth Smith, and especially Julie Chu, who offered support and comments until the bitter end. Leo Hsu has been a long-standing support in matters existential, intellectual, and technical. My colleagues at the Watson Institute for International Studies at Brown University provided an intellectual home during my fellowship in the Politics, Culture, and Identity Program. Among the many Brown colleagues who deserve my thanks are Peter Andreas, Keith Brown, James Der Derian, Cathy Lutz, Simone Pulver, and particularly Kay Warren. I have also benefited from thoughtful comments following public presentations of pieces of this work at the Watson Institute faculty seminar, the Pembroke Center at Brown University, the Anthropology of Media Lecture Series at Wellesley College, and the Department of Anthropology at the University of Texas at Austin. Ramiza Koya offered thoughtful comments on many drafts, as well as many hours of conversation and reflection; I have been fortunate to have had her outstanding editorial assistance. Lori Allen, Chuck Call, Arturo Carrillo, Robin Kirk, Eleanor Douglas, Juanita Sundberg, María Clemencia Ramírez, Mary Roldan, and Kimberly Theidon commented on parts of the manuscript when it was a work in process. I am also grateful for the comments of the two anonymous readers for the University of California Press, where Naomi Schneider has provided unfailing support. I deeply appreciate the work of the professional staff at the press, in particular Jacqueline Volin and Valerie Witte. I am especially grateful for the patient attention of the copy editor, Sheila Berg. Thanks to Annelise Grimm for her assistance in compiling the index.

Financial support for my fieldwork was provided by the Wenner Gren Foundation; a subsequent Peace Scholar Dissertation Fellowship from the U.S. Institute for Peace funded the writing process. My work as a research consultant for a number of organizations, including the Centre for Humanitarian Dialogue, the John Merk Fund, the Latin American Working Group, and the Lawyers Committee for Human Rights (now Human Rights First), provided both monetary support and the opportunity to engage with new issues and institutions. Earlier work for Human Rights Watch and UNICEF (many thanks to Bjorn Petterson, Robin Kirk, and Frank Smyth) also taught me a great deal about international research and advocacy and also subsidized research in Colombia.

During my fieldwork, I received institutional support from the Social Sciences Department of the Universidad de los Andes, the Colombian Institute of Anthropology and History (Instituto de Antropología e Historia), the Colombian Commission of Jurists (Comisión Colombiana de Juristas), and the Center for Grassroots Education and Research (Centro de Investigación y Educación Popular). I was fortunate to have the friendship and fresh perspectives of many journalists during my time in the field, including Steve Ambrose, Sibylla Brodzinsky, Steve Dudley, Doug Farah, Quil Lawrence, Jeremy McDermott, Karl Penhaul, and Kirk Semple. Volunteers with Peace Brigades International (PBI) and Witness for Peace offered their insights and analyses; during my fieldwork, PBI also provided housing during my trips to Barrancabermeja.

This work has been indelibly enriched by my friends and colleagues in the human rights community. While at the Washington Office on Latin America, I was extremely fortunate to have as colleagues Adriana Beltrán, Peter Clark, Rachel Farley, Laurie Freeman, Dave Mattingly, Rachel Neild, Eric Olson, Bill Spencer, Geoff Thale, George Vickers, and Coletta Youngers. Colleagues at the Colombia Steering Committee, especially Lisa Haugaard, Adam Isacson, and Alison Giffen, kept me laughing even as we lost most legislative battles. Many of the insights I have about international human rights work I learned from them. Ann Mason, Arlene Tickner, and Leslie Wirpsa offered wise counsel on adapting as an American woman in Colombia. Finally, among the others who deserve thanks for their sustaining friendship are Madeline Church, Mario Barbosa, Haidy Duque, Gloria Flórez, Daniel Garcia-Peña, Olga Gutierrez, Juan Ibañez, Alice Jay, Neil Jeffrey, James Lupton, Nancy Sanchez, Gabriel Rivera, and Xan Young.

My parents, Bill and Sue, and my sister, Frances, were unwilling witnesses from afar to the early years of my work in Colombia; they remain the best examples I know of intellectual curiosity and ethical commitment. Scott Beale arrived relatively late in the process but has rarely questioned my commitment to Colombia and human rights work. He has given me the best gifts of all: the space and time to write and reason to leave my study. My daughter, Beatrice, arrived two months after my book contract; hours of revising were lightened by her laugh, and her presence has infinitely improved my corner of this troubled world.

My greatest debt is to the Colombian human rights professionals who took time from their busy lives to offer their reflections. I am especially indebted to the activists who took me into their lives and hearts in the many years I have spent trying to find my way in Colombia. While the conclusions—and the errors—are my own, whatever wisdom is contained in these pages belongs to them.

Abbreviations

AAA	Alianza Americana Anticomunista (American Anticommunist Alliance)
ANAPO	Alianza Nacional Popular (National Popular Alliance)
ASFADDES	Asociación de Familiares de Detenidos y Desaparecidos (Association of Relatives of the Detained and Disappeared)
AUC	Autodefensas Unidas de Colombia (United Self-Defense Forces of Colombia)
CCJ	Comisión Colombiana de Juristas (Colombian Commission of Jurists)
CINEP	Centro de Investigación y Educación Popular (Center for Grassroots Education and Research)
CODHES	Consultoría para los Derechos Humanos y el Desplazamiento (Council on Human Rights and Displacement)
CONGO	Conference of Non-governmental Organizations in Consultative Relationship with the United Nations
CPDDH	Comité Permanente para la Defensa de los Derechos Humanos (Permanent Committee for the Defense of Human Rights; known as the Permanent Committee)

CREDHOS	Corporación Regional para los Derechos Humanos (Regional Human Rights Corporation)
CRS	Corriente de Renovación Socialista (Socialist Renovation Current)
CSPP	Comité en Solidaridad con los Presos Políticos (Committee in Solidarity with Political Prisoners)
DFID	Department for International Development
ECOSOC	United Nations Economic and Social Council
ELN	Ejército de Liberación Nacional (National Liberation Army)
EPL	Ejército Popular de Liberación (Popular Liberation Army)
FARC	Fuerzas Armadas Revolucionarias de Colombia (Revolutionary Armed Forces of Colombia)
HRW	Human Rights Watch
IAHRC	InterAmerican Human Rights Commission
ICRC	International Committee of the Red Cross
IHL	International humanitarian law
IPC	Instituto Popular de Capacitación (Grassroots Training Institute)
M-19	Movimiento 19 de Abril (April 19 Guerrilla Movement)
MINGA	Asociación para la Promoción Social Alternativa (Association for Alternative Social Education)
MORENA	Movimiento de Renovación Nacional (National Renovation Movement)
OIDHACO	Oficina Internacional de Derechos Humanos Acción Colombiana (International Office of Human Rights Action on Colombia)
PC	Partido Comunista (Communist Party)
PCML	Partido Comunista Marxista-Leninista (Marxist Leninist Communist Party)
PEPES	Perseguidos por Pablo Escobar (People Persecuted by Pablo Escobar)
UNHCHR	United Nations High Commissioner for Human Rights

UNIR	Unión Nacional de Izquierda Revolutionaria (National Revolutionary Leftist Union)
UP	Unión Patriótica (Patriotic Union)
URS	Unión Revolucionaria Socialista (Revolutionary Socialist Union)
USAID	U.S. Agency for International Development
USCR	U.S. Committee for Refugees
USO	Unión Sindical Obrera (oil workers' union)
VIDA	Comité Nacional de Víctimas de la Guerrilla (National Committee of Victims of the Guerrillas)
WOLA	Washington Office on Latin America

Colombia

Introduction

In fall 1994 I moved to Colombia to be a professional human rights activist. My qualifications were slim: eighteen months as a volunteer in Colombia during the late 1980s, a college degree in Latin American studies, assisting with political asylum cases in Texas, and six months in Guatemala bouncing through several ill-fated research projects. I yearned for the intense emotional rush of my first year in Colombia five years before, when I had found my way through the bewildering complexity of Bogotá as an anthropology student at the National University and an intern at the human rights office of a Jesuit grassroots think tank. Committed to a vague platform of social justice but suspicious of institutional politics, I believed that human rights activism offered a life of excitement without moral compromise.

My efforts to secure permanent employment with a Colombian non-governmental organization (NGO) were unsuccessful, however, so when I was offered the opportunity to work with a regional human rights committee located just a short plane flight from Bogotá, I swallowed my misgivings and packed my bags. For the past decade a rotating nucleus of activists had braved broiling tropical heat, official indifference, death threats, and the assassination of several of their members in the effort to document abuses committed by the army in pursuit of guerrillas nestled just out of sight in poor neighborhoods and rural hills. The committee was interested in developing an in-depth research project on the growth of paramilitary groups in the area, I was told. I suspected that they were more interested in the possibility of fostering international connections and the potential protection of having an American on staff, but absent a better offer and intrigued by the opportunity to spend some time on the front lines, I accepted.

I spent weeks alternating sweaty hours attempting to divine my purpose in the office and swimming laps in the cloudy pool of the one real hotel in town, finally coming to the realization of how complicated my new workplace was. The Colombian director of the committee, unwilling to confess her opinions to her local colleagues, sat with me for hours on the poured concrete steps of her small house as her young son raced up the hilly street. Omaira, a tall black woman whose open gaze belies her strong opinions, told me stories: about her youth as a radical student activist, fights with her husband over time spent in meetings away from home, the impossible hope of finding safe passage for vulnerable staff trapped by army movement in distant villages, and divisions over how to respond to the recent murder of a teenage girl by guerrillas as punishment for dating a policeman from the barrio.

The conversation that I remember most vividly from those days began when I asked about a trip to Europe the year before, during which Omaira had spent several weeks raising money and speaking about human rights. She had been impressed by the iconic role assigned to Isabel, the committee's secretary, who had been gunned down in front of the office three years before. Theories abounded about why Isabel had been killed. The then-director had published an editorial in the *New York Times* the day before Isabel's murder criticizing the military, and some said it was payback. Another senior staff member claimed the hit had been intended for her, a much better known activist with a similar hairstyle. A picture of Isabel, who is now venerated as the archetypal human rights victim, was featured on posters and published in international reports. To my surprise, Omaira objected to this celebration of Isabel. Of course she should be mourned, Omaira explained, but she wasn't one of us. Isabel had been a secretary, a member of a privileged class whose command of office machinery and protocol set her apart from the largely lower-class radical activists. She had simply followed the then-director from his law practice into human rights activism in office space he had donated to the committee. Though celebrated as a martyr killed for her beliefs, she was in fact just doing her job—and not very enthusiastically at that, Omaira said. She was not *comprometida*, committed to the ideals of social justice and radical transformation. Seeing

Isabel's face printed on posters and in reports made Omaira shake her head. They don't own our dead, she told me. The European activists can say what they want about the struggle, but we know what the real fight is.

I returned to Bogotá shortly thereafter, lured by the promise of a brief and lucrative consulting job that did not require any travel outside the capital, and more doubtful than ever that I could make sense of the complicated politics swirling around me. Although I did not know it at the time, Omaira returned to Europe later that year, this time to stay, fleeing death threats variously reported as originating from either the military or the guerrillas, possibly both.

I have never forgotten those stories in that sweltering town. More than office gossip, they, as well as countless hours of conversation with friends and colleagues, reached the heart of the questions that came to drive my research as I continued to work as a human rights researcher and advocate over the next decade. How did people come to have radically different ideas about the nature of human rights work, and how did these ideas shape their activism? What drove these activists to persist despite the dangers? What kinds of partnerships were forged among activists in Latin America, Europe, and the United States?

I examine these issues here by exploring how an idea—the idea of human rights—has been used in Colombia by different and sometimes competing groups to mobilize political action. This is not an intellectual history, tracing how ideas about human rights have emerged and evolved. Rather, I am interested in how these ideas have moved in the world. Beginning with the fact that they have been written into international treaties and covenants, I explore the wide range of ways that activists and human rights professionals have employed them to understand the experience of violence and generate public support for their aims. This is an ethnography of ideas in action: I explore the different ideas of what constitutes human rights violations and the daily practices of human rights professionals.

Colombia, given the increase in both political violence and human rights bureaucracies over the past decade, offers an unfortunately ideal opportunity to study activism by human rights organizations. Institutions using the rights framework remain bitterly divided over its interpretation. Colombian governmental human rights offices portray themselves as being a part of weak institutions and offer a diffuse notion of rights as "everyone's responsibility." The human rights offices of the

Colombian military produce diverging rights narratives, at once attacking human rights NGOs as politically motivated subversive groups and embracing a rights discourse that represents their own forces as victims. NGOs have been divided over what kind of violence to include in the rights framework, debating whether simply to address acts carried out by state agents, as defined in international legal human rights norms, or to adopt the additional frame of international humanitarian law, which covers violence by guerrilla groups as well. Few human rights groups address the fact that the vast majority of violence in Colombia is not included in the rights framework at all; for example, more than 85 percent of violent deaths are generally classified as common crime.

This study does not focus on acts of violence themselves—I do not attempt an exhaustive recounting of Colombian violence or human rights violations—but on the process of classifying certain kinds of violence as human rights violations and on human rights activism itself as a critical site for generating collective identities, relationships, and social obligations. Violence is a slippery category that has been used to describe an expanding universe of experiences ranging from name calling to structural poverty. Here, my focus is on violence understood as physical harm to another, or the threat of such harm.

Human rights violation is a category that makes violence socially legible, understood by the public to establish accountability and locate specific acts within broader histories. Classifying violence is a contested and complicated business, producing both cultural meaning and material rewards for those who can impose their interpretations on violent acts. This work—the production of knowledge about violence—is of particular urgency because of the high stakes involved in authenticating specific versions of history and facilitating specific outcomes. Other categories in the taxonomy of violence include combat, common crime, domestic disputes, and organized crime. These categories are comparable to the concept of frames used by sociologists and social movement scholars to describe how participants organize their experiences and justify their actions. Rather than focus on competing frames, or changes in frames over time, I examine the use of the same frame—human rights—by different groups. I demonstrate that different social actors can use this frame to advance profoundly different ideological projects. For all the Colombian human rights professionals I discuss here, the focus is on how to protect human lives. However, their ideas of which human lives to give priority and how best to achieve their protection result from widely divergent views on the nature of power, on understandings of the role of the state, and on the origin and possible resolution of the Colombian conflict.

Human rights activism draws on the international legal standards enshrined in multilateral treaties and documents that hold the individual as the ultimate rights-bearing subject. This activism, regardless of the focus, shares a repertoire of practices. These include the public reporting of wrongs to spur social action, or denunciation (Sp. *denuncia*), and an orientation toward an amorphous international public sphere, an imagined foreign public of governments, international agencies, multilateral institutions, and transnational social movements. For all the actors involved in these debates, human rights activism is a means of achieving international legitimacy, as well as cultural and material resources, for their divergent political projects. In Colombia, groups using the human rights framework include nongovernmental activists identified with the left, governmental agencies mired in bureaucracy but striving to embody the modern ideal of the nation-state, and military officers incorporating human rights language into existing institutional culture as part of their military strategy.

According to international standards, human rights claims are made against the state; the state is party to the multilateral treaties that enshrine rights, and it is the state as an institution that promises specific protections to its citizens. In the making of human rights claims, activists thus articulate their vision of the ideal state and the kinds of relationships that should exist between state and citizen. Nongovernmental activists work to create a public imaginary of a state invoking the Weberian ideal of a state monopoly on violence. Though relatively powerless, these activists use human rights claims as a means to force state representatives to claim responsibility for abuses and thus enact an accountable state. In their human rights practice, state agents emphasize the power of social and economic relationships that foster violence outside of the state; for them, human rights practice both reinforces state institutional power and undermines the state's claim to legitimacy by acknowledging its failure to effectively monopolize violence. Military officials involved in human rights programs argue that a state under attack is not obligated to uphold human rights obligations that would protect the enemy but only those standards that will advance the expansion of state authority. For all these actors, the imagined state is not contained within the human rights standards themselves but is expressed through the practice of human rights activism and the articulation of certain kinds of political claims.

LEGAL FRAMEWORKS

While efforts to codify rights dates back centuries, the modern history of human rights begins with the signing of the Universal Declaration of Human Rights in 1948. U.S. diplomats, working with other international delegates and writing in the shadow of World War II and the Jewish Holocaust, authored the Declaration as one of the founding documents of the United Nations, which had been formally established three years earlier (Brucken 1999; Donnelly 1993). The Declaration lays out in thirty articles universal minimal standards for the "inherent dignity and the equal and inalienable rights of all members of the human family." Later U.N. treaties codified a series of additional rights frameworks, including social, cultural, and economic rights and the collective rights of indigenous peoples (Ishay 1997).

The Universal Declaration of Human Rights, the foundational text of the human rights movement, is a product of the United Nations, a collection of states that have signed a series of treaties and covenants committing themselves to protect the rights of citizens. For activists working within this framework, only states can violate human rights, as only states have the obligation to protect them. Heinous acts committed by private citizens are considered common crimes, and it is the responsibility of the state to investigate and prosecute those responsible. But when it is the state agents themselves who commit these acts, citizens have no recourse, so the international human rights system emerged to address them. Activists confronting totalitarian or authoritarian states, whose leaders cement their own absolute power at the expense of their citizens, used this focus on state agents to bring international attention to their cause.

International humanitarian law (IHL) is used by activists or nonstate actors hoping to prompt redress during wartime. Also known as the rules of war, international humanitarian law dates from the 1899 Convention with Respect to the Laws and Customs of War on Land, adopted at the Hague to formalize generally accepted principles prohibiting mistreatment of soldiers hors de combat and protecting civilians and civilian targets. After World War II, in 1949, the Geneva Conventions established certain acts as war crimes and further stipulated the treatment to be accorded civilians and combatants during wartime. In 1977 the two Geneva protocols were enacted to expand their reach (Neier 1998). The first added to the list of offenses considered war crimes; the second expanded the Convention to include internal conflicts. Though the idea of human rights has passed into much wider general circulation, these treaties have been used primarily by humanitarian groups aiding victims of war, most famously in the development of the International Red Cross.

In some cases the differences between war crimes and human rights violations are clear. When a cop beats a suspect while questioning him, that is a human rights violation: a state agent abuses the power he holds over other citizens, particular to him as a state agent, in the course of his professional duties. When Japanese soldiers raped and killed women in Nanking, China, in 1937, this event was a war crime: during an invasion of one nation-state by another, soldiers abused civilians. Peacetime is clearly established by the absence of war, and wars are fought between clearly defined nation-states in combat operations.

In many cases, however, the circumstances are not so clear, and neat legal divisions are hard to maintain. Civil wars, entrenched conflicts, and even such amorphous struggles as the "cold war" and the "war on terror" blur the lines between peacetime and wartime, making the categorization of abuses more difficult. At what point does the emergence of localized armed groups become a civil war? How do the amorphous security threats of the turn of the twenty-first century—drug trafficking, illegal immigration, terrorism—fit into the framework of war? Activists, policy makers, and scholars have yet to define consensus positions on these issues, complicating the debates surrounding how and why human rights frameworks should be applied.

BEYOND LEGAL FRAMEWORKS

Many of the current debates about human rights focus on philosophical and legal issues. Where do rights come from? Are rights really universal? How do rights affect issues of sovereignty? Historians are beginning to explore how different rights have been bundled together at different times. Lynn Hunt (1966) has shown, for example, that the current linkage of civil and political rights did not exist in nineteenth-century debates over, for example, voting (not granted to women) and property ownership (granted to women). Contemporary human rights activism remains marked by the cold war politics that divided rights into two categories, with their respective super-power backers: individual civil and political rights, defended through official U.S. activism against Soviet persecution of political dissidents, and economic and cultural rights, defended through the Soviet Union's military and economic support of liberation movements around the world. How this division affected activists attempting to transform diverse national contexts has been part of all accounts of Latin American activism and is only now being explored in terms of struggles in other places, such as the movements to desegregate the American South (Anderson 2003).

Even discussions that do not explicitly focus on the legal and philosophical rights debates issues often take the international legal framework for human rights as the center of their inquiries. This is particularly true for the current discussion of the kind of subjectivities produced by rights activism. Employing the rights framework is part of the neoliberal package, some scholars argue, and necessarily leads to the production of atomized subjectivities, focused on the individual rather than the collective (Brown 2004; Spivak 2004). Many of those writing in this vein are especially troubled by the use of the rights framework by governments to justify military action. They provide important histories of the legal and philosophical roots of rights discourses and examine ideologically troubling uses of rights talk. However, to conclude that these examples encompass the entire universe of possibilities presented by rights talk is to fail to historicize evolving rights activism in the United States and beyond, as well as the ways in which, like many flexible frames used to mobilize political action, rights talk can be employed to multiple ideological ends.

The approach taken by scholars exploring the multiple registers of rights activism is useful for ethnographic histories of rights activism such as mine. For example, scholars working with Sally Merry and Peggy Levitt's project examining the localization of women's rights discourses have found that there are at least four distinct human rights discourses: legal focused (centered on documents and enforcement and characterized by instrumentalism), process focused (stressing participation, accountability, and transparency), values focused (in which human rights are felt to be aspirational, holistic, principled, and normative), and social change focused (incorporating social movement activism and a critique of law, offering a vision of the just society and how to get there) (Yoon and Serban 2006: 29). Though I do not follow this template of discourse clusters, I am interested in exploring precisely how the multiple uses of rights discourses by Colombian activists have evolved over time, how nongovernmental activists have drawn on a repertoire of political action developed by several generations of Latin American activists, and how state agents have employed rights discourses to serve their own bureaucratic and ideological interests.

The stated intention of much human rights activism as practiced in the

United States over the past three decades has been to reveal the secrets of hidden violence, connecting observers to violent abuses and inspiring their action to prevent it; such activism relies on the assumption that witnessing results in understanding and requires response. In this paradigm, the revelation of the unknown acts upon us, and the changes wrought by knowledge require action. Knowledge transforms both our internal selves and our relations in the world and brings with it responsibility to bear witness to that knowledge in the world and take action. Often this action is framed in terms of the connection between victims and the newly knowledgeable and organized according to the categories most likely to inspire response: citizens shocked to learn their government could be complicit in human rights violations; Christians moved to act by the persecution of their religious brethren; mothers unwilling to stand by while other mothers plead for their sons; and others, aligned by profession (doctors, journalists, lawyers) or activist identities (gays and lesbians, labor, leftists). This paradigm of transformative witnessing is a fundamental tenet of numerous varieties of Christianity, and many human rights organizations have roots in church-based organizations.

These ideas about the relationship between knowledge and action have resulted in, among other things, a presentational genre and political activist repertoire with deep roots in American and European political and religious traditions.[1] For more than a century, abolitionist campaigns, temperance movements, suffragists, and reformers of all stripes appealed to possible adherents with literally missionary zeal. Organizations such as Amnesty International, often described as an almost spontaneous response to the news of injustices in the world, have deep roots in these histories of activism (Clark 2001; Hopgood 2006; Power 2001; Rabben 2002).[2] Other episodes in this history include antislavery and, later, antilynching campaigns (Crawford 2002; Hochschild 2005); Roger Casement's efforts to raise awareness about mistreatment and torture of indigenous slave labor in the rubber trade at the turn of the twentieth century in Putumayo (Taussig 1987); international concern about colonial abuses in the Belgian Congo (Hochschild 1999); and campaigns to free the Scottsboro Boys (nine black men falsely imprisoned for rape), the Italian anarchists Nicola Sacco and Bartolomeo Vanzetti, and Ethel and Julius Rosenberg (Rabben 2002).

A comprehensive history of Latin American human rights activism has yet to be written. These activist groups have developed rich and varied experiences over the past four decades, and several important generalizations can be made about the development of the repertoire of human rights practice that inspired Colombian activists. The brutal repression that followed the military dictatorships of the Southern Cone inspired the first human rights networks (Paraguay in 1954, Brazil in 1964, Chile and Uruguay in 1973, and Argentina in 1976).[3] For them, and for subsequent generations of activists, authoritarian states were the target of activism focusing on the state as the central actor in political violence.[4] Activists employed human rights discourses as a response, in reaction to political violence. Strong personal networks were crucial, as was the support of transnational institutions such as the Catholic Church. Most groups emerged from complex oppositional political cultures, including political and solidarity activists fighting for widespread social transformation, with complicated legacies for postdemocracy and postconflict human rights groups. Human rights practice included documentation and public reporting of abuses, material aid to victims and their families, popular, or grassroots, education efforts, and street protests and marches. Many groups also employed the use of symbolic actions to maintain the images of the dead, disappeared, or imprisoned in public space. Creative legal innovations, including the development of the United Nations and Organization of American States (OAS) human rights mechanisms, remain characteristic of ongoing activism.[5]

The relationship between United States and Latin America is fundamental to the development of rights activism on the continent. Human rights discourses have been used to contest the actions of repressive Latin American governments but also the policies of the neocolonial power that supported those governments, in this case the United States. As in the boomerang model of human rights activism, developed by Margaret Keck and Kathryn Sikkink (1998), activists called on the U.S. government to put pressure on Latin American governments to improve their practices, but they also used human rights discourses to pressure the U.S. government to change its own policies supporting those governments. For many based in the United States, the U.S. government's support of repressive regimes with taxpayer dollars made these issues not an abstract international concern but directly connected to their identities as citizens.[6]

EMBEDDED ANTHROPOLOGY: POSITIONING IN THE FIELD

The intersections of multiple understandings of activism, and the relationships between activists in the United States and Latin America, are of particular interest to me because of my experience as a human rights researcher and advocate and my decision to focus my academic research on human rights activism. Over the past fifteen years, I experienced and participated in human rights activism from within a number of institutions and from varying positions of power. After graduating from high school, I lived in Colombia from 1988 to 1989, where I was a volunteer intern at a human rights organization. After graduating from college, I returned to Bogotá in 1994 and stayed through 1996 to do volunteer work with women displaced by political violence; I also worked as a consultant with Colombian human rights groups, Human Rights Watch, and UNICEF. After completing the coursework for my master's degree, I accepted a full-time position with the Washington Office on Latin America (WOLA), an advocacy organization that lobbies to change U.S. foreign policy. After two years, I completed my Ph.D. coursework and exams while continuing to work part-time in Washington. At WOLA I wrote policy memos, conducted research trips and led delegations to Colombia, briefed members of Congress, and gave innumerable media interviews, including appearances on CNN, Frontline, and BBC television, and was quoted in the *New York Times* and the *Washington Post,* among others. Since then I have worked as a research consultant with a number of organizations, including the Centre for Humanitarian Dialogue, the Latin America Working Group, and Human Rights First.

My interactions and knowledge were shaped by my previous relationships and by having been embedded in activist processes. This does not mean that when I returned to Colombia everyone recognized me or that they were unable to distinguish between my new agenda and my previous work. However, these experiences did profoundly influence my analysis of human rights activism and my perspective on the history of Colombian human rights institutions. Rather than focus on a single institution, I emphasize the connections and networks operating between and among institutions. Rather than see the "international" and the "local" as separate and distinct spheres of activism, I focus on the ways activism is a spectrum of evolving practices. Rather than view power as static and unidirectional, I explore power as fluid and relational, in the microdynamics of individual encounters and the macrodynamics of institutional positioning.

From the time I entered graduate school, the relationship between my professional and academic experience generated conflicting reactions, including my own uncertainty about how to integrate academic research with policy activism. Some academics were less than sympathetic to my insistence that advocacy experience would enrich my scholarship, viewing participation in policy debates as at best unintellectual and at worst producing second-rate scholarship. Others dismissed my concerns about the compatibility and contradictions presented by combining theoretical and applied research, insisting that academic research could be easily incorporated in advocacy campaigns.

As I prepared for my departure for fieldwork, the impact of my previous work with the very institutions I was now preparing to study was impossible to ignore, and I searched for inspiration among scholars who focused on the practice of anthropology. The school of reflexive ethnography that flourished during the 1980s offered often-scathing critiques of the colonial legacy of anthropology, which imagined an ethnographic encounter that erased the role of governmental and colonial authority in guaranteeing access. Scholars of this school offered useful meditations on the impact of ethnographers' ethnicity, race, and national identity on the research they carried out (Altorki and Fawzi El-Solh 1988; Behar 1993; Rosaldo 1989). I sought suggestions for fieldwork practice in the works of scholars advocating "studying up," the use of ethnographic methods to study powerful elites (Gusterson 1997, 2000; Nadar 1969, 1997), and "homework," the study of anthropologists' home countries in the West (Visweswaran 1994), as well as in the work of medical anthropologists, who perform the institutional tasks involved in the practice of medicine but also write from the distanced observer perspective of anthropology (Das et al. 2000; Farmer 1992).

Taking the ethnographic method into new arenas of transnational bureaucratic practice required considering issues of access and location in new ways, and I was unsure what the "participant" part of participant observer fieldwork would look like when the field was not a village but a network of institutions. Some of the central contributions of ethnography—the focus on the construction of meaning by participants and the critical examination of practice rather than simply outcomes—can provide insights into the workings of contemporary institutions and organizations. Yet the structures of such institutions and the policing of their boundaries can make ethnographic research extremely difficult to carry out.

The concept that best seemed to address these issues was embedded ethnography, which I first heard discussed in a paper presented by Stephen Jackson at a seminar on studies of humanitarian aid. This concept highlights the issues of institutional positioning as a central factor in the production of knowledge about modern transnational processes. Ethnographers assuming positions within institutions not simply as academics but also as participants in different kinds of institutional practices over time can enrich, rather than degrade and debase, anthropological analyses. From his own experience as an aid worker in Africa, his research in the Congo, and his current position at the Social Science Research Council, Jackson noted the need to capture "compound talk," the conversations that reveal both the contradictions and the critical analysis occurring within apparently monolithic institutions. Ethnography that included research "embedded" in institutions could illuminate "the dialectical relationship between 'head quarters' and field, principles, policy and practice" and explore "how the changing external environment is internalized and enacted within organizations."[7] I found the phrase tremendously useful for thinking about my own ethnographic practice and my complex positioning within the institutions that I studied.

As a play on the then-current phrase "embedded journalists," widely used to describe the reporters who traveled with U.S. military units during the 2003 invasion of Iraq, the idea of embedded ethnography is deliberatively provocative. By using it, I do not intend for the discussion of anthropological methodology in the twenty-first century to be derailed into a fruitless debate over the role of the media in that conflict. Rather, I want to focus on the partial nature of any account and the ways in which perspective is limited through the institutional positioning of the research. These observations are hardly revelations to the discipline, but they are worth keeping in mind, particularly given the methodological difficulties inherent in research in complex transnational bureaucracies.

In stressing the "embedded" and insider nature of my research, I do not want to suggest that I went—or could have gone—native. While proud of my Colombian vocabulary and pleased on the occasions when my Colombian colleagues would introduce me as "almost Colombian," I never denied or doubted my identity as an American. During my first years in Colombia, as I was trained as an activist by Colombians immersed in the leftist culture I explore in chapter 3, I experienced the "stranger effect" that is the hallmark of traditional ethnographic research. Many of the insights and questions I developed about human rights activists first occurred to me during those early years, as I was struck by the differences in the activist culture I encountered in Colombia and the assumptions I brought from the United States. Undoubtedly, engaging with these issues as an activist as well as an ethnographer has transformed my own political consciousness and identity. While my focus is on Colombian activists and institutions, some part of these personal transformations are also present here.

My work history was crucial to gaining access to Colombian NGOs. Two prominent human rights NGOs agreed to sponsor my research, the Center for Grassroots Education and Research (CINEP), founded in 1974 by Jesuits, and the Colombian Commission of Jurists (CCJ). I had first interned with CINEP's human rights office in 1989. Their human rights team provides assistance to local human rights groups across the country and offers human rights education workshops. CCJ publishes yearly human rights reports and provides legal assistance to victims of human rights violations and has led Colombian NGO lobbying efforts before the U.N. Human Rights Commission. Both offered letters supporting my research and facilitated interviews with staff. My history of collaboration with Colombian NGOs was instrumental in gaining initial contacts with almost all the persons I interviewed.

This is not to suggest, however, that I enjoyed free passage within these organizations because of my history. The executive director of CINEP refused to approve my attendance as an observer at staff meetings. Staff members at other institutions also voiced concerns about my presence and observation of possibly sensitive material. In part, this was the result of the general fear of persecution lived by human rights NGOs. Widespread rumors of infiltration by spies for armed groups and widely believed stories of governmental informants' involvement in the assassination of several prominent human rights activists during the late 1990s contributed to these fears. Immediately before and during my research, two foreign graduate students were accused of misrepresenting their research and undermining, possibly jeopardizing, the human rights work of the organizations they studied. I was well aware that my presence generated significant concern. Numerous people confided that they were willing to speak with me and allow me into their offices and homes only because of the trust generated by my previous experience.

The military was the institution with which I had the least "embedded" relationship, other than in the broadest sense of being engaged on different sides of the same debate. I was concerned, however, about conducting research into an institution that I often criticized in press statements and written reports (Tate 1997, 2003). But even with this notoriously closed institution, I relied on my network of contacts built through my professional experience. As a research analyst for WOLA from 1998 to 2001, I had met with a number of Colombian colonels and generals. During trips of the military high command to Washington, the Colombian ambassador would summon a small group of NGO representatives to the embassy's conference room where we would trade interpretations of the Colombian conflict, often with veiled accusations of lack of impartiality or outright falsehoods. While in Colombia I would meet officers at the Defense Ministry, or in local battalions, to raise concerns about specific human rights cases and ask probing questions of their views of human rights.

Because of my consistent criticism of the military's human rights record and lobbying against additional military aid, the military's supporters often accused me of not understanding the armed forces, of failing to take into account the difficulties of battle and the armed forces' historic alienation from power. Thomas Marks, a former U.S. Army Special Forces officer and a counterinsurgency expert (and correspondent for *Solider of Fortune* magazine) summarized these concerns in a note he passed me when we appeared on a panel together at Boston University. "If HR groups want to up their credibility, they *must* begin to ground their analyses in the realities of the situation, particularly numbers, time and space," he wrote. "What they present now is like academic theory which attempts to impose itself on data. Cynically, I *know* they will not do so—it goes against their organizational imperatives" (Marks, pers. com. 2000; original emphasis). While I knew that many would question my ability to view the Colombian military objectively, I was intrigued by the opportunity to understand these officers on their own terms. When I explained my new project, Marks graciously sent me copies of his *Soldier of Fortune* articles and spent several hours talking with me in a suburban Virginia Starbucks about his travels with the Colombian military.

My first real military interview occurred haphazardly, organized over my objections. Although I had intended to interview Colombian military officials since arriving in Bogotá, the idea of sitting down with armed officers as an academic researcher and asking them about human rights unsettled me. I worried that they would remember my history of activism and accuse me of going undercover, perhaps even detain me for interrogation. But my concerns were wildly misplaced, as I learned during a trip to a human rights forum in a small riverside town midway through my fieldwork. As I sat, wedged in a patch of shade, against the wall with several Spanish human rights volunteers, a government lawyer I had interviewed several times approached me. "Hey, let me introduce my brother," he said, jokingly referring to the incessant gossip and speculation among NGOs of secret communications between the lawyer and the colonel in charge of counterinsurgency operations in the area because they shared a last name. "No, that's OK, maybe later," I said, in a transparent show of cowardice. I was not sure that I was ready for such an introduction, or how to manage my public associations that day. Always calculating the possible repercussions of any witnessed proximity, I attempted to circulate among the government officials, NGO activists, and international volunteers at this public event, although I was sure my allegiances, real or imagined, had already been broadcast (I was staying in the house of the international volunteers and spent my days traveling among the NGO offices). The lawyer brought the colonel to my side, and as I struggled to gracefully stand up he pumped my outstretched hand enthusiastically. "Come by any time," he said. "We are always eager to talk." I took him at his word, and later that week he spent several hours talking with me in his office.

Emboldened by my initial success, I began exploring my military contacts. At WOLA I had periodically met with civilian military analysts, and I called on them now and explained my new research project. They offered me the telephone numbers of some of the well-known retired generals who now spent their time writing op-eds, commenting on current events, and advising politicians. From journalist and NGO friends I got the names and numbers of colonels in far-flung battalions and began cold-calling them, using my unpronounceable, undeniably Anglo name and "la Universidad de Nueva York" to get my foot in the door. I took the colonel's breezy offer to help me any way he could as an invitation to visit his new posting in a southern town and, to his evident surprise, showed up for a three-day visit.

I also prepared an official letter to the Ministry of Defense, requesting permission to attend human rights training programs. One of the U.S. embassy's human rights officers provided me with the name and contact number of a former staff member of the International Red Cross, now working for the military's human rights program, and I arranged for a meeting. While initially welcoming, she was never able to procure for me the official permission and military transportation to visit the military's human rights course at the southern base of Tolemida. The military interviews I obtained were developed through my contacts.

The chapters that follow are based on my previous experience and the fieldwork I conducted between November 2001 and December 2002. While based in Bogotá, I conducted research in four other Colombian cities and spent a month observing the United Nations Human Rights Commission in Geneva, Switzerland. I visited six battalions in five cities. I attended NGO human rights workshops and public forums in which human rights activism was debated and performed, as well as two human rights conferences organized by the military, a program organized for international human rights days, and a conference on the Inter-American human rights system organized by the Defense Ministry. I conducted life history interviews with more than forty nongovernmental human rights activists, as well as open-ended interviews with numerous other NGO activists, officials from the Ministry of the Interior, the Foreign Ministry, and the National Human Rights Ombudsman's Office (Defensoría del Pueblo) and U.N. officials in Colombia and Geneva. I spoke with six retired generals, the result of a "snowballing" list of names chosen because of their leadership role in current debates on military policy, and with more than fifteen active duty military officers. These interviews ranged in length from twenty minutes to over two hours; most were tape-recorded but all included off-the-record discussions.

I collected extensive files on human rights reporting in the Colombian media and reviewed NGO archives. I also collected newspaper articles on human rights issues from the Human Rights Database Project of Justicia y Paz (Justice and Peace) and CINEP, which has organized clipping files from all Colombia's major newspapers since 1991, and reviewed special interest magazines (including *Alternativa,* a leftist journal, and publications by the Colombian Armed Forces) for articles on human rights issues. I consulted Colombian military human rights course materials and human rights reports published by military human rights offices. Through the Low-Intensity Conflict and Colombia document collections at the National Security Archives, I was able to consult declassified U.S. embassy and military documents. I gathered copies of Colombian congressional debates on human rights issues and specific legislation (including Law 288, allowing for state reparations in human rights cases and the debates surrounding the adoption of the Geneva Convention Protocols). I also collected reports by NGOs such as Amnesty International, Human Rights Watch, and Colombian groups, government reports from Colombian civilian and military human rights offices, and U.N. office reports.

STUDYING UP, DOWN, AND AROUND

I arrived in Bogotá for my fieldwork on November 9, 2001. Almost fifteen years earlier I had shared a tiny two-room house perched on a hill above the bustling downtown in a working-class neighborhood built a century before to house brewery workers. Before departing Washington, I had signed a lease faxed to me by a friend for an apartment in the exclusive Torres del Parque building complex, an architectural landmark overlooking Bogotá's bullring, home to Colombia's intellectual bohemian elite, and only four blocks from the tiny house where my original roommate still lived. The friend who helped with my lease was from one of Colombia's oldest political families, a former cabinet member, and one of a new generation of cosmopolitan elites. Among his siblings were an artist in New York, a lesbian activist in Norway, and a bartender in Washington; his cousins included a senior editor of Colombia's major newspaper and an anchor on the evening news. While I conducted interviews, he directed an NGO, ran for Congress, and managed the presidential campaign of the democratic left candidate (now mayor of Bogotá); he would occasionally invite me to join them for long weekend lunches, bodyguards included. This life was a world away from those early years of student poverty.

Similarly, during my time in Colombia, I had gone from an unpaid intern to a staff member of a well-regarded Washington-based organization. Several of the people I interviewed for this project had first met me when I was nineteen years old and barely conversant in Spanish. I got to know many others while trying to make ends meet doing consulting jobs while living in Colombia during the mid-1990s. Some saw me as being very powerfully positioned, with access to highly desirable international organizations and funders; others viewed my failure to find a permanent position as evidence of my general inadequacy. Over time, my personal and professional relationships with people changed. Some friendships deepened while others faded; some differences were resolved while others grew. I saw people and issues from multiple perspectives as time passed and I moved through different institutional positions, and I saw how people's attitudes toward me changed.

Returning to Colombia as an ethnographer once again changed my status. No longer in an international advocacy position, I had to rely on the personal connections I had made and the recognition that I retained many previous institutional connections. Working at WOLA had allowed me to expand my contacts in Colombia. During my frequent trips, I talked with academics, policy analysts, journalists, embassy personnel, and government officials. I was seen as a valuable commodity because, regardless of my position on human rights topics, I offered an "insider's view" of Washington. Everyone I talked to was interested in understanding the dynamics of policy debates in Congress and governmental agencies, and I could offer them my perspective. By the time I returned as a graduate student interested in asking an entirely new series of questions,

I had developed a reputation as someone who could traffic in useful information. Being known as a political actor in my own right, as someone who could contribute useful insights and knowledge, was critical to gaining interviews with many high-status people. During the course of my fieldwork, I interviewed former cabinet members, congressional representatives, a former president, and executive directors of NGOs; many of these people had Ph.D.'s from international universities, numerous graduate degrees, high-ranking positions, and extremely limited time.

Paradoxically, my status as an American from the United States played an important role in my ability to gain access to people within closed institutions by serving as transparent evidence of my ignorance and lack of connections to Colombia. Because I was from the United States, not organically connected to partisan debates, each Colombian had the opportunity to instruct me in the ways of Colombia. Gender also played into this equation: many government officials and all the military officers reacted to me as a woman, commenting on my physical appearance and generally appearing pleased with themselves for being able to explain such complicated issues to such a "lovely young woman." Despite my discomfort, I exploited these reactions for greater access; like Jennifer Schirmer during her interviews with Guatemalan military officers, I was "assumed to be in need of instruction in the male world of security matters" (Schirmer 1998). But while gender certainly shaped my interactions, it was my "Americanness" that got me in the door. My physical self, like my blue U.S. passport, was a constant reminder of the privileged weight attached to the idea of "America." While Colombians were assumed partisan and thus suspect, I was granted free passage, expected to inquire and advise as part of a general category of imperial American. I am sure that for many Colombians, the carefully policed distinctions among U.S. embassy personnel, journalists, human rights activists, and academics blurred together as we blustered our path through security checkpoints, watchful secretaries, and Byzantine bureaucracies to announce our opinions and demand details.

This account of the history of Colombian human rights activism focuses on the power of stories to shape action and define possibilities. My retelling of it is grounded ethnographically, examining the people who tell the stories and the space of individual encounter, between peasant and bureaucrat, between activist and U.N. official. This focus on individual agency, however, should not obscure the ways in which particular stories are promoted by institutions and circulated among nations and their representatives. These stories illuminate the workings of structural power, "manifest in relationships that not only operate within settings and domains but also organizes and orchestrates the settings themselves, and that specifies the direction and distribution of energy flows" (Wolf 1999: 25). Considering the stories that institutional representatives tell about their own work and relationships allows an exploration of the relational power between institutions: how U.N. officials can be both extremely powerful in the eyes of community leaders and powerless before their U.S. congressional funders.

This zooming perspective, focusing close-in for detailed descriptions of events and conversations while drawing back for transnational institutional mapping, offers a more complete understanding of the dynamic of activism. There is a danger of vertigo in the shifts: attempting to track multiple processes and perspectives can leave analyst and reader dizzy. By using a variety of ethnographic and expository techniques from a range of disciplines, I hope to keep such dizziness to a minimum. The voices of people within these institutions, expressing their ambiguous positioning, paradoxical activism, and evolving practice over time keep both lived experience and institutional structure within the frame. Our collective accounts of violence must include both historical roots and the individual authors.

ETHICS AND POLITICS

This is by no means a complete retelling; among the notable absences are the voices of victims and illegal armed actors. In part this was a security issue. I did not believe it would be safe during my fieldwork to spend the amount of time required with these groups to adequately address their views. Primarily, however, this reflects my choice in defining the scope of my project. The effort to make violence part of coherent national stories is not limited to the victims and perpetrators. My study is not about the experience of violence but public efforts by human rights professionals to classify violent events. I did interview members of one group of armed actors, the Colombian Armed Forces. As a group legally constituted to engage in combat operations, finding and interviewing military officers did not pose legal issues. More important, I did not focus on their attitude toward human rights from the perspective of a party in the conflict but as a group of self-proclaimed human rights professionals.

Like all Colombians, everyone described in my narrative has lived with violence. Small-town activists and local human rights officials face daily confrontations with men with guns, military men go into combat, well-known human rights activists and national bureaucrats confront the distorted voice threatening from the end of the phone line. But this is not a story about those experiences or about the victims, to whom the experience of violence most completely belongs. Such a story would require a distinct kind of fieldwork, located in other spaces, asking different questions of other people.

Part of my argument is that the story of violence does not belong just to the victims; it belongs to all society. As a society, we make collective sense of these acts. As history and as the present, we assign them meaning. National narratives of violence are crucial for refashioning national identities after violent conflict (Osiel 2000; Stern 2004). These debates over collective violence usually focus on the motive of the perpetrator. Is it a crime of passion, self-defense, elimination of a national enemy? Defining the motive of the perpetrator allows for the creation of consensus about reincorporating—or not—violent actors into the national body politic. The most visible public debates on these issues have occurred regarding the truth commissions established throughout Latin America following sustained political violence (Hayner 2001).

This process of making meaning out of violence is necessarily incomplete. The personal experience of violence, the excess of meaning and inevitable sorrow no matter the motives, is often at odds with this national meaning. The parents of a dead child, the wife or husband left behind, do not primarily feel the meaning of their loss as defined by the motive of the perpetrator but by the meaning of the victim in their lives. For the perpetrators themselves, the experience of motive is rarely pure. Motives are hard to parse, difficult to determine. The soldier after combat may be plagued with nightmares and bitter visions of the enemy he has killed even while being celebrated as a national hero of a just war. Perpetrators have different roles and identities and participate in multiple social processes. The boundaries between actors may be fluid, as individuals move from one category of perpetrator to another. In the Colombian case, guerrillas are involved in domestic disputes, paramilitaries in drug trafficking, the soldier in corruption. The guerrilla commander becomes a paramilitary, or the soldier a guerrilla.

Violence, and the romance of danger, has become part of Colombian identity and the *berraquera*—defiant courage—to navigate its dangerous shoals a badge of pride. Celebrated with Colombians' famous black humor, the willingness to stand up and fight is literally a double-edged sword, as the creative and competitive spark fueling Colombian art and business also lights the flame of conflict. To be *muy viva*—literally, very alive—is to be sly, sharp, on the make and on the move. For most observers, violence appears to be the constant backdrop, the context in which all other discussions—politics, love, travel, business, painting, or poetry—occur. Violence becomes *the* problem of Colombia, the central issue that plagues the body politic, for which other conditions—weak state, repressive state, excessive wealth, poverty, inequality—are offered as explanations. Each individual death is explained as *algo debía,* something was owed.

Of course, Colombians also resent this relentless focus on violence and ongoing assessment of their national character. The focus is distorting, blurring the contours of everyday life, the ebb and flow of sleeping, waking, eating, working, playing that occupies the vast majority of the nation's citizens. Even I, deliberate in my attention to these issues, spent most of my days in the calm and safety of my apartment or in the offices of my informants, only occasionally traveling through the dusty backroads where violence remained out of sight but with a more palpable presence.

Another distorting effect of this constant verbal reworking of violence is that the very attempt to articulate meaning and define such acts suggests articulation and definition are possible. This account erases the ways in which human rights activism functions in a continual state of emergency (Taussig, pers. com. 2004). As one reads this account on the page, much of the daily desperation and frantic fear are lost. The multiple meanings, the excess of emotion and rationalization produced by violence, cannot be reduced to categories. Michael Taussig, not coincidently one of the few U.S.-based anthropologists to focus on Colombia, has been the most eloquent and influential theorist of the emotional work of violence and our ultimate inability to confine its meaning. His articulation of the "culture of terror, space of death" as a place of transformation has been widely employed (quoting Conrad) "to penetrate the veil while maintaining its hallucinatory quality" (Taussig 1987: 10). He emphasizes the difficulty of fixing the meaning of violence, as an inherent quality of terror is confusion (Taussig 1987, 1999). He returns to these issues throughout his work on Colombia, most recently in a moving meditation on the paramilitary takeover of the small town where he has based his fieldwork since 1969 (Taussig 2004). In less genuinely reflexive hands, such conclusions collapse the major debates of Colombian political life into an analytic throwing up of hands, in which there can be no accountability for nothing can be known. Countless bureaucrats have told me that Colombia is complicated, smugly resting on their assertions that no one can pierce the veil.

It may appear that I have focused too much on what can be known, neglecting the emotional weight of terror and the brutality of the events behind the debates. In my focus on debates and meetings, my recounting of interviews in calm offices and reflections offered over cups of coffee or glasses of wine, the impression may be one of excessive structure and neatness. The desperate quality of much of the activism I observed and participated in and the impact of operating in a constant state of emergency may be lost. Though I discuss some of the negative repercussions of this environment of pressure and violence, the improvised, immediate scramble for responses that constitute much of the daily practice of human rights activism is hard to capture in the order of chapters and words on the page.

In writing this project, I insist that the hallucinatory terror that is endemic in Colombian life, particularly in small towns and rural hamlets, can itself be part of a political project, and there is much about the violence that occurs that can be known. For researchers working in Latin America, discussion of violence, what is known and what is reported, has been a contentious issue for several decades. Orin Starn caused an uproar among Andean ethnographers when he took several established scholars to task for failing to anticipate or document attacks by the Maoist guerrilla group Shining Path in areas where they conducted fieldwork (Starn 1994). David Stoll's well-publicized allegations that the Nobel Peace Prize–winning indigenous activist Rigoberta Menchú lied about her past brought the issue of what scholars knew and when they knew it into the limelight (Stoll 2000). In her book *Paradise in Ashes,* a history of the Guatemalan village where she has conducted research for decades, Beatriz Manz accuses ethnographers and archaeologists of doing research with "blinders on," noting that "much scholarship of the 1970s and early 1980s missed the growing mobilization and discontent among the Mayas [and] raises a challenge to the narrowness of perspective among many scholars" (Manz 2004: 5). In Colombia strategic silences by scholars are an issue as well.

Certainly in Colombia this is a major concern at a time when human rights NGOs are under attack from right-wing and mainstream politicians. As of this writing, NGOs are constantly being accused of being guerrilla sympathizers, guerrillas in disguise, or generally leftist, in an apparent effort to undermine their work. Activists themselves argued that these *señalamientos* (accusations) endangered them, making them military targets by linking them to illegal armed groups. I present a nuanced argument about the role and legacy of leftist political culture in ongoing activism but do not endorse such political attacks or the use of my research to support such claims. I write of activists' origins in the left and internal debates over the use of violence by guerrilla forces, and about how to frame their activism, hoping to contribute to a more informed debate about how human rights activism can contribute most effectively to reducing violence.

Writing about violence in the context of an ongoing conflict requires silence as well as stories from my informants reluctant to name and blame and from myself as an author unwilling to risk possible retaliation. Perpetrators of violence as well as those privileged by violent regimes go to great lengths to suppress research assigning them responsibility. Conversely, other scholars point to the incommunicability of experiences of violence and the inability of language to articulate shareable memory (Langer 1997; Scarry 1985). In this work I have attempted to illuminate the complicated debates over controversial subjects—the nature of paramilitary violence, the legacy of the left in current activism, reactions to guerrilla violence, and activism by gays and lesbians—in sufficient detail to contribute to their analysis but without compromising the safety of the individuals involved. On some issues I have maintained silence at the request of my informants and colleagues, on others because of my personal judgment that certain revelations would not contribute to debate but derail it.

In many ways embedded ethnography presents the same ethical challenges of all fieldwork. Complicated political alliances, friendships, gossip, and even scandal are integral parts of all ethnographic endeavors. The boundaries of the "field" are inevitably difficult to establish. In my own practice of embedded ethnography, I came to the "field" with a well-known history, benefiting from more than a decade of experience and knowledge, well versed in many of the code words and back stories of the people I interviewed. I benefited as well from the compound talk that Jackson described, the endless hours of critique and rehashing among friends and colleagues that were among the most useful intellectual discussions I had.

The central problems of embedded ethnographies emerge from the benefits: how to define and manage the personal and institutional boundaries and allegiances. The interior lives of institutions are hidden and strongly policed; shifting position from participant to researcher can leave that boundary difficult to establish and hard to maintain. In my writing, I draw widely on the notes and recollections of my previous work experience. Because of the nature of my work, most if not all of the meetings I participated in were defined by the standards of journalist practice: the conversations were established as on or off the record as a matter of course. Nevertheless, to safeguard the participants and avoid the ethical problems presented by writing about these experiences without explicit permission of the participants, I decided to generally conceal the identities of the individuals involved. I did not intend to use my history as a means of circumventing institutional boundaries but rather to deepen my understanding and presentation. Additional complications arise while attempting to research and represent opposing viewpoints in a particular debate. I have struggled to represent the conflicting viewpoints of human rights professionals as accurately as possible.

The issue of allegiances in fieldwork is very complex, including the question of what is "owed" to those who chose to spend their time and energy assisting in the research, especially when it involves violence and attempts to raise international awareness. Many of my former colleagues who helped me during the course of this project probably thought my time would have been better spent producing human rights reports. Pursuing embedded ethnography requires confronting expectations based on former roles and performances with a new kind of project that often appears amorphous and certainly of little benefit.

In her moving and nuanced account of her move from the position of solidarity activist to anthropologist, Diane Nelson writes, "I have found 'the people' to be rather more heterogeneous, 'the state' less clearly bounded, *gringas* less magically welcome, and my accounts to be far more 'partial' in the sense of incomplete than I had acknowledged" (2000: 46). For scholars working with peoples basing their claims to political legitimacy and access to power on essentialist identities, critiques can be challenged and rejected (Hale 1994; Warren 1993, 1998). Research into the arena of heroic resistance to repression can spring from the various forms of nostalgia to which anthropologists and others fall prey—nostalgia for the politically pure activist or the culturally pure savage (Rosaldo 1989), or the *revolucionostalgia* found in Latin Americanists (Nelson 2000: 71). Such identification can be productive and even essential, however (Marcus 1997). While at times oversimplifying the divide between activism and academia, calls for engaged anthropology remind us of the real life-and-death stakes at issue and the importance of keeping power and ethics in the frame (Scheper-Hughes 1995).

The larger issue is the contradictions that often exist between institutional interests and the production of ethnographic knowledge. Groups and movements have a vested interest in presenting their aims and actions as transparent, natural, and coherent. Ethnographic explorations focus on the contradictions and constructions of such groups and movements, the fissures and disagreements. Anthropologists have explored these issues elsewhere in Latin America, where calls to solidarity by the leadership of repressed peoples often compete with the dictates of academic research (e.g., Nelson 2000; Starn 1999; Warren 1998). Despite the best intentions of the ethnographer, such accounts can and often are seen as profoundly threatening simply by virtue of the fact that they expose internal divisions and "weaknesses."

What I present here is not intended as the final word. In a postconflict situation (such an optimistic phrase!), there may be space for discussing sensitive issues; continuing violence in "postconflict" El Salvador and Guatemala suggests that imagined future openness may be more partial than scholars had hoped. The ongoing discussions in the Southern Cone on how to address the legacies of the military dictatorship and the violence it perpetrated do suggest, however, that these are long-term debates whose outcomes are never closed. Some will argue, as they have in reaction to other recent books addressing the complicated history of the left in Colombia, that now is not the time even to air the controversies addressed here (Dudley 2004). I believe, on the contrary, that beginning to address these contradictory legacies and practices is necessary to fully understand the present and begin to work toward a less violent future.

WHAT FOLLOWS

The title of this work comes from the derogatory phrase often used to describe human rights work as the relentless cataloging of depressing statistics, *contando muertos,* counting the dead.[8] However, the practice of human rights activism involves more than simply counting the dead; it is also making the dead count. This work, and the categorization of violence in general, is concerned with giving deaths meaning, making them socially legible, filling out the narrative arc that explains why people died and how to prevent such violence in the future. This is the real work of human rights activists and all those who have struggled to define the reasons for Colombian violence. Throughout this account of activism in Colombia, by NGOs, by military officers, and by state bureaucrats, I have attempted to show that making the dead count is a difficult, sometimes deadly task, even among those who claim ownership of the human rights frame. Examining these disputes illuminates the differing ideological projects that rest behind them.

Throughout the institutional histories presented here, I use the voices and deliberations of activists and officials to emphasize their agency in defining the meaning of their activism, despite the extremely limited opportunities for political success. There are several recurring themes in this book. The first is an obvious focus on political culture and the production of meaning for individual activists. In the course of writing, I found it increasingly difficult to separate the "local" from the "international," as the relationships between U.S.- and European-based organizations (often identified as "international" organizations) and their Latin American counterparts (often identified as "local" organizations) are characterized. Finally, ideas and strategies are not fixed but shift over time, particularly as modes of political violence change over time and new political resources become available to activists.

Most of my attention in this book is given to Colombian nongovernmental activists. In part, this is due to access: I have spent the better part of the past fifteen years working alongside, debating, and studying this activism. A different level of field data is reflected in the chapters on military and civilian state institutions. Rather than attempt to grapple with officers' and officials' emotional identities and global imaginaries, I have focused on institutional and organizational culture. In part, however, these differences also result from the fact that the NGO activists were the first to employ a human rights framework in their efforts to respond to political violence in Colombia and have embraced the contradictions, possibilities, and limitations of this activism for more than three decades. Their emotional investment in this work is profound; for most of the NGO activists I profile here, "human rights" is not a job but a vocation. Though there are some exceptions among civilian state human rights bureaucrats, in particular those who began their careers with NGOs, this identification with activism was not the rule for state officials and military officers employed in human rights agencies.

To protect those who shared their reflections with me, I employ pseudonyms throughout the text as follows: first-name-only pseudonyms are used to identify nongovernmental activists; active duty military officials are identified by rank and pseudonymous last names. I identify public figures, published authors, and retired military officers by their full, correct names. I have also used real names for the nongovernmental activists who are profiled in greatest detail or whose roles as public figures make them easily identifiable, including Gloria Flórez, Carlos Rodriguez, Gustavo

Gallón, Jael Quiroga, and Fr. Javier Giraldo. With a few exceptions, the interviews cited here were conducted in Spanish; all translations from those interviews and from Spanish-language texts are my own.

I begin this book with an examination of the categories used to define Colombian violence since Independence: partisan struggles, insurgency, counterinsurgency (military and paramilitary), and organized crime. In showing how these have evolved over time, and the multiple ways they intersect, I stress the difficulty inherent in attempting to definitively separate violent episodes into discrete historical boxes. Next I explore one of Colombia's best-documented cases of human rights abuses, a series of brutal murders that occurred in the small town of Trujillo, Valle, and became the subject of one of the country's most successful joint NGO-government investigations, the Trujillo Commission. How certain murders came to be considered human rights violations, after two centuries of periodic political violence in the region, exemplifies the possibilities and limitations of rights activism. The Trujillo Commission has left a divided legacy, with many unintended consequences. The final sections of this chapter address the competing narratives used to understand the Colombian crisis, which allowed for certain kinds of international interventions throughout the 1990s.

Chapters 2 through 5 explore the history and evolution of nongovernmental human rights organizations. Chapter 2 begins with the first generation of human rights activists in Colombia, focusing on their origins in solidarity organizations rooted in radical leftist politics, including liberation theology and student and union movements. I examine the early debates over the use of the human rights framework, including concerns over "bourgeois" rights, alternative rights frameworks focusing on collective rights, and the role of armed revolutionary movements. I also explore the role of popular education workshops in establishing networks of local human rights committees. Chapter 3 examines the transition of these groups into increasingly professionalized NGOs in the 1990s. I begin with a brief review of the growing scholarship on NGOs, the institutional evolution of these groups, and the role of international funding. I emphasize that while documenting abuses according to international legal standards was their most visible work, for this group of NGOs, human rights practice included various forms of participation in radical politics. I conclude the chapter with an examination of the paradoxes of human rights practice in evidence at a human rights documentation training workshop.

Chapter 4 examines the emotional and ideological debates over human rights practice in the 1990s. I argue that the activist identity constructed through human rights activism by NGOs in Colombia emerged from the political culture of the Communist and Catholic institutions that dominated the early human rights movement. This activist identity has been a source of profound strength for NGOs as the foundation for resistance to ongoing political persecution. I trace how activists struggle to resolve the conflicts between a professional advocacy based on legal standards promoted by international funders and the emotional commitment of Colombian human rights defenders to social transformation. In chapter 5 I explore how Colombian activists view the international sphere and their myriad experiences of transnational activism. By focusing on Colombian activism before the United Nations Human Rights Commission, I show how professionalized human rights activism was successful—within the limitations of the U.N. system—in motivating the commission to create a new human rights mechanism, an office of the High Commissioner for Human Rights in Colombia. I explore the critiques of this work by activists with alternative global visions, who insist that to focus international activism on foreign governments and multilateral institutions misses the critical site of transnational solidarity as a means of promoting human rights and social justice.

The final section considers the use of the human rights framework by two actors who have attempted to harness its power for radically different projects. In chapter 6 I consider the relatively new phenomenon of state human rights institutions created by weak or partial democracies in conflict situations where nonstate political violence is a significant factor. Profoundly shaped by transgovernmental activism, and in many cases staffed by former NGO activists, new state human rights agencies have opened up avenues for state action on individual cases. By channeling concern about human rights cases into an endless loop of repeating cycles of bureaucratic programs, however, state human rights agencies often contribute to the production of impunity. In chapter 7 I trace the shifting appropriation of human rights activism by the Colombian military. I demonstrate that the Colombian military attempts to harness the power of human rights, including international legitimacy and funding, by proactively adapting human rights discourses and practices into existing military cultural conceptions of the state, society, and military institutions. After initially rejecting all human rights activism as part of guerrilla warfare against them, the military began advancing officers as victims of human rights violations, arguing that accusations of human rights abuses launched in the public sphere violated their due process rights by failing to proceed through the court system. A new generation of colonels has promoted human rights standards—understood as respect for physical integrity for local populations—as an integral part of psychological warfare efforts.

I conclude with reflections on how human rights activism works to move discussions of violence from being public secrets—what is known but cannot be said—to the public transcripts—the hegemonic discourses shaping political life. I return to the example of the Trujillo Commission, which functioned through the creation of a new public consensus about violent acts that had been investigated before the commission convened. I briefly explore new scholarship on human rights activism and the changes in the political landscape that followed the September 11, 2001, attacks.

As both academic and activist, I have been amazed by the stories people have shared with me in the course of my work, stories that are incredible, tragic, inspiring, infuriating, patently false, heartbreakingly true. One of my greatest frustrations has been the number of narratives I could not include, for reasons of space and clarity or political sensitivity and requests for silence. Ultimately this is my story; there are many other ways this history could have been told, and certainly many of the participants portrayed here will argue with my conclusions. I hope at the very least to have honored the stories entrusted to me, the diversity of truths they hold, and I hope that the accounts presented here will contribute to the ongoing conversations about Colombia, about activism, and about how we think about violence.

Personally and professionally, I remain committed to human rights work in Colombia. I still believe that the government should fortify the rule of law, not repressive security forces, and that the best way to reduce violence and end impunity is for the government to bring perpetrators of abuses to trial. I can offer no miracle cures for the entrenched violence in Colombia. But I also believe that understanding the history and deeply held convictions of human rights professionals in Colombia across the political spectrum can lead to a more reflexive and effective human rights practice. My perhaps utopian hope is that my research can contribute to moving forward in the sometimes bitter debates about justice, human rights, and violence in Colombia.

CHAPTER I

Colombia: Mapping the Eternal Crisis

For most international observers, violence remains the primary evidence of Colombian national failure. For the past two decades, debates about Colombian national identity have focused on Colombia either as a country in progress or as a failing state. Popular culture references consistently portray Colombians as criminal; the State Department warns U.S. citizens that travel to Colombia is dangerous. Inside Colombia, academics, artists, politicians, and cab drivers spend hours debating why, where, and how the country went so terribly wrong. By most measures, Colombia has been counted among the most violent places in the world, yet this is not the reason that it is a useful place in which to consider violence. Many other countries have experienced the dramatic spikes in political violence that are characterized by observers as a human rights crisis; the death toll in the Balkans and Central Africa during the 1990s dwarfs the number of Colombians who died in such circumstances.

What makes Colombia's case illuminating is not that it is the site of the worst violence but rather that multiple forms of violence exist in the context of a relatively wealthy, established democracy. Throughout the twentieth century Colombia has experienced periodic waves of political violence in which murder and torture were used to ensure electoral outcomes, guarantee property rights, and solidify economic power. Over the past three decades, Colombia has also had one of the world's highest murder rates and entrenched organized crime. The kinds of violent acts committed in Colombia—political, domestic, common, and organized crime—coexist and commingle, making the classification of violence and the production of accountability a highly contested public process. Despite the inability of the Colombian state to monopolize the use of force, to control national territory, or to guarantee its citizens basic rights, Colombia has a wealth of democratic institutions, a stable economy, and a relatively well financed media and educational infrastructure. Colombians have traditionally enjoyed one of the highest per capita incomes in Latin America, and the country is defined as a "middle income" country by the World Bank (although poverty and inequality levels are growing) (Vélez 2002).[1] The persistent levels of violence combined with the wealth and educational levels enjoyed in major cities have created generations of policy makers, activists, and scholars devoted to analyzing and arguing over the causes and consequences of Colombian violence.

Here I want to sketch the broad outlines of Colombian history in order to locate debates over human rights activism within the history of debates over violence, focusing on the categories used to classify the episodic violence that has erupted since Colombian independence: partisan struggle, insurgent violence, counterinsurgency efforts, and organized criminal violence. The dynamics of these types of violence have varied over time and by region: the changing nature of capital accumulation privileged certain actors over others, and the shifting structure of political institutions facilitated new kinds of power accumulation. In my tour through discussions of Colombian violence, I draw on some of the most insightful studies, which have explored these changes in particular places over limited windows of time (Carroll 1999a, 1999b; Roldan 2002). For readers unfamiliar with Colombia, I paint with broad strokes the most prevalent evolving forms of violence over the past six decades. From this history, I turn to the example of complicated violence in one place, Trujillo, Colombia, where a specific set of murders came to be investigated and eventually categorized as human rights violations. I examine the factors that made this possible, factors that are the focus of much of the rest of this book: the increasing professionalization of human rights groups (and their corresponding greater credibility and research capacity), the growing acceptance of human rights in the post–cold war era, and the new state human rights agencies. Despite the achievements of the commission established to investigate these murders, which produced a consensus document finding local military commanders and drug traffickers responsible, the case demonstrates the limits of human rights activism. Finally, I examine two frames according to which the international community responded to the violence during the 1990s: Colombia as a humanitarian crisis and the need for a culture of peace. Each frame catered to different institutional interests and constituencies, and while some organizations employed both frames, many groups viewed the human rights focus on justice and accountability as an obstacle to humanitarian assistance and the search for peace.

BASIC STATISTICS ON VIOLENCE IN COLOMBIA

A central point of this book is that the production of statistics on violence is a profoundly political and contested act. The debates among and between groups about which deaths to count in what category are explored throughout. Understanding the basic universe of figures being debated is important for understanding the wider context for these debates. Colombian homicide rates peaked in the early 1990s at more than 28,000 violent deaths a year (86 per 100,000 inhabitants). Since then the death rate has declined but still remains extremely high; during my research in 2002, the homicide rate was 66 per 100,000 inhabitants, almost eleven times that of the United States.[2] Kidnapping is a major industry; half of all the kidnappings in the world occur in Colombia. Colombia is home to the longest-running civil war in the western hemisphere and currently suffers from the highest rates of political violence. According to the Colombian Commission of Jurists, on average, ten people were killed daily in political violence in 1990; by 2000 that figure had risen to almost twenty a day (CCJ 2001: 4). The Council on Human Rights and Displacement (Consultoría para los Derechos Humanos, CODHES), an NGO that researches the Colombian conflict and internal displacement, reports that the number of people fleeing their homes has climbed dramatically, to an all-time high of 412,553 people in 2002, a 20 percent increase from the year before (CODHES 2003: 2). There are currently three Colombian groups on the State Department's list of terrorist organizations: the two Marxist guerrilla groups, the Revolutionary Armed Forces (Fuerzas Armadas Revolucionarias de Colombia, FARC) and the National Liberation Army (Ejército de Liberación Nacional, ELN), and the largest umbrella organization of right-wing paramilitary forces, the United Self-Defense Forces of Colombia (Autodefensas Unidas de Colombia, AUC).[3]

RELIGION, RACE, ETHNICITY, CULTURE, AND GEOGRAPHY

Colombian violence does not fit into the model of internal conflict most prevalent during the post–cold war period, which focused on ethnic and religious divisions. Religious institutions, in particular, the Catholic

Church, and ethnic divisions within society have shaped how violence was deployed and mobilized, but these factors were not the primary motor of the conflict. The vast majority of Colombians are Catholic, and the Catholic Church has played a privileged role in Colombian history, having been granted special rights, including control of the educational curriculum, by the 1886 Constitution (which was replaced in 1991). The church has also occasionally taken sides in the conflict. Historically, it was identified with the Conservative Party, and the hierarchy backed the Conservative government during moments of political violence. Despite the conservative hierarchy, many priests were involved in liberation theology and promoted grassroots organizations that were targeted for repression.

While significant discrimination is practiced along racial divisions, Colombia does not experience significant violent ethnic or racial tensions. Unlike the Incan Empire to the south or the Aztecs and Mayans to the north, Colombia's indigenous population lived in relatively isolated small groups and today accounts for approximately 2 percent of the population, one of the smallest percentages of any Latin American country. Despite their small population, indigenous communities control almost 25 percent of Colombia's territories through the *resguardo* system (comparable to the system of Indian reservations in the United States). This has contributed to the targeting of indigenous groups by all the actors in the armed conflict (Jackson 2003).[4] Scholars have only recently begun to examine the racial dimensions of Colombian violence, particularly in terms of the Afro-Colombian population. Colombia has one of the continent's largest African-descendant populations, approximately 26 percent of the population. Between 1580 and 1640 as many as 170,000 African slaves were brought through the port of Cartagena de Indias, the only slave port in Spanish America besides Veracruz, Mexico, primarily to work in plantation and cattle ranching and gold mining on the Atlantic and Pacific Coasts (Arocha 1998). While slavery was abolished in 1821, total manumission was only gradually achieved over the next three decades (Lohse 2001). Afro-Colombians remain concentrated on the Pacific Coast, especially the department of Chocó, where freed and escaped slaves established independent communities; over the past two decades, however, Afro-Colombians have migrated throughout the country, in part because of the internal conflict. Racial identity remains a slippery category in Colombia, and most Afro-Colombians do not identify themselves as such, despite incipient efforts to organize around Afro-Colombian rights to combat ongoing discrimination (Wade 2002). In the current conflict Afro-Colombians are disproportionately victims of forced displacement (Jeffery and Carr 2004). Although systematic demographic surveys do not exist, Afro-Colombians appear to be well represented among paramilitary combat troops (but not the command structure) because of their extensive recruitment along the Atlantic Coast.

"Culture," understood as a national essence or identity, is often used as the default commonsense explanation for Colombian violence: Colombians are violent because violence is inherent in Colombian culture. In addition to being a dangerously reductionist and static view of culture, this view suggests that there is no possibility for transformation, or any need to address structural inequalities and injustices. Such a view of culture should not be confused with the more nuanced efforts by anthropologists and historians to understand the relationship between Colombian violence and political culture.[5] For example, the historian Marco Palacios argues that "Colombian political culture inasmuch as it is pseudolegal, ambiguous, and *tramposa* [deceitful], is not born of the matrix of modernity, Enlightenment, and Independence but from the matrix of tradition, conquest, and Baroque institutions" (Palacios 1999: 256). Most of those analyzing and reflecting on Colombian violence consider culture to varying degrees; here I focus on political culture broadly conceived, including how individuals imagine their relations to the state as well as the institutions that channel political power and participation.

The geographic distribution of mountains, rivers, and flood lands has contributed to Colombia's strong regionalism as well as the ongoing conflict (Park 1985; Safford and Palacios 2001). The interior is cut off by the three Andean cordilleras, making land travel extremely difficult. The major rivers flow northward, and their passage is often obstructed by marshy wetlands and seasonal flooding in the northern regions. Almost two-thirds of Colombia's landmass, the Amazon jungle and the flooded eastern plains, house less than 12 percent of the population. Much of this region remains to this day accessible only by plane or river during large parts of the year. Similarly, the Pacific Coast remains undeveloped, with few roads, as did the Atlantic Coast until the mid-1980s. The human geography of institutions, settlements, and infrastructure has been the decisive factor in shaping the patterns of Colombian violence, but this physical geography makes addressing conflict and promoting national integration more difficult.

PARTISAN VIOLENCE

The first one hundred fifty years of Colombian independence were characterized by three major periods of violence: early coups and conflicts;

the War of a Thousand Days in the early 1900s; and La Violencia during the 1950s. Until the emergence of the leftist guerrillas in the 1960s, most of the violence was defined as partisan struggle between the Liberal and Conservative Parties, which continued to dominate Colombian political life until the 1990s. However, political life was characterized by sporadic violence throughout the past two centuries. While the fighters identified with Liberal red or Conservative blue, many scholars have pointed to conflict over resources, particularly land, as being the primary motor of these conflicts.

In many ways the parties were indistinguishable; that they inspired such passionate allegiances has been one of the great mysteries of Colombian political science. Both were led by members of the elite, with little difference between their economic and political platforms. Some scholarly explanations for the strength of party allegiances have focused on symbolic identification akin to a religious identity; party allegiances ran in families and were inherited from one generation to the next. Strong clientalist relationships led to intense rural and lower-class identification with parties, as the vertically linked networks of privilege and patronage were the only channel connecting remote rural regions to national politics. One of the few significant differences between the two was the issue of power and privileges accorded to the Catholic Church, with the Conservatives strongly backing Catholic legal and economic privileges and control over the public education curriculum (Bushnell 1993). As was common throughout Latin America, political debates centered on three major divisions, protectionist or free trade, centralist or federalist, and pro- and anticlerical, although in practice the positions of the parties varied from region to region.

The winner-take-all political system encouraged conflict to control bureaucratic resources, and those shut out of the political system often used violence to gain political power. The political structure established by the 1886 Constitution significantly contributed to Colombia's entrenched clientalism and conflict by creating a hierarchical system of political appointments. Departments (similar to states) were headed by presidentially appointed governors, who in turn appointed local mayors, and elected legislative assemblies were subject to strict review by national politicians (Park 1985: 265). This distribution of power remained in place until the electoral reforms of the 1980s, described below, and created a structure in which strong local leaders interacted directly with the national government rather than with locally based governance networks such as department-wide assemblies.[6] This system encouraged backroom dealing and consolidated the power of local strongmen who functioned outside official electoral hierarchies. Regional powerbrokers were known as *gamonales,* while their local counterparts were called *caciques,* from the local slang for "Indian chief."

Colombian political life was characterized by the use of violence to effect political change and control resources. The early years of Colombian independence were marked by political upheaval—one historian counted at least thirteen coups and armed insurrections during the last decades of the nineteenth century (Bushnell 1993: 13). While most were skirmishes with little impact on political order, "what is inescapable is the sheer frequency with which political factions in this land, which paradoxically always has prided itself on its adherence to civil government and strict legalism, made use of force, or the implied threat of force, in the hope of effecting a change in the rules" (Bushnell 1993: 12). Combat during the poetically named War of a Thousand Days (1899–1902) killed an estimated one hundred thousand people, about 2 percent of the population, and displaced hundreds of thousands more, pushing land colonization into new areas. Generated by partisan struggles (the Liberal revolt against the Conservative government) and exacerbated by an economic crisis caused by a sharp decline in world coffee prices, the guerrilla tactics developed during this conflict were a taste of things to come.

La Violencia, as the partisan violence of the 1940s and 1950s is known, burst forth with the April 9, 1948, assassination of the dissident Liberal populist Jorge Eliécer Gaitán in downtown Bogotá. Gaitán had formed his own third party in 1933, the National Revolutionary Leftist Union (Unión Nacional de la Izquierda Revolucionaria, UNIR), and was the front-runner for the 1950 presidential elections. The assassin was caught and lynched in the street, but the sponsor of the crime remains unknown. Enraged Liberals began a three-day riot, known as El Bogotazo, resulting in the near-total destruction of downtown Bogotá. In an effort to parlay the general unrest into a revolutionary movement, Communist and Gaitainista leaders created "revolutionary juntas" in Bogotá and small-town radical strongholds (most notably Barrancabermeja and Puerto Berrío) but failed to galvanize cohesive support. Political violence had increased throughout the 1930s, despite the economic recovery fueled by high coffee prices and U.S. compensation for the Panama Canal.[7] With polarizing absolutism, Liberals accused Conservatives of wanting to physically liquidate the poor; the Conservatives in turn accused Liberals of moral filth and being Communists, Jews, Protestants, and Masons (Perea 1996).[8] Conservative leader Laureano Gómez had

spent years in exile in Franco-ruled Spain and returned to Colombia with
an apocalyptic vision of a threatening mob—led by an indistinguishable
mass of Communists, Liberals, and Gaitanistas—on the verge of engulf-
ing Colombian civilization. Violence dominated political life; during one
debate, a Conservative shot and killed a Liberal on the floor of Congress.
In the countryside the conflict was much worse.

El Bogatazo escalated to large-scale violence. The main agents of rural
terror were the *pájaros* (lit., "birds"), assassins who traveled throughout
the country carrying out the dirty work of their urban, elite sponsors,[9]
and the Chuvalitas, peasants recruited from the Boyacá district of
Chuvalita to replace Liberal policemen dismissed by Conservative politicians. Much of the violence involved torture and bloody public displays;
killers developed elaborate mutilation techniques. To cite just one example, the *corte de corbata,* or necktie cut, involved slicing the victim's
throat and pulling the tongue through (Uribe 1990). Land conflict, particularly in areas of lucrative coffee production, fueled the struggle: the
three most violent states (Viejo Caldas, Antioquia, and Tolima) produced
two-thirds of Colombian coffee and 60 percent of the deaths during this
period; coffee also provided approximately 80 percent of the foreign
exchange revenues for the Conservative government (Chernick 2005).
Over the coming decades the struggle to control resources, including oil,
land, coca, and cocaine, increasingly shaped the geography of Colombian violence.

La Violencia was ended by Colombia's only modern military dictatorship, when General Gustavo Rojas Pinilla took power in 1953 with
significant civilian support. Four years later the traditional parties re-
established their power by removing Rojas Pinilla and instituting a
power-sharing agreement, known as the National Front, that would
shape Colombian political life for the next half century. By alternating
power between the two traditional parties while maintaining the system
of political appointments whereby presidents appointed governors, who
in turn appointed mayors, the possibility of any third-party participation
was precluded.

POLITICAL EXCLUSION

Colombians and Colombianists alike have been interested in understanding and categorizing La Violencia. The first studies, produced in the
1960s, suggested that the conflict was the result of the transition from
premodern to modern politics, while others focused on the rivalries

between patron-client networks.[10] The American sociologist Paul Oquist (1980) stressed the competition between Conservatives and Liberals for control of the resources of the increasingly powerful state; the French political scientist Daniel Pécaut (1987) posited the inability of the state to articulate a cohesive national identity and resolve conflicts in the face of the expanding "subcultures" organized along party lines. In his work focusing on the Gaitán movement and the immediate aftermath of el Bogotazo, the historian Herbert Braun (1985) focused on the degree to which political power and decision making was channeled through elite backroom deals rather than open political debate. The political scientist Gonzalo Sánchez stressed the connection between different phases of Colombian violence: "The Violence was an ambiguous process resembling both a 19th century style civil war and an embryonic peasant revolution, and as the former problem was resolved, the second took the fore. In theory a negotiated way out of the Violence, the National Front in practice actually inaugurated a new phase of it" (Sánchez 1992: 114).

Colombia's closed political system has been one way to explain ongoing political violence. The National Front agreement ushered in decades of paradoxical results. While Colombia remains widely touted as Latin America's oldest democracy, having missed the periods of repressive dictatorships that plagued its neighbors to the south, the strict limits on political participation imposed by the country's political elites hobbled the political process. Scholars have stressed the partial nature of the country's democracy, characterized variously as "elitist pluralism" (Bailey 1977), "exclusionary democracy" (Pécaut 1989), "*democradura*" (Leal 1989), and a "limited democratic consociational" arrangement (Hartlyn 1988, 1989). Leftist historians and activists argued that by preventing the participation of third parties the National Front pushed participation into illegal channels, including banned strikes and armed opposition movements. Palacios concluded that the National Front agreement embodied the paradox of desire for reform combined with the inability to enact it. He writes, "Trapped by the logic of oligarchic control and the cold war, [the National Front] meant the exclusion of popular interests in the central decisions of the state and repression of political dissidents, and the co-optation and absorption of popular sectors and emerging middle classes through the expansion of clientalist and patronage networks" (Palacios 1999: 58).

Political violence and electoral fraud continued to dominate political contests throughout the years of the National Front. In a classic example of the dramatic turns famous in Colombian political life, Colombia's only military dictator, Rojas Pinilla, returned to political life as a populist champion of the democratic process through the creation of the National Popular Alliance (Alianza Nacional Popular, ANAPO). Rojas Pinilla's dream of returning to power was denied, however. Many analysts contend that Rojas was the winner of the presidential elections of April 19, 1970, but the minister of the interior named Conservative Misael Pastrana Borrero the new president after a suspiciously timed massive power outage. Though ANAPO failed to garner significant political support in subsequent campaigns, the 1970 election was widely viewed by the left as definitive proof that there was no point in pursuing electoral politics; a group of nationalist guerrillas adopted the date as their name (the April 19 Guerrilla Movement, or the M-19) to focus attention on the alleged fraud and the closed nature of Colombia's political system.

Another limit to Colombian democracy throughout the second half of the twentieth century was the use of state of siege legislation by the executive branch to justify the assumption of extraordinary powers. From 1958 until 1991, when the new Constitution redefined and limited state of siege powers, Colombia was governed under almost continual decrees of "state of siege." The incidents that prompted months and even years of state of siege powers were often episodic outbreaks of violence or civic strikes, but the long-term impact was to strengthen the executive branch. The president also frequently appointed military governors and mayors in areas suspected of harboring guerrillas or strong civic associations (Gallón 1979).

Despite political reforms during the 1980s and 1990s to open the electoral system, participation in Colombian political life continued to be limited by violence. Reforms in 1986 led to the direct election of mayors, and the 1991 Constitution allowed election rather than appointment of governors. While opening local offices to popular election initially generated significant opportunities for third parties, paramilitary violence targeting legal leftist organizing wiped such efforts off the political map. The most famous attempt to garner significant support for a leftist alternative was the Patriotic Union (Unión Patriótica, UP), created during frustrated peace talks with the FARC in 1985. Activists claim that more than three thousand of their members were killed. Violence targeting politicians continued over the next decades. In the late 1990s the FARC began targeting mayors, forcing over 200 of the total 1,091 to resign. Many who remained in office were forced to abandon their towns and govern from capital cities. The political scientists Ana Maria Bejarano and Eduardo Pizarro Leongómez describe the Colombian political system as going from "restricted to besieged." They go on to write, "At the regime level, we claim that it is no longer the system's 'closed' nature that affects prospects for democratic consolidation, but instead the excessively lax rules of the game created by the political reform initiated in the mid-1980s. This set of rules has engendered additional incentives for party fragmentation, leading to an extremely atomized and personalistic party system" in which powerful criminal syndicates and illegal armed groups now pose the most serious limits on political participation (Bejarano and Pizarro Leongómez 2002: 2).[11]

INSURGENT VIOLENCE

Colombia is home to the longest-running guerrilla war in the hemisphere. Like most countries in Latin America, numerous small guerrilla forces emerged during the 1960s and 1970s espousing varieties of Marxist doctrine. However, some Colombian insurgencies differed in important ways from their counterparts throughout the hemisphere before and after the cold war zenith of such revolutionary groups. The FARC, for example, traces its history to peasant defense groups that emerged in the 1930s and 1940s. Rather than negotiate following the collapse of international support after the cold war, Colombian guerrilla groups were able to expand their operations by tapping into the revenues of one of Colombia's most lucrative enterprises, the drug trade. Here I focus on the two largest remaining insurgent groups in Colombia: the FARC, which emerged at the beginning of the twenty-first century militarily stronger than any time in its history even as political support for their operations had dramatically declined at home and abroad; and the ELN, which has shrunk due to military defeats and desertion but remains a significant force in several regions.

The FARC's origins in early peasant self-defense forces is the basis of its claims to political legitimacy and ability to represent the marginalized rural peasantry. These rural communities organized in part by the Communist Party developed into armed enclaves, often fleeing en masse into previously unsettled lands, a process later described as "armed colonization" (Molano 1989). Their leaders were larger-than-life Robin Hood figures who combined armed robbery with peasant resistance in an amorphously defined political banditry, with profound consequences for political activism in the coming decades. In the words of one of Colombia's most famous historians, himself the son of persecuted Liberals, "In this subculture of violence that was transforming social conduct, language, and values, and spawning leaders of the Liberal resistance with nicknames such as *Desquite* (Vengeance) and *Sangrenegra* (Blackblood), an entire generation was growing up whose attitudes toward their condition oscillated between fatalism, a thirst for vengeance, and repressed rebellion" (Sánchez 1992: 90).

Over the next decade, these poorly trained self-defense forces developed into Colombia's first guerrilla organizations. In the process they were disavowed by the national Liberal Party, targeted by ferocious counterinsurgency campaigns, and isolated from Colombia's industrializing economy.[12] Although weakened by amnesty offers from the government that enticed many leaders into civilian life and battered by overwhelming counterinsurgency campaigns, these armed enclaves survived into the 1960s as "independent republics" operating outside the control of the central government. Guerrilla leaders, radicalized by the military campaigns against them, formalized their vision in a meeting on July 20, 1962, declaring themselves the southern bloc and issuing a national agrarian platform. Two years later, at the second national conference of guerrilla groups, the leadership adopted a Marxist platform and announced the birth of the Revolutionary Armed Forces of Colombia. The FARC remained a loose federation of poorly organized peasant fronts for its first two decades of existence, but increased resources from its "taxation" of the illegal narcotics trade and other criminal activities financed its expansion into the country's largest guerrilla force by the late 1990s.

The next generation of guerrilla organizations emerged in the 1960s and 1970s. Students, union organizers, and other activists were inspired to take up armed opposition by the examples of colonial liberation movements around the world and the Cuban Revolution closer to home. Che Guevara and the leftist journalist Regis Debray popularized the *foco* theory of guerrilla warfare, which conveniently allowed would-be revolutionaries to circumvent tedious political organizing (in the form of a mass movement led by the Communist Party) in favor of a vanguard-sparking revolt. These ideas inspired a multitude of primarily urban, youth-led armed movements throughout the world in the 1960s (Colburn 1994; Varon 2004). Despite passionate—and sometimes lethal—sectarian disagreements among these groups in Colombia, the myriad armed radical organizations that arose throughout this period generally shared central elements of a political vision: the revolution was imminent, any possibility of national development was totally blocked by the oligarchy, and a monumental political crisis was brewing. Many of these groups were more concerned with establishing the proper theory to explain the struggle's master plan than with establishing contact with the oppressed. Early organized efforts were characterized by extreme militarism and even brutal internal purges of young volunteers accused of insufficient commitment (Broderick 2000).

One of the most important of the second-generation guerrilla groups, the National Liberation Army, was the brainchild of a small group of Colombian scholarship students who had traveled to Cuba at the height of the missile crisis in 1962. Inspired by the revolutionary moment, a number of them requested military training and vowed to re-create the Cuban Revolution in Colombia on their return. Their first combat operations commenced on January 7, 1964. The group, boasting only sixteen men, opened fire in Simacota, Santandar, and distributed their first manifesto (the "Simacota Manifesto"). The ELN was closely linked to the liberation theology movement within the Colombian Catholic Church; three of its original leaders were Spanish Catholic Worker priests. Despite attracting one of Colombia's most promising and charismatic leftist leaders to its ranks, the Jesuit priest and sociologist Camilo Torres, the ELN suffered from divisive internal purges and had few combat successes during its first years. Torres was killed in his first combat operation on February 15, 1966, and the group was almost completely annihilated following a series of successful counterinsurgency operations in the early 1970s.[13]

Other guerrilla forces coming to prominence during the late 1970s included the Popular Liberation Army (Ejército Popular de Liberación, EPL) and the M-19. The EPL grew out of the Communist Youth and the Marxist-Leninist Communist Party (Partido Comunista Marxista-Leninista, PCML), a legal political party that sided with the Chinese during the Sino-Soviet split. Both the PCML and the EPL were often on the verge of total extinction because of the army's counterinsurgency campaigns and their own deep internal schisms, which generated spin-off groups that included the Marxist-Leninist League and the Marxist-Leninist Tendency, among others. The M-19, by contrast, emphasized nationalism and democracy, distancing itself from the dogmatic ideological debates that characterized its counterparts. Many of the group's leaders had been expelled from the Communist Party, the FARC, and the socialist wing of ANAPO. Its strength lay in dramatic symbolic gestures: stealing Simón Bolívar's sword as its first official act (vowing to return it when real democracy returned to Colombia, although the sword was then lost), stealing milk to give to the poor, a daring nighttime theft of weapons from the army's northern Bogotá arsenal, and taking fourteen ambassadors hostage at the Dominican embassy during a dinner party were only a few of their major exploits.[14]

Most of these groups laid down their arms during peace talks in the late 1980s. The M-19 suffered a spectacular defeat when, in hopes of bringing attention to government intransigence and the torture of M-19 cadres in jail, they took over the Palace of Justice, the seat of the Supreme Court, in 1985. When the military stormed the Palace in what analysts later called a forty-eight-hour coup, eleven Supreme Court justices and more than one hundred bystanders were killed. Widespread rumors that the M-19 had been in the pay of the cartels, who wanted their case files destroyed to circumvent extradition efforts, contributed to the guerrillas' plunging popularity. Along with a host of smaller groups, the M-19 attempted to transform itself into a legal political party. The M-19 Democratic Alliance enjoyed a brief groundswell of popular support and was instrumental in rewriting the Colombian Constitution in 1991 but was unable to sustain a coherent national political organization.

In the 1980s the ELN was able to rebuild its organization thanks in part to the petroleum boom; a German multinational construction company, Mannesmann Anlagenbau AG, admitted paying more than $2 million in ransom in 1985 during the building of the Caño Limon pipeline along the Venezuelan border (long an ELN stronghold). The ELN claimed to have received more than $20 million in total ransom during the construction project (Chernick 2005). During the 1990s, however, the ELN was hard hit by paramilitary violence. A dissident wing known as the Socialist Renovation Current (Corriente de Renovación Socialista, CRS) laid down its arms in 1994; according to a December 2005 report in the Colombian newsweekly *Semana,* only approximately thirty-five hundred armed ELN combatants remained in the field, many divided between entering into peace talks with the government, continuing the armed struggle, or joining the ranks of the FARC. A surprising number of former ELN fighters, as well as combatants from other guerrilla groups, have joined the paramilitary forces.

During the 1990s, the Colombian guerrillas increasingly relied on criminal activities to fund their military and political operations. Of the more than 3,700 people reported kidnapped in 2002, approximately 70 percent are attributed to guerrillas and two-thirds of those motivated by extortion.[15] According to Colombian governmental statistics, the FARC and the ELN received approximately $1.2 billion in ransom between 1991 and 1998.[16] The drug trade provides the majority of the FARC's revenues, however, with estimates ranging from $100 million to $200 million a year.[17] Initially the FARC was solely involved with taxing coca production by small farmers, but it has progressively moved up the production chain. The FARC used this money to more than quadruple its forces to approximately 18,000 by the end of the 1990s, as well as build substantial urban militias.[18]

COUNTERINSURGENCY VIOLENCE AND THE COLOMBIAN ARMED FORCES

The Colombian military's response to the long-running guerrilla conflict has differed substantially from that of other Latin American militaries in many respects. Colombia has not endured the military coups that have been common in the Southern Cone; compared to the conflict in Central America, combat operations were limited, due in part to the "containment" policy promoted by U.S. mentors. In other ways the Colombian military response has been typical of other instances of low-intensity conflict. In one of the primary examples, the military has resorted to the use of paramilitary forces (explored in greater detail below) that were responsible for the majority of human rights violations during the 1990s. To understand the differences and similarities, however, requires examining the institutional evolution of the military and its role in Colombia's political life.

Colombia's military has historically played a very different role in society from that of its counterparts to the south and north. Consolidated as a national, professional force only with the creation of the Military Academy in 1917 (a generation later than its military colleagues in the Southern Cone), the Colombian military has never been a primary receptacle for national identity and pride. After independence from Spain, the army was "not a pillar of the nation, a privilege reserved for political parties and the Catholic Church" (Blair Trujillo 1999: 10), but remained fractured under the authority of regional bosses until well into the twentieth century. In her groundbreaking study of the partisan violence of the 1950s, Mary Roldán concluded:

> Unsure of their legitimacy or strength, Liberal and Conservative party leaders had historically proven unwilling to create viable forces of public order for fear that these might challenge or usurp civilian authority. Such public order forces consequently fulfilled the state's repressive functions but were never allowed to grow into sufficiently coherent entities bound by a code of ethics or professional identity. Poor pay, lack of discipline, and the subordination of public order to the interests of private parties and the shifting winds of political influence ensured that the armed forces would never compete for moral or physical parity with civilian rulers. (Roldán 2002: 145)

As the country was consumed by partisan violence in the 1940s, the military remained largely neutral, refusing to respond to pressures from local party bosses interested in capturing land and resources. Even as the violence escalated, President Laureano Gómez (1950–53, elected as the only candidate when Liberals boycotted the elections) made the controversial decision to send a battalion to fight alongside the United States during the Korean War in 1952, the only Latin American country to do so. Viewed by some as pandering to the United States and as a convenient means for the Conservative president to rid the corps of Liberal officers, the Korea Battalion was a telling example of how removed the armed forces were from the ongoing domestic disruptions. The Colombian police, at the time still appointed by local politicians, served as the basis of death squad operations at the behest of Conservative leaders in many areas. By the mid-1950s, however, the army was pulled into partisan violence in some areas as well. Small groups of soldiers were sent into conflictive areas, causing a breakdown in the chain of command, morale, and logistical supplies.

La Violencia ended with Colombia's brief and only modern military dictatorship. Unlike the later wave of military dictatorships that swept the continent in the 1960s and 1970s, General Rojas Pinilla did not seize power as part of a plan orchestrated by a cohort of military officials. Afraid the violence was spiraling out of control, party leaders played a key role in organizing the *golpe de opinión* (lit., public opinion coup; refers to the widespread support for Rojas Pinilla) as a means of establishing an interim leader outside the traditional party structure but still under their control. Rojas Pinilla's efforts to develop an autonomous political movement and his increasingly heavy-handed censorship and repression of protests led to his removal from power by the Liberal and Conservative leadership. Rojas Pinilla was stripped of his political rights in a theatrical trial in the Senate (setting the stage for his comeback a decade later as a populist representing Colombians disenfranchised by elite political wheeling and dealing).[19] After a transition government called the Military Junta (1957–58), the National Front mandated that the parties alternate the presidency and equally distribute all public posts, including legislative offices, until 1974; informally, the deal lasted well into the 1980s. Enshrined in a constitutional amendment and approved by a plebiscite, the National Front limited political participation to the two traditional parties.

The perception of military neutrality during La Violencia was central to the subsequent political role of the armed forces. In exchange for its ongoing neutrality, understood as a refusal to intervene with civilian leadership, the military was granted authority to design and implement national security policy largely independent of any civilian oversight. Originally known as the Lleras Doctrine, from the 1958 speech by then-President Alberto Lleras to the armed forces, this doctrine defined the *no deliberante* character of the military. "I do not want the armed forces deciding how the nation should be governed, instead of what is decided by the people," Lleras told the crowd of officers, "but I also do not want, by any means, that politicians decide how to manage the armed forces, in their technical functions, their discipline, their rules, their personnel" (quoted in Pardo Rueda 1996: 319). This historic trade-off was instrumental in Colombia's subsequent democratic transitions and lack of coups and established military expectations for almost complete autonomy in defining security policy.

During the early years of the insurgency, the Colombian Armed Forces followed a strategy of containment. Given a cost-benefit analysis of the scale of military operations required to eliminate small guerrilla forces, officials concluded that these groups should be allowed relative freedom in remote rural areas so long as actual combat operations were minimal. In areas where the guerrilla presence increased, the army often opted not for direct confrontation but to train and arm local civilians as "paramilitary" forces. However, the military has been extremely effective in lobbying to ensure that its privileges and policy prerogatives remain enshrined in Colombian legislation. Military officers have also not remained silent when in disagreement with civilian policy decisions over issues they believe are in the military's domain. The primary example of such episodic "saber rattling" has been over the series of peace initiatives, established by each successive administration since 1982, intended to promote negotiated settlements with guerrilla groups. Military officers have strongly opposed these efforts and consider them examples of undermining counterinsurgency efforts and as civilian meddling in security policy; they often make their opposition to civilian policies known through media interviews.

ORGANIZED CRIME AND DRUG TRAFFICKING

The illicit drug trade has generated multiple forms of violence in Colombia. Revenue from drug production and trafficking has allowed for the expansion of all armed groups, including the military, which has received billions of dollars from the United States as part of counternarcotics programs. The dynamic of violence associated with the drug trade has shifted, however, as the illicit drug business has evolved. What is called "drug trafficking" in the United States is in fact a major, multi-faceted, and global industry with deep roots in Colombia's economic development. Colombians have long enjoyed a reputation for creative commerce and as well-connected middlemen for contraband. Benefiting from their strategic location at the crossroads of Central and South America, Colombians also enjoy access to both the Atlantic and Pacific Oceans. Since the time of the Spanish colonial monopoly on tobacco and salt, Colombians had profited by circumventing tariffs and trade laws. To this day, illegal trading of otherwise legal goods, including cigarettes, gasoline, and liquor, is a major motor of the Colombian economy. The most profitable of all contraband markets remains the illegal drug trade, first driven by the U.S. market and now expanded to European and Colombian users.

Colombia's role in this industry has changed over the past decades. Beginning with the 1970s, a marijuana boom along Colombia's Atlantic coast created a class of newly rich traffickers that radically altered local political and economic hierarchies. The serendipitous meeting in a Connecticut jail cell of George Jung, a small-time pot dealer from New England, and Carlos Ledher, a Colombian car thief who would rise to be a founding member of the Medellín Cartel, led to the dramatic expansion of cocaine sales along the West Coast of the United States (Bowden 2002; Porter 2001). Soon the Colombian role in the drug trade shifted to the more profitable—and easier to handle—cocaine trade, as dealers began shipping and processing coca grown primarily in Bolivia and Peru.

Led by a small number of powerful drug kingpins, the Medellín and Cali family-based empires came to control a billion-dollar cocaine industry. The flamboyant personalities of the Medellín Cartel embodied the contradictions of the Colombian drug trade during the 1980s. The traditional economic elite tolerated the growing power of the cartels as long as they were not perceived as rivals. Pablo Escobar, elected congressional alternate in 1982, became a flamboyant public figure who built subsidized housing and soccer fields as head of the Medellín Cartel. The Cali Cartel, led by the Rodriguez Orejuela brothers and José Santacruz Londoño, emerged as the Medellín Cartel's main rivals. The Cali Cartel cultivated an image as sophisticated businessmen, in contrast to the Medellín Cartel's rougher and more violent reputation, and invested heavily in legal businesses. Their violent competition with the Medellín Cartel escalated throughout the late 1980s, culminating in the creation of

People Persecuted by Pablo Escobar (Los Perseguidos por Pablo Escobar, PEPES), a shadowy group dedicated to attacking the Medellín Cartel's businesses and associates, as well as allegedly secretly supplying the DEA with information about their adversaries.[20]

The power and violence of the illicit drug industry came to permeate all facets of Colombian society, demonstrated by the saying "plata o plomo"—silver or lead—meaning "take the bribe or take a bullet." By 1988 *Fortune* magazine reported that "the illicit drug trade is probably the fastest-growing industry in the world and unquestionably the most profitable" and estimated that Colombia's illegal exports were worth $4 billion a year, more than coffee and oil exports combined (quoted in Dudley 2004: 71). Drug lords achieved unprecedented political influence through threats, bribery, and political contributions. Violently opposed to extradition treaties pushed by the U.S. government, a group of drug lords known as the *extraditables* declared war on the Colombian government and used what became known as "narcoterrorism" to cow officials into denying extradition attempts.[21] Drug traffickers from all groups began buying up land as a means of money laundering and buying their way into the respect of the elite; according to one estimate, as many as 6 million hectares changed hands from 1985 and 1995 in what some analysts called a "reverse agrarian reform" (Reyes and Gómez 1997).[22] This new role for drug traffickers was instrumental in the development of paramilitary groups. During the late 1980s, cartel mercenaries bombed public buildings, assassinated high-ranking officials, and blew up an airliner en route to the United States. To avoid judicial investigations, cartel-financed hitmen killed hundreds of judges, police investigators, journalists, and public figures.

During the 1990s, ties between illicit drug operations and paramilitary organizations solidified, with several high-level traffickers becoming paramilitary chiefs. Despite the U.S.-assisted breakup of the two largest cartels, Colombian drug trafficking continued unabated. These drug syndicates have been replaced by smaller, more vertically integrated trafficking organizations whose nimble, independent traffickers are much more difficult to detect and infiltrate. These traffickers employ new and constantly changing shipping routes through Central America, Mexico, and the Caribbean for moving cocaine and, increasingly, heroin.

The cultivation of both coca and poppies (used to make heroin) has expanded enormously in Colombia since the mid-1990s. Unlike in Peru and Bolivia, where peasants have for centuries grown and chewed the coca leaf (a mild stimulant, compared to the processed form, cocaine), in

Colombia this practice was limited to a very few small indigenous groups. While coca cultivation declined in Peru and Bolivia as a result of U.S.-financed eradication programs, cultivation in Colombia increased 54 percent from 1996 to 1998, leaving overall Andean coca production constant. By the late 1990s, Colombia was the world leader in both illicit drug trafficking and the production of coca. Guerrilla groups active in areas of increasing coca cultivation, primarily the FARC, funded their dramatic military expansion by taxing coca crops and by protecting drug processing labs and other illicit installations. U.S.-sponsored counter-narcotics programs, including the massive spraying of chemical herbicides, pushed coca cultivation into new regions of Colombia without significantly diminishing overall cultivation levels. Paramilitary leaders, who have long been tied to drug trafficking, moved to increasingly control coca production as well.

THE EVOLUTION OF PARAMILITARY GROUPS

"Paramilitary groups" and "self-defense groups" describe a range of different groups active in Colombia over the past fifty years. Colombian paramilitary forces, like similar groups throughout Latin America, worked covertly with military forces in counterinsurgency operations characterized by death squad operations that targeted activists and opposition political parties. Unlike these groups in other countries, however, Colombian paramilitaries were able, thanks to the influx of drug money, to develop offensive military capabilities with large numbers of troops, in some cases better financed than the military; a series of charismatic regional spokesmen have argued that Colombian paramilitary groups now represent a significant independent political project (Aranguren Molina 2001; Tate forthcoming).[23] Despite wide regional variations, the evolution of paramilitary groups can be divided roughly into three major, at times overlapping, phases: death squad operations in the 1970s and early 1980s, private armies funded by the drug trade in the late 1980s and early 1990s, and the consolidation of paramilitaries into a single coordinating body represented by national spokesmen claiming to share a political platform in the late 1990s.

Paramilitaries historically have acted in concert with and have been supported by the state military apparatus rather than in opposition to the state (an important exception is paramilitaries' violent repression of state judicial efforts to investigate their crimes, particularly in relationship to the drug trade). Paramilitary groups have periodically been incorporated legally into counterinsurgency efforts, and the links between legal and illegal paramilitaries have historically been pervasive. The legal basis for state sponsorship of paramilitary organizations was Law 48, approved by the Colombian Congress in 1968, allowing the government to "mobilize the population in activities and tasks" to restore public order.[24] International pressure and additional attacks against government officials led President Virgilio Barco to declare the creation of paramilitary groups illegal in 1989. The expansion of paramilitary groups in the 1990s coincided with the organization of legal rural defense forces, known as the Convivir. Officially launched in 1995, the Convivir were enthusiastically supported by Colombia's current president, Alvaro Uribe, during his tenure as governor of Antioquia (1995–98). In 1997, after numerous complaints that Convivir groups were involved in human rights abuses, the Supreme Court continued the organization's legal status but prohibited it from collecting intelligence for the security forces and from receiving military-issued weapons.[25]

According to human rights groups and government investigators, during the first phase of paramilitary activity there was considerable overlap between the civilians legally trained by local military forces in the 1970s and illegal paramilitary death squads such as the American Anti-Communist Alliance (Alianza Americana Anticomunista, AAA), active in the Magdalena Region. The first qualitative shift in Colombian paramilitary groups occurred in the 1980s, when money from the drug trade allowed them to grow from small groups linked to local military commanders to private armies. Unlike the death squad operations in other Latin American countries, the paramilitaries benefited from the spectacular resources provided by the drug trafficking industry. The fusion of counterinsurgency ideology and illegal narcotics revenue produced one of the most lethal fighting forces in Latin America. As the owners of vast haciendas, drug traffickers needed protection from the guerrillas, whose primary fund-raising techniques involved *boleteo* (extortion), *vacunas* ("vaccination" against guerrilla attack), and, increasingly, kidnappings of the rural elite. Paramilitary groups linked to drug cartels (especially the Medellín Cartel) worked closely with Colombian military officers to eliminate suspected guerrilla sympathizers, while at the same time they attacked Colombian authorities who tried to investigate drug trafficking. Throughout the 1980s paramilitary groups were implicated in the assassinations of high-ranking government officials, including those of Minister of Justice Rodrigo Lara Bonilla in 1984 and hundreds of police officers and judges. Paramilitary groups were particularly vicious in targeting activists from the leftist parties, who enjoyed considerable support after the 1986 reforms allowing popular election of mayors and other local officials previously appointed to their posts.

By the end of the 1980s a loose network of paramilitary groups covered the country: Henry Perez and Gonzalo Rodriguez Gacha operated in the Middle Magdalena Valley; the Eastern Plains region was split between Rodriguez Gacha and emerald baron Victor Carranza; Fidel Castaño controlled Cordoba and northern Antioquia; and Pablo Escobar funded a Medellín-based group of young assassins for hire, known as *sicarios*. Though primarily focused on economic control, some forward-thinking paramilitary groups also developed a political platform, the National Renovation Movement (Movimiento de Renovación Nacional, MORENA; modeled in part on Salvadoran death squad leader Roberto D'Aubuisson's ARENA party). The party won six mayoral seats in the Middle Magdalena Valley in 1988, thanks in part to support from the Association of Middle Magdalena Ranchers and Farmers and to backing from the Liberal mayor of Puerto Berrío, the self-proclaimed counterinsurgency capital of the country. Behind a network of health clinics, "patriotic" education, and agricultural cooperatives, paramilitary operatives conducted deadly assassination campaigns (Dudley 2004; Medina Gallego 1990). The paramilitaries failed to develop a national political network or overcome entrenched regional differences; their primary focus continued to be ensuring their profits were safe from Communist-inspired attack.

The third phase of expansion was marked by the creation of a national coordinating body of paramilitary groups, the United Self-Defense Forces of Colombia.[26] Under the umbrella of the AUC, the paramilitaries transformed themselves from regional renegades into political operators respected in many quarters and viewed as valid interlocutors worthy of sitting at the negotiating table with the government. This metamorphosis involved changes in paramilitary tactics as well as a substantial public relations campaign aimed at changing public perceptions at home and abroad. These groups began new and wider military operations in the late 1990s, dramatically expanded their troops from an estimated 2,500 in the early 1990s to more than 15,000 by the end of the decade, and embarked on offensive military campaigns to conquer new territory. Following a summit in July 1997, the AUC issued a statement announcing a military offensive into new regions of the country "according to the operational capacity of each regional group." Newly created "mobile squads"—elite training and combat units—carried out these operations, which included a series of massacres targeting the civilian population in these areas. The July 1997 massacre in Mapiripán, Meta, was the first step in implementing this new plan.[27] AUC fighters carried out similar massacres throughout Colombia. Paramilitary leaders undertook a public relations campaign employing a range of strategies to engender political legitimacy and acceptance as political spokesmen by the government and international funders. These efforts were a critical component in the domestic and international support for the current negotiations between the government and paramilitary leaders. Through these negotiations the Colombian government officially demobilized 31,671 paramilitary fighters by the end of 2006, using classic conflict resolution strategies based on the collective disarming, demobilization, and reintegration of combatants (Alto Comisionado para la Paz 2006).

CONNECTIONS AND CONTRADICTIONS IN COLOMBIAN VIOLENCE

As the history of the practice of violence in Colombia demonstrates, definitively classifying Colombian armed actors is difficult. The complex connections among these groups and the difficulty of parsing their motives feed debates over how to best resolve the Colombian crisis. Paramilitary and guerrilla groups have undergone profound shifts over the past three decades and exhibit marked regional differences. Guerrillas claim the mantle of revolutionary violence and representation of an oppressed and neglected rural poor but devote few resources to political education, while their increasing criminality further erodes their popular support. Paramilitary leaders have claimed that paramilitary violence is part of state-supported counterinsurgency efforts, yet they also want to be considered insurgents; they are at once defining themselves as independent of the state, a substitute for the state in some areas, and supportive of the state (even as they threaten and murder judicial representatives investigating their crimes). Guerrillas and paramilitaries employ violence in the struggle to control resources, including land, drug production and trafficking routes, and other business enterprises; they are deeply involved in petroleum contraband trade and the fight to control coca production, although to different degrees in different regions. Military corruption in many areas deeply implicates state security forces in the drug trade. The paramilitaries have worked closely with military officers to coordinate military operations and select targets and have benefited from the tacit approval of much of the Colombian elite. Paramilitaries have also adopted guerrilla strategies to build political legitimacy, and have even brought former guerrilla opponents into their ranks. These examples demonstrate both the difficulties of developing simplistic models and the importance of tracing these complicated histories and exploring regional variations.

There are many other dimensions of violence that I have not explored here, including the role of gender in shaping Colombian violence. Women are both participants in and victims of violence in Colombia. Several high-profile leaders of the guerrillas were women, among them María Eugenia Vásquez and Vera Grabe in the M-19; as many as 30 percent of the FARC's members are estimated to be women, although they are not proportionally represented among the commanders. Female combatants constitute a very small part of paramilitary fighters, between 2 percent and 4 percent according to most observers. According to an interview in January 2004 with the paramilitary commander Jorge 40, most women involved in the paramilitaries are "dedicated to social and political projects."[28] Thanks in large part to the efforts of Colombian women's organizations, violence against women by illegal armed actors is beginning to be examined by human rights organizations.[29] A high percentage of internally displaced people are women. In its report focusing on violence against women, Amnesty International noted numerous cases of female community activists who were captured and raped by paramilitary forces, even during the declared paramilitary cease-fire. Paramilitary and guerrilla efforts to enforce social control are also highly gendered. Women accused of socializing with suspected enemy sympathizers, wearing suggestive clothing, or engaging in inappropriate behavior are targeted for public punishments. Violence against women is underreported; many cases involving sexual violence are closed without investigation.

I have mapped the history of Colombia according to kinds of categories usually described as political violence: partisan, insurgent, and counterinsurgent violence that also at times intersects with criminal violence and the struggle to control resources. Each of these categories is defined according to the motives and intentions of perpetrators. There are many other ways to map this history, for example, through the identities of the victims rather than the aspirations of the perpetrators, tracing the violences experienced by women, indigenous groups, Afro-Colombians, and other minorities. Much of those histories remains to be written, and will, I hope, guide future research on Colombia.

MAKING HUMAN RIGHTS NARRATIVES:
TRUJILLO AND MODERN COLOMBIAN VIOLENCE

The human rights groups that I examine in Colombia attempt to use the category "human rights violations" to highlight particular instances of violence within this pantheon of aggressive acts. In doing so, they focus on certain characteristics of the act itself: the motives of the perpetrators, the credibility of the evidence, and the degree to which this example represents a larger universe of events. Institutional and historical shifts were instrumental in making the use of the human rights framework possible. This process was exemplified by the "Trujillo case," the torture and murder of more than one hundred people, which became one of the most widely discussed human rights cases in Colombia in the 1990s. The Inter-American Human Rights Commission (IAHRC) of the Organization of American States (OAS) ruled on the case. The Trujillo Commission, a mix of government, military, and NGO representatives named to investigate the murders, was called a mini–truth commission for Colombia. Its investigation found a lethal mix of military commanders and drug traffickers responsible for the violence, which had included the dismemberment of living victims with chainsaws and the decapitation of the local priest.

The work of the Trujillo Commission typifies many of the issues I explore in this book. Out of the complex panorama of multiple armed actors, the commission crafted a narrative using the human rights frame to establish accountability of state agents. Its work was possible because of the increasingly credible and professional investigations undertaken by NGOs, the state human rights institutions created in the early 1990s, and the Colombian military's willingness to participate (and attempt to co-opt) human rights spaces. The perpetrators of the murders in this case were a mix of state agents (military officers) and economically powerful businessmen (drug traffickers), and common criminals, just as they had been throughout Trujillo's history. But now they could be labeled "human rights violators" in an effort to publicize the case and bring the guilty to trial. In that effort, the activists who pushed for the commission largely failed. Nevertheless, they participated in the dramatic transformation of the political landscape of human rights activism in Colombia and the efforts to understand and address Colombian violence throughout the 1990s. To understand the complexity of their task requires first a brief mapping of the dynamics of political violence in the decade before the commission began its work.

Power Disputed: Trujillo in the 1980s

While human rights violation as a category for understanding violence was applied to events in Trujillo, a small town west of Cali, only at the beginning of the 1990s, violence has long played a central role in the town's political life.[30] At the end of the nineteenth century, like much of the Colombian countryside, the land that became Trujillo was first emptied of its sparsely settled indigenous occupants and then filled with the second-generation sons of Spanish adventurers, who founded the first official settlement in 1922. In a pattern that would be repeated along the agricultural frontier throughout Colombia's history, settlers were driven by a desire for economic opportunities and to escape political violence. Political bosses employed violence to control their patronage system and consolidate their ownership of land and other economic resources, channeled through divisions between the traditional Liberal and Conservative Parties.[31]

The violence that was the subject of the Trujillo Commission emerged from the new actors that began to dominate political and economic life during the 1980s: guerrillas, paramilitaries, and drug traffickers. In Trujillo, as in many small towns across the country, the military was deeply implicated in supporting paramilitary activity, which was in many cases financed by drug traffickers. The guerrillas had first arrived in the region in the early 1980s. The ELN sent periodic political and military excursions into the mountainous outskirts, composed primarily of students and union activists from Cali and Medellín, as part of the Frente Luis Carlos Cardenas Arbelaez. By the time they arrived in the mountains of Trujillo, the ELN was slowly rebuilding its ranks after a near-total defeat in the early 1970s.[32] Its effort to consolidate a rural power base coincided with the arrival of a new priest to the area, Tiberio de Jesús Fernández Mafla, known simply as Father Tiberio. By all accounts, he was a charismatic native son, from a neighboring small village, committed to the growing radical Catholic movement that focused on solidarity with the poor, liberation theology. He had been a youth leader in the Jesuit rural training program (Universidad Campesina, or Peasant University) and had traveled to Israel to learn cooperative farming on a kibbutz. Father Tiberio promoted lay organizations, supported community businesses and cooperatives, and became an active voice in local politics. From the pulpit, he used his homilies to condemn the *acciones pistoleras* (gangster actions) of the most important political bosses in the region, the Giraldo family.

The ongoing shifts in power relations with the guerrillas were one of the many factors that would ignite the new outburst of violence at the end of the decade. According to Adolfo Atehortúa, for much of the early 1980s Father Tiberio's ministry and activism coexisted peacefully with the ELN. He managed a "tacit agreement" with the ELN following long conversations; the guerrillas agreed not to take over the town and to respect the autonomy of the community groups organized by Father Tiberio and the Instituto Mayor Campesino, a Jesuit-led education and community development cooperative. Atehortúa admits, however, that Tiberio did not have much leverage in these informal negotiations: he "could not oppose them: they had arrived first, were in the zone with his parishioners, and they were armed" (Atehortúa 1995: 240).

The importance of drug money in shaping local politics and violence was personified by Henry "The Scorpion" Loaiza. Local legend has it that Loaiza was "an illiterate peasant, [employed] before as a driver, who left one good day for the Putumayo, and then one day returned with his pockets full of money and ready to become the patriarch of the area" (Atehortúa 1995: 276). Loaiza eventually became head of security for the Cali Cartel and one of the largest landowners in the region, one of many who rose from peasant to near-king on the tide of drug money that washed across Colombian's small towns.

In addition to the ELN, M-19 dissidents arrived, their political and economic prospects badly battered. After frustrated peace talks with the administration of Belisario Betancur (1982–86) and the M-19's unsuccessful attempt to take the Palace of Justice in 1985, M-19 combatants returned to the area where they had once hopefully made plans for peace. Desperate for economic resources, they kidnapped Rogelio Rodriguez, an up-and-coming power broker who supported Father Tiberio's peasant organizing projects. Because of Father Tiberio's "understanding" with the ELN, neither believed that he would become a target.

The fragile, unwritten agreements between these complex, competing forces had been broken, and the conflict between groups escalated throughout the mid-1980s. The ELN, attempting to expand its base of support while staving off increased army incursions, fought M-19 influence. Drug traffickers felt increasingly threatened by the guerrillas, as they bought up land to consolidate a strategic shipping corridor up the western Andes. Traffickers spread their bribes to police and military forces, hoping to replace the traditional agricultural elite as the main power brokers in the region and reduce the influence of the reformist politician Rodriguez and the radical priest Tiberio. After his kidnapping by the M-19, Rodriguez was unwilling to trust the guerrillas. The Giraldo family hoped to maintain their power against the multiple threats of Rodriguez, drug traffickers, and guerrillas. The poor peasants saw their access to land threatened by the drug traffickers' land grab. The small "middle class," made up of independent tradesmen, coffee farmers, and *inspectores de policias* (police inspectors; civilian officials who are often the only government representatives in small hamlets), were pressured from all sides.

In the Cauca River valley, Loaiza and his Cali Cartel cohorts developed alliances with the local military. They were convinced that the peasant organizing going on in the guise of Catholic solidarity was simply a cover for the guerrillas. The final straw was local participation in a series of protest marches, including local organizing to support the National Strike on October 27, 1988. Several of the banners demanding state action on agricultural credit bore the insignias and slogans of the ELN. The following March local peasants again protested the lack of state services, and on April 29 they occupied the central plaza. The army responded by cordoning off the area and declaring a curfew; a negotiating commission that included Father Tiberio, the mayor, and other local officials was established to mediate with the protesters. Peasant leaders accused the army of mistreatment, and the protest ended with a shootout in which fourteen people were wounded. Tensions increased again during the mayoral elections a year later. To prevent violent disturbances during the voting on March 11, 1990, the army militarized the area.

Local inhabitants reported a notable increase in the disappearance of their neighbors and the appearance of unidentified, mutilated bodies. By the end of the month a series of incidents involving the army and the ELN left seven soldiers dead and a number of civilians dead and disappeared. On March 29 two army patrols began searching for an ELN camp in La Sonora. In confused circumstances, an ELN ambush and possibly other combat left seven soldiers dead and six civilians wounded. In the middle of the night of March 31, soldiers rounded up ten local farmers from their homes; the farmers were never seen again. The first week of April, five carpenters were detained, tortured, and killed by the army. Selective assassinations were also on the rise, with increasing numbers of mutilated bodies washing up on the banks of the Cauca River. Prominent locals did not escape the violence. Among them was *gamonal* José Noe Giraldo, a *concejal* (councilman) and congressional representative, who was shot dead in Cali. The final straw was Father Tiberio's brutal killing. He disappeared, along with his niece and two parishioners, while returning from a funeral. His decapitated and mutilated body was found on April 23, 1990, on the banks of the Cauca River.

The Trujillo Commission

The Trujillo Commission was a response to the number and brutality of the killings that occurred during the first months of 1990, but before and after, massacres similar in scale did not enjoy such treatment. A number of factors conspired to focus attention on Trujillo and facilitate the work of the commission. Human rights NGOs viewed the case as an opportunity to raise international awareness. The leadership of the new governmental human rights agencies created by the 1991 Constitution, many of whom had previously worked with the NGOs, saw the case as the chance to demonstrate their capacity to take on sensitive investigations. The increased profile of human rights in the international community in the post–cold war political climate opened new avenues for transnational activism. Closer to home, personal commitments and the political crisis made human rights a priority for the Samper administration.

The first important factor was the increasing ability of NGOs to carry out credible research. The Trujillo murders were first investigated by a Catholic NGO, Intercongregational Commission of Justice and Peace (Comisión Intercongregacional de Justicia y Paz), known as Justice and Peace. An influx of international funding, including major grants from the Ford Foundation, had allowed the expansion of several large organizations and professional training for staff and other activists. Father Javier Giraldo, a radical Jesuit priest with a long history of human rights activism, founded Justice and Peace in 1989. He made documenting paramilitary expansion a priority. He could also marshal significant resources from the Catholic Church in cases of persecuted clergy and was particularly touched by Father Tiberio's brutal death.

The Trujillo case itself was seen as an example of the growing number of massacres being carried out around the country. As such, it served as an archetype that NGOs could use to demonstrate national patterns of political violence. At the same time, researchers were able to gather enough specific evidence to build a compelling case. The NGOs had another critical advantage in this case: they had a witness, someone who was not simply a surviving victim or a local peasant who had seen the events. Daniel Arcila was a participant in the murders, a paramilitary informant who had turned himself in after overhearing paramilitary leaders plan to kill him precisely because of what he had witnessed.[33] Arcila gave a detailed account of the full history of the murders, including incidents that left no survivors, and implicated drug barons, among them Loiaza, and local military commanders. His chilling tale included a gruesome recounting of victims stuffed into burlap sacks and dismembered with chainsaws while still alive (the many nicknames for paramilitary groups included the *monchacabezas*—headsplitters—and the *motosierras*—chainsaws). Beginning on April 19, 1990, Archila testified at least six times before three different government agencies.[34] Despite this testimony, the Colombian courts absolved all the implicated military officers of any responsibility.[35]

Newly organized NGOs such as Justice and Peace were also involved in developing new strategies for transnational activism that began pushing multilateral human rights mechanisms for action. In March 1992 the NGOs decided to try a relatively new tactic, taking the case to the InterAmerican Human Rights Commission. Based on the evidence produced by the NGOs, the IAHRC was prepared to rule against the government, but the head of the governmental Ombudsman's Office (Defensor) and the director of one of the NGOs bringing the case before the commission advocated a different outcome. Rather than present a formal statement finding the government responsible, one that would simply be reported in the press and filed away, they argued that a consensus agreement *(arreglo amistosa)* between the government and the NGOs promising follow-up to victims would provide real closure to the case. That agreement resulted in the Trujillo Commission: an investigative body including both state and civil society representatives charged with clarifying the events, determining responsibility (state and otherwise), and recommending compensation for the victims. Nineteen representatives of civilian state agencies, military branches, and NGOs were named to the commission.[36] The commission addressed events occurring from the end of 1988 to 1990, with special attention to events during March and April 1990, from the ambush of a National Army patrol by a guerrilla column of the ELN until the day Father Tiberio Fernandez's body was recovered from the banks of the Cauca River. Sixty-three victims were named in the original documents, with a total of 107 victims named in the final report.

New state human rights agencies gave crucial support to the commission and to NGO human rights initiatives during this period. As part of the democratic reforms and the negotiated settlement between the M-19 and the government in the late 1980s, a broader movement for political reform led to a Constitutional Assembly, resulting in the 1991

Constitution. The final document stressed human rights and offered an expansive list of guarantees for a range of civic, political, economic, social, and cultural rights while leaving the system of military privileges largely intact. The 1991 Constitution also created a series of new judicial bodies. The Fiscalía (Attorney General) and Procuraduría (Inspector General) were given separate functions; the latter was charged with investigating official misconduct by state agents. The new Constitution also established a central governmental human rights agency, the Defensoría del Pueblo, a type of ombudsman's office, which was charged with assisting victims of abuse but lacked specific investigative and enforcement powers. The first *defensor* was charged with establishing institutional procedures and defining a work program for his vague mandate; many of the first staff attorneys were drawn from NGOs. The presidential human rights adviser, a cabinet-level position established in 1987, also played a critical role in promoting the commission among reluctant governmental officials.

The Trujillo Commission was made possible by a favorable international and domestic political climate. In the post–cold war decade, before the war on terror, human rights played an increasingly prominent role in international relations. Absent the defining conflict between the superpowers, some analysts argued that diplomatic relations could now be driven by the moral imperatives of protecting citizens rather than the crass commerce of national interest. The human rights bodies of international organizations, including the OAS and the U.N., took on more prominent roles in discussing particular national cases. Having the IAHRC offer to provide institutional support for the Trujillo Commission, in place of the public censure of the Colombian government, undoubtedly played a role in the willingness of the Samper administration to participate. The Samper administration in general was open to human rights concerns, and its position on these issues marked a decided shift in government rhetoric. Whereas previous governments had rejected the suggestion that Colombia had a human rights problem, President Samper took a different tack: Colombia had a problem, but it was not his fault. The government was a victim of the extremist violence of the left, the right, and organized crime and needed the help—not the criticism— of the international community. When I interviewed former President Samper at his international business consultancy office, he was proud of his human rights record. "We had to admit that we had a human rights problem," he told me. "It was a reality, and what we had to change was not the image of the problem abroad but the reality itself. That was the philosophy that I worked from." According to Samper's aides, this was in part an ideological conviction and in part a reflection of the cyclical nature of Colombian politics, in which presidential administrations alternated between negotiations and military campaigns; Samper was consciously distancing himself from the "total war" approach of the previous president, Cesar Gaviria.

The profound political crisis that shook the Samper administration from its inception also influenced its policy. Immediately after Samper's election, the DEA released alleged proof that he had received campaign contributions from the Cali Cartel. Much of the first two years of his administration was spent refuting rumors of his imminent resignation, and his power as a political broker was infinitely weakened. Samper's campaign manager (then minister of defense) was forced to resign and was ultimately jailed, Colombia was "decertified" by the U.S. Congress, and Samper's visa to the United States was revoked.[37] Becoming a champion for the human rights cause was one way to win back a margin of political capital for his embattled administration. "The crisis was so extreme that everyone could do whatever they wanted," one former senior official told me. "Which meant that the military had a lot of freedom, but the human rights people had a lot of freedom too."

TRUTH AND CONSEQUENCES:
THE LIMITS OF HUMAN RIGHTS REPORTING

The publication of the Trujillo Commission's final report was itself a great achievement: a consensus document, produced by NGO, civilian state, and military representatives working together to clarify the events surrounding sixty-three brutal murders. On January 31, 1995, President Ernesto Samper officially accepted state responsibility for the Trujillo murders, concluding, "The attitude which we have assumed today will serve as an example for all public servants in Colombia with regard to the unwavering commitment of my government to respect and to enforce respect for human rights" (quoted in ICCHRLA 1997). According to the final report, the paramilitary death squad operated in coordination with the army's Palacé Artillery Battalion No. 3 under the command of Major Alirio Antonio Ureña Jaramillo. As a result of the report, Ureña was removed from active duty; Henry Loaiza had surrendered to Colombian authorities in Bogotá on June 19, 1995, and had been tried on drug trafficking charges.

The lasting legacy of the Trujillo Commission remains uncertain. After its findings were released in 1995, President Samper publicly accepted state responsibility for specific human rights violations—a first in Colombia's history. His public apology was heralded as a major triumph for the human rights groups that had pushed for the commission. For the remainder of the decade, the case remained a major point of reference for both its supporters and its critics, an example of the success of human rights activism and its dismal failure. For the NGOs who participated, the failure to try high-ranking military officers remained a vivid example of impunity. For governmental human rights officials, the commission was an example of the extreme fragility of the compromises required by working in coalition, never to be repeated despite efforts to revive the model to address abuses in other regions. For the military, witness to the demotion of a rising colonel, the commission was a demonstration of how its commanders were scapegoats and contributed to the emergence of a human rights discourse developed to advance military programs, from its own perspective. Perhaps most tragically, the nature of political violence in Colombia itself shifted in part as a result of the commission and other pressures from human rights groups. In the decade after the commission, violence by private actors—paramilitary forces—replaced abuses committed directly by the armed forces as the single largest kind of human rights abuse committed in Colombia. Paramilitary commanders gave their troops lectures on how to escape the attention of human rights groups—by avoiding the publicity of a massacre by killing their victims individually or scattering the bodies, for example—and developed sophisticated public relations campaigns. Ultimately, examining Trujillo, the town and the commission, illuminates both the history of Colombian violence and the way in which human rights activism functioned in response.

The Trujillo Commission brought the issue of state responsibility for brutal human rights violation in Colombia to the attention of the Colombian public and to the world at large in an unprecedented fashion. As a result of the commission, and of lobbying by NGOs and state human rights officials, the Colombian Congress passed Law 288, which ensures the compensation of victims in cases where the InterAmerican Human Rights Commission finds the government responsible. In the long term, the commission set the stage for the evolution of governmental human rights agencies into major players both in terms of international lobbying and in defining the domestic human rights agenda. The commission also began a slow shift in the political culture of NGOs as they moved toward closer cooperation with state agencies.

The commission also contributed to a number of unintended, less positive effects. Its failure to effect jail sentences radicalized many NGO participants; Justice and Peace repeatedly described the outcome as "Truth without Justice" in its publications. Despite the exhaustive investigation and the consensus report naming five individuals responsible for at least thirty-five murders, no one spent a single day in jail as a result. The failure of the commission to bring about legal accountability was used as a justification for refusing to cooperate with governmental initiatives in the future. There was no follow-up to the commission's recommendations. The efforts of Justice and Peace to continue to assist the families who were victims of violence met with ongoing repression, and its Trujillo branch office was forced to close as a result of death threats in 1997.

The civilian state representatives were disappointed in the results as well. According to one such representative whom I interviewed at length, the Defensoría staff viewed the governmental refusal to invest in follow-up as a betrayal of their own hard work. Subsequent efforts to replicate the commission's experience in other regions failed. Almost immediately after the commission concluded its work in 1995, NGOs pushed for a similar investigation of violence in Meta. After a few months of bitterly divisive meetings, however, the effort disbanded, with all sides unwilling to invest political capital in compromises.

The military leadership's resentment of the commission arose from different reasons. Colonel Ureña's ruined military career signaled to many officers that they were to be the scapegoats in the new era of human rights activism. In response, over the course of the 1990s the Colombian military established a network of human rights institutions in order to influence the human rights debates at home and abroad (see chapter 5). "One of the most important things that came from Trujillo was that it opened the way for the state [human rights] agencies to begin a relationship with the [military] leadership," former President Samper told me. "The truth is that it began a consciousness-raising campaign with the military, human rights offices were opened in all the departments, a special human rights adviser was named, and a military human rights curriculum was established."

COMPETING NARRATIVES:
THE HUMANITARIAN CRISIS AND SUPPORT FOR PEACE

Human rights work is a slippery category that both blurs into and conflicts with other categories of the newly emerging "international helping operations." These include humanitarian aid, peace keeping, nation building, conflict resolution, and political advocacy. In practice, such operations can often be very similar, involving establishing bureaucracies, delivering material assistance, fund-raising and public relations, and ensuring staff security. One of the major similarities, however, is also the element that produces the most conflict: all these operations involve the production of knowledge and the categorization of violence, making suffering socially legible in particular ways in order to generate specific kinds of social obligations. Where these operations differ is in their reading of violence and in the nature of the social obligations they generate, so that despite their similarities, in practice these categories are often felt by the people who enact them to be different, even contradictory. These conflicts are generated in part from the kind of social response they require. In traditional NGO human rights activism, the central focus is on the perpetrator and on establishing accountability. For activists involved in other kinds of international interventions, such efforts can seem frivolous (worrying about laws when people starve) or counterproductive (undermining efforts for negotiated settlements by insisting on trials for leaders). A number of institutions devoted to these operations began to operate in Colombia during the late 1990s, offering support as well as competition for human rights NGOs. These institutions operated with their own frameworks for categorizing and addressing the violence in Colombia.

Within the humanitarian aid community, the issues of accountability and prosecution have emerged as highly controversial, and possibly even counterproductive, for organizations that define their primary mandate as providing assistance to reduce suffering and protect life. The largest and oldest humanitarian network, the Red Cross movement, was developed in the late 1800s, following the first Geneva Accords, to protect civilians, medical personnel, and noncombatants during wartime. Absolute neutrality and impartiality, defined as providing assistance without supporting any of the parties in conflict, was the touchstone of its operations, and arguably what allowed the International Committee of the Red Cross to continue to operate in many entrenched conflict situations. By the end of the cold war, however, this approach to humanitarian operations was increasingly scrutinized by critics who concluded that in practice neutrality actually resulted in a political position that favored one party over others during conflicts. Famines and other so-called natural disasters were increasingly seen as the result of human intervention, bringing the issue of accountability to the fore in order to prevent future disasters. Frustration with treating the result (starving people and structural poverty) rather than the cause (local power structures, war, and economic policies) led many humanitarian agencies to develop advocacy and lobbying programs to address the perceived causes.[38]

The "humanitarian crisis" frame that emerged in the late 1990s was a new one for Colombia, despite the long-running internal conflict. The traditionally high relative per capita income and stable economy prevented Colombia from qualifying for most international development funding and programs. Colombia's level of conflict has also been low, particularly compared to Central America and Peru. Yet by the mid-1990s conflict, displacement, and the production of refugees in those areas had largely ended, while in Colombia combat and political violence was on the rise. The worst economic crisis in a century threw Colombia into a tailspin, with almost 20 percent unemployment, growing poverty, and negative growth. Agencies working former hot spots in Latin America were looking for new institutional mandates and ready to expand into new program areas, and they were eager to open programs in Colombia.

Internal displacement first became a visible issue in Colombia in the mid-1990s. The Catholic Church, through its Office on Human Migration, was instrumental in bringing the issue to public notice. Though periodic earlier press coverage and a few NGO reports focused on the issue of displacement, there was little international attention to the issue and almost no major agencies working in Colombia (Kirk 1993). The Office on Human Migration published one of the first comprehensive studies of internal displacement, based on a nationwide survey of parishes, in 1995.[39] In the first evidence of major governmental concern, the Samper administration created the position of presidential adviser on displacement. This position has since been abolished, but the issue now takes up considerable bureaucratic space within the Ministry of the Interior and the Social Solidarity Network, the government agency currently charged with providing assistance to the displaced. By the end of the decade, the U.S. Committee for Refugees (USCR) had named Colombia as one of the major humanitarian crises in the world, on par with the Sudan. After staff visits the USCR issued several reports examining the situation of Colombian refugees and the internally displaced.

With higher visibility, and a subsequent increase in available funding, the number of international NGOs operating in Colombia focusing on humanitarian aid expanded dramatically. The ICRC renegotiated its mandate in 1996, expanding its ability to meet with illegal armed actors and dramatically increasing its field presence.[40] Doctors without Borders (the Dutch, French, and Spanish chapters) and other humanitarian organizations established field presence and programs in Colombia. Project Counseling Services, a coalition of European and Canadian aid organizations, began with one project in Colombia in 1992 and by 2000 had relocated its Latin American headquarters from Lima to Bogotá.[41] The United Nations High Commissioner for Refugees opened a Bogotá office in 1998 and established three field offices by 2002; last-minute negotiations limited its mandate to monitoring the "situation of internal displacement" and small aid delivery projects. At least three coordinating coalitions of humanitarian agencies developed during the last years of the 1990s: the Inter-Agency Dialogue (Diálogo Inter Agencial, or DIAL, made up of Oxfam, Christian Aid, Save the Children, the Norwegian Refugee Council, Diakonia, Project Counseling Services, and PBI as observers) and two groups coordinating southern European and Nordic humanitarian agencies. The U.S. aid package passed in 2000 also pumped tens of millions of dollars into humanitarian projects and assistance to the displaced.

The expansion of humanitarian agencies in Colombia occurred simultaneously with growing debates within the field over the relationship between the role of neutrality, human rights, and political advocacy in aid provision during conflicts. Sharp controversies within and among leading agencies led to widely different positions. Some groups saw humanitarian aid as a means of assisting populations at risk while avoiding messy political commitments in the context of entrenched internal conflicts. Others, like Oxfam, came to see their role as increasingly political and began advocacy programs to target policy makers to change what they viewed as the origins of these conflicts. The result was a surprising new landscape of competition and opportunity for Colombian human rights NGOs. While some humanitarian agencies dismissed these NGOs as too overtly political and partisan, others provided funding for human rights advocacy campaigns or incorporated human rights issues into their initiatives.

PEACE AND HUMAN RIGHTS

The use of a culture of democratic or peaceful coexistence *(cultura de convivencia democrática or pacífica)*, not to explain violence, but as a way out of it, was first forcefully articulated during the public debates surrounding the writing of the 1991 Constitution and is reflected in a number of its articles. For example, Article 70 states, "Culture in its diverse manifestations is the foundation of the nation. The State recognizes the equality and dignity of all who live within the country."[42] This demonstrates a new emphasis on the "diverse manifestations" of culture, reflecting a previously unacknowledged multiculturalism in this new imagining of the Colombian nation. President Samper suggested that such a culture could be institutionally stimulated through the Ministry of Culture. As he stated at the Forum of Culture in Bogotá on March 23, 1995: "The Ministry of Culture will help us replace the culture of conflict that characterizes our social relations today for the culture of democratic co-existence [conviencia democrática]. The Ministry of Culture will enable us to remember always and for always that we are richly different. . . . But above all the Ministry of Culture will help us achieve peace for Colombia. The peace of identity, the peace of return to the basics of conviviality, the peace of equality based on differences" (quoted in Ochoa 1996: 26–27).

This process is not unique to Colombia. During the 1990s, the decline of the socialist model, the end of armed opposition movements, and the continued economic decline in spite of democratic reforms have engendered a deep crisis of both state institutions and leftist movements throughout Latin America. With the absence of clear alternative political platforms, "culture" is increasingly being emphasized as a site of political identity and activism. As Ana Maria Ochoa explains, "With the disenchantment produced by the failure of left-wing movements of the sixties and the emergence out of dictatorial regimes the inquiry over the role of culture in the current processes of democratization in Latin America has taken central stage" (Ochoa 1996: 169).

In Colombia this vague exhortation for a culture of peace has been championed by numerous networks, including many organizations backed by the Catholic Church that have adopted a conflict resolution approach as a means of reducing the conflict in Colombia. Their political platform has largely centered on supporting guerrilla negotiations, and these groups experienced a dramatic resurgence during Pastrana's frustrated peace talks with the FARC in the late 1990s. Their major international allies included staff of the U.N. missions that were being slowly phased out of Central America following the culmination of peace treaties in El Salvador and Guatemala; for several years Colombia was rumored to possibly be the next large-scale mission should peace talks succeed.[43] Despite an important attempt to build alliances within the human rights community based on protesting specific kinds of abuses, tensions about differing political agendas and priorities led to an eventual rupture.

One of the largest civil society peace organizations was Redepaz (lit., "peace network"), founded in 1993 as a loose coalition of organizations from throughout the country, with strong backing from the Catholic Church. According to Monsignor Leonardo Gomez Serna, bishop of the province of Socorro and San Gil in the Northeast and a leading proponent of the initiative, the main objective was "defeating the war." The initial group received an important influx of ex-combatants from the M-19 (reconstituted as the Democratic Movement M-19 after peace talks that resulted in a negotiated settlement in 1991). Later successive groups of reincertados, guerrillas who accepted a series of amnesties and negotiated settlements, were also influential in peace activism, among them the CRS, a dissent group from the ELN, which laid down arms in 1994.

During the mid-1990s, Redepaz was one of the main organizers of a series of marches and symbolic actions in support of peace. A primary, and unexpected, ally was País Libre (lit., Free Country), an organization that supported the family members of kidnap victims and whose major constituency was middle-class businessmen. The organization was inspired by then-journalist Francisco Santos, who had been kidnapped and help captive by the Medellín Cartel for almost nine months during its "narcoterrorism" campaign against governmental prosecution. In an El Tiempo editorial, Santos complained that greater understanding of the phenomenon of kidnapping—and support for the victims—was needed.[44] País Libre remains the primary NGO dedicated to assisting kidnap victims and their families.

In 1996 País Libre, Redepaz, and other peace groups organized a series of peace marches in five cities, with a massive turnout that surprised even the organizers. In Bogotá nearly fifty thousand people marched under the banner "For the country that we want, no to kidnapping." Redepaz agreed to work with País Libre on the condition that the protest include forced disappearances (abductions carried out by state agents) and that the call to end guerrilla violence be broadened to a blanket rejection of war and support for a negotiated settlement. Redepaz also participated in the organization of a number of symbolic votes for peace, including the Children's Mandate for Peace and Rights in October 1996 and the Citizen's Mandate for Peace, Life, and Liberty, which resulted in more than 10 million votes in support of peace in late 1997.[45] Critics decried these efforts as so symbolic as to be meaningless. Peace was not defined; the ballot simply offered a choice between war and peace, so the vote did not advance any larger social consensus regarding specific policies to promote peace. However, the process of organizing the referendum encouraged interaction among persons and sectors that rarely had the chance to share a common cause, such as members of the Business Council and trade union leaders along with members of human rights organizations and representatives of economic groups. The high-profile peace campaigns made negotiations with the guerrillas the central issue in the 1998 elections and a clear factor in Pastrana's election.

Media coverage and publicity sound bites reduced these efforts to a slogan, *No more!* (No más). The more nuanced position of the citizens' campaign for liberty and against kidnapping and forced disappearance was lost, and the marches developed into a distinctly antiguerrilla affair. Redepaz and other organizations were profoundly critical of this shift. Despite the advances, many complained that the oligarchy stole the movement, in the person of the leader of the Santos family, the powerful owners of *El Tiempo*. The organizing coalition no longer convened a broad spectrum of organizations, instead beginning to function as another NGO in its own right. For their part, businessmen and economic associations organized an NGO based on the "No more" campaign. For these groups, the primordial objectives were to stop the war and end kidnapping; they did not support the broader social justice platform advanced by Redepaz.

Human rights NGOs continued to participate in peace efforts through a series of umbrella organizations convened to foster civil society participation in negotiations. Trade union groups, human rights NGOs, and activists from the left organized the Comité de Búsqueda de la Paz (Search Committee for Peace), which held seminars on peace and civil society in the main departmental capitals. These seminars included representatives from the "organized sectors": workers, indigenous people, women's groups, youth groups, and environmentalists. In 1996 this committee was absorbed by the Permanent Assembly of Civil Society for Peace, organized to galvanize Catholic leadership on the peace issue and to broaden participation. This was a particular concern in light of what some leaders called the "jet-set" civil society (primarily business representatives) who played a crucial (some would say steamrolling) role in the civil society discussions with the ELN and the paramilitaries. The first Permanent Assembly meeting had support from international organizations including the Red Cross and the United Nations Development Program; Danielle Mitterrand, widow of the former French President François Mitterrand, was the keynote speaker at the first national conference.[46]

For Colombian human rights NGOs, concern that the human rights agenda would be sacrificed in the name of peace became a significant concern. During the Pastrana administration, the focus on peace translated into neglect for state human rights programs; Pastrana's message stressed that human rights abuses could be dealt with only after the war was ended. This view of human rights was widely shared by groups involved in the burgeoning field of conflict resolution, which commonly view efforts to ensure human rights accountability as an impediment to peace agreements between warring factions. Amnesty legislation and guarantees of immunity are often viewed as fundamental for trust building at the negotiating table; warlords have little incentive to lay down their arms if they will immediately be tried for war crimes or other abuses. Human rights activists point out that such amnesties can fail to ensure lasting peace, with criminal elements within political factions frequently returning to armed actions.

Confronted with the complex panorama of Colombian violence, activists began using the human rights framework to classify the violent homicides that years earlier had been considered partisan violence, or part of insurgent and counterinsurgency campaigns. However, human rights is only one of the frameworks used to prompt specific responses from the international community. Other NGO actors and government officials were deeply invested in documenting the humanitarian crisis in Colombia and the growing number of internally displaced people to generate increased assistance. Groups focusing on negotiations and prospects for a settlement with the guerrillas advocated for the creation of a culture of peace that required support from groups focusing on conflict resolution strategies. Other rights frameworks were also deployed in Colombia throughout the 1990s, including women's rights, children's rights, indigenous and Afro-Colombian rights, and economic, social, and cultural rights. International concern about child soldiers and the forced recruitment of minors spurred the creation of new NGOs and networks focused on the particular needs of this population. These groups offer important sites for further research. My focus for the remainder of this book is on the human rights professionals who employed the human rights framework to focus international attention on politically motivated homicides.

CHAPTER 2

Solidarity with Our Class Brothers

The First Wave of Colombian Human Rights Activism

Over lunch in a cavernous, once-elegant Chinese restaurant in bustling downtown Medellín, Doña Eugenia told me her life story, which is also the story of the first generation of Colombian human rights activists.[1] The daughter of victims of the partisan violence of the 1940s, Doña Eugenia was a young widow in the growing shantytowns of 1960s Medellín when a cohort of young radical priests introduced her to a new world of political activism and changed her life. She distributed an underground guerrilla newspaper hidden under bushels of *plátanos*, collected medical supplies, and began assisting peasants detained after the ELN's first military operations in the early 1970s. Her collections of food and clothing from local unions for the prisoners evolved into one of the first major Colombian organizations to adopt the human rights framework: the Committee in Solidarity with Political Prisoners (Comité en Solidaridad con los Presos Políticos, CSPP). Now in her seventies, Doña Eugenia had survived death threats, exile, and the waves of political violence that claimed the lives of many *compañeros*. For her, human rights work remained a radical vocation, born of the political consciousness-raising of 1960s *militancia*. She exemplified many of the characteristics of the first wave of human rights activists: she was marginalized, lower middle class, and touched by political violence, and she was pulled into the radical transformations of Colombian society as the new urban majority gained access to higher education and joined new community networks that exposed them to new paradigms of political analysis and participation. Like her colleagues, by the late 1980s Doña Eugenia had adopted the human rights framework to describe her work but continued to view solidarity with her class brothers and the radical transformation of society as the foundation of her activism.

Human rights entered the political repertoire of the Colombian left in the 1980s. Activists learned about human rights, and how to use them, from other activists, many from the Southern Cone. They then spread the human rights framework throughout the country by making it the focus of popular education workshops and consciousness-raising efforts. Human rights frameworks were simply the latest of a series of "traveling theories," such as different strains of Communist ideologies and the international circulation of cultural production that have flowed throughout Latin America (Hale 1999). They were used to explain and resolve a specific kind of Colombian violence: violence perpetrated by the state against the left. Despite the dramatic rise in drug-related violence during the 1980s, these human rights discussions did not view the narcotics trade, or the accompanying criminal violence, as a central factor in the escalating violence. Sympathetic to revolutionary struggles at home and abroad, these activists also largely viewed violence as employed by the Colombian guerrillas as the legitimate expression of the "right to rebellion" and collective defense.

Human rights groups in Colombia first began documenting abuses after the massive detentions and jailings of urban leftists in the late 1970s and early 1980s; these were followed by assassinations and massacres in the late 1980s.[2] For the vast majority of self-defined human rights activists, however, activism was not simply a response to political violence but was profoundly shaped by the political culture inherited from this legacy of radical activism. One of the only exceptions to this rule was the family members of radical activists, who became human rights organizers on behalf of their detained and disappeared relatives. Learning to navigate the complicated terrain of Colombian leftist politics was a central element in their involvement with human rights groups.[3] For both human rights activists and victims' family members who joined the vast majority of organizations, however, activism was defined in the terms of the Colombian left. In their view, Colombian history was an unbroken line of state repression against popular organizations, which justified revolutionary violence and focused on state responsibility.

When I arrived in Bogotá in May 1989, ten months into my first year of volunteer work in Colombia, I unwittingly landed in the center of this growing human rights community. After completing a year volunteering in educational programs for poor children, rather than return home, I decided to stay in Colombia, start college, and continue my volunteer work with a human rights group. I began classes in the anthropology department of the Universidad Nacional, Colombia's largest and best-known public university. Through the exchange program that originally brought me to Colombia, I contacted the director of the human rights office of the Jesuit think tank CINEP and began a volunteer internship, my duties ranging from assisting human rights education workshops with union activists to baby-sitting the director's six-month-old son.

What I did not realize at the time was how fortuitous my location and timing were, for I spent the next six months immersed in the debates and struggles of the emerging network of human rights organizations. I shared a tiny house in the downtown working-class neighborhood of La Perseverancia with one of a series of students who leased the house from a political activist living in exile in France. Gabriel, who had served with my philosophy student boyfriend during their obligatory military service, was an actor and humanities major at La Distrital, a public university up the hill from our house. His two sisters were political activists who would eventually go on to work with a number of human rights NGOs, and his brother was an archaeology classmate of mine. The house was filled with a rotating crowd of activists, artists, and students. At the Nacional the political debates were no less intense. Periodic student strikes and violent clashes with the police shut down class; for much of the semester, antiriot tanks were stationed outside the campus gate. The professors were not immune to the politicized atmosphere; the chair of the anthropology department had recently returned to Colombia after ten years in Moscow completing his Ph.D. on a Communist Party scholarship. I first met Flor Alba Romero in her class, "Contemporary Social Problems in Colombia"; her then husband was the director of the Committee in Solidarity with Political Prisoners, and her sister was the director of the human rights office where I volunteered. The circle of friends and colleagues I stumbled into those first six months began more than a decade of work and study in and about Colombia.

At the time I did not imagine that far ahead; I was simply consumed with absorbing my new life. As a white nineteen-year old American high school graduate, self-described vegetarian, Quaker pacifist, I was clearly a novelty for the Colombians with whom I lived and worked. But in many ways I was much like many of the activists who began their careers in politicized universities and radical Christian organizations; I had been raised with a deep suspicion of authority and institutions and identified with a vague vocation for social justice and radical transformation. Now I was thrust into a complex network of personal and political attachments that were rarely publicly acknowledged. I was schooled in Colombian history as taught by the left and made my home in an activist culture that connected us to political struggles around the world through Cuban music, Spanish poetry, and the slogans of the African National Congress. Immersed in a tightly knit community of human rights organizations that grew in international influence over the next decade, I witnessed firsthand the expansion of the first wave of human rights activism in Colombia.

THE EMERGENCE OF HUMAN RIGHTS GROUPS

Doña Eugenia was just one of many veteran activists who shared their life stories with me as I attempted to piece together the largely unwritten history of the first human rights groups. For many hours, activists sat with me in offices, my apartment, restaurants, or their homes and told me the origin stories of their activism. Most were still active with human rights organizations; some had become directors of their own groups, receiving international recognition and death threats as a result of their efforts. Some had left their activist days behind them and now worked for the government or in private companies. From those stories, I have chosen those of Carlos Rodriguez, a lawyer; Gloria Flórez, a college dropout and now NGO executive director; and Doña Eugenia, a working-class mother with a fourth-grade education. Despite their differences, they shared a commitment to radical social transformation, shaped by their participation in consciousness-raising groups organized through the Catholic Church, universities, and unions. Their life stories are the stories of the first human rights organizations, of the networks of relationships and the development of strategies that would shape early activism and the human rights agenda for more than two decades.

The formative political experience of the first generation of Colombia's NGO human rights activists was *militancia*, participation in the semiclandestine leftist parties of the 1960s and 1970s. For this generation, being a part of the militant left meant participation in a single spectrum of political struggle that ranged from community organizing to armed revolution. Deeply divided by ideological differences, hierarchical, and largely clandestine, this organizational experience also infused a generation with hope for radical change and the belief that a relatively small group of dedicated individuals could achieve social transformation in their lifetimes. Militants positioned themselves in the context of a global struggle for social justice, through passionate ideological debates that assume an intricate knowledge of international politics and cultural production. In practice, being a militant involved a range of activities. One activist explained that *militantes* "did political work that was assigned by the party, *trabajo de masas*, work with poor, marginalized urban and rural communities, or political propaganda or training and education, different kinds of work that was assigned according to the party's strategy and the directors of the party." While degrees of party affiliation varied with time, strictly defined *militancia* involved a direct and explicit connection with an organization. Not all activists were militants, but all those I interviewed espoused a general leftist sympathy shaped by the political milieu in which *militancia* was the dominant standard.

Doña Eugenia Goes to the City and Begins Working with Priests

Many first-generation human rights activists traced their political awakening to the persecution of their parents during the partisan violence of the 1950s. As we sat in the Chinese restaurant, Doña Eugenia began her story with her arrival as a child in Medellín, after fleeing with her family from the political persecution faced by her father, a member of the Liberal Party. "My family is from the Urrá Valley, and because of the violence in 1948 we had to come to the city. My father was a Liberal, he was the tailor in the town, with a very low salary, and he had ten children. So my childhood was very hard, sometimes we didn't have enough to eat and we would go out to the hamlets to bring back what we could find," she told me over steaming plates of limp chop suey. "My father got a job in the local government and they sent him to Sonsón. That is when La Violencia arrived. Fortunately he wasn't there. But they persecuted the wives and children of Liberal people. With two sisters, we managed to get out. We were very poor when we arrived in Medellín, in El Corazón barrio in Belencito." This slum, like hundreds of others ringing Medellín and other cities in Colombia, swelled with the displaced from the Colombian violence of the 1950s.

This origin story has become a central narrative in the history of Colombia as told by the left, connecting past violence to the present. In this telling, La Violencia was an example of the political repression of small farmers (Liberal peasants) by state-controlled security forces (police agents), part of a historical continuity that continues to the present day. This version of history has been reproduced in numerous publications, including such books as *El libro negro de la repressión* (The Black Book of Repression), one of the first publications of the CSPP, and is frequently woven into activists' stories, even by those too young to have directly experienced the persecution of the 1940s. These stories remain part of the living narrative of human rights activism for many older activists; during a human rights workshop in Medellín, Doña Eugenia began her comments to the guest speaker with an emotional appeal to collective memory, reminding the audience that political violence in Colombia started with the torture and murder of Liberals by paid assassins backed by the Conservative government in the 1950s.

Doña Eugenia's life in the city was hard. Married at sixteen to a man twice her age, she was left with three young children when he died. As she described her life, she worked "day and night" to support her family sewing underwear and cooking for children studying at a local Catholic school. Already a neighborhood leader among local housewives, she was deeply influenced by a chance meeting with Camilo Torres. One of the luminaries of the Colombian left, Torres was a Jesuit priest and sociologist who founded a broad left movement called the United Front. He became disillusioned with the limits of electoral politics and joined the ELN, only to be killed in his first combat operation in 1966. At the time Torres was visiting striking factory workers in the neighborhood, and Doña Eugenia offered the charistmatic speaker the use of her phone. While waiting for his phone call to go through, Torres began Doña Eugenia's political education.

> He would dial the phone, but it was busy, and he would talk to me. Why are there so many children here? And I would explain, and he would dial the number and it was busy again. What are you doing in this neighborhood? And I would explain, and he would dial again. Do you know what the Frente Unido [United Front] is? I didn't, and he explained to me that *Siete* [Seven] was their newspaper. He talked to me for a long time. That day, I became a different person from the woman I was. He awoke something very large in me.

Doña Eugenia began to work with Torres's movement and then with the radical priests who supported him: "Working with the Frente Unido I met many people. I worked with Vicente Mejía, he became the priest in my parish. He had worked with Golconda, and he opened another world to me." Golconda was Colombia's most prominent early expression of liberation theology, first named in a 1971 book by the Peruvian theologian Gustavo Gutierrez. Liberation priests preached a doctrine of action against poverty and for the poor, emphasizing the need for social change and employing Marxist categories of class, conflict, and exploitation as a basis for critical social analysis. They extended changes begun by Vatican II, which in 1965 directed the church to become more engaged with community activities and prescribed a series of liberalizing reforms, including performing the liturgy in local languages instead of Latin. In 1968 the Bishop's Conference in Medellín proclaimed the "preferential option for the poor" as the root of the church's ministry and urged an expanded role for lay clergy in forming Christian base communities (CEBs), small groups that used biblical readings as the basis for consciousness-raising, reflection, and community organizing.[4]

Liberation theology played a smaller role in Colombia than in other Latin America countries such as Chile and Brazil. Colombia's Catholic hierarchy has been one of the most conservative and historically powerful on the continent, linked to the institutional power of the state through control of educational curriculums and privileges (fueros) and backed by the Conservative Party (González 1977; LaRosa 2000). Although the 1968 Bishop's Conference was hosted in Medellín, the Colombian Catholic hierarchy remained largely hostile to transformations in church practice and doctrine. To cite only one example, Conservative Colombian Bishop (and now cardinal) Msgr. Alfonso López Trujillo aggressively opposed liberation theology in the 1970s, first as the secretary general and then as the president of the Latin American Council of Bishops.

The influence of liberation theology was widely felt, however, by a generation of priests, nuns, and lay leaders who devoted themselves to nurturing community development efforts. Some of the most radical established Golconda, a short-lived Catholic community. Many members were jailed for their activities, and a small but influential cohort of radical priests joined the guerrillas, primarily the ELN (Medina Gallego 2001; Restrepo 1995).[5] For many of the un- and undereducated rural and urban poor, participation in these groups was their first experience with political activism (Levine 1992). Participation expanded members' social networks and created a new activist identity, especially for poor women previously defined solely through their family relationships. Marxist notions of solidarity and struggle with the oppressed replaced the traditional Catholic teachings of passive acceptance of poverty and the understanding of charity as giving to the poor. Doña Eugenia described this transformation as it affected her sense of herself as an activist working within the church:[6] "With Father Vicente I learned the difference between solidarity and charity. If I give you the food that is left over, that I don't want because I am full, or the clothes that I don't need anymore, that I no longer wear, that is charity. Solidarity is when I share what I have with my class brother. I began working in the jails as solidarity work."

Doña Eugenia began carrying out clandestine errands for the United Front, including distributing their newspaper, which, although technically legal, was viewed with extreme suspicion by government officials: "I would take the newspaper and put it in a basket and cover it with plantains on top. I would take the paper as far as Itaguí, to all the unions. I had to hide it, because everything is forbidden here, anything that talks against the state is illegal." She lowered her voice as she sat across the table from me, and admitted that she distributed the outlawed ELN newspaper, *Simacota,* as well, and collected medicine for injured activists and guerrillas. These jobs were not without risk; on at least one occasion her house was searched, and she was detained and questioned for days at time, but she described with pride resisting army attempts to intimidate her during her interrogation.

Doña Eugenia's first foray into human rights activism, an ad hoc effort to bring supplies to jailed ELN suspects, like much early human rights work, depended on already organized members of social movements—in this case, unions—to provide material support. During a visit to a jail in 1972, she discovered that detained guerrilla suspects lived in terrible conditions without the minimal food and clothing necessary for survival; to this day, prisoners in Colombia often depend on family and friends for food and clothing while imprisoned. Doña Eugenia explained, "The peasants don't have anyone to visit them. They were from rural areas, that is where the ELN was operating. The families couldn't come visit them because from their *vereda* to the road was a day's walk, and then from the road to the town was another day, and they had no one to stay with in the city and no money. These peasants didn't even have a change of clothes, they were in the same clothes they had been captured in."

Doña Eugenia was profoundly moved by their state: "I looked at those people with a lot of tenderness, I remembered what Camilo Torres had said about how we had to act with our class brothers, and so I told them that I would come back and visit them. This is how the Committee in Solidarity with Political Prisoners began." Despite her inexperience in public speaking, Doña Eugenia convinced the doctor's union to support her newfound cause. "I went to the unions, the doctors' union, who were having their meeting, and told the head about these prisoners who didn't even have a change of clothes.[7] And at their assembly, he said, you have to get up and go tell these people your story. I said, no, you go, but he told me I had to go. I got up, and my hands were trembling, I had never talked like that before people." The next weekend they took clothes, food, toothbrushes, and soap to the prisoners.

The Committee in Solidarity with Political Prisoners was officially founded in 1973. As the name makes clear, the organization did not initially adopt a professional human rights profile but clearly identified itself with (as in solidarity with) individuals jailed because of their anti-state actions. Typical of early human rights work in Colombia, the CSPP had an all-volunteer staff, close links with wider social movements (especially the union and student movements), and, as its name would suggest, a strong symbolic identification with the guerrillas.[8] As Doña Eugenia explained to me, "The visit to the jail every week was sacred. I would go to union meetings, and I began to understand what a political prisoner is. We didn't work for just one sector, to name one, the FARC, no. We worked with all of them. I was like the mother to them all." The CSPP remained a small organization with only a handful of volunteers during the first five years of its existence. In addition to its direct work in the jails, the CSPP published pamphlets and reports on political violence in Colombia. The CSPP was instrumental in the first Colombian congressional debates of a human rights issue; it provided documentation of peasants accused of belonging to the ELN and tortured to sympathetic congressional representatives. The debate was widely covered in the leftist press. In 1977 the CSPP sent the first international urgent action to Amnesty International; for the next decade, international human rights work was limited to sending information to the emerging international human rights nongovernmental organizations (primarily Amnesty International) and periodic visits to Colombia from Amnesty staff.

As Doña Eugenia recalled her early days of activism, the work was incorporated into her daily routine. "When I worked with the *presos* [prisoners], I had a notebook, and all the time when I would walk down the street I would say to people, you, what are you going to give? A pair of socks, some clothes, some food. And I would write it down in my notebook." But despite the dangers and setbacks, the 1970s were a time of great hope: "You have to realize that it was one big party, *una fiesta*." By the end of the decade, their trips to the jails were widely supported by other groups in Colombia. Early on, the CSPP benefited from the widespread popularity of the left among intellectuals. Among its first high-profile members were Enrique Santos, from one of Colombia's most prominent political families (he is now an editor at *El Tiempo*, which his family owns), and Nobel Prize-winner Gabriel García Márquez and other intellectual luminaries, earning them publicity and legitimacy.

The repression faced by guerrillas and activists alike, however, was about to change. Doña Eugenia recalled the dramatic shift in government response in the late 1970s: "In 1979 I was going to all the unions, I didn't need any letters of introduction because everyone knew me. This was during the Turbay administration, when he went to Europe and said that he was the only political prisoner. This is when Amnesty International made their first visit, when everyone was thrown in jail and Omaira Montoya was disappeared."[9]

Carlos Joins a Party, Gets Arrested, and Starts Thinking about International Law

Carlos was one of the people thrown in jail in 1979; later he became a founding member and deputy director of one of Colombia's best-known human rights groups. He sat down with me early one morning in his uptown Bogotá office to tell me the story of how he began working in human rights. Like Doña Eugenia, Carlos traces his human rights work to his past as a *militante,* in his case as a member of the Revolutionary Socialist Union (Unión Revolucionaria Socialista, URS).

I began our interview by asking him to explain to me what exactly a *militante* was. "To be a militant is a person who pays his dues, who goes to party meetings. More than that, I was a leader, a member of the URS command," he said. His future human rights career was born in the URS analysis of the Colombian situation and what the appropriate response should be: "We broke with traditional Colombian Marxist thought, and we characterized the political regime as a civilian dictatorship. It was a civilian regime but with an authoritarian power structure." Focusing on the extensive use of state of siege powers by the president, these activists argued that despite the formal trappings of electoral democracy—and even the expansion of democratic possibilities following the end of the National Front in 1974—the extraordinary powers used by the Executive and the military made Colombia essentially a dictatorship. Carlos continued, "So our political action should focus on recovering these liberties. I remember we said that we had to recover the street for the citizens and not just for military parades." In 1974, after a Communist Party town councilman was assassinated, leftist parties and unions came together to form the Democratic Front for Liberties and began lobbying the government to ensure the safety of leftist activists. Carlos joined them: "One of our tasks was to go meet with the president at the time, López Michelsen, to demand guarantees. In the Front, I represented the URS at the working group, and the Communist Party representative was Hernando Hurtado; he was later very important, he was a congressional representative, and he was very important in creating the Permanent Committee for the Defense of Human Rights [Comité Permanente para la Defensa de los Derechos Humanos], whose political origin was this Front." While the United Front quickly fell apart due to persecution and political infighting, one of numerous ephemeral coalitions characterizing Colombian political life, the Permanent Committee went on to play a major role in human rights activism in the 1980s.

The Permanent Committee was founded following the first national human rights forum in 1979. A series of restrictive laws and mass detentions brought the issue of human rights to the forefront of Colombian political debates. During the 1970s, the military court system was allowed to try civilians in secret hearings known as *consejos verbales de guerra*, military hearings in which the accused had none of the due process rights allowed in the civilian court system. In 1978 the rights provided by the judicial system were further eroded by the National Security Statute, issued by President Julio César Turbay, which extended extraordinary powers allowed by the state of siege to the military. At the same time the guerrillas, in particular, the M-19, conducted a number of dramatic operations. The largest single incident was the December 1978 theft of weapons from the national armory in northern Bogotá (Morris 2002). This audacious attack on military installations, and the poor planning by the M-19 that left a long trail of involved family members and friends, led to more than two thousand arrests in little more than a week in Bogotá alone. The military took advantage of its powers to carry out massive sweeps, leading to a dramatic increase in the number of political prisoners—from an average of only 200 to more than 5,000 a year. Detainees were held in military barracks without benefit of counsel, and many were severely tortured. Carlos was one of those caught in the sweep after soldiers raided the office he shared with two other lawyers. He recalled what happened:

> They searched our office in an impressive operation, they took over the block, soldiers arrived. They were looking for weapons, or things related to weapons, papers, documents. They found copies of the *Manifiesto*, they found copies of [the Communist Party newspaper] *Voz*, they found an Opus Dei newspaper called *Diálogos Universitarios*, but this edition had a cover

photo of a policeman hitting a student, so that seemed suspicious to them too.[10] From our office, we were working with the union movement and we participated in courses and there were flyers advertising a course by the union committee. This was the so-called subversive material they captured, in other words, absolutely without any relationship to their supposed objective. But they made me go with them, my two colleagues no, because my name was on the lease for the office.

Carlos refused to talk in detail about the torture he underwent but commented that those days shaped the rest of his life. It was during his time in jail that he had an inspiration that would guide the rest of his legal career:

> I was held there for seventeen days in really bad conditions, it was a torture camp, but there, during a moment during a torture session, I asked if there was a judge. They told me, of course, you can write to the judge, and they gave me a piece of paper and a pen—that was the moment when I realized they had stolen the pen that I had inherited from my father—and I wrote several pages to the judge, asking him to set me free. I told him, look, you have to pay attention to the international human rights treaties, that was when I still didn't know much about what I was talking about because we had never appealed to international law before. I still have a copy of what I wrote, because it didn't make the judge pay attention to the international treaties, but it did make me realize that international law was very important, that it was something we could use when we had no possibilities of appealing to an internal organism. At that point you had two choices, you could take up arms or you could take the road of appealing to institutions outside the state, that were superior to the state and that somehow would force them from outside, that had authority and power. That is how, with other colleagues, I saw the necessity of thinking about how international law applied to the situation in Colombia.

The lawyer who eventually took his case, Gustavo Gallón, argued successfully for his release and eventually became a pioneer in the use of international law in his own right. Carlos and Gustavo had first met at law school, in student protests and through an organization known as the Group of 33. The Group of 33 included the future political luminaries Carlos Pizarro (later commander of the M-19 who demobilized only to be assassinated as their presidential candidate in 1990), his brother Eduardo Pizarro (who went on to write numerous books about political violence and the history of the guerrillas in Colombia), and a number of future Jesuit priests. After graduating, they maintained an intellectual connection, particularly on the issue of use of state of siege powers by the Colombian state. Gustavo's research on the topic was published as

Quince años de estado de sitio en Colombia: 1958–1978 (Fifteen Years of the State of Siege in Colombia) (Gallón 1979).

In addition to defending Carlos, Gustavo helped organize the first human rights forum, held in April 1979, and one of the first major human rights groups, the Permanent Committee for the Defense of Human Rights. Public sympathy for the left and rejection of what was widely viewed as excessive force and unjustifiable use of torture by the armed forces, led to participation by a broad cross section of the Colombian intellectual and political elite. The Permanent Committee pioneered attempts to raise awareness of human rights issues with both the public and the government by holding public forums and meeting with government officials. This was facilitated by the membership of several highly educated lawyers and the participation of Alfredo Vázquez Carrizosa, a member of Colombia's political elite and former *canciller* (secretary of state). Radicalized by his experience as Colombian ambassador to Chile during the 1973 coup, Vázquez Carrizosa remained an active presence in the Permanent Committee and, as the public face of the organization, stressed their political plurality. Over time, however, the Permanent Committee was increasingly dominated by the Communist Party (Partido Comunista, PC). In part this was the result of logistical necessity: the PC had the national network and organized cadres capable of mobilizing significant grassroots support for the new organization. However, the PC also remained deeply involved in the Permanent Committee because the former's membership was increasingly targeted for political violence by expanding paramilitary groups throughout the 1980s. One founding member who requested not to be named recalled:

> The [first] forum was guaranteed to work because the Communist Party organized it. After that a lot of people withdrew, and the sectors of the left were the ones who remained, along with the PC. Other sectors started feeling that they didn't have a place within the committee. They kept having forums, and each time there was less and less participation of the nonleft sectors. They didn't feel really committed to the issues. They didn't feel affected by the repression, they didn't feel like it was their thing, *lo nuestro*. The PC and the Patriotic Union, which was created later, they kept on being touched, being affected by political violence, so they stayed involved in human rights issues. The others, they left because they didn't feel committed to the issue, or because they didn't feel there was political space for them to participate in human rights groups, they felt excluded.

Carlos also left his activism in Colombia behind during the 1980s but not by choice. In addition to his psychological and physical scars, his time in jail had left him another legacy: his name and picture appeared on a wanted poster of suspects accused of attacking a police station. Harassed by police although he did not match an eyewitness account of the perpetrator, Carlos packed his bags and left for Spain, where he began doctoral studies in human rights law.

Gloria Raises Consciousness and Reads Poetry

The executive director of her own NGO and the mother of a young son, Gloria made and broke numerous interview appointments with me before finally arriving at my apartment one sunny Saturday morning. On her way to an afternoon of work at the office, she sat at my table, drinking coffee and pausing frequently as she tried to reconstruct her life as a student activist in the early 1980s. Plump and pretty, she had pale features that were a legacy of her ancestors, German tradesmen who had settled in the Magdalena Valley several generations before. Like Doña Eugenia, she traced her openness to activism to her Catholic education but her political awakening to student debates: "Inside the university, political conflicts were very dynamic, not just general student conflicts but social conflicts in general. At the university, I had the opportunity to participate in different groups. The first was the University Solidarity Committee, which included workers, students, and professors and carried out solidarity events for political prisoners."

She was not alone. Student activists were one of the primary motors of leftist organizing during this period, and there were more students in Colombia than ever before. The number of students continuing education beyond grade school was one of the most important demographic changes of the second half of the twentieth century. A generation of modernizing policy makers, many funded by U.S. programs including the Alliance for Progress, expanded the number and quality of both high schools and public universities. "The importance of the increase in the student population between 1960 and 1980 cannot be overestimated," according to the Mexican historian Jorge Castañeda in his history of the left in Latin America (Castañeda 1993: 191). He goes on to describe how "millions of Latin American students entered a university system seeking answers to questions their parents had never known well enough to ask. They found most of the satisfactory responses in the teachings, writings, and preachings of social scientists . . . [that] provide a coherent, all-encompassing explanation for the status quo—what later came to be known as dependency theory—and a blueprint for a better world. It featured continental heroes—Che Guevara first among them—and national second stringers—Luciano Cruz in Chile, Camilo Torres in Colombia" (Castañeda 1993: 192).[11]

For most of these students, the first in their families to go on to higher education, negotiating college life meant participating in passionate political debates and eventually aligning themselves with a particular political group. While defined by a political line *(línea),* these groups organized and directed a range of activities, including study groups, volunteer work with neighborhood committees, and "cultural work," including concerts, poetry, and theater.

At the time, none of this activism was defined in terms of human rights; Gloria told me she thought of her activism as a general response to the "dramatic social situation." The few references to human rights in the 1970s in *Alternativa,* a major left-wing magazine, referred not to Colombia but to the Southern Cone dictatorships, particularly Chile. Chileans were among the first on the continent to use the human rights framework to mobilize support for persecuted activists, working with the support of the Catholic Church and a large international network of Chileans in exile following the 1973 military coup (Loveman 1998). Colombian leftists learned of this activism through left-wing publications and the direct accounts of exiles, and their example proved influential for the spread of the human rights framework in Colombia.

First through the University Committee, then the Bogotá-based Committee in Solidarity with Political Prisoners founded by Doña Eugenia, Gloria began regular visits to jailed activists and was a founding member of the branch of the CSPP in her town. "The solidarity work in the prisons was linked to consciousness-raising [*trabajo de sensibiliza-ción*] in many sectors of the population, especially the unions," she said. Like Doña Eugenia, she collected money for political prisoners to supply them with food and clothing and to pay for family visits, traveling by bus for weekly workshops in the work camps of the heavily unionized African palm plantations. The unions began creating solidarity committees of their own, in addition to receiving training courses from and organizing activities with university activists. Gloria explained:

> I gave talks, training, what you could call now human rights work, but then we didn't call it that. It was more a consciousness-raising work, how to strengthen solidarity, how to understand what is happening. What was the National Security Statute, what needed to change. This was in 1980, 1981, 1982, during the election. We explained why these kinds of laws went against the Constitution and our rights. It was that kind of educational

work. We did talks with the workers in their camps, each week to the camps, gathering the workers and giving talks about the reality of the country.

At the same time, she traveled to other cities, working with the oil workers' union and the teachers' union, as well as with community and neighborhood groups.

Gloria described the cultural work of singing and performing with a musical group as a central part of her political education efforts:

> We combined the solidarity work with the musical work because we reached people [*sensibilizamos*] through music as well. For example, we had a recital called "For Liberty." We performed a show that had poetry and music sung by Joan Serrat, Silvio Rodriguez, Pablo Milanes, songs with a social content, and through these recitals we also did consciousness-raising work. We also read poems by Neruda, Benedetti, poems by Spanish poets like Miguel Hernandez, Machado. It was a good show. Many of the solidarity activists had music, theater, and poetry. All this was part of consciousness-raising and education strategy.[12]

When I arrived in Colombia, my friends and colleagues introduced me to these artists, as my cultural education was an integral part of my political training. The first book I read in Spanish was the Uruguayan writer Eduardo Galeano's alternative history of Latin America, *Memory of Fire*. The posters lining the narrow hallway in the house where I lived included the iconic image of Che Guevara, next to a Charlie Chaplin poster, next to a surrealist collage featuring the slogan of the French barricades, *l'imagination au pouvoir*. The music we played included the generic Andean folklore popularized by Chilean bands in exile. I puzzled through translations of Bruce Springsteen, Paul Simon, and the Beatles at the request of my friends, who in turn explained the lyrics of Silvo Rodriguez's "Playa Giron" to me.[13]

In part these artists offered actual history lessons for budding activists. The history of leftist struggles, including the Spanish Republican war against the fascist Franco regime, the Popular Unity government of Salvador Allende, the Haymarket Rebellion of the U.S. labor movement, and the Vietcong resistance to U.S. forces in Vietnam were all mentioned in the music and poetry circulated among Colombian activists in the 1970s and 1980s. In the retelling, the artists made this history a living discussion. In areas where public education was chronically underfunded and public libraries largely nonexistent, and decades before the Internet, the posters, pamphlets, poetry, and cassettes that passed from hand to hand among activists were often a major source of information and education.

This cultural production also contributed to an activist identity locating individuals in a worldwide network of social movements. In Latin America, this cultural production centered on the primary Spanish-language centers of culture: Cuba and Spain and, to a lesser degree, the Southern Cone and included music, poetry, and theater. The music and poetry made by Cuban revolutionaries, radical Spaniards, and Chilean protesters were used throughout Colombia in what was openly referred to as "cultural work" to build political consciousness and construct new political identities. Colombians identified themselves as *hippies* (the English word directly incorporated into Spanish vocabularies with a variety of phonetic spellings), listened to Janis Joplin, and debated politics in terms of Albania, the Sino-Soviet split, Vietnam, and the Paris Revolt of 1968 (López de la Roche 1994: 13).

Gloria finally began to work full time for the CSPP in 1985, doing educational workshops around the country, moving to Bogotá, and leaving college behind. The core of the work of the CSPP, and that which most motivated its volunteers, was the direct service work in prisons. Its methodology was developed by a core of activists, including Gloria, who then traveled around the country teaching the volunteers, primarily student and union activists, how to carry out work in the prisons and the basics of the human rights framework.

The CSPP expanded its prison work to include casework and legal representation of detainees. With five lawyers, the organization began to focus on legal rights and reform, in particular, the issue of habeas corpus (lit., "finding the body"; this is the legal mechanism that obligates state authorities to reveal where they are holding detainees, and it was instrumental in attempts to safeguard prisoners at risk of torture or forced disappearance). By the end of the decade the CSPP was instrumental in getting a few sentences overturned on grounds of lack of evidence and proof that confessions were obtained through torture. It was also instrumental in bringing before the Supreme Court the 1986 case that resulted in the ruling that trying civilians in military courts was unconstitutional; such trials were definitively prohibited by the 1991 Constitution.

When she arrived in Bogotá in 1985, Gloria found what she described as a "weak network" of human rights institutions. In addition to the CSPP and the Permanent Committee, several smaller groups had emerged, including the newly created human rights office of the Center for Grassroots Education and Training. Despite ideological differences, there were numerous connections among these groups. To name only one example, when Gloria arrived at the CSPP, she replaced Amanda Romero, who left to direct CINEP's first human rights office, where I worked as an intern four years later. The earliest incarnation of this office, called the Center for Grassroots Legal Defense, was devoted to the "study of critical legal theory and law as running counter to the legitimate asiprations of the popular classes because of its bourgeois connotations" (Pérez 1998: 210). The center was created as a part of efforts to organize a neighborhood of squatter families being evicted because of the construction of a major highway along the eastern ridge of Bogotá, Avenida los Cerros. After a former CINEP worker was accused of involvement in the assassination of a former cabinet minister, CINEP was investigated by the state intelligence agency, and two member Jesuit priests and the staff librarian were detained. This was the catalyst for establishing the organization's human rights office.

The CINEP human rights office developed a two-pronged approach, documenting human rights abuses, particularly in rural areas, and supporting the development of local human rights groups. One of its first publications was a study of military operations in response to the presence of the M-19 in the southern state of Caquetá, *Muerte y tortura en Caqueta* (Death and Torture in Caqueta); the report was also translated and published in the United States by activists based in New York. In part because of the international institutional links provided by the Catholic Church, CINEP developed a strong relationship with human rights activists in the Southern Cone, in particular the Madres de la Plaza de Mayo, the Argentine association of family members of the disappeared (Perez 1998; Romero 1992). In part because of this relationship, CINEP was instrumental in the creation of the Colombian Association of Relatives of the Detained and Disappeared in 1982. ASFADDES was the earliest self-identified organization of family members of victims of human rights abuses; its first members were the families of fourteen National University students disappeared during a student protest. ASFADDES became an independent organization in 1984, but CINEP continued to play an important advisory role for another decade.

LOCAL COMMITTEES

The CSPP, CINEP, and the Permanent Committee all shared a primary goal by the late 1980s: building local human rights committees through *concientización,* or consciousness-raising. Despite differences in political orientation and ideology, all these groups shared a commitment to radical pedagogy and participatory education as a means of inspiring a critical mass of new activists. By 1984 a loose coalition of human rights groups that met monthly in Bogotá prioritized "human rights education for the promotion and defense of the popular sectors" (Romero 1992: 118); the participating groups included the CSPP, the Colombian League for the Rights and Freedom of the Pueblos, the local Amnesty International chapter, and CINEP. Many were inspired by similar efforts throughout Latin America, in particular, the work of the Brazilian educational theorist Paulo Freire (Freire 1990). According to the translator of his seminal work, *Pedagogy of the Oppressed, concientizaçao* was "learning to perceive social, political and economic contradictions, and to take action against the oppressive elements of reality" (Freire 1990: 19). The underpinning of Freire's theory is that critical consciousness linked to radical practice would end oppression. Many groups, ranging from Christian base communities to the incipient women's movement, adopted similar philosophies to direct work with grassroots communities.

Early human rights activists used these theories to design their workshop methodology. Giving participants a new framework for understanding their experiences of marginalization and oppression was intended to enable new kinds of action and organization. A senior staff member of the CSPP who began her career as a volunteer organizer with the local hospital union described her early training from Bogotá-based activists. Their workshops generated "big interest," she said, "because really what we knew how to defend was workers' rights, but we didn't know anything about other rights, and no one had told us. People started coming from Bogotá, the people who worked with us, for education, how to create the committee, to explain all the things to do."

CINEP began a human rights education program in 1984. The "basic workshop" tried to unite a conception of human rights with a conception of popular education, incorporating ideas from Freire and liberation theology. The workshop consisted of three major sections: the diagnosis of the "life conditions" of participants; a discussion of the human rights situation in Colombia and information about human rights, including the origin and evolution of the Universal Declaration and different legal instruments; and specific steps for acting in cases of human rights violations. In 1986 CINEP introduced *etnodramas*, in which participants enacted different human rights situations, such as an illegal detention or trial without due process. Between 1984 and 1990 CINEP activists conducted approximately two hundred workshops. While the CSPP worked primarily through the unions, CINEP based its community contacts on networks of Catholic priests and nuns, who viewed these workshops as part of their pastoral work.

The ultimate aim of the workshops was not simply to educate individuals about human rights but also to create a human rights infrastructure consolidated through local committees throughout the country. Concentrating exclusively on state abuses, these local committees received training in Colombian and international legal mechanisms for denouncing excessive force and the state's failure to comply with human rights standards. According to one of the trainers, "The common idea was to create on a local and regional level a group of people who could immediately attend to victims of human rights violations, who could take legal action, and who could write up *denuncias* and circulate them on a national and international level and to different state agencies."

The Regional Human Rights Corporation in the Magdalena Valley

The founding of CREDHOS (Corporación Regional para la Defensa de los Derechos Humanos), the Regional Human Rights Corporation in the Magdalena Valley, was typical of the local human rights committees being set up around the country. Based in Barrancabermaja, an oil refining town on the Magdalena River with a violent history of both civic opposition and guerrilla operations, CREDHOS at its zenith had an office in the city and a network of members in the small towns along the river. Barranca is the unofficial capital of the Middle Magdalena, twenty-nine municipalities in five departments that surround the river in the valley between the Andes. For more than four decades, Barranca was famous as a hotbed of radical politics; during the rioting after Gaitán's assassination, the town council declared a revolutionary city government. The ELN, the FARC, and other splinter guerrilla groups were active in the town for many years. The oil workers' union there, the Unión Sindical Obrera (USO), has long been one of the country's largest and most combative. CREDHOS was officially founded in 1987. What made this group exceptional was its longevity; it is still known and funded internationally, and although its membership has shrunk, it continues to operate out of the founder's law office despite ongoing death threats and the assassination of six people affiliated with the project. I had briefly worked with CREDHOS in the mid-1990s designing a research project. Despite my earlier work with the organization, I was ignorant of its early history until I sat down to interview the founding members in Bogotá and on several trips to Barranca during my field-work. They first organized, they told me, after meeting while "collecting bodies," and they decided to create a human rights committee so they could carry out the gruesome tasks together.

Jahel, a founding member, was always impeccably dressed in the tailored suit dresses and large gold jewelry favored by executive women in Colombia. We met first in her office in downtown Bogotá and then in her sunny apartment, where we talked over lunch as Jahel sighed over the ineptness of her maid. Although a lifelong self-described Marxist, she does not take pains to hide her love of luxury and status; the revolution, after all, is "so we can all live well, not so that we can all be poor!" she told me with a laugh. Like Gloria, she began her activism in college; she was a Maoist militant and involved in theater productions. "Being a *militante* was being part of a study group, people studying different thinkers and reflecting on things. We studied Marxism, Leninism, and Stalinism; people then were studying Stalinism too. You belonged to that group and did work, did popular work for the people," she recalled. In her case, this popular work was theater. "I believed myself to be an artist of the people," she told me, smiling ruefully as she remembered her youthful enthusiasm. "From the Forum of Yenan, a speech by Mao about being cultural workers. I remember my friend had the little red book and I was so excited to borrow it and read it. I believed it. I believed that the revolution was coming tomorrow, was right around the corner."

Her husband, a petroleum engineer, was not politically active, and Jahel's life changed when he accepted a job at the Barranca refinery. After a year hanging out in the executive walled compound, "being the *señora* and playing golf," she got involved in local politics, working for the mayor's office. Eventually she was elected as a *concejal*, not for the Maoist party, which she found too ideologically divided, but for the newly formed Patriotic Union. This new progressive party did very well in the local town council and mayoral elections in the areas where the FARC and other guerrilla forces had been strong. But paramilitary death squads, in a shifting alliance between drug traffickers and local military commanders, targeted the civilian supporters of these legal parties.[14] Barranca was changing, becoming flooded with displaced peasants fleeing paramilitary attacks in rural communist strongholds. "That's when my career as a human rights defender started," Jahel told me. "We all met on humanitarian missions, when we would go help displaced people. So we saw the need to create a committee that didn't have any other purpose except human rights. . . . Of course the women in my old neighborhood, they didn't like what I was doing."

The people she met on those missions included the radical lawyer Jorge Gómez and the union activist Rafael Gómez (no relation). Jorge, tall and pale, with a baleful gaze and sardonic sense of humor, arrived in Barranca in 1974 as a judge but resigned two years later to defend labor activists and political prisoners. He lent his office and his secretary for committee meetings; outside the door of the CREDHOS office a brass nameplate announces his legal practice to this day. He was back in Barranca when I met him, a government human rights ombudsman after a decade in exile spent working with the United Nations in Central America (see chapter 6). He recalled the violence of the early 1980s:

> Many of the threats at that time were converted into reality, into deaths. Hernando Posado, a leader from the Communist Party, was the first political killing in Barranca, that was 1982 or 1983. This was followed by an escalation of violence, Gustavo Chacón,[15] others. . . . In 1985–86 I decided that this work was not just for one lawyer but for a collective, a stronger group. . . . The municipal council created a human rights committee, which was linked to CREDHOS. It was a preventative effort. We tried to get the civilian population out of [range of the] bombings and confront the paramilitary strategy.

This effort was not invented by local activists but learned through training. Union activist Rafael was one of those involved in applying human rights activism to local violence. Since starting his job at the refinery in 1975, Rafael had risen through the ranks of the union, eventually becoming president of the Barranca section. Then, as now, the union was dominated by leftist factions and bitterly divided by sectarian infighting. A Trotskyite, Rafael spent a year in Bulgaria studying organizing after a series of divisive strikes split the union in Barranca. When he returned in the early 1980s, he recalled learning about human rights from the national groups in Bogotá: "In 1985–86 we started using the term *human rights*. I was going to Bogotá, and that is where I got all the information from the Permanent Committee. . . . [They] were invited to give us talks, as the recognized experts in those issues in the 1980s. They convened events where many people participated, they were invited to the USO. This was in 1980–82, when the bodies were coming down the river, from Puerto Boyacá, from Puerto Berrió."

Like all human rights groups at the time, CREDHOS operated on a shoestring budget, with volunteer staff. In addition to the donated office space from Jorge's law practice, the USO contributed a mimeograph machine for a monthly newsletter, as well as office supplies and transportation. Rafael recalled that they began documenting military abuses:

> We received *denuncias,* people would come and tell us their problems. We would accompany communities, for example, during the bombing in Yondó. We published the bulletin and sent out urgent actions. At this time no one went to Barranca; we started organizing the first international commissions, with the Quakers and DFID.[16] We did three workshops through an agreement with CINEP, and then we got invited to national events. The Colombian Commission of Jurists had an event about national and international mechanisms, CINEP had events, Funprocep [a regional group based in the state's capital] had a worksheet about how to write up *denuncias* and urgent actions. Jorge had an advantage because he was a lawyer, so he knew a lot about these issues.

By the end of the 1980s a number of the Bogotá-based groups were involved in supporting activism in Barranca. Gloria recalled helping to organize a human rights forum held at Barranca's exclusive Club de Infantas. In 1987 and 1988 civic strikes had been met with repression and the assassination of many leaders, generating further protest marches. According to Gloria, thousands of peasants were mobilized in the towns of northeastern Colombia (including Ocaña, Valledupar, Barrancabermeja, San Vicente de Chucurí, Tibú, Cúcuta, and Pamplona). Because of the repression against protest leaders, and the counterinsurgency campaigns throughout the region, the forum focused on the human rights situation in northeastern Colombia. She described the event:

> It was huge. At the forum, the organizers received reports about the human rights situation from all the states and the most vulnerable regions. That is where I established my first contacts with all the regions, and so then, from the CSPP, I started to do follow-up [*segimiento*] with all these contacts. During that time, there was the first forced displacement of peasants from Filogringo in Catatumbo and el Tarra to Tibu. Some of the displaced people occupied the installations of the Club Barquito of the ECOPETROL employees. They were there for a month, about thirty-three days, and their return was negotiated with the local government, the bishop, the Procuraduría.

Almost all activists had some contact with local committees during this period. I spent several hours discussing the early human rights committees with a lawyer, now working as a consultant for an international agency, who had worked with several NGOs in the 1980s, providing legal counsel and helping establish local human rights committees. He recalled the risk run by local activists even as the support for these com-

mittees grew, echoing the critical appraisal of the kind of training offered
to local committees, and their ultimate impact, that had been expressed
in interviews:

> There was a big boom in creating municipal human rights committees. Peo-
> ple would say to the peasants, why don't you create a human rights commit-
> tee? Everyone, everywhere you would go, was creating human rights com-
> mittees. This was at the end of the 1980s and the beginning of the 1990s,
> the big boom in local human rights committees. People even started human
> rights committees inside the jails, when I was with the CSPP that was one of
> the things that we would do.
>
> They were an important tool. The more committees were created, the
> more people thought that they were doing something. Someone from the
> NGO in Bogotá would go to some zone and spend a week indoctrinating
> them. The leaders of the local committees quickly learned about *denuncia*.
> The first work of the NGOs was *denuncia, denuncia,* everything was *denun-
> cia,* they never did anything proactive [*propositiva*]. Now that has changed
> a little, there is work that is more professional [*calificado*]. This vision of
> human rights work, that it was just *denuncia,* was transmitted to the local
> committees, and that is what the local peasant leaders learned. They took
> on the human rights discourse, and they would go see if the local police were
> mistreating people, and of course they were, and then they would denounce
> them. A large number of these local leaders were disappeared and assasi-
> nated. You have to wonder to what point this was a well-thought-out
> strategy, did this help to create local committees. They really left the local
> leaders abandoned to their own luck. . . . In the *foros,* they gave really fiery
> speeches. There was nothing *propositivo,* nothing. Some would go so far as
> to give speeches in favor of the armed actors. There were many reasons why
> the armed forces would oppose these committees, for them to say that some
> of them were being manipulated by the subversion. There was always some-
> one who would scream, *"viva!"* whatever group. And then the entire event
> would be marked [*quedaba marcado*].

DEFINING THE ROLE OF ARMED REVOLUTION

For a generation of Colombian activists in the 1960s and 1970s, the central focus of political debates and of organizing was the armed struggle.
They were a part of a continent-wide preoccupation with revolutionary
social change, spurred by the success of the Cuban Revolution in 1959
and fed by radical intellectuals who championed violence as the only
path. Throughout the continent, armed guerrilla groups kidnapped political and business leaders, led rural raids and bombed urban targets.
Although these guerrilla groups achieved significant political and military
power in only a few cases, they played a dominant role in shaping the

political landscape. According to Castañeda, "The impact of the hemi-sphere's armed left was far greater than its actual political importance in any one country at any time. For more than a decade, the urban, middle-class, university-educated, politicized youth of an entire continent was mesmerized by the armed struggle" (Castaneda 1993: 16). Even for the vast majority who never actively participated in violent guerrilla training or attacks, the *opción armáda* (armed option) remained the major fault line of political life, against which all activism was judged.

During this time, most of these *militantes* were focused on the romance of revolution, inspired by the heroic figure of martyrs such as Che Guevarra (killed by CIA-trained Bolivian soldiers in 1967) or the Colombian guerrilla priest Camilo Torres (killed in his first combat oper-ation in 1966). Profoundly sectarian and deeply influenced by identifica-tion with international political groups, the debates among the left focused on the proper road to revolution—*foco* or prolonged popular war? Tito or Hoxha?[17] Vanguard or alliance with the middle class?—a debate that occurred largely without questioning the ultimate goal of Marxist revolution. The dark side of these revolutionary groups, which included violent internal purges, criminal activities, and the "collateral damage" of civilian deaths, was justified, ignored, or downplayed.

For many activists who traced their political awakening to the politi-cal persecution of the 1940s and 1950s, the guerrillas were simply the expansion of the armed peasant resistance that emerged during that period. Historians have debated extensively the degree to which these armed peasant groups represented political resistance or were simply an expression of local banditry (see chapter 1). For the activists raised in these areas, the guerrillas were a natural part of the political landscape. One veteran activist told me that, though not of the same *línea,* her fam-ily had been politically active in the left for generations:

> I arrived [in Bogotá] very young from Chicorral, a town where the guerrilla was born. My mother and her family were Communists. I was different, I was a Maoist, and you know how much the Communists and Maoists fight and don't get along. They thought they were so different. But I never fought with my mother, my aunts who were Communists. They didn't differentiate between the Communists and the Maoists. They differentiated between the right and the left. We knew who they were, the guerrilla was the same peo-ple from the town, our cousins, sisters, brothers, neighbors, the people we all knew. They weren't strange [*ajeno*].

Over the past decade Colombian scholars have produced a number of important works in a variety of genres examining the origins of the

Colombian guerrillas, including memoirs, biographies, and scholarly texts. Many address the shifting and troubled relationships between guerrilla groups and social movements in the 1960s and 1970s. These works emphasize the degree to which these relationships were fraught and contested, as guerrilla strategies shifted to emphasize urban tactics and links with organized social movements and these movements more or less successfully struggled to maintain degrees of autonomy from armed groups. Among other issues, these works explore the relationship between guerrillas and banana plantation unions in Urabá (Garcia 1996) and with the student movement (Vargas Velásquez 1992) and peasant unions (Zamosc 1989). Histories of the colonization of new areas of Colombia have included reflections on the complicated relationships among settlers, new forms of social organization, and guerrilla groups (Molano 1987, 1989, 1994; González Arias and Marulanda Alvarez 1990; González Arias 1992; Ramirez 2001); M-19 memoirs (Vasquez 2000; Grabe 2001); and studies of the early history of the ELN (Broderick 2000; Medina Gallego 2001), the FARC (Pizarro Leongómez 1991, 1996; Alape 1994), and the EPL (Villarraga and Plazas 1994). Despite their limited distribution and often descriptive bent (with only minimal analysis), these works are an important foundation for any consideration of the relationship between armed groups and social movements in Colombia.

The decision by the guerrillas to combine all the forms of struggle determined the basic framework of the relationship between them and Colombian social movements. Essentially, the guerrillas decided on the tactic of simultaneously embracing the full range of legal and illegal means available to attack state power; armed groups would thus back both legal protest movements and military campaigns. The Colombian Communist Party traced its adoption of the "combination" strategy to the writings of Vladimir Lenin, who wrote that "as the class-consciousness of the masses grows, as economic and political crises become acute, the struggle continually gives rise to new and more varied methods of defense and attack" (quoted in Dudley 2004: 24). According to Steve Dudley, author of the first history of the Patriotic Union, "The Colombian Communist Party interpreted Lenin's words as meaning it should use all forms of struggle at all times," with armed "self-defense groups" protecting Communist-affiliated settler groups in the countryside while the Party organized urban groups in the cities (Dudley 2004: 66). He concludes that this ultimately had a devastating effect on the development of Colombian social movements, as leaders who attempted to develop genuine political independence were targeted by the guerrillas for failing to adhere to the guerrillas' *línea* and by paramilitary groups for being a front for guerrilla organizations.[18]

For a range of legal community organizations and social movements, this position severely complicated attempts to attain political autonomy. "With this ambiguous strategy, the agrarian self-defense regions were isolated, making them lose legitimacy, political standing, clarity in their initial objectives and their capacity for political opposition to the National Front" (González Arias and Marulanda Alvarez 1992: 11). Because the combination strategy acknowledged guerrilla involvement in a range of legal political and protest movements, the military felt justified in viewing these movements as legitimate targets. For their part, political activists struggled to define autonomy and chafed under hierarchical command structures that often privileged military over movement objectives.

Many of the activists I interviewed described passionate and tense discussions during their early years as militants over whether to join armed movements. One lawyer named Alonso who worked with several NGOs in the 1980s and 1990s described the attraction of revolutionary movements when he became frustrated by slow-moving reforms and escalating political violence. Even after deciding not to join the guerrillas, he remained convinced that they were fighting for a just cause and saw his early human rights work as supporting their struggle:

> After 1984, when I was working more on human rights, and had my legal training, I was really motivated by seeing the state of things as abhorrent, the need to change structures. This was a time of much reflection. Then I started to think that the legal struggle [*lucha jurídica*] doesn't give any results, that there is no way for it to work, and that the only solution might be the armed struggle. I saw that nothing was changing, that nothing was happening in the way we wanted it to. Change wasn't coming as fast as we thought. Maybe because of my Christian background, I didn't take that [armed] option. I had many friends that did go into the armed struggle, and we remained friends, but I didn't take that path. But my own commitment only got deeper, from there, everything proved that the nature of the state was to violate human rights, that the legal struggle was with the NGOs and was based on denouncing this state. We also worked to get some international support for what we were doing. I decided that working to support those who had the same kind of commitment, who fell in their struggle to do this, would be to defend political prisoners.

Many of the activists who began work with individuals detained and accused of being guerrillas did so not because they believed those individuals had been falsely accused of crimes. Like Alonso, many of them saw the defense of so-called political prisoners as the defense of the right to armed rebellion and as an extension of the guerrillas' struggle. One activist described her high school activism as "solidarity with the sectors in conflict."

Another lawyer recalled his youthful debates cynically, as a "waste of time." Like several of the human rights activists I interviewed, he described his decision not to join the guerrillas as the result of a vague "feeling," not an articulated political response against the armed movement:

> I worked as a lawyer for three years and in leftist projects in [the poor neighborhoods of] southern Bogotá, as part of the civic movements that were related to the church. I had friends from the university that were very close to the people working with Christian base communities, part of the Camilista Movement, which was an attempt to create a political party that was a complete failure. They were close to the ELN, and had a completely stupid discourse, *muy bobo*. We spent a long time discussing if we should support the armed movement or not—a complete waste of time. People gradually left; some people went into the ELN, some people into the human rights movement.

When I asked him why he decided to work with human rights NGOs instead of joining the guerrillas, he did not have a clear answer. "That is a question that I asked myself a lot," he told me. "I guess it just felt natural, it felt like it was what I wanted to, and also because that is where I got a job."

No one I spoke with would comment in any detail on the actual history of relations between guerrilla groups and specific NGOs. Some would speak in vague generalities if they positioned themselves as struggling for more autonomy. For example, Alonso recalled the debates at the organizations he worked with on how to relate to the guerrillas: "Within the NGOs, there were people on one side or another. Now, I don't like divisions, but within the NGOs there were a lot of political differences. Some had their positions, some received direct orders from other latitudes. They didn't decide what to do based on their board of directors or their director but from orders, from *el monte* [lit., "the mountain"; refers to remote guerrilla headquarters]. Some of us, we wanted something else, we wanted to be a little more independent from the armed actors."

One woman I spoke with described the distinction between participation with the guerrillas and with state-recognized grassroots organizations as the "clandestine life" and the "legal life," but she also emphasized the connection between the two. For her, the guerrillas were a natural response to Colombia's closed political system in the 1970s, as well as part of the hemispheric struggle for power: "As a consequence of this [political] exclusion, guerrilla groups were formed, part of an international movement, for example in Cuba, that were trying to fight for political changes. But they weren't able to ensure that the political discourse led the military discourse. In practice, these groups were very military, and [did] little about political practice. But even everyone in legal life, in their hearts, had hope that the guerrillas would defend us, because we never won anything politically."

The issue of sympathy for the guerrillas sometimes generated controversy in the human rights training courses. "There was always a lot of discussion in the workshops about why we defended *guerrilleros*," one veteran activist told me. Part of the human rights training workshop explained that armed revolution was a natural response to Colombia's exclusionary economic and political system: "They [the Bogotá activists doing human rights training] had many arguments for explaining why, of course, many arguments why the group should do so, and they presented why the armed struggle emerged in Colombia, what the consequences were, it was very interesting talk *(carreta)*." Others summarized the relationship between legal political parties and different guerrilla groups by talking in code—using kinship terms to describe armed groups as being more *(los hermanos,* the brothers) or less *(los primos,* the cousins) related to their organization.

Relationships between the guerrillas and legal social movements became more complicated as the guerrillas lost wider political support and began to escalate their criminal activities. High-profile scandals generated public concern about the worsening conduct of the guerrillas, including the massacre by their paranoid commander of more than one hundred members of the FARC dissident split-off, the Ricardo Franco Front. The M-19's 1985 takeover of the Palace of Justice was perhaps most damaging to the public view of guerrilla violence. The extremely poor political judgment demonstrated by the M-19 during the takeover, and the bloody results, undermined what had been relatively widespread political support for the group. Escalating criminal activity, including increasing numbers of kidnappings (justified by the guerrillas as "taxation"), and the FARC's strategic decision to finance its expansion by skimming profits from drug production and trafficking also eroded their base of support. Throughout the 1980s human rights groups continued to debate the continued perception of the guerrillas as part of the spectrum of social struggle and the focus on the guerrillas' origins as part of an international revolutionary movement. The attitude of human rights groups toward the use of political violence, how to understand the actual tactics of Colombian guerrilla groups, and the role of the *opción armada* in social transformation have remained extremely controversial topics in Colombia.

HUMAN RIGHTS AS BOURGEOIS

Colombian leftists were initially reluctant to adopt the human rights framework. For many identified with Marxism, "human rights" was simply a bourgeois concept, originating in the West to strengthen the hegemony of the United States and distract attention from real (i.e., class) mobilization. These activists emphasized the focus on individual rights—particularly civil and political rights—in the Universal Declaration of Human Rights rather than the collective rights of communities for autonomy and for economic and cultural rights.[19] Various metaphors have since been developed to describe the different kinds of rights as distinct but related. In his 1941 address to Congress, President Franklin Roosevelt described the "four freedoms"—freedom of speech, freedom of worship, freedom from want, and freedom from fear. Subsequent activists described first-generation rights (political and civil) and second-generation rights (economic, social, and cultural), or "baskets" of rights. In the 1970s and 1980s, however, many activists questioned outright the appropriateness of the human rights framework. Gloria recalled bitter debates in her first human rights training workshops, especially among union activists: "The first human rights workshop, I think it was in 1984, that CINEP organized on a national level, they invited people from all of the regions. [Human rights] generated resistance in the beginning. People especially from the union sector said, no, these human rights, [this] is a bourgeois discourse, all about private property. We could go so far as to say that for several years the issue was not well received in many venues, but later people understood what it was about." For militants in Marxist parties, the universal aspirations of rights language were unconvincing. Many simply rejected the idea that rich people had rights, focusing on abuses experienced by peasants and workers during the course of their class-based organizing efforts.

In part, this resistance was increased by the human rights rhetoric of the Carter administration in the late 1970s. For many Latin American activists, the official adoption of human rights as a central thrust of U.S.

foreign policy was simply a facade to cloak military expansion and neo-colonialism in the region. According to Amanda Romero, "For these intellectuals [influenced by ideologies developed in the then Soviet Union, China, Albania or European socialist parties], the struggle for human rights is taken as part of the perverse inheritance of the bourgeois order: mechanisms to lull [adormecer] the population. Because of this, they emphasized constant denuncia of the regime; the victims produced by the confrontations among political militants, peasants or workers is the price that must be paid to achieve social change" (Romero 1992: 14). These positions began to change as leftist intellectuals living under the military regimes throughout the continent themselves began to feel the brunt of persecution, first in Brazil after the 1964 military coup and then in the subsequent Southern Cone dictatorships. The relative success of groups employing the human rights framework in raising international attention and sanctions against these military regimes, particularly in Chile, also contributed to its increasing acceptance elsewhere on the continent.

Some activists recalled that even as ideological objections made some reject the human rights label, in practice the work of the newly formed organizations was focused on human rights issues, such as the torture and repression of activists. According to Gloria's friend Pablo, one of the CSPP staffers first based in Medellín, there was "great demand" for the basic human rights workshop offered by the CSPP, which included "the diagnosis of the national social reality and statistics about unemployment and foreign debt" as well as "training about protection measures, legal measures, and what to do in case of a search." At the time the CSPP adopted as its institutional mandate solidarity with oppressed peoples and the rights of the pueblos. Pablo recalled:

> There were a lot of Marxist discussions, following the era when Carter launched his human rights proposal for Latin America, the issue of human rights for the Colombian left, it was an issue as people said, or as they say still, that was stained [marcado] by Carter's imperialism. It was seen as very bourgeois. So we worked in favor of the rights of the pueblos; but the reality that we lived was different, we had to work on human rights issues every day, because of the searches, the torture, that was the daily work that led us to work on human rights.

The development of an explicitly anti-imperialist and alternative human rights framework is often omitted in histories of human rights activism, which focus on the development of international law. Alternative rights declarations focusing on collective rights and the so-called people's tribunals are two examples of such frameworks. The

1976 Universal Declaration of the Rights of Peoples, known as the Algiers Declaration, was widely taught in Colombian human rights workshops throughout the 1980s as a fundamental text. This declaration, written and signed by nongovernmental representatives and thus without even the symbolic weight of U.N. treaties, stressed collective rights and autonomy. Beginning with "Every people has the right to exist" (Article 1), the Algiers Declaration goes on to assert that "every people has an unalienable right to self-determination" (Article 5) and that "every people has the right to break free from any colonial or foreign domination" (Article 6). For these activists, rights were designed not only to safeguard individuals against the actions of a repressive state but also to protect communities from the oppressive impositions of a colonial—or in the case of Latin America, neocolonial—power. The Algiers Declaration was promoted by the International League for Liberation and the Rights of Peoples, which established a Colombian chapter in the late 1980s.

"People's tribunals" used the Algiers Declaration, and other human rights documents, as the basis for establishing alternative judicial systems outside state authority. One of the best known was the Russell Tribunal, established by Bertrand Russell in 1967 to judge the United States and other nations that supported war crimes in Vietnam. A second Russell Tribunal, convened from 1974 to 1976, focused on the military dictatorships in Latin America, with an additional session held during 1989–91 (Tribunal Permanente de los Pueblos 1991). In fall 1989 the tribunal sessions were held in downtown Bogotá; visiting experts on human rights in Latin America offered comparative expertise. Colombian NGOs organized public presentations and devoted significant resources to research for tribunal publications. While some scholars argue that the Russell Tribunals' explicitly partisan agenda lessened their impact, for many activists on the left they were a critical space for using the human rights framework to raise the international profile of political violence (Klinghoffer 2002).

THE LEFTIST LEGACY OF
EARLY HUMAN RIGHTS ORGANIZING

Like the Colombian left as a whole, early human rights groups were profoundly divided over issues of ideology. While most adopted similar human rights strategies (expanding local human rights networks and documenting and denouncing abuses), early groups' allegiances to differing political groups generated significant internal divisions. According to Romero, early attempts to coordinate human rights activities were limited by perceived political differences. Many groups did not participate because of the "political sectarianism of those who considered that human rights organizations were 'representatives' or 'controlled' by one or another position or political party; and the prevalent conceptions in the popular movement about the issue of human rights, which was indiscriminately categorized as 'social democratic,' 'reformist,' 'conciliatory,' or as the opposite, as 'extreme leftist,' or confrontational" (Romero 1992: 115).

Regardless of affiliation, the vast majority of early human rights groups shared a view of the state as the enemy and the primary source of political violence. In this period the "predominant vision of human rights was marked by a radical commitment to the victims, politicization of the discourse, conception of the law as an instrument of the repressive dominant classes and of human rights as a tool for confrontation and reaction against the state," one veteran activist told me. This view was widely taught by radical professors to the expanding student population of public universities; the sociologist Alejo Vargas Velásquez writes that the Colombian state was viewed as a "dictatorship similar to Batista in Cuba" (Vargas Velásquez 1992: 216). Colombian activists used the almost constant state of siege legislation granting extraordinary powers to the Colombian Executive to argue that despite formal democracy, the country was characterized by authoritarian rule similar to the military dictatorships of the Southern Cone (Gallón 1979). One veteran activist neatly summarized the position of these groups in the 1980s: "We were organizations against the state, we were never nongovernmental organizations. Everything that had to do with the state was bad: repression, inequality, lies, and corruption."

These views profoundly shaped the kinds of violence on which early human rights campaigns focused. For some groups devoted to legal activism, the ambivalence toward guerrilla violence extended from defending individuals accused of participation in guerrilla groups to defending the rights of guerrilla groups themselves, using the so-called right to rebellion. Lawyers, building on just war theory and the established legal recognition of the rights of oppressed peoples to rebel, relied on many of the anticolonial arguments developed by Asian and African intellectuals during the 1960s and 1970s.

Another consequence of the focus on the state's role in perpetrating violence was that early human rights groups often minimized the vio-

lence generated by other powerful social actors outside the state. In the
case of Colombia, the most glaring omission was the refusal to view
drug trafficking cartels as anything but simply an extension of the oligarchy, as working in the service of the Colombian elites and armed
forces. In part, this view recognized an important reality, inasmuch as
wealthy drug traffickers played a pivotal role in financing right-wing
paramilitary death squads (see chapter 1). However, it failed to address
the degree to which drug trafficking in Colombia, and the unprecedented
opportunities for wealth outside the official economy, dramatically transformed class and power structures. During the 1980s, the cartels had
shifting relationships with state power; drug lord Pablo Escobar was
elected as a congressional alternate *(suplente)* in 1984 but by the late
1980s had declared "war" on the state and was paying more than
U.S.$300 a head for the assassination of policemen in Medellín. During
the 1980s' "dirty war" in Colombia, paramilitary groups linked to drug
cartels (particularly the Medellín Cartel) worked closely with Colombian
military officers to eliminate suspected guerrilla sympathizers, while at
the same time they attacked Colombian authorities investigating drug
trafficking and paramilitary activity. Hundreds, even thousands, of
judges were threatened and killed during this period. Throughout the
1980s these paramilitary groups, working with security forces, were
implicated in the assassinations of high-ranking government officials
(including the murders of Minister of Justice Rodrigo Lara Bonilla in
1984 and hundreds of police officers and judges). Most human rights
groups ignored drug-sponsored attacks on the state, viewing drug trafficking as primarily a U.S. issue and public discussion of the issue as an
attempt by the right to mask the real situation of political violence.[20]

The history of the first years of Colombian human rights groups is only
one of the cultural, intellectual, and political projects of the 1970s and
1980s that have had a profound impact on contemporary politics and
activism. Much of this history remains to be written; many of these stories are still extremely sensitive in places like Colombia where internal
conflicts and political violence persist. Excavating this history, however,
is critical for understanding shifting modalities of political violence and
collective responses to it.
    The Colombian activists who first used the human rights framework
in Colombia faced tremendous challenges: escalating political violence,
entrenched resistance to political reform, deep sectarian divisions, and
serious persecution. From their experience with leftist organizations, they

linked a vision of transcendent social change to the new and expanding repertoire of political activism made possible by international human rights. During the 1980s, Colombian NGOs succeeded in applying the human rights framework to understanding Colombian violence, beginning what would be consolidated as significant national and international alliances to mobilize responses to violent repression carried out by the state and its allies. The roots of this activism in Catholic and Communist-influenced organizations left a lasting legacy on Colombian human rights groups, contributing to the development of a resilient activist identity while also sowing the seeds for divisive conflicts as pressures on professional human rights practice increased during the 1990s.

CHAPTER 3

The Production of Human Rights Knowledge and the Practice of Politics

Throughout the 1990s human rights work became increasingly professionalized, and new institutional norms and practices developed. Solidarity groups staffed by volunteers were replaced (or in some cases, augmented) by nongovernmental organizations staffed by well-trained, full-time paid professionals, often lawyers. Written documentation that circulates abroad conforming to (or at least approximating) international legal evidenciary standards remains the most visible dimension of this kind of human rights work. Activists participating in these transformations remained deeply embedded in oppositional political cultures, however. Often in remote localities far from the urban cosmopolitan sites of human rights conferences, activists continued to engage with efforts to promote broad social and political transformation. This work was ephemeral, involving local partnerships and initiatives that were often invisible to the international observers (both supporters and critics) of human rights work. Here I explore the new forms of partnerships as well as contradictions produced as activists attempted to negotiate the political landscapes, and sometimes competing demands, of their local constituencies and international counterparts.

The Colombian solidarity groups that had organized under the human rights banner to protest the persecution of their members and allies became NGOs in the 1990s.[1] Activists responded to the pressures and opportunities created by the shifts within Colombia's political landscape and funding and training offered by international partners to create these

NGOs, with new mandates and new rules of information production. This professionalization of human rights knowledge production centered on objective reporting that depoliticized human rights knowledge, adhering to legal standards and using a dispassionate tone rather than explicitly expressing alliance with leftist programs. These changes generated serious internal debates among activists committed to social transformation but unsure of the shape of radical politics at the close of the twentieth century. Despite these changes, activists did not abandon their participation in the Colombian political left, but this participation shifted in response to the challenges of ongoing political violence, the complexities of Colombian party politics, and the opportunities presented by political reforms. This work was often invisible to Colombian NGOs' international partners, and in some cases purposely minimized by groups invested in ensuring the dominance of professionalized activism. However, it allowed Colombian human rights groups to build new political relationships and networks as they struggled to articulate an ongoing project of social transformation. This chapter traces the institutional transformations of this generation of human rights organizations and the shifts in how they practiced human rights activism. I consider three examples of activists' evolving political participation: support of the local political movements that followed the electoral reforms of the late 1980s, lobbying efforts to shape the 1991 Constitution, and promotion of political reforms in the context of a negotiated settlement with the guerrillas.

In the ethnographic recounting of a human rights workshop that concludes the chapter I trace the institutional and organizational transformations that occurred even as new groups emerged over the course of the decade. A central concern in this chapter is how the process of professionalization transformed the production of human rights knowledge; international partners that funded and supported Colombian organizations demanded new kinds of human rights narratives. It was in the workshops, the legacy of popular education campaigns and local human rights committees of the 1980s, that the production of those narratives was taught. Like their predecessors (and in some cases, themselves in earlier days), professional activists taught their local counterparts how to interpret Colombian political reality, educated them about international human rights standards, and offered human rights activism as a means of achieving some measure of social justice. They differed, however, in their focus on producing human rights accounts that conformed to the standards of international law and their shifting relations with the state. These workshops brought together not only local activists but also elected and appointed local officials who came to power through the electoral reforms of the late 1980s or were hired to staff the new human rights institutions created by the 1991 Constitution. The relationships forged between NGO activists and these officials were evidence of the new relationships between activists and the state that offered both opportunities and challenges. As a space for encounter, these workshops also served to establish powerful personal networks among activists confronting complicated panoramas of violence.

PROFESSIONALIZATION IN ACTION AND THE NEW HUMAN RIGHTS NGOS

The transformation of solidarity organizations linked to social movements into professionalized NGOs was the most important institutional shift of the 1990s. This shift involved myriad changes on multiple levels. The organizational structure changed as new resources allowed for paid staff rather than volunteers. Increasing staff specialization meant organizational hierarchies, including salary differentiation, which exacerbated class tensions. Some groups received more international funding than others, setting up rivalries, competition, and class tensions between organizations. The need for accountability to donors led to new institutional practices involving staff supervision, fund-raising and proposal development, evaluation and accounting procedures, and operational changes. Groups were required to submit work plans outlining objectives and delineating measurable outcomes (with specific indicators) and schedules. The availability of international funding allowed some groups to expand their focus in certain areas but forced cutbacks in others and in some cases brought about the redirection of mandates and work.

Human rights groups were not the only organizations undergoing transformations. The professionalization of social movement–based voluntary groups has become the subject of considerable scholarly attention (Fisher 1997). To generalize about NGOs is very difficult, however, as this designation includes a huge range of groups that have different orientations and address different issues, among them, development, education, housing, health, civil society and democratization, media access and production, and environmental protection. Despite this range, there are several general schools of thought about the expanding field of NGOs. Supporters, among them many political scientists and sociologists, argue that NGOs will allow broader political participation in policy making, foster stronger civil society, and allow services to be provided in a more direct, efficient, and accountable fashion. Critics, among them many anthropologists, view NGOs as symptomatic of the depoliticization and political co-optation of social movements as members move from being political activists to being service providers as part of the privatization of state functions that is fundamental to the neoliberal transformation of the welfare state. These scholars focus on the lack of accountability of NGOs to the larger constituencies they claim to represent, finding them instruments of states on the one hand and international donors on the other. They focus on the ways in which professionalization exacerbates class differences and tensions within movements and increases corruption (for nuanced discussions of these changes in the women's movement, see Alvarez, Dagnino, and Escobar 1998; Ewig 1999; Markowitz and Tice 2002).

Most of the recent anthropological considerations of human rights work have stressed the complex ways in which activism intersects with neoliberal projects (Speed and Sierra 2005). Sally Merry, in her work on the transnational circulation of women's rights projects, has similarly stressed the contested terrain of negotiating local activism: "Human rights create[s] a political space for reform using a language legitimated by a global consensus on standards. But this political space comes with a price. Human rights promote ideas of individual autonomy, equality, choice and secularism even when these ideas differ from prevailing cultural norms and practices. Human rights ideas displace alternative visions of social justice that are less individualistic and more focused on communities and responsibilities, possibly contributing to the cultural homogenization of local communities" (Merry 2006: 4).

Even in the context of these broad schools of thought, however, scholars stress the importance of recognizing the heterogeneous nature of NGOs and their potential for multiple ideological positioning. A decade ago William Fisher urged scholars to consider the "diversity of the NGO field"; to consider "focusing on fluid and changing local, regional, national and international processes and connections, which both potentially support and suppress 'an insurrection of subjugated knowledges'; such studies avoid simple generalizations and reveal the rich ideological and functional diversity of NGOs" (Fisher 1997: 449). In their examination of women's groups in the United States and Latin America, Lisa Marcowitz and Karen Tice remind us that "professional activists, no more monolithic than any other occupational category, encompass a broad and fluid spectrum of ideologies, interests and motivations in their work" (Marcowitz and Tice 2002: 951). This full diversity of organizations and histories is represented in Colombia, which has thousands of self-defined NGOs with almost as many different mandates and agendas (Villar and Confederación Colombiana de ONGs 1998). These Colombian groups share many characteristics with NGOs throughout Latin America. Many have their origins in Catholic Church–sponsored projects, while others emerged directly from government-created projects, and many are sustained through foreign funding.

My discussion of NGOs is limited, however, to organizations with a different historical trajectory: those that emerged from the radical leftist movements of the 1970s and became the major oppositional human rights voices of the 1990s. Their largest umbrella organization began as the Coordinación Colombia-Europa (henceforth Coordination, described in greater detail below). These organizations view their role not as providing technical services for improving the human rights performance of the Colombian government but as promoting social transformation achieved through advocacy for the rights of the oppressed and disenfranchised in Colombia. According to its Web site, Coordination currently has 106 member organizations, with a range of perspectives on issues including professionalization, which remains tremendously controversial and contested among these NGOs. Some of the most controversial debates— over activist identities, class differences, and mandates—are explored in the next chapter.

Progressive NGOs were not the only ones to attempt to harness the power of human rights. Some self-proclaimed human rights NGOs operated as service providers for the government and joined the largest NGO umbrella organization, the Colombian NGO Confederation (Confederación Colombiana de ONGs), which was founded in 1989, with over 1,000 member organizations and 18 state-level federations. According to the Confederation's Web site, their mandate is "to link and facilitate communication [interlocución], lobbying [cabildeo], and negotiation between NGOs, the public and private sector and international agencies for the creation of public goods." According to the database on the Web site, 49 member organizations define their mandate as promoting human rights, justice, or international humanitarian law.

Right-wing NGOs have denounced the activism of Coordination members while using the human rights framework to defend the rights of those victimized by guerrilla violence as well as those accused of perpetrating abuses. The earliest such NGO was the National Committee of Victims of the Guerrillas (Comité Nacional de Víctimas de la Guerrilla, VIDA). Established by Fernando Vargas, VIDA was vocal throughout the 1990s in condemning the activism and research carried out by Colombian human rights NGOs.[2] According to the brief biography that appears on the jacket of his book, *A Country without Rights,* Vargas is a lawyer, "expert in human rights, international humanitarian law and analyst of the Colombian conflict." He attended "hearings before the InterAmerican Commissions and the Human Rights Commission of the U.N., and the NGO World Forum for Human Rights in Vienna, 1993." The rest of his résumé details his service with the Colombian army, including his role as adviser to the army, the Joint Chiefs of the Armed Forces, and professor at the Military Academy and the Intelligence Academy of the army.[3] A number of similar organizations have appeared on the Internet, for example, Colombia Objectiva (Objective Colombia) and Tradición y Acción (Tradition and Action).

While these groups appear to have little or no substantial program work, their media campaigns have gained significant attention. One of the best examples is the media campaign against NGO human rights activists in the case of El Carmen, San Vicente de Chucurrí. Justice and Peace, a church-based group led by Jesuit Father Javier Giraldo, had published a report documenting the paramilitary takeover of the region. Several high-profile journalists began publishing articles and columns alleging that Justice and Peace was linked to the ELN. Manuel Vicente Peña, director of *La Prensa* (a daily newspaper that folded in the late 1990s), wrote a series of critical articles titled "The Private Justice of Father Giraldo." *El Tiempo* columnist Plinio Apuleyo, in a published open letter to the attorney general, wrote that the report was "scandalously false" and that the violence in El Carmen resulted from peasant rebellion after twenty-five years of ELN, not paramilitary, control.[4] Apuleyo's political influence was demonstrated by his later appointment as Colombia's ambassador to Portugal by President Uribe. His final column before his departure to Lisbon, published on November 24, 2002, in the Bogotá weekly *El Espectador,* is typical of his vitriolic commentary: "The prosecutors of the Human Rights Unit [of the Attorney General's Office] found their twin in the Chilean Marxist José Miguel Vivanco, director of Human Rights Watch. . . . The problem is, driven by a secret vindictive fervor, this phobia has become extensive against the Colombian military. Thus, they have tried [*enjuiciar*] the best officials of the army, to the joy of Tirofijo and Mono Jojoy [two senior FARC commanders]." Apuleyo's perspective is repeated in the columns of ultra-conservative Mary A. O'Grady in the *Wall Street Journal* and periodic editorials in the *Washington Times.* This kind of commentary has contributed to the polarization of the debate about human rights in Colombia.

COLOMBIAN TRANSITIONS

The transition from solidarity groups to the new NGO organizational structure can best be seen in the lived experience of activists such as Pablo. He began as a volunteer with the Committee in Solidarity with Political Prisoners and became one of its first paid staff members. Over several small cups of *tinto*, Colombia's ubiquitous sweet black coffee, Pablo told me his history of activism. Pablo is small and round, with the dark skin and crinkled hair of Afro-Colombians, and of short stature, probably as a result of childhood malnutrition. His eyes are quick and bright behind his round glasses, and he smiled often at his own quiet sly jokes made in the *paisa* drawl characteristic of the Antioquia region. I had known him for several years, and we had met occasionally during conferences in Bogotá and with friends, but it was not until I sat down with him in his office on a sloping hill in a pleasant neighborhood above downtown Medellín that he revealed to me his history and how he had come to reconcile the challenges presented by professional human rights activism with his life as a political activist. Like many activists, Pablo began as a student, community activist, and performer with a theater troupe; he and his *compañeros* divided their time between studying political philosophy and presenting their plays during strikes and protests. Named "secretary for solidarity" by the Coordinadora de Barrios (Coordinator of Barrios), he became active with the CSPP in the early 1980s, participating in the human rights workshops taught by Bogotá-based activists. At the time, his life revolved completely around activism: "I was very activist, I lived at home [to save money], eating lunch and drinking coffee all day at the union offices."

In 1988 Pablo became a professional human rights defender, an official staff member of the CSPP in charge of the direct services program, working first in Medellín and then in Bogotá. The CSPP was undergoing a dramatic shift in its institutional culture. "When we formalized the committee, we abandoned the clandestine life to work in the public sphere," Pablo explained. Full-time activists were finally given regular paychecks and benefits and allowed to affiliate with state-run social security and welfare programs. Benefits and paychecks were not the only difference: the newly public role brought an increase in threats, harassment, and attacks. Pablo said that the intense fear of persecution—and the experience of threats and the forced disappearance of a colleague—shaped the experience of working within this new organizational structure (see chapter 4). But he continued human rights work for the next decade, leaving the CSPP a few years later to work for another NGO, the Institute for Grassroots Training (Instituto de Capacitación Popular, ICP), several of whose staff members left to create yet another NGO, the Regional Studies Corporation (Corporación Región).

The numerous splits and reconfigurations were caused in part by political disagreements, exacerbated by close personal relationships. "One of the big errors [of the NGOs] was mixing the personal and professional. The NGOs were practically family organizations, with a very special character, everyone was someone's brother or uncle or relation, or were friends," one activist who had worked with several NGOs recalled. "It was too domestic, the personal relationships weighed too much." Generational differences also contributed to tensions within the NGO landscape. "We were more trained, more specialists in human rights, earlier people had mainly learned from their experience," he went on, focusing on the differences between the new generation of formally trained human rights professionals and the previous volunteers. "In my generation of activists, this was at the end of the 1980s, we all had university degrees. We wanted to work near certain organizations, but we didn't fit into armed groups. We wanted to find new spaces to do what was possible. Of course, there were some of the established activists involved too, Umaña and others with more experience."[5] Pablo's experience was typical of the institutional reorganizations going on throughout the 1990s. Many new NGOs were created from splinter groups as staff left because of political and personal disagreements with their former colleagues. Activists that had begun their careers in the solidarity groups, including the Permanent Committee for the Defense of Human Rights, the CSPP, and CINEP's human rights office, now went on to create new institutions, with new mandates and professionally trained staff.

Carlos, the lawyer forced into exile in Spain after being falsely jailed in the late 1970s, returned to Colombia to cofound one of the most important of the new institutions, the Colombian Commission of Jurists with his friend and lawyer Gustavo Gallón and other lawyers. According to Gustavo, the CCJ was imagined as a new kind of professional human rights organization from the outset.[6] "The CCJ was created as a professional organization, of permanent, full-time, paid work on these issues by people who had specialized training. Without ignoring politics, we focused more on legal work at the national and international level. The contribution of the group, what we did which was new, was trying to exploit the potential of international mechanisms in relation to Colombia," Gustavo told me.

> Our specific objective was to contribute to the improvement of the human rights situation in Colombia. That was not the same as what other groups were trying to do, other groups had other objectives, which were very valid and important, they were just different. The CSPP was focused on solidarity, CINEP wanted to contribute to social change. . . . We were the first to focus on international organizations so they would work on Colombia, like the InterAmerican Commission and Court and the U.N. Human Rights Commission. We also did activities focused on the country, so that people would understand and work on international mechanisms. We worked with judges, the courts, Congress, the administration, and the population.

Jesuit Fr. Javier Giraldo was another former CINEP researcher who went on to found the influential Intercongregational Commission for Justice and Peace. Extremely dry and serious, Father Javier managed to marshal an impressive team of Catholic clergy and lay workers committed to working with local organizations and priests based in some of the most violent areas in the country. An admirer of sociologist priest turned guerrilla fighter Camilo Torres, Father Javier wrote his thesis on liberation theology and completed a Ph.D. in France, where he was active in solidarity committees during the 1970s. He returned to Colombia and began working at CINEP, while pressuring the Catholic Conference of Bishops to take a more active stance on human rights. In part as a result of his efforts, in 1986 the Conference of Religious Superiors of Colombia approved the following resolution: "To promote, support and encourage the Christian prophetic signs which are present in religious communities, through the creation of a Commission of Justice and Peace which will channel and disseminate information and protests throughout the country" (Giraldo 1996: 21). The board of directors of the Bishop's Conference blocked the initiative, however. Two years later a group of twenty-five of the most progressive provincials led by Giraldo founded Justice and Peace, which was later adopted as one of the official commissions of the Bishop's Conference. In a 2003 interview Father Javier described the founding of Justice and Peace this way:

> Among progressive religious orders we began exploring how we might protect the human rights of victims of the Colombian state. The bishops were not interested in helping, but in early 1988 the superiors of 25 orders [which we call congregations] came together to found the Comisión de Justicia y Paz. Its goal was to provide humanitarian and legal support, especially in

areas of intense conflict—Santander, Valle del Cauca, Magdalena Medio, Putumayo, and Urabá. We would gather facts about human rights abuses in a databank and would publicize situations of crisis. Some cases we would take to the courts. Our staff developed close relationships with some impoverished communities that were suffering in the midst of the armed conflict and that gained courage to declare themselves peace communities. (quoted in Goring 2003)

Originally staffed by a small cohort of radical nuns, priests, and laypeople active in the Catholic Church, Justice and Peace soon moved to the forefront of human rights groups for its reporting of what they called the "dirty war" in Colombia. The group first received national attention for its reporting on paramilitary activity in El Carmen, including the attacks from right-wing commentators described above, and played a leading role in the Trujillo Commission.

Gloria, the cultural activist profiled in chapter 2, was also looking for an institutional setting to continue her work with rural displaced communities. After quitting the CSPP at the end of 1989 because of frustration with the internal divisions and limited mandate, she had been thrilled at the new opportunity to work in the Catatumbo region along the Venezuelan border. The foundation where she found work, however, was also split by internal divisions and funding problems. "The foundation dissolved, but we still wanted to work there, we still had connections and commitment to the people in the region," she told me. "We couldn't abandon them, we had to do something." One of her mentors, the human rights lawyer Eduardo Umaña, told her that another NGO had just split and suggested a merger of former staff from both organizations. Umaña had been a founding member of the José Alvéar Restrepo Lawyers' Collective and was well known for his abrasive personality and his long history of human rights activism (his father had been one of the authors of the first study of state-sponsored violence during the 1940s). He was a mentor to an entire generation of radical young university students. Gloria explained, "Eduardo called me and the others, and suggested that we get together, telling us, you are all doing committed work for human rights and I care about you four, why don't you create your own organization." Over lunch in a downtown restaurant, they decided to call their organization MINGA, the name for collective work in rural communities.

MINGA's team built on the work each had previously established. Lourdes, a slim, dark-haired lawyer whose youthful appearance belied her heavy caseload of political prisoners (including some senior members of the ELN), led the legal division. Gloria, working with several others, continued her work with regional human rights committees in eastern Colombia, expanding into Catatumbo and the Sur del Cesar and establishing contacts with a Belgian priest who was working with peasant organizations in southern Bolívar. Gloria was focused on her passion for work with grassroots community organizations by devoting her time to training the local committees established throughout the region.

Another of the new organizations, CODHES, founded in 1992 by a group of academic researchers and journalists, was among the first to focus on internal displacement, which would become one of the most pressing humanitarian and human rights issues in Colombia over the course of the next decade. CODHES president Jorge Rojas would also be a leader in integrating human rights work into support for peace and a negotiated settlement with the Colombian guerrillas.

One of the most important human rights groups in the 1990s did not fit the NGO model: the José Alvéar Restrepo Lawyers' Collective, named for one of the radical ideologues of the Liberal peasant guerrillas in the 1950s. The Collective was created in the early 1980s by a group of lawyers providing legal services to peasants and workers detained during protests and representing victims of human rights violations. During the 1990s, they expanded into international work, lobbying at the United Nations and bringing cases before the InterAmerican Human Rights Court. Unlike other NGOs, part of their operating budget comes from paying clients. They have also received significant funding from Law 288, passed in 1996, which forces the government to pay monetary compensation to victims of human rights violations after rulings in their favor by the InterAmerican Commission on Human Rights and the U.N. Human Rights Committee. Because the Collective receives a portion of the compensation for their representation of the victims, one member joked that they are funded in part "by the Colombian military." Like other NGOs, they have sustained their pro bono legal work with additional funding through grants, primarily from European governments and foundations.

While their mandates differed, all these groups shared one characteristic that profoundly shaped human rights work over the coming decade: all relied on international funding, from U.S. and European foundations and European Union governments, to sustain their organizations. The relationship between NGOs and their international partners was instrumental in allowing these Colombian NGOs to develop strong institutions with trained staff. They were also forced to negotiate new kinds of institutional practices, particularly the production of human rights knowledge about Colombia.

INFORMATION POLITICS

The new model of human rights knowledge was based on legal standards and focused on credibility, on making quantifiable and verifiable claims. The production of credible statistics, including percentages of kinds of violations and kinds of perpetrators, became an extremely controversial and contested issue. Because of the reliance on legal standards, human rights reporting focused on individual events, producing analyses that were comparable across conflicts and cultures and limiting the exposition of context and multiple social causal factors in order to highlight narratives of individual victims and perpetrators. The veracity of specific claims—including dates, time lines, places, and responsibility—was critical.

The importance of reliable information was a constant refrain of the international partners and funders of these new NGOs. The clearest example was the Ford Foundation's role in establishing the CCJ. The Ford Foundation has been a principal funder of human rights NGOs throughout Latin America and developed the "Ford model" of "flagship organizations."[7] These institutions were designed to be the "one place where you could go if you wanted to know about the human rights situation," according to Michael Shifter, now a vice president of the InterAmerican Dialogue, a Washington, D.C.–based think tank. During the 1980s, he was the director of the Ford Foundation's governance and human rights program for the Andean Region and the Southern Cone, based first in Lima and then in Santiago from 1987 to 1993. He described flagship organizations as "groups with very high credibility and good connections internationally, and very reliable with information."

Shifter described Colombia as "the hardest case to fund in the Andes." By the late 1980s Colombia and Peru were funding priorities for the Ford Foundation, but there was little enthusiasm among its staff for funding existing Colombian organizations. Shifter viewed many as too "politicized," others as too closely attached to the hierarchy of the Catholic Church, which was largely controlled by conservative bishops and could not be relied on to support human rights work. Shifter's solution was to create and fund a "flagship organization" in Colombia. He began by approaching Gustavo Gallón, who was then working as a human rights lawyer, a volunteer with the Permanent Committee, and the editor of the

CINEP publication *Cien Días* (One Hundred Days). Shifter arranged a meeting between Gustavo and Diego García Sayán, director of the Andean Commission in Peru in 1988, and urged them to work together to set up a Colombian branch of their organization. His encouragement included $50,000 in seed money from the Ford Foundation, with the promise of more money to come. Shifter recalls his role with pride: "From my perspective it was great, one of the few things I funded instinctually in my grant making career, I felt it was right." Through Shifter, the Ford Foundation also paid for consulting with Chilean activists to help them organize the institution. A falling out over the political direction of the institution led to the Colombian Section of the Andean Commission becoming an independent organization, the Colombian Commission of Jurists, in 1996. According to Shifter, the Ford Foundation got what they wanted: "It did become the flagship organization, different from other institutions. Obviously it hasn't solved the human rights situation in Colombia, but . . . the point is to draw more attention to the situation."

The CCJ established close international ties, particularly with Human Rights Watch (HRW). According to former HRW researchers, CCJ staff was their "main contact" in Colombia, even scheduling all their in-country meetings during HRW research trips. "They were by far the most important source of information for us," the former staffer said. The relationship was not one-sided: CCJ had a strong interest in international work and used its HRW connections during advocacy trips to Washington. HRW also helped them raise funds for their research. CCJ published HRW reports on Colombia in Spanish and worked with HRW on cases before the InterAmerican Commission. HRW researchers stressed how they also worked with other NGOs, but the importance of transparency in their reporting remained a critical point for their long-term relationship with CCJ. "There was more willingness to address our questions on methodological issues, to see them not as an interrogation, not to criticize them publicly, but to get a sense of if the information was sound, if we could use it or not," one former researcher concluded. Other groups were less willing to make their research processes transparent.

International concern about the availability of timely, credible information also led to the creation of new networks that transformed the landscape of human rights activism in Colombia. European funding agencies, solidarity committees, and other NGOs working on Colombia decided they needed a better mechanism to ensure the flow of credible information and a space to coordinate lobbying efforts in Europe. This concern came to a head during a large human rights conference organized in Brussels in 1995 to lobby the European Parliament. One result was the International Office of Human Rights Action on Colombia (Oficina Internacional de Derechos Humanos Acción Colombia, OID-HACO) based in Brussels with two full-time staff members, one Colombian and one European. The Colombia-Europe Coordination (the United States was later added to the mandate, with a corresponding office in Washington) was also created that year as OIDHACO's counterpart in Colombia, a coalition of NGOs that produced a consensus statement for lobbying at the United Nations Commission.[8] The Coordination published a regular bulletin and came to serve as a bridge between local activists in Colombia and the international sphere. Throughout the late 1990s their workshops became a prime space for the education and socialization of new activists. The mandate of the Coordination was specifically designed to prevent the network from becoming another NGO; instead, the technical secretary was restricted to organizing events and ensuring information flow. A separate coordinating body, the London Agreement, was established to allow European funding agencies to develop public statements for lobbying through a consensus process.[9]

According to activists involved in the founding of the Coordination, the initiative was generated as a response to general concern about redundant work (including receiving multiple urgent actions from different organizations on the same case), the lack of follow-up, and insufficient or unclear information. In one example, organizations sent out a human rights urgent action about an extrajudicial assassination; in fact, the case involved a guerrilla combatant killed in combat. In another incident, the U.N. Working Group on Arbitrary Detentions sent an official inquiry to the Colombian government in the case of an urgent action regarding the detention and fear of disappearance of four protesting coffee farmers during 1994 mass mobilizations. Forced to research the matter, activists found that the four farmers had been released after several hours in the police station, but no follow-up had been sent to the recipients of the international urgent action. Such cases damaged the credibility of both the Colombian NGOs and their international partners and gave the Colombian government cause to disregard the allegations of human rights abuses reported by NGOs.

"The main purpose of the office was to improve the quality and fluidity of information," one of the office's founders told me. "People say that the information flow doesn't work because of emergencies and the stress that everyone works under, but that is not all true; it's also because people don't understand the value of information, how to produce information. So the office was created because they thought it would be a good idea to improve the credibility of the NGOs and to have everyone's opinion consulted." One of the NGOs would send bundles of newspapers to European counterparts via express mail—unclipped, because the Europe-based staff wanted to make sure that they could see everything. The office also relied on a toll-free phone line, prepaid postage envelopes, and faxes to elicit information from distant NGO partners. Email and Web-based information exchange did not become widely used until the early 2000s.

The Coordination was also tasked with educating their Colombian members on the production of credible human rights information. "The problem with the information was that it was too general—everything is the fault of the neoliberal system—or it was too specific—such and such happened in the *vereda* Santa Rosa last weekend, and no one had any idea what you were talking about," one of the Coordination's founders told me. To address the issue of information production, the Coordination organized periodic workshops, with a large annual meeting to produce consensus documents for U.N. lobbying, and additional regional workshops to share information and train activists.

Though one of the most important, the Coordination was not the only space for training activists to produce human rights information that conformed to the demands of international partners. Many activists were also educated through informal channels, such as mentoring by senior activists, as well as conversations and lessons learned abroad. I was part of this process during my work at WOLA. A fundamental part of the lobbying strategy employed by WOLA and other members of the Colombia Steering Committee, a coalition of U.S.-based NGOs interested in Colombia, was to invite Colombian activists to share their perspective and concerns with policy makers through public conferences and lobbying meetings. At the beginning of each visit, Washington-based staff would instruct Colombian activists on the best manner in which to present their case. They were instructed to be extremely concise and to present linear narratives focused on specific incidents. Activists were told to reduce their complicated stories of Colombian violence to a single anecdote that could be understood and sympathized with by young congressional staffers who could spare at most fifteen minutes for a meeting. In addition, activists were taught the mandates of different agencies, and their roles in policy debates, in order to tailor the message to their concerns. For example, Colombian activists were forced to address the drug trade, despite their at best marginal concern with it, because of many

U.S. policy makers' overriding interest in the issue. Through these informal training sessions, numerous activists were taught the basics of American constituency-based politics and political advocacy and were trained in presenting certain kinds of human rights narratives.

Activists were also taught how to produce human rights claims at formal workshops that brought together professional activists in Colombia. A small number of activists were able to participate in international training courses held abroad, such as courses at the Inter-American Institute of Human Rights in Costa Rica. In Colombia governmental human rights agencies as well as international organizations such as the United Nations also offered periodic human rights training; an increasing number of universities now grant advanced degrees or certificates in human rights. Many of these training workshops were organized by NGOs, however. In some cases workshops focused on aspects of international human rights mechanisms, such as the U.N., OAS states, or European human rights system. Occasionally, human rights activists from other countries would share their experiences and strategies; those from the Southern Cone and Central America, for example, were instrumental in the development of national truth commissions. The vast majority of workshops, however, featured professional Colombian activists, most from Bogotá, instructing new recruits and activists from smaller towns and rural areas on developments on the national scene, such as new legislation or court rulings and how to make a human rights claim. One such workshop is discussed in detail below.

HUMAN RIGHTS NGOS AND POLITICAL PARTICIPATION

In addition to illuminating the process by which the construction of human rights narratives is taught to activists, workshops illustrate one of the most important changes in NGO practice during the 1990s: activists' growing engagement with the state and the assumption of a role in public political debates. Unlike the *denuncias* circulated internationally, much of this political work consists of ephemeral encounters that rarely leave any written records. While previously NGOs had little or no direct contact with state representatives and focused on denouncing state abuses, during the 1990s NGO activists became enmeshed in a much more complicated field of contested relationships with certain officials and agencies. In part, this reflected the shifting attitude of the Colombian state toward human rights and the dramatic expansion of the state human rights bureaucracy. Here my interest is in how Colombian activists became engaged in exchanges with Colombian officials and their efforts to support democratic left politicians and participate in public debates on social policy more broadly. While continuing to locate ulti-mate responsibility for political violence in the state and to denounce neoliberal reduction in state welfare programs, activists attempted in practice to orchestrate a new kind of state through political participation on multiple levels. To explore these efforts, I discuss three political moments: work with local politicians elected after the political reforms of the late 1980s, participation in the writing of the 1991 Constitution, and NGO work on the peace agenda.

NGO activists developed multiple forms of engagement with state representatives, including individual or periodic meetings to address spe-cific issues and commissions organized to work on specific problems.[10] The most visible, and controversial, engagement with the state took the form of service provision, such as human rights education, as part of con-tractual agreements with governmental agencies (including department and municipal education departments, mayors' offices, governors' offices, the Defensoria del Pueblo, the Culture Ministry, the Interior Ministry, the Planning Ministry, and the *personerías,* local officials charged with oversight and human rights protection). The majority of NGOs saw such efforts as a threat to autonomy and as posing the greater danger of co-optation; most members of the Coordination did not accept direct funding from the Colombian government. Opportunities to work with the state varied over time. The largest specific increase in govern-mental funding for human rights NGOs came from the United States at the end of the 1990s, when millions of dollars were appropriated for human rights funding through the Plan Colombia assistance programs. This money was administered through USAID and its contractors, and only a fraction was destined for NGOs (the majority was destined for Colombian governmental programs). The issue of U.S. governmental funding generated a huge controversy among NGOs, which did accept European governmental funding. The majority of the NGOs discussed here decided to reject U.S. funding on the grounds that it endangered institutional autonomy. But many NGOs benefited from the indirect sup-port of governmental agencies. NGO representatives took advantage of government-financed transportation to remote rural areas during inves-tigatory commissions, for example, and used government buildings and transportation for meetings.

For the vast majority of human rights NGOs who chose to engage the state on multiple levels outside of direct contractual agreements, these spaces for political participation were a critical site for the articulation of human rights work as part of an ongoing political project founded on the need to transform Colombian society through participation and reform as well as radical opposition and denunciation. This political work complicates the conceptualization of human rights work as NGOs working with international partners to target abusive governments (the "boomerang" model developed by Keck and Sikkink) and disrupts the critique of NGOs as being in the service of a hegemonic state.

In his evaluation of the work of the Coordination, longtime activist Jaime Prieto emphasized the new engagement between NGOs and the state. After more than twenty years as the director of the CSPP, Prieto resigned, first to lead a protection program for threatened activists and then to become a consultant and researcher examining the institutional development of human rights groups in Colombia. He was hired in 1999 to write a comprehensive evaluation of the Coordination. The first half of the hundred-page document is devoted to the relationships between NGOs and the Colombian state. He described two general ways in which NGO activists engage with the state: advocating specific services for particular people (e.g., groups of internally displaced people from a single town needing health care, education, and food) and lobbying for general human rights policies and legislation. No longer simply denouncing and confronting the state, these groups used direct engagement as a means of influencing state policies, to take on a more proactive role in the construction of a democratic society.

In his study, which included extended interviews with more than fifty activists, Prieto found that for all NGOs, engagement with the state remained controversial. Most NGO activists, however, welcomed this engagement as "an advance, a substantial jump forward that increased their capacity for influential advocacy, [giving them a] less marginal role in demanding that the state fulfill their human rights obligations," even while recognizing the limitations of their advocacy efforts (Prieto 1999: 11). Some activists critiqued this engagement as risking co-optation and distraction from the central issue of state responsibility for political violence, which could improve the image of an abusive state. Even those groups that counted engagement with the state as an important element of their work acknowledged that the purported changes within the state were primarily public relations. One activist described state efforts as "shallow and unstable." According to this view, any of these superficial changes resulted from international pressure and the work of specific bureaucrats and institutions but did not entail a demonstrable shift in the hegemonic practices of the state. Activists also described multiple motivations for their engagement. Some who were critical of ongoing relationships with state bureaucracies reported participating in engagement in order not to be isolated from the NGO community. Others were motivated by gaining public recognition for their work while spotlighting the hypocrisy of the state, calling engagement a "resource that must be employed without expecting any effective result, whose only use is leaving a record [*dejar constancia*] in order to show international agencies or demonstrate to public opinion the lack of results, the absence of political will, and the inefficiency of the state in the protection and guarantee of human rights" (Prieto 1999: 9).

For state officials, engagement with NGOs resulted from widely divergent positions (an issue explored in greater detail in chapter 6). One important if unexpected factor was the reliance on NGOs for support that local officials did not receive from their state counterparts. Especially on the local level, state representatives often had less power and lower class standing—lower education levels, a poorer standard of living, certainly fewer international connections and opportunities—than many of the urban NGO activists they encountered. In some instances, local officials relied on NGO activists to support their efforts to promote human rights, pursue investigations of specific cases, and work with local communities; their colleagues in state institutions often did not support, or even undermined, their efforts. A typical example was the *personera* (municipal human rights official) from a small town in Antioquia whom I met at the human rights workshop described below. She was one of a number of people appointed or elected to local government offices who had either responded to the invitation of the NGO coordinators or asked to participate.[11] A quiet woman with a dark shiny bob, she told me shyly that this was her first workshop. She described the situation in her town, a municipal capital of six thousand people eight hours from Medellín "at the end of the road," as complicated. To get there, she told me, you have to pass through five roadblocks set up by the army, paramilitaries, and the FARC. She had worked in the Personería for nine years, starting as a secretary. "One of those jobs is a good thing in a small town," she explained. She was frustrated that "no one really want[ed] to talk about human rights," describing the office as more "community focused, humanitarian." They provide assistance, for example, to peasants that showed up with their families in tow, silently fleeing from somewhere and trying to find a way to get somewhere else. She concluded, "We don't really do any human rights work." A human rights NGO from

Medellín had traveled to the town to investigate the situation, and now they talk on the phone, and she sends some information. She has tried all avenues, the Ministry of the Interior, the vice president's office; she has sent her reports everywhere. She was not optimistic about this lobbying. "Things are just going to stay on the paper they are written on," she glumly concluded, but she was interested in learning more about human rights from the NGO activists who welcomed her analysis and offered her more training. In many areas of the country, NGO activists introduced local officials to representatives of international NGOs, who in turn used their access and greater credibility (as government representatives) in their reports to substantiate their claims. International activists provided protection—in some cases facilitating political asylum—for local officials threatened because of their work.

ACTIVISTS AND THE FIRST WAVE OF ELECTORAL REFORM

Human rights activists' first widespread engagement with electoral politics began with the leftist parties that flourished briefly following the electoral reforms of the 1980s. When local offices were opened to electoral contests, many smaller political parties, including those on the left, came into power at the local level. These reforms were part of a larger push for decentralization of political power and financial resources from the national state to local governments. Many scholars and officials thought such reforms would resolve ongoing political instability and reverse the closed, clientalistic, and corrupt political system established by the National Front agreement. The first stage was fiscal decentralization during the 1970s, which increased local government authority over spending and returned more state revenue to the local level. The second stage was a series of political and administrative reforms during the 1980s, culminating in Law 11 of 1986, which provided for the direct election of mayors and created mechanisms for community participation in local decisions (among them local administrative boards) (Hoyos and Ceballos 2004: 4).

In many areas where inexperienced leftist politicians came into power, experienced activists from the major cities became vital in instructing them on civic duties and opportunities, including connecting them to national and international networks when conservative local elites and unresponsive national state bureaucrats did not support their initiatives. This political opening provided the first real opportunity for small, leftist parties to gain significant local power through direct elections. One of the major beneficiaries of these reforms was the Patriotic Union, created in 1984 during frustrated peace talks with the FARC. A legal political party with complicated relationships with the FARC command structure, the UP brought together a number of reform-minded organizers and won significant electoral gains. Localized civic movements that united social movement organizations, community development groups, and opposition politicians also flourished in some areas, gaining political power through local elections that challenged the corrupt traditional party power structure. These political reforms coincided with growing political autonomy for leftist social movements, legal left parties, and human rights groups, as activists became more independent from the armed left. In part this reflected the general crisis of the left as a result of the collapse of the Soviet Union and was most directly felt by groups affiliated with Communist Parties, but these issues were widely debated among the left.

In the small towns of Antioquia and Meta and in other regions, human rights activists became deeply involved in these local political movements. In addition to working with alternative parties, some activists ran for office themselves. Jahel, a founder of CREDHOS (see chapter 2), first began to work for human rights when she was elected as a *concejal* for the newly formed UP. Like other activists elected to local office, Jahel used her position to provide humanitarian assistance—with state resources—to victims of abuses: "Because I was on the town council, I got the whole council involved. Horacio [Serpa] was involved, the church, the governor, it was a broad range of people involved."[12] In similar ways elected officials throughout the country provided critical support to the newly formed local human rights committees that were the backbone of NGO regional activism.

Gloria recalled that human rights work in many small towns developed in concert with the local elected officials who supported a reformist platform. She described the optimism of the time:

> Human rights work could develop a lot because when there were the first mayoral popular elections, the people decided, the community leaders decided to launch campaigns for the mayor's office. They formed civic associations to support these candidates, and so in several towns there were mayors elected who represented the community. The control of the traditional political elite was broken, with the political bosses, the *caciques* who stole from the communities—there was terrible corruption throughout Cesar. These new mayors were community leaders who opened up a lot of political space and facilitated all our work with human rights. We coordinated with the mayor's office, they gave money for our workshops budget, they helped transport people from the rural areas to the town centers, the *casco urbano*.

It was a very interesting time because of the emergence of new social and political processes. People who had been community leaders before were in charge of the mayors' offices in several municipalities in Cesar, Norte de Santander, in the Catatumbo that also started to happen.

In Medellín the Permanent Committee was established in part in response to the persecution of civic movement leaders protesting the high cost of public services in the early 1980s. The first president of the group, Liberal doctor and professor Hector Abad, is now primarily remembered by the human rights community as an activist, but at the time of his assassination in 1987 he was also a candidate for mayor of Medellín. One of the group's founders remembers how they would work with local officials during the 1990s. "People from different towns would send letters, and we would go and help them set up the committees," she told me. "Jesús [Valle; the group's president at the time] had a lot of relationships with the *personeros*. We would give workshops and courses. We covered the Universal Declaration of Human Rights, all the different kinds of treaties, how to write a *denuncia*, how to get to the Procuraduría, how to make sure that everything was documented."

This rich and complicated political history was largely forgotten after the devastating violence that decimated this generation of local activists. Paramilitary and military repression escalated during the end of the 1980s, some argue, in direct response to the threat to local elites and military forces posed by the possibility of political reform (as well as the specter of increased insurgent military power) (Romero 2002). Since the violence that destroyed these early efforts to implement political reform through electoral support for progressive parties, activists have taken different roads. Jahel now leads Reinciar (lit., "to begin again"), a group dedicated to supporting the survivors and family members of assassinated members of the UP. They also continue to push for the government to accept responsibility for the party's destruction, through negotiations with governmental human rights agencies, cases in the Colombian judicial system, and a case at the InterAmerican Human Rights Commission. Together with other former UP activists, they argue that the definition of genocide, currently restricted to the attempt to destroy a national, ethnic, racial, or religious group, should be expanded to include political affiliation. Gloria, on the other hand, has remained active in political organizing on a national level. In addition to directing her human rights NGO, she was elected one of six members of the board of directors *(mesa directiva)* of the Polo Democrático de Izquierda, Colombia's leading democratic left party. At a rally in support of Lucho Garzón, the Polo's 2002 presidential candidate and now mayor of Bogotá, Gloria told the assembly that she refused to abandon the idea that Colombia could be made a better country, that peace with social justice and human rights could still be created. "Even if we lost in the polls, we are planting the seeds of a hopeful change for Colombia," she said, explicitly linking her human rights and political activism.

HUMAN RIGHTS ACTIVISTS
AND THE WRITING OF THE 1991 CONSTITUTION

During the late 1980s, Colombian human rights activists were instrumental in the campaign to rewrite the national Constitution. The resulting 1991 Constitution dramatically expanded the human rights protections offered by the national charter. The Constitution itself was in part the result of broad popular mobilization, in particular the student movement known as the "seventh ballot" after a nonbinding referendum in the March 1990 legislative elections. From that, an official plebiscite was authorized by President Barco during the May 27, 1990, presidential elections, with five of the six million participants voting in favor. The 70 delegates to the Constitutional Assembly were elected on December 9, with only about 25 percent of eligible voters participating. The low turnout was in part responsible for the large leftist representation in the Assembly: 25 delegates from the Liberal Party; 19 from the newly demobilized M-19 guerrilla movement; 11 from the Conservative Party's dissenting leader, Álvaro Gómez Hurtado, and his National Salvation Movement; 9 from the main Colombian Conservative Party; and 2 each for the indigenous peoples, the evangelicals, and the Patriotic Union. In addition, the government assigned four more delegates: 2 for the demobilized EPL, 1 for the Revolutionary Workers' Party, and 1 for the Quintín Lame indigenous guerrilla movement. The Assembly was inaugurated February 5, 1991, with the presidency shared by Liberal Horacio Serpa, M-19 representative Antonio Navarro Wolff, and National Salvation leader Hurtado (see Kline 1999 for details on the process).

The opportunity to write a new charter for the country galvanized human rights activists. "We decided with this new bill of rights, let's give an opportunity to the Constitution, work with the Constitution, we will play it that way," Pablo recalled. "We studied the Constitution a lot, working on the new rights established there with the Colombian Commission of Jurists and others. So they were included [in the final draft of the Constitution]. We did a lot of lobbying with the Constituyente [Constitutional Assembly], with advising from the Human Rights Institute in Costa Rica." Juan Méndez, then director of Human Rights Watch/Americas, recalled working with the NGOs on lobbying strategy: "[There was] a very broad and open discussion in Colombia. It was a very interesting time to be involved in the work."

Among the important innovations were the limitations placed on the use of the state of siege, which previous presidents employed to such an extent that most of the previous forty years of governmental rule had occurred under various forms of exceptional powers. Alfredo Vázquez Carrizosa, head of the Permanent Committee, played an important role in these debates. The new Constitution advanced human rights guarantees in a number of ways—including new legal mechanisms such as the *tutela,* which allowed any individuals to bring a lawsuit against the government if they felt their fundamental rights were being violated, and new institutions such as the Office of the Human Rights Ombudsman (see chapter 6)—and enshrined rights as a foundation for democracy.

The new Constitution did have limitations. According to Juan Méndez from HRW, "The worst aspect of the Colombian constitution, which was generally very good, was the due obedience clause." This provision allowed soldiers accused of abuses to claim that they were only acting under orders and therefore should not be held responsible for human rights violations. Human rights groups argued that soldiers should not be required to follow orders that would result in (presumably illegal) abuses and therefore should be held responsible even if acting under military orders. An Argentine national who had been persecuted and forced into exile by the military dictatorship, Méndez had counseled the Colombian NGOs on use of the due obedience clause in Argentina, "why it was wrong and what the consequences were." The 1991 Constitution maintained other special rights for the military, including the military *fuero,* a series of privileges that included a separate military justice system to hear cases involving military personnel. While designed only to try cases involving military service, such as issues of military discipline, many cases involving human rights violations were tried in the military court system despite the objections of human rights groups. The inability of NGOs to successfully establish greater civilian control over the military and limit its special rights in the new constitution was in part the result of the military's lobbying efforts. One governmental human rights official recalled, "It was very curious, because on the one hand you had a series of guarantees, but when it came time to confront the mechanisms that encouraged human rights violations, the Constituyente couldn't [carry out reforms]. So that was a failure." Some officials involved in the process also reported rumors of secret deals during the negotiations, including an alleged agreement between the M-19 representatives to block reforms targeting the military in exchange for promises that they would not be the target of violent reprisals. "The army wouldn't touch their people, and in exchange, the new Constitution wouldn't touch the army's privileges," one participant told me.

NGO lobbying during the Constitutional Assembly had paradoxical results. The 1991 Constitution dramatically expanded the role of human rights in the national charter as well as creating numerous new specific mechanisms for the protection and promotion of human rights in the country. They were unable, however, to touch the privileges of the military, widely believed by human rights groups to be a decisive factor in abuses. Many of the reforms have been only partially implemented, and many politicians have attempted to undermine many of the human rights provisions. Participation in the drafting process, however, gave a new generation of activists direct experience with lobbying government representatives and with working within the democratic system. Since then many NGOs have lobbied before Congress on human rights legislation. NGOs were instrumental in efforts to codify forced disappearances as a crime instead of having to try cases under existing kidnapping laws, and the 1996 passage of Law 288, which forced the government to provide monetary compensation in cases decided in favor of victims of human rights violations by the InterAmerican Human Rights Commission and the U.N. Human Rights Committee. In addition, NGOs became more involved in ongoing efforts to shape human rights policy instead of simply denouncing violations.

PROMOTING POLITICAL PEACEMAKING

By the mid-1990s NGO activists were searching for new ways to engage in public policy debates. Participation in progressive local electoral politics was largely impossible due to political violence, and efforts to implement the human rights protections written into the 1991 Constitution were under way. Violence and human rights abuses, however, continued apace. President Pastrana made peace the focus of his campaign platform in the 1998 elections and sanctioned talks with the FARC in five southern municipalities. The ultimately unsuccessful discussions provided an opportunity for human rights groups to weigh in with their prescriptions for peace.

For the NGOs that focused on state-sponsored and paramilitary violence against community activists, simply ending the guerrilla conflict was not enough. They argued that without ameliorating the root causes of the conflict—poverty, inequality, and political corruption—the dissolution of the guerrillas' military machine would not lead to a reduction in violence.[13] Many human rights defenders viewed the peace activists' slogans, such as blanket rejections of violence and generic statements in support of peace, as a competing discourse that undermined efforts to ensure justice and accountability. In fact, many of the early peace initiatives, such as the mass demonstrations against guerrilla violence and the symbolic votes for peace, did not address the issues of social reforms that NGO activists viewed as the foundation for a lasting peace (see chapter 1).

Some activists developed the concept of political peacemaking, which focused on the need for political reforms in the context of a negotiated settlement with the guerrillas and not simply on a cease-fire. Jorge Rojas Rodriguez, director of CODHES, was one of the senior advocates; senior members of the CCJ and Gloria were also very active in leadership for this vision of peacemaking. They and other human rights activists participated in the Permanent Assembly for Peace, an umbrella organization of peace efforts founded in July 1998. During their first meeting, approximately three thousand representatives from a range of civil society organizations promoted a reformist agenda in which civil society organizations, not simply the government and the armed groups, were proclaimed major participants in negotiations. Through periodic meetings for several years, the Permanent Assembly sought to both promote negotiations and develop a civil society agenda for peace agreements. Meetings have been held every year since.

Colombian activists were also motivated by increasing U.S. intervention in the Colombian conflict. In the 2000 U.S. aid package Plan Colombia and subsequent yearly additions, approximately 80 percent of the funding was earmarked for military assistance and training. International partners pushed Colombian activists to articulate an alternative policy to increasing militarization and to develop proposals that included the possibility of long-term reform. Human rights NGOs that questioned Plan Colombia from its inception as a dangerous obstacle to the negotiations joined forces with peace initiatives and social movements in a civil coalition called Paz Colombia (in an obvious play on Plan Colombia, which then becomes "war Colombia" by default). One of Paz Colombia's major efforts was the International Conference for Peace, Human Rights and International Humanitarian Law, held in San José, Costa Rica, in October 2000. Delegates from thirty-two governments attended, along with a sector of the insurgency and broad representation from sectors of Colombian society. With similar intent and in the midst of the breakdown of talks between the government and the FARC (February 2002) and the presidential elections (May 2002), the National Congress for Peace and Country was organized. This was a last desperate attempt by civilians to restart dialogue and negotiations and to create a joint platform for a social and political response to stop a candidate from successfully campaigning for total war.

In an article titled "Political Peacemaking: A Challenge for Civil Society," Rojas Rodriguez described both the movement's objectives and its internal divisions:

> [E]xamples of civilian action for peace in Colombia have a common agenda: a politically negotiated solution to the armed conflict, full respect for human rights and IHL, political and social changes in favor of equity and inclusion, international aid for peace and the democratic participation of society in voting on eventual accords. However, there are tensions and difficulties that weaken capacities and affect credibility. The most fundamental difference may be between those who justify and those who reject the armed struggle of the insurgency. There are also many deficits in understanding, especially on issues such as the representativeness and the legitimacy of organizations involved in civil peace coalitions; the political changes occurring around the armed conflict; the role of the international community, the logic of their actions and their contradictions and differences; and the role of specific social sectors and of the regions (with regard to centralism and exclusion). Finally, there are deficits in coordination, such as the absence of alliances with diverse sectors of Colombian society, and a lack of a national and international communication strategy in a country at war. (Rojas Rodriguez 2004)

The Paz Colombia initiative collapsed following the suspension of peace talks in February 2001. Human rights activists continued to actively promote a negotiated settlement to the conflict, however, through umbrella organizations such as the Alianza (Alliance; officially called the Alliance of Like-Minded Social Organizations for International Assistance for Peace and Democracy in Colombia). This coalition was founded in 2003, after a meeting of the London Accord. The human rights activists who had been involved in the Paz Colombia meetings were among the primary forces behind the organization. Their platform included a clear rejection of guerrilla violence and a broad agenda that included human rights, peace, and democratization issues; their stated objective was "influencing the policies of international assistance such that it is directed toward peace, democracy, human rights and international humanitarian law, protection and strengthening of ethnic groups (including indigenous people and Afro-Colombians) and the peasantry, and toward agrarian reform, as well as toward sustainable integral human development, environmental protection, including a gender perspective and strengthening civil society." In 2006 the Alliance continued to meet weekly and sponsor periodic workshops, organized through a coordinating committee of twenty-two organizations.

LEARNING TO TELL THE STORY: NGO WORKSHOPS

Colombian human rights activism remained grounded in the international legal norms that defined human rights standards, particularly as professionalized institutional practices expanded the focus on this legal foundation. The same NGOs struggled to link the radical aspirations for social change that characterized the first generation of human rights activism with their work in the 1990s though different forms of attempting to advance political change, including electoral politics, Constitution writing, and political peacemaking. They opened up to dialogue with new sectors, including state representatives, and worked alongside rural and marginalized communities that confronted complex violence from multiple armed actors. These two impulses—professionalization and adherence to international norms and agitating for social change and political transformation—were fraught with contradictions. Pointing out this lack of coherence is not intended as a critique. Rather, I want to locate these tensions as part of what made human rights activism in Colombia such a rich and productive field during the 1990s, as activists attempted to negotiate these often-competing demands. This ongoing, contested process is clearly visible in the workshops where small-town activists attempted to fit the complex realities of Colombian violence into the linear narratives required by international human rights activism.

Human rights education workshops were often the places where these contradictions and struggles were most transparent. Those groups with greater access to training and professional standards often traveled throughout the country offering presentations and exercises devoted to teaching activists how to appropriately report human rights abuses. The "professionalization" of documentation included greater vigor in fact-checking, the standardization of presentation, tone, and language, and the inclusion of contextual details and framing. Such efforts were an explicit goal of the Coordination. I attended one such training, held as part of a larger workshop for activists in Medellín and the surrounding towns. The training was attended by approximately thirty activists, and participants included new recruits to established organizations, small-town activists with few opportunities for training, and low-level local government officials who received little official support in their efforts to promote human rights. The workshop, held in the conference rooms of a dingy downtown hotel in the bustling center of Medellín, had been organized by the Coordination as part of a yearly series to facilitate discussion among the groups and to develop consensus positions to present to the international community. Several of the two-day sessions were devoted to producing human rights documentation and were led by Rodrigo, a veteran activist from Bogotá. A university-trained sociologist, he was the author of numerous reports about violence in Colombia and had coauthored several that were published in book form. His presentation was divided into three sections: a lecture on how to write a human rights report, a small-group exercise in which we were asked to discuss how to write up complicated real-life cases, and a plenary discussion in which he critiqued the conclusions of the small-group presentations. This presentation demonstrated the merging of two workshop styles, the participation-focused model of popular education and the lecture style of professional training sessions.

Rodrigo also embodied the often-tense relationship between Bogotá NGOs and "the regions," as the smaller, locally based groups were known. Since the first human rights groups emerged in the 1970s, activists from Bogotá had traveled throughout the country to raise consciousness, train new activists, and encourage the creation of new organizations. Bogotá-based groups enjoyed considerable advantages over those located in smaller cities and rural areas in terms of access to funding, educational resources, and opportunities to engage with Colombian governmental and international officials. Bogotá groups were often criticized for being out of touch with local realities, hogging the limelight, and squandering resources, and for using the activism and commitment of local activists to fund their international adventures. "The regions," in turn, were accused sotto voce of being poorly trained, divisive, and enmeshed in local political conflicts.

Rodrigo appeared to personify the condescending attitude attributed to the Bogotá groups in his rapid-fire approach. He was dismissive of questions and began with the directive, "I'll pass out some information later, I recommend that you don't take notes so you don't get distracted." He began his presentation by saying he was "leaving aside political discussions" to focus on methodology. "Reports coming from the field are full of information about the situation, but don't have structure or order, making them hard to read." He proceeded to give a lecture that was full of explanations and exhortations about how to write a professional human rights report. What he did not acknowledge, however, was that these demands were explicitly political in how they shaped the kind of information—the content itself—of the reports that were to be written, and that such discussions were at the heart of the controversy over the professionalization and political positioning of human rights work. For many activists, who viewed their activism as rooted in a radical vision of social transformation, efforts at professionalization contradicted the underlying purpose of their work.

Rodrigo's words echoed the workshop's previous speaker, who had emphasized the role of the consensus position adopted by the Coordination in international advocacy. The consensus position was a short statement, adopted during the annual Coordination national meeting, developed to present at the United Nations Human Rights Commission meetings and as a guideline for the year's lobbying efforts. "It is very few words, 1,500 words, so you have to synthesize, in the least number of words," Rodrigo told us. Long-winded and overly rhetorical statements were a major point of contention between Colombian and foreign activists. "We the NGOs are very given to criticizing," he said, repeating "criticizing" five times to emphasize the degree to which Colombian NGOs were perceived by foreign NGOs and governments as focused on the negative and unwilling to present practical solutions. "People are very good at criticizing, but you have to think, people, what do you suggest, so that they can't say that the NGOs just criticize and that we are proactive [*propositivo*]," meaning able to present proposals for future action.

The majority of his presentation, however, focused on the structure and content of longer human rights reports. Reports must be clearly structured, he told us, with an introduction outlining what will be contained therein. Most of this discussion was devoted to the issue of context and sources. Rodrigo told the gathered activists that human rights reports must include context and clarity about sources explicitly as a means of producing new kinds of knowledge about Colombian reality. "If you look at bulletins from academia, history, we don't agree with them, with their version of history, with their heroes," he said. Rodrigo explicitly positioned human rights documentation as presenting a dissenting version of Colombian history, with similar intellectual rigor and requirements: "Just like a thesis, we have to include information about sources and the region." This included a discussion of armed groups. Rodrigo criticized human rights reporting in which "we say they are there but not why or what relation they bear to the *dinámica* [dynamics] in the region." To understand that *dinámica,* activists must include a wide range of sources, including the statements of the armed groups themselves: "We can't refuse to read Castaño's book or the books by the FARC.[14] We have to be ready, we have to know what the other side is saying about themselves. We have to do interviews with people from the region; interviews with armed actors, which is a very controversial issue."

Rodrigo advocated a fundamental change in how activists approach information, exhorting them to develop a more professional practice of documentation that was oriented to the long term. "We can't use lack of resources as an excuse" but have to develop "press archives," he told the audience, many of whom lived in small towns where national and even regional newspapers arrived days late. He advocated a "culture of newspaper reading" that involved not simply passive reading but constant note-taking for archives. These archives should contain not only press clippings but previously published reports and notes from events as well. "We talk every day with the *compañeros*"—referring to other activists— "but we don't structure our work. Because of the rhythm of the work we lose the opportunity to systematize our experience." Here he was repeating a common critique—that the improvised nature of work focusing on emergency cases, rather than strategic planning, made the achievement (or even the articulation) of long-terms goals more difficult. "We need to keep better notes [*memorias*] from workshops and forums . . . and records of what we produce."

In this clear exposition of the commonly held standard of professional human rights documentation, Rodrigo was glossing over a number of profound controversies within the human rights community. A basic and evident contradiction was one of material circumstance. Rodrigo placed documentation alongside academic research and implicitly promoted a measured, reflective production of knowledge. Most of the activists in the room were volunteers, however, and few had more than a small-town high school education. Almost none had access to regular funding for their human rights-related activities. In addition, his call for including multiple sources was dangerous: interviewing armed actors was illegal and exposed activists to accusations that they were supporting the guerrillas. Several well-known bishops had been publicly accused of being guerrilla supporters after news of meetings with local commanders became public; the bishops maintained that they were attempting to get information about kidnap victims and work out local humanitarian accords. Rodrigo himself had been the subject of controversy after allegations that he facilitated contact between the guerrillas and the author in a book published about the FARC.

The difficulties of conducting human rights research was brought home by the opening chants after the participants returned from a break. "José María Valle, ¡presente!" was repeated several times as we took our seat for the afternoon session. The ¡presente! chant was commonly heard in protests and marches, used to invoke the presence of dead comrades and colleagues through the calling of their names and a roll call response of "present." Like the classroom ritual "Here," the chants affirmed that the dead were present and not forgotten, that the cause that justified their sacrifice lived on. Valle had been a friend and colleague to many in the room, a prominent local lawyer who had taken over the presidency of Medellín's Hector Abad Permanent Committee for the Defense of Human Rights. The committee had taken the name of its first president, Hector Abad, who was assassinated in 1988; Valle was killed in his downtown office ten years later, on February 27, 1998, four years before the meeting at which his name was chanted. While it was unclear to me if the originators of the chant had intended it to be a direct challenge to Rodrigo's vision of professional human rights documentation, the ringing cries invoked the martyr status of assassinated activists and linked their struggle to the broader leftist political movements that had used such chants in protests since the 1960s.

The difficulty of categorizing violence, and of limiting the retelling of these violent events to a single coherent narrative, was made amply clear by the small-group assignments. We were split into groups of five to ten participants, assigned a real-life case from the surrounding towns, and told to write a human rights *denuncia,* presumably using the morning instruction to guide our discussion. The discussions within the group and the presentations of the case to plenary made painfully clear the divisions and difficulties inherent in cramming the complicated events into a single narrative structure.

My group was sent off to work on the following case: El Carmen, we were told, was a small town near Medellín, home to a ceramics factory that had been the major source of employment but that was forced to close after the "economic opening," shorthand understood by all to refer to the neoliberal reforms of the early 1990s that reduced tariffs and increased imports in Colombia.[15] Three hundred workers, members of a union affiliated with the Central Unitaria de Trabajadores (CUT), Colombia's largest labor federation, were left without jobs. Owed back wages and severance pay from the owners, the workers took over the factory, an action that marked the beginning of the violent persecution of the union. Two union activists were killed. After reading this brief case synopsis, Rodrigo left us to write up the case. Because it was a real event from a local town, however, the participants in our small group knew a great deal more about the details and context of the event than was revealed in the synopsis.

"I know that town well," the man sitting next to me announced. "Two years ago, in the *vereda* La Chapa, where the Ninth Front, the Iván Uribe Buitrago Front of the FARC, was in control, the *autodefensas* from the Magdalena Valley came in and ran them out. There were 150 people assassinated in the past year. All this—the paramilitary takeover—didn't happen overnight, they are still struggling over who will control that area. La Unión [a neighboring municipality], that is completely taken over by the *paras* [paramilitaries]."[16]

Across from him, a thin man with the wiry build and stilted formal cadence of an unpracticed, newly recruited peasant activist began denouncing the violence suffered by local communities. He stood, his hands grasping the back of the chair in front of him, leaning forward and swaying slightly with the rhythm of his words. The defenseless peasant is always the one to fall, he announced dramatically. His passionate condemnation of official indifference ran on; each time, as he appeared to wind down, he would begin again, taking up another repeated theme. I had heard such speeches perhaps hundreds of times during interviews and in the countless similar workshops and conferences I had attended; generally, they filled me with frustration because of the repetitious empty rhetoric. Now, as an ethnographer, I sat back with a more measured eye. The man sitting next to me leaned close to my ear. He—with a nod to the speaker—is from the Hector Abad Committee, he confided. I discovered later that this newly formed human rights group was well known for its opposition to the sterile professional standards promoted in workshops such as this, explicitly linking its activism to radical politics. As the speaker continued, it became clear that the speech was not intended for us—who clearly agreed with his passionate defense of the rural poor—

but instead was a rehearsal, a stump speech of sorts for a young activist who could then return to his membership and tell them how he lectured us. This activist was not simply talking to hear himself speak: he was also voicing another kind of human rights narrative. This narrative with the repetitive cadence and angry rhetoric was not the detached language of professional documentation but the political outrage of a community organizer. Although equally stilted and confining in its own way as the professionalized narrative, his narrative expressed emotions rarely exposed during the workshop: anger at repeated government failure to fulfill their promises, despair at the economic transformations that decimated the rural poor. As his speech continued, circling around the issue and repeating the theme of the defenseless peasant, the other participants became restless. Finally, one woman called out, "This is not the time for political speeches [*discursos*] but to do our assignment." The man reluctantly took his seat.

It turned out that others in the group knew even more about the case assigned to us. A soft-spoken man told us that he was a *personero* in the region. He said that as part of the local *alcaldía* (mayoral administration), they had to carry out *diálogos* with "them." "We talked to them," he said—never identifying "them," even with any of the vague slang used to name the paramilitary forces common in the region. "They said they did it, and even told us why they killed them," he explained. The paramilitaries had "done intelligence" and discovered that the town council met frequently with the FARC commander in the region; to avoid attack, the council members had to report their activities to the insurgents. The woman who had earlier urged the politician in training to end his speech disputed this excuse for the violence, noting that the paramilitaries frequently use allegations of guerrilla connections to justify their attacks without any real evidence.

The *personero* told us that as state representatives they "represent human rights but also to ensure that the laws are enforced." Thus he felt that although the murders were not justified, the union activists should not have taken over the building but instead used the legal system to ensure their rights were respected. One of the men in the group disagreed, saying that paramilitaries had gained too much control in the region to allow the judicial system to function.

"They were going to kill the entire town council," the *personero* told us, his detailed recollections overwhelming the discussion. Our group efforts were abandoned as the *personero* revealed the local dynamics. In order to reduce violence in the area, he and other local officials had been carrying out humanitarian dialogues with illegal armed actors, including talks with local guerrilla leaders after they had issued a blanket threat against mayors. The issue became a national debate, with the federal government declaring such efforts illegal. Local politicians labeled them humanitarian dialogues and claimed they were the only hope for establishing temporary reprieves for embattled communities, liberate kidnapped hostages, and recover bodies for burial. "There were 149 deaths, with no investigation, no one named responsible," the *personero* continued. "Only the case where it was very evident, everyone saw them with the victim, that would be the only case that was ever solved." He told us that things had been very different in the 1980s, when UP members were being targeted by political violence and, he insisted, were well covered by the media. "Now, it's just one more death." The current violence did provoke a new kind of human rights violation: internal forced displacement. Communities had fled their homes in search of safe haven in neighboring regions but did not qualify as refugees because they did not cross a national border. In this case, the *personero* explained, "these incidents didn't cause a lot of displacement because everyone had already left. Month by month, everyone had already left because of the ongoing political violence." As he described it, the underlying motor of the violence is the struggle to control land and resources: "This is a strategic corridor, along the highway that ends up in the Middle Magdalena Valley. In the lower part, everything is controlled by the guerrillas, nothing is stolen. But part is now controlled by the *paras*." Although he was himself a state official, he concluded, "There is no state, the state is finished."

The *personero* finished with a description of the changing political dynamics in the region. "When you look at the *paras*, at first, during our conversations, they had no political advisers, now when you go, they call the political adviser, someone who has a lot of political training," he told us. He had observed firsthand the push for paramilitary political recognition, while the guerrillas became more abusive: "The other group, the FARC, they do things that makes them lose political credibility with the people, in the beginning, they were very violent but they had political work. They continue to be very violent [*muy asesino*]."

The group time almost up, the *personero* agreed to present our report. Rodrigo had started us off with the barest outlines of the context: a closed factory, a union, paramilitary groups, two assassinations. Now the context appeared much more complicated, including not only those factors but also guerrilla groups, secret meetings, allegations of corruption, and the shifting political profile of the armed actors in the region.

Conflict over land and resources, paramilitary politicization, and increasing guerrilla abuses, as well as the efforts by local officials to negotiate with armed actors, had no place in the linear human rights narrative focused on individual assassinations, which the activists were being trained to produce.

We returned to the plenary, and each group presented its case. The first case was the well-known disappearance of two Medellín activists with ASFADDES, Claudia and Angel. The group presented the minimal facts of the case: they had been last seen on a bus, taken off by armed men and never seen again. The second case revealed additional dangers involved in the production of human rights narratives. Dealing with certain kinds of populations requires special considerations. As in the United States, for example, minors, those under the age of eighteen or in some cases fifteen, are subject to special laws protecting their identity and specifying limited punishments (factors contributing to the employment of minors by criminal groups). This case involved a fourteen-year-old girl tortured and killed by a fourteen-year-old boy on November 9, 2001, as part of a "promotion" requirement within the AUC, the paramilitary umbrella group. In its presentation the group offered a detailed recounting of the day's events. The nature of these details generated concerns from Rodrigo and others: with too much detail, the people involved in the case could be identified and any witnesses or survivors endangered. You have to be very careful when you refer to witnesses, Rodrigo told us. The victim and the perpetrator were both minors, further complicating the case. Then there were the questions of motive. The girl knew the boy—some people said they had dated—so what was the motive in the killing, personal or political? Was the individual responsible, or the group? Was the boy organically attached to the AUC, acting under orders, or had he been acting alone? Despite the detail offered about how the case had unfolded, the motive, and thus the classification, of the case remained unclear.

The rest of the cases were presented with minimal details. There was the 1994 case of two bodies found tortured in the road, with a sign left on the remains reading "ACCU," the initials of a powerful regional paramilitary group. The next was the 2000 case of army soldiers who told the townspeople of Santa Ana that they were from the ACCU, took over the school as their base, and burned down twenty-three houses and one business, causing nearly eight hundred people to flee to the nearby town of Ituango. Finally came the 2001 case of a young man who was killed and beheaded, reportedly by the AUC and the police working together, and his head sent in a package to his family.

During our group presentation, the *personero* stood and read a brief *denuncia:* two union activists were killed by presumed paramilitaries. The group had run out of time to plan the final presentation; the *personero*'s final report was his personal invention based on Rodrigo's instruction (and probably his familiarity with other human rights narratives). His presentation fit into the structured lessons of the day but ignored his elaborate retelling of the local power struggle and the active role of local political leaders—himself included—in addressing the violence, parsing the motives of violent actors, and encouraging local negotiations. Even as Rodrigo stressed the importance of a sophisticated understanding of local dynamics—an understanding that undoubtedly allowed the *personero* to continue to function in his daily work—there was no room for those details of the story in the human rights narrative. Our discussion served as an example, although perhaps not in the way he intended, of the complexity of fashioning out of daily experience in such violent towns a human rights narrative focused on the legal framework of guilt and on establishing clear state responsibility.

Comparing the *personero*'s accounts before our small group and at the workshop's conclusion was instructive on several levels. He told of complicated violence but also of complicated responses to violence; he emphasized not the passivity of the victims but the actions of local authorities to address violence, using a wide repertoire of tactics, including some that were illegal at the time. As a representative of the local state speaking at an NGO meeting, the *personero* highlighted how the local state is located in a liminal position, in this case receiving instruction from NGOs while being alienated from the national government and clearly in need of support. In both recountings, the security forces were completely absent, erased from the narrative of violence that occurs between illegal forces, paramilitary, and guerrillas.

In this workshop and others, small-town activists demonstrated a sophisticated awareness of the limitations and possibilities of professional human rights narratives. They were unwilling to openly express dissenting views of what should be contained in these accounts because of their desire to claim the political capital made available through the use of international human rights frameworks. According to Rodrigo's lecture, human rights reports can be made credible through correct training in knowledge production: the right use of language, context, and tone; the necessary details without extraneous information. By design, these accounts are unable to contain diverse narratives, including those of outraged community activists and local officials trying to negotiate conflicts, but instead promise access to a sphere of international action on human rights cases. Through their participation in human rights training, where activists with greater experience translated stories of local violence into acceptable human rights cases, small-town activists demonstrated their hopes that their stories, however truncated in the telling, could transcend their regions and reach the vaulted spheres of international activism.

The 1990s were a time of dramatic transformations for Colombian human rights activists, providing both opportunities and challenges. Activists created new groups that addressed new issues such as forced internal displacement. Financial support from international foundations and European governments provided the resources for the transition from solidarity groups to human rights NGOs, with paid staff largely replacing volunteers and new regimes of work discipline and institutional practices accountable to institutional funders. The central shift in human rights practice during this time was the increasing emphasis on the production of credible human rights documentation. These narratives relied on a linear structure, verifiable claims, and singular motivations to be considered a human rights abuse actionable by international partners. In doing so, the intricate complexities of violence, including multiple causalities, rumor, public secrets, and entangled actors, are trimmed from the accounts.

Critiques of NGOs often point to the ways in which they depoliticize movements, replacing the state with technocrats who are accountable only to distant funders. The anthropologist James Ferguson labeled development NGOs in Zambia "the anti-politics machine" in his now-classic ethnography of the same name. Certainly such a critique is warranted for many of the self-defined NGOs currently operating in Colombia. For the human rights groups I examine here, the political landscape is more complicated, however. Rather than simply becoming service providers, these activists struggle to define a political practice that continues to strive for radical political transformation in the radically different political landscape of post–cold war Colombia. The contradictions of and controversies over these issues are explored further in the next chapter; my focus here has been on three moments of political participation that demonstrate the multiple ways in which these activists have attempted to continue their activism despite the increasingly limited open political debate in Colombia. Paradoxically, in many ways this participation has required the creation of new forms of relating to the state, whether through supporting local officials, lobbying for a new constitution, or attempting to articulate the political reforms necessary for a lasting peace. The activists portrayed here do not attempt to replace the state through their efforts but co-construct a state that fulfills its obligations to its citizen.

These contradictions are displayed as activists demonstrate the appropriate forms of professionalized activism in settings where the multiple forms and meanings are undeniable, such as the human rights education workshop described here. Among themselves, the intricate complexities of Colombian violence are constant fodder for discussion, gossip, and jokes, even while they produce expunged versions for use by their international counterparts. While rarely openly acknowledged, activists must be fluent in multiple genres of production of knowledge about violence. Survival in the small towns and rural back roads requires complete mapping of the circuitous histories and relationships surrounding violence, while the possibilities of international action, such as public pressure on specific cases or the intervention of multilateral bodies of the United Nations, require staccato summations of specific incidents. Such inconsistencies are not resolved in the course of activism but put into evidence once more the complexities of political action.

CHAPTER 4

The Emotional Politics of Activism in the 1990s

The emotional dimension of activism and the ideological platforms that guide both the objectives and the strategies of activists intersect in the debates over how to define human rights activism at the turn of the century. While much of the work on social movements has focused on their ideological dimensions, emotion also shapes activists' employment of political practices as well as the nature of their aspirations. These emotional dimensions are often obscured, erased by the focus on formal documents, diplomacy, and political power; for many, the emotional dimensions of such work invalidates the serious business of politics. Many activists and scholars prefer to think that those who make policy are rational political actors; to focus on the emotional dimension of oppositional activism makes such work suspect. However, all dimensions of political life have an emotional component: cold rationality is itself an emotional posture. To explore how political activism occurs requires illuminating the messy and contested terrain of emotions and identity. This chapter examines the complicated intersections of the emotional and ideological dimensions of many of the most controversial aspects of human rights activism, including debates over professionalization, identification with victims, and confronting the danger and loss inherent in work in areas beset by political violence.

Scholars of social movements are increasingly turning their gaze to the

issue of emotion and personal identity as critical locations for understanding how and why individuals become and remain involved in high-
risk social action. The social theorist Craig Calhoun wrote that risks
may be borne "not because of the likelihood of success in manifest goals
but because participation in a course of action has over time committed
one to an identity that would be irretrievably violated by pulling back
from risk" (Calhoun 1991: 51).[1] Several recent works examining the
role of emotion and identity in social movements have developed this
insight in a number of illuminating case studies. In her article about the
Southern Cone human rights organizations, Mara Lovemen stressed the
importance of "dense yet diverse interpersonal networks . . . embedded
within broader national and transnational institutional and issue networks" as well as external support (Loveman 1998: 477). In his introduction to the edited volume *Passionate Politics: Emotions and Social
Movements,* the sociologist Jeff Goodwin argues that "strong feelings for
the group make participation pleasurable in itself, independently of the
movement's ultimate goals and outcomes," and "protest can be a way of
saying something about oneself and one's morals, of finding joy and
pride in them" (Goodwin 2001: 12) He points out that the negative emotions associated with shame and guilt can also be powerful forces in
forcing activist identity. Goodwin concludes that "the 'strength' of an
identity, even a cognitively vague one, comes from its emotional side"
and that "elaborately processed" emotional reactions to political issues
are profoundly shaped by cultural and historical factors (Goodwin 2001:
18). Elizabeth Wood, in her new study of "insurgent *campesinos,*" peasants who were not combatants with the guerrillas during El Salvador's
civil war but actively collaborated with them, concludes that moral outrage and emotional identity were extremely important factors for
explaining peasant participation in dangerous activism: "One [reason
for participating] was the expression of moral outrage at state violence
and defiance of state authority. Participation per se expressed outrage
and defiance; unlike other possible reasons for participating, its force was
not negated by the fact that victory was unlikely and in any case was not
contingent on one's participation. The second was the pride taken by
campesinos in their successful assertion of their interests and identity,
what I term here the pleasure of agency" (Wood 2003: 20). In these
accounts participation has its own emotional rewards, independent of
the outcome; understanding these rewards helps explain why people
remain involved in activism when the results are not favorable.

ACTIVIST VOCATIONS AND THE LEGACY OF THE LEFT

In Colombia, the emotional rewards of activism are central precisely because the material benefits of human rights activism in Colombia are so few and the dramatic drawbacks—threats and harassment, even death—loom so large. During all of my oral history interviews with long-term activists, they reflected on their personal commitment and identity forged over the course of a lifetime of activism. The construction of a deeply held activist identity was one of the major factors that allowed NGO activists to continue their work despite violent repression. Human rights activists who traced their roots to *militancia* in the 1970s and 1980s drew on a repertoire of cultural meanings for their activism based on the two major cultural influences on the Colombian left—the Catholic Church and Communist parties (see chapter 2). In addition to serving as ideological and political resources, these institutions provided cultural frameworks for appropriate activist emotional responses. During my oral history interviews, Colombian activists most often described this revolutionary consciousness in human rights practice as *mística*, loosely translated as "mystique," which captures the connotation of otherworldliness, romance, a commitment beyond rationality, while losing the political dimension of vocation. Activists used the word *mística* to describe the profoundly motivating emotional force that defined human rights activism for them, a commitment to this work as both a connection to the victims of political violence, a covenant with them, and a means of articulating the broad hope for justice and social change. In this vision, risk becomes part of the emotional appeal, as sacrifice, suffering, and even martyrdom were celebrated among radical Catholics and Communist Party activists as central signifiers of true vocation.

Activism was not simply about sacrifice, however, but also offered profound rewards to activists. Doña Eugenia gained valuable skills and recognition for her efforts to help political prisoners. Despite the dangers and setbacks, she described work with the committee as "one big party, *una fiesta.*" Among the skills she learned was public speaking. Her social status increased as she became widely recognized, and praised, for her work in the prisons. She described her political transformation into activism as involving profound personal transformations as well. Of her encounter with the priest (and later guerrilla) Camilo Torres, she said, "That day, I became a different person from the woman I was. He awoke something very large in me [*disperto algo muy grande en mi*]." She concluded the interview by telling me that despite the tremendous difficulties and sacrifices she has made, including death threats and exile, she was happy and satisfied with her life. "I have been a very privileged woman" she told me. Doña Eugenia was particularly proud of having been part of history and of having known such luminaries of the Colombian left as Torres and the priests of Golcanda.

Other activists blossomed as they took advantage of the opportunities provided by human rights work. Gloria was awarded the Robert F. Kennedy Memorial Human Rights Prize in 1998 (along with three Colombian colleagues). The awards ceremony featured Tom Brokaw and the Dali Lama and was followed by a luncheon at Ethel Kennedy's home. Gloria was later named one of Colombia's one hundred most influential women in history by the leading news magazine *Semana*. Many other activists received similar recognition—numerous human rights awards given in the United States and Europe and travel abroad to lobby foreign governments and educate international audiences about the human rights situation in Colombia.

Some of the most emotional debates about human rights activism that occurred during the 1990s, however, focused on the transition from solidarity groups to professional human rights NGOs, a transition that involved institutional mandates and practices as well as the emotional identities of activists. Did adapting to the codes of professional activism signify abandoning activists' historic commitment to radical social transformation? This question was one of the most contentious issues over the next decade.

Simply discussing these issues was extremely difficult in the polarized and dangerous times of the 1990s. "In the current conditions of the country, there is no room for these debates to happen," Pablo told me. In part this is because of the lack of information and independent media coverage; most of the leftist alternative press has been forced to close or has been silenced by threats. Almost any critical discussion of public policies was immediately condemned as support for the guerrillas, frustrating activists interested in exploring these issues. "It is not an issue of defending the insurgents," Pablo said, "but rather how to open space for political debate about how to transform the country." Activists who supported denouncing guerrilla abuses were in turn accused by radical activists of being apologists for an abusive state, or worse, paramilitary infiltrators.

These mutual accusations were described by one veteran activist as the struggle between the *iluminados* (wise ones, who felt they had all the answers) and the *brutos* (dumb ones, who questioned the human rights orthodoxy). The *iluminados* are human rights purists "who know what the country has to do, who have all the answers, and anyone who questions them is 'in crisis,' 'is a traitor' [*se torció*], gone to the right [*derechista*]." The *brutos,* accused of "not understanding what is happening in the country," are open to critiques and discussion. During one conversation, Oscar drew extensive diagrams on a series of paper napkins to demonstrate the complex web of relationships among NGOs, grassroots organizations, local politicians, and armed opposition groups in one area of the country where he had worked for several years in a Catholic community outreach program. He described the past years as "a time of decision and definition," with people being forced to take sides in bitter internal discussions.

For activists who embraced professionalization, the new codes of knowledge production and institutional practices made work more effective, enabling them to achieve victories otherwise unavailable through more parochial strategies. For some, it was also an issue of moral authority. Pablo responded to those who had suggested that guerrilla violence should be ignored by bringing the discussion back to the central question of who is a victim and what responsibility activists have to the victims: "We can't take the side of just some of the victims, in this country there are many victims, from all sides. . . . Human rights is a short-term vision if we only defend a certain kind of people and leaders. We need to be on the side of the victims of the insurgency, and they do exist." These activists believed they were taking the essence of their work—the violent abuse of the innocent and defenseless as indicative of larger patterns of social injustice—and adopting the new language and practice of professionalized lobbying to bring the perpetrators to justice. This activism was not dispassionate but distilled passion, using the outrage and the *mística* that fueled activism in a form that could be productive within the limitations of transnational activism. The emotional strength of *mística* was not abandoned but disciplined by the vigor of professionalized practice into more effective activism. I was reminded of this during a discussion with Jorge, a human rights lawyer who was educated in the United States and employed first by the United Nations and then by the Colombian Commission of Jurists. Jorge insisted that even the most "professionalized" human rights lawyers remained profoundly motivated by their emotional connection to the victims of human rights abuses. "We drew strength from the victims," he told me. Jorge mentioned several occasions when people he had worked with had been assassinated, and he had drawn on their lives and deaths for motivation as he lobbied the United Nations, telling their stories and keeping their memories close as he traveled to Geneva.

Similarly, many activists were able to navigate the difficult waters of NGO human rights activism in the 1990s by maintaining their commitment to the *mística* of human rights work as vocation while simultaneously adapting to the demands of modern international human rights groups. The lawyer and now U.N. consultant Alonso described holding on to this profound motivation through a number of positions—at NGOs, state human rights agencies, and international organizations. "I started human rights work because of wanting to work with the community, trying to contribute something that would be for the good of the community, trying to achieve what I think is just," he told me. "I can feel the same things working with NGOs or the state, the same dynamic, the same *mística*." While defending his decision to work in different institutions, he noted that some former colleagues had changed when they took new jobs. "Some of the *compañeros* were very radical when they worked in NGOs, then they went to work with the government and they *burgesiaron* [became bourgeois]." But, he insisted, his passion remained the same: "I have the same *mística* of the work that I have always had, I haven't cut the cord. This isn't a political position, it is the nature of the work."

Pablo explained to me how NGO activists had most successfully redefined their activism in the twenty-first century. Like many of his colleagues, Pablo was profoundly aware of the contradictions presented by these conflicting claims to an authentic human rights practice. Prior to and during my fieldwork, I spent many long hours in conversations with friends and colleagues about activists' sense of themselves in relation to these claims and their own trajectories of political awakenings and shifts over the years. For Pablo, human rights activism did not betray former political convictions; it replaced them: "I have taken up the struggle for human rights as my political *militancia*, because *militancia* has helped us survive many difficult moments. The idea of utopia, of continuing to insist that change is possible. Despite not seeing any light, continuing to walk on." He recalled his childhood debates with his mother: "She said that the *pueblo* doesn't pay, no one recognizes or values anything you do, and you are going to get yourself killed. But all my experience has served me extremely well, because I consider the struggle for human rights as the central base of my *quehacer*, my reason for being." Finally, expressing his values in terms of human rights helped him overcome his fear: "Ideologically, this helped me a lot. Before, there was a lot of fear. There [still] is. Because of politics, because when you belong to a political group, in Colombia you feel afraid. Now, I feel it to be something higher, I feel more free, with a greater right [to be doing what I'm doing]." Pablo told me that many of the people he has worked with over the years had expressed similar sentiments. Ultimately, his commitment to human rights involved the same passion for social change but with a different vision: "As a paradigm, human rights is different from the paradigm of taking power. We are trying to build an *imaginario* based in the paradigm of human rights."

CRITIQUES OF PROFESSIONALIZATION

Many activists rejected Pablo's articulation of human rights work and saw the move toward professionalization as a betrayal of the early political commitments to radical transformation that had been the hallmark of the early years of organizing. Doña Eugenia had harsh words for Pablo during a human rights workshop. "You were a boy from the slums who was committed to defending the people," she told him during the question-and-answer period when he had supported efforts to professionalize human rights documentation and address guerrilla abuses. "Now, you are in *otro cuento* [something else]." She elaborated on her bitterness toward her former colleagues during our interview. When forced to flee to Ecuador after death threats and barely escaping capture herself, she angrily reported, she was "completely abandoned by everyone." Her lifetime of service had been cast aside, and she blamed the class differences among human rights groups created by international funding: "How can it be that when you are in exile, people don't look for you, make sure that you are all right? The CSPP, now that they are an NGO with money, don't care. It is like we are friends if we are in the same position, but once you go up in the world, we can't be friends any more because you have a new position, you are comfortable, and you have different interests."

Doña Eugenia was not the only one who stressed that international funding transformed the structures of the NGOs that came to dominate human rights activism. "The 'NGO discourse'—creating nongovernmental organizations rather than social movements—started in the middle of the 1980s. It is all imported, from the north," one activist who has worked as an employee for international agencies, including Oxfam, told me. "Accountability, governance," she said the words in English, then returned to Spanish, "all these things are imported. They have to be assimilated with their context." She described serious conflicts between local organizations and what people viewed as paternalistic attitudes from international funders, as well as conflicts among them, but concluded that the situation had improved. "Today, there is not as much division, there are joint platforms, and we share more information. But the international NGOs are more reluctant [to work together], there is no unity among them, or any coordination. With local NGOs and the internationals, there is still a difference in the level of resources and in the *protagonismos* [public recognition and status]. . . . There are also ideological differences, especially in terms of human rights, what collective rights are and how programs should be developed," she told me.

Professionalization, particularly as a result of international funding, highlighted the growing class differences between groups. For example, even after the transition to an NGO-style organization, the CSPP staff was relatively low paid, the office was still in a shabby downtown commercial district, and Che Guevara and other revolutionary heroes remained enshrined on posters on the wall. Thanks in part to a special grant from the Ford Foundation, the CCJ was able to buy two floors of an office building in northern—wealthier—Bogotá. CCJ's waiting room is coldly corporate marble and sofas, and the walls are adorned with posters from UNICEF and U.N. campaigns. Class differences were reflected in the use of public space in the offices. The CSPP, MINGA, and the Lawyers' Collective had large waiting rooms, often filled with people hanging out, waiting, drinking tiny cups of coffee, and planning events. No one would think of using the CCJ waiting room as a base of operations. The CCJ's decision to spend a month each year before and during the commission meetings in Geneva has also generated much speculation about its finances and lack of dedication to "frontline" human rights work, encapsulated in the derisive nickname "the Alpine Commission of Tourists."

There was also concern that the performance of professionalism would manipulate the actual positions of NGOs and impose particular perspectives on the human rights situation. In the words of Jaime, a lawyer who objected to the use of international humanitarian law, U.N. lobbying resulted in "too much of a focus on official advocacy, directed toward governments and intergovernmental organizations; . . . [such lobbying] depends on the rhythm of the embassies and must remain within the realm of the 'diplomatically possible.'" In the name of professionalism, activists were forced to use diplomatic, officialist language, "light" language, and weaken their critique of the state, hiding the seriousness of the human rights situation and the depth of state responsibility. One clear example for these activists is the controversy over guerrilla violence and international humanitarian law. Jaime insisted that the position adopted by some NGOs to oppose guerrilla abuses does not reflect the authentic concerns of NGOs but is the result of pressure by foriegn embassies in Colombia and serves the government's interest in presenting a confusing panorama of violence in which it appears as simply another victim. Advocacy with governmental organizations is considered "dirty work"; though no one is willing to abandon it, many do not hide their reluctance to do it and their suspicions of its effectiveness.

Activists were not the only ones to critique the NGOs; public opinion as represented by general media commentary often accused NGOs of getting rich off the country's tragedy, enjoying benefits denied the general population and traveling abroad to abandon the difficulties of Colombian daily life. Gladys, a leader of the Association of Relatives of the Detained and Disappeared, one of the only victims' groups among the human rights groups, reflected on a campaign that they had organized to increase public support for human rights work. "The lack of respect [*desprestigio*] is intense, you can be on the bus and hear people talking about NGOs, [saying] all they do is channel money," she told me. "They are a bunch of *naranjas podridas*" [lit., "rotten oranges," slang for corruption]. As a response to this widespread perception, they had designed a campaign for a human rights day in support of human rights defenders. Gladys explained, "So the campaign for [human rights] defenders [was] not to present them as victims but as people who are working for you, for everyone's rights. For two weeks, we were doing TV, radio, and press interviews." Among the other supporters of the campaign were the CSPP, the Permanent Committee, and the Lawyers' Collective.

ACTIVISTS CONFRONT VIOLENT PERSECUTION

In addition to internal division, new forms of public activism generated significant risks for activists who were targeted by military and paramilitary forces. Pablo described his intense fear as he began his work as a paid CSPP staff member: "I felt that every policeman I passed was going to grab me, I had this constant feeling, that it wasn't valid work that we were doing." These feelings were not paranoia; in 1989 the CSPP was thrown into crisis when Jesús Alirio Puerta, a senior lawyer on staff, was disappeared from downtown Bogotá. "This was the first period when we felt pressure for doing human rights work," Pablo told me. As activists came to openly define human rights work as the documentation of government abuses, they were increasingly the target of reprisals. Paramilitary groups, often working with military officers and soldiers, targeted human rights activists in retaliation for their investigations into specific crimes, to prevent the completion of investigations, and because of the widespread view that human rights activism was simply a facade for guerrilla supporters. Though no comprehensive statistics exist, it is certain that hundreds of activists were threatened and dozens killed throughout the decade (Amnesty International 2000; Human Rights Watch 2000; Tate 1997).

Activists volunteering with local committees in remote rural areas were particularly vulnerable. Gloria described the violent attacks against the human rights leaders they had trained:

> Parallel to our training program, they started to develop a serious counterinsurgency campaign in the region that was based on breaking the social fabric. Really, that was the objective. We knew that the army had a list of the leaders, all the leaders who had been in the protest marches appeared on lists. Many of the people whom we worked with were afraid to go through the roadblocks because they were afraid they would be taken. That was the reality. And the paramilitary groups began spreading in Cesar, San Martín, and Ocaña, that was in 1993. In 1994 the paramilitary project spread to southern Cesar and the city of Ocaña. They started killing a lot of leaders. The paramilitaries established themselves in Cesar . . . [and] then the paramilitary project began. The first thing they did was eliminate and assassinate those leaders who were in the mayor's office or had promoted a new kind of political leadership through the popular election of mayors. For us it was really hard because it was a brutal change. First, because before there had been human rights violations but not in this form. There were lists of threats, they started to kill people, the people we worked with, in Pailitas, in Aguachica, in San Alberto, in San Martín, in Curumani. MINGA had to focus a lot of effort on the legal work, in the *denunica* work, in the protection work, and we had to combine the education project with the legal project. . . . At the same time, the Second Mobile Brigade moved into Catatumbo, which also generated serious human rights violations. We had to dedicate ourselves to *denuncia,* to collecting evidence, to organizing humanitarian and investigation missions. In 1992, 1993, and 1994 we managed to get international and national agencies to visit the region so they would have the firsthand testimonies of the population. The profile of MINGA changed. Now we worked not just on training but also in *denuncia, denuncia* of the action of the military. This impacted the team a lot.

By the mid-1990s a series of fatal attacks against high-profile human rights activists left the community reeling. On October 13, 1996, Justice and Peace lawyer Josué Giraldo was gunned down while playing with his two young daughters at his home in Villavicencio, Meta. On May 19, 1997, CINEP staff members Mario Calderón and Elsa Alvarado were killed by gunmen in their Bogotá apartment; Elsa's mother and the couple's two-year-old son survived by hiding in a closet during the attack, but her father also died. Their killings were particularly shocking—they occurred in the heart of Bogotá—and touched a large number of people. The well-known couple had also worked on environmental projects and taught at local universities. Mario Calderón had begun his career as a Jesuit priest and had been forced to flee his parish in the late 1980s because of death threats. Many other NGO activists would die in similar incidents before the decade's end, including lawyers Eduardo Umaña, CSPP staff members Jesús Puertas and Julio Ernesto González, and Jesús María Valle, president of the Hector Abad Permanent Committee for the Defense of Human Rights in Medellín. For many surviving colleagues, these attacks against the human rights defenders recalled the bitter years of the late 1980s, when thousands of political activists were targeted by paramilitary gunmen.

In her account of the Patriotic Union, which uses UP member and human rights lawyer Josué Giraldo's life and death as a central narrative, former Human Rights Watch researcher Robin Kirk described participation in the doomed movement as bordering on pathological, saying activists would have to be "painfully naive or suicidal" (2003: 117). Josué survived an assassination attempt when he was a member of the UP but was killed several years later, presumably in retaliation for his human rights activism. "Joining the Patriotic Union was like sending an embossed invitation to MAS to schedule your murder; six of her [a psychiatrist the author interviewed] patients had come to her after being diagnosed as mentally ill by other psychiatrists. One element of the diagnosis was their membership in the Patriotic Union party. . . . [A]fter speaking with [a Colombian psychologist], I had to wonder if being crazy was not a metaphor but an actual prerequisite for membership in the Patriotic Union. Perhaps that was what it took, the kind of crazy, illogical hope" (Kirk 2003: 118).

In his history of the UP, journalist and former Peace Brigades volunteer Steve Dudley reflected on the impact of sustained violence on party activists, many of whom became involved in human rights activism as the party was decimated. He also frames his narrative around the life and death of Josué. In one passage Dudley describes a conversation with Father Omar Garcia, a priest who knew Josué well and described his struggle as a "religious compromise":

Garcia said the same was true for other UP members. They pretended to disregard the church, but their struggle closely paralleled their belief that their sacrifice would be rewarded. Within the party it was. Garcia said that the UP functioned using a strange honor code. "To be threatened was to get more prestige," he explained. "That's why they took risks. Risk is what gave them importance. The one who was the most threatened would be the most important. . . . I don't know what it was, sympathy for death; sympathy for martyrdom." Josué's virtually unprotected house, Garcia said, was a perfect indication of his attitude. (Dudley 2004: 222)

For most Colombians, the vast majority raised in the Catholic Church, church teachings about suffering and martyrdom resonated deeply with the experience of political repression. The Catholic conceptions of martyrdom and suffering were expanded in the popular teachings of liberation theology to encompass the experience of activists persecuted for their political activities. In focusing on the struggle for justice and oppression experienced by the "historical Jesus," liberation theologians highlighted Christ's humanity, and his life and suffering, as a model for human experience. Popular theology developed in CEBs and other liberation theology teachings stressed that repression is the inevitable response of the wicked and powerful. The extensive persecution of religious leaders and activists in Central America and the Southern Cone seemed to bear out this vision, and in response many local activists expanded their conception of religious martyrdom to include political persecution.[2] For the local activists who viewed themselves as following in Jesus' footsteps as he championed the poor and disenfranchised, persecution and martyrdom seemed the natural outcome.[3] In her study of progressive Catholicism during El Salvador's civil war, Anna Peterson concluded that the "fruits of martyrdom" included strengthened commitment, recruitment of new members, and demonstrations of defiance. "Political killings [were viewed] as a test, necessary for social justice to give fruit, . . . that when understood properly, suffering enriches both their faith and their lives. Martyrdom dramatizes the Christian paradox: ultimate victory can be won only through defeat; death must give way to eternal life" (Peterson 1997: 143).[4] These attitudes were not limited to Catholics; activists I interviewed who had begun their political activism in Communist factions also recalled an extreme valorization of suffering and an ascetic life. Like the Catholic focus on poverty, Communist activists were urged to identify with the proletarian masses and model their lives after theirs. Their aim was not suffering per se but political solidarity, and many reported that the performance of poverty through the rejection of material comfort was rewarded by party leaders as sign of political worthiness.

When talking about her activism among political prisoners, Doña Eugenia drew on her established religious and gender identities, describing her weekly jail visits as "sacred" and stressing the bond she developed with the prisoners. She "was like a mother to them all," she said. The strength of this identification can be seen in Doña Eugenia's reaction to Camilo Torres's assassination. After describing their conversation while he used her phone, she recalled her strong emotions at the news of his death in his first combat operation as an ELN fighter. "I remember when they told me that he had been killed, I was furious. I couldn't believe it. I took down the sacred heart of Jesus, that is what everyone has in their houses here, and I put Camilo Torres's picture up. When people asked me, why did you take down the picture, it is a sacred picture? I said, 'Camilo Torres is more sacred than the *corazón de Jesús* [heart of Jesus].' "[5]

The focus on death and martyrdom was reflected in the ritualized commemorations of assassinated activists, who were often remembered primarily in terms of the circumstances and date of their deaths. One activist showed me an *agenda,* the ubiquitous datebooks widely used by Colombian office workers, produced and sold by an NGO to raise funds; almost every day was marked as the anniversary of an activist's violent death. Many organizations issue posters to commemorate those killed, with inspirational quotations, artwork, and photos of the dead activists alongside the date of their deaths. The rallying cry of a name followed by *"presente, presente, presente"* has been largely abandoned at professional conference–style public forums, but this passionate invocation of the names of the dead and disappeared are common in grassroots workshops and forums.

Assassination can resignify the meaning of individuals' lives, granting them status and respect denied in life. One controversial and extremely contentious lawyer, who had been working almost alone after being asked to leave the organization he helped found, was lionized after his assassination; one colleague remarked that had he died a natural death, no one would have come to his funeral. Conversely, two of the most senior members of the human rights community, Hector Pinzón and Alfredo Vázquez Carrizosa, both founding members of and lifelong activists with the Permanent Committee, died at advanced ages of natural causes during my fieldwork. Their passings went virtually unremarked.

Reflecting on the sacrifice of victims of political violence can serve as a source of strength for activists. Activists frequently spoke of being inspired by the memories of their dead colleagues. For many, a change in career would have been seen as a betrayal of those who had died. Alonso told me:

> Thinking of those dead also helps me go on, thinking of our common dreams. I look at the old books I have at home, and sometimes I find photos, things they have written, some mention of them, and I feel nostalgia, but it also gives me a lot of strength. That we have to keep adding to the work, that if I leave, if we all leave, we are not ever going to get what at one time we thought we were going to get. I don't know what I would do with my life if not work for human rights, what I would do.

At the same time, Alonso expressed his anger, frustration, and even despair at the lack of progress in the face of such sacrifices and loss. Maintaining a professional demeanor in front of representatives of the institution they believed responsible for their colleagues' murders—the military—was extremely difficult for activists who were required to meet regularly with them. Alonso went on to say:

> If only you could be with all the people who are gone, hold out a hand, and say, here we are together, but no, those people are gone, because of the violence in this country, most because of the violence of the state. I am filled with rage sometimes, and can only think of criticism, how am I going to coordinate with these people, how am I going to sit at the same table with the military who are responsible for killing so many peasants? This has caused me to question what I do, has generated many crises for me. But I do what I have to, led by my conscience. This country's impunity hurts me greatly, it produces a great crisis in me.

This focus on death produced other emotional problems for activists. The pressure of political persecution and violence took a heavy toll in self-destructive behavior among activists. "People think they have to be tireless workers, fundamentalists in terms of human rights, almost like martyrs, always with the communities," Pablo told me. "It is harder and harder to do this kind of work." Alcohol abuse, fractured personal lives, and recklessness were frequently mentioned during my interviews as one result of the pressure felt by activists. Gloria recalled the difficulties of dealing with the many attacks suffered by colleagues:

> The team was deeply affected by the death of so many people, so many families, the displacement. It affected us internally. In 1993 Lourdes had to leave the country because of death threats. We had to live with threats at the office, with the telephone calls. MINGA had to start resolving very serious human rights problems, to observe and to feel the impact of how this social

fabric was being destroyed, and all the people displaced. . . . We were
strongly affected; we suffered a lot, of course. It was very hard because
it was as if it was happening to us, because we had such a strong regional
work. We would spend two or three weeks in the region working with people. At that time we spent more time in the regions than in Bogotá, or on
the national or international work. So emotionally [*animicamente*], the
team was deeply affected. We were working Saturdays and Sundays, we
didn't have any time to rest. And I think that our mental health was deeply
affected.

Daily routines were disrupted by constant emergencies. "When you tried
to talk to someone, saying, listen, can I talk to you, the person would
respond, No, I can't, I have to save someone, I have to go to the jail,"
one activist told me. "Or we would let ourselves [practically] die, the director would be bleeding [from an ulcer], he was so sick, but he wouldn't
go to the doctor because he had to go take care of the shelter or get I
don't know who out of the country." She described this sense of self-
righteousness as "perverse," ultimately undermining human rights practice by contributing to staff burnout and conflicts.

The violence confronting activists and communities where they
worked was one of the factors that drove these vitriolic discussions.
"This fight becomes focused on the cycle of death, that it is all right, if
while defending life you find death," another activist concluded. "But
death is becoming an end in itself." The despair of constant violence, and
the celebration of sacrifice, has led to the glorification of violence and the
view that death is the only option. "The slogan has become, 'they kill us
or they kill us' [*nos maten o nos maten*], which gets activists and communities into the logic of death—death as inevitable and desirable," he
said. Organizations that do not experience the same persecution are
viewed with suspicion as betraying their ideals, possibly harboring paramilitary informants or covertly supporting military programs. "If people
aren't threatened or killed they are suspect; organizations whose members aren't killed are suspect," he went on to say.

As a result of these attacks, human rights activists themselves became
the object of an increasing amount of international human rights work,
much to the discomfort of some NGO activists who preferred to speak
on behalf of victims rather than be perceived as victims themselves.
Amnesty International, Human Rights Watch, and WOLA wrote reports
and organized campaigns focusing on the situation of human rights
defenders. While there had been previous attacks against human rights
groups, "human rights activists" as a category of vulnerable victim only

became the object of specific activism campaigns in the mid-1990s. Logistical factors contributed to the popularity of these campaigns, including the increasing difficulty of receiving accurate information from outlying regions about abuses against the general population and the complicated dynamics of local political violence. Human rights defenders, operating out of urban areas and with (relatively) transparent institutional connections, were less potentially controversial than inaccurate or politically compromised local accounts of rural violence. Organizational mandates also played a role, especially for Amnesty International. Amnesty's limited mandate focused on prisoners of conscience and was expanded to include the "disappeared," wrongly imprisoned, and tortured. Throughout the 1990s these methods of political violence declined (with the exception of torture) throughout the world, while assassinations increased. As a membership organization, responding after the fact in the case of massacres and assassinations was a limited mobilizing tool, compared to the appeal of supporting living prisoners where the activists had the possibility of having a direct impact on their conditions and fate. Human rights defenders offered a category of victims that did not require Amnesty to broaden its mandate—an arduous consensus process—that appealed to grassroots activists.

DEFINING THE HUMAN RIGHTS MANDATE

International human rights organizations were not the only groups redefining their mandates. In the mid-1990s Colombian NGOs also began debating the best way to orient their programs. The focus on death, poverty, and suffering produced profound schisms within human rights groups and among activists over the best ways to direct their programs and confront persecution. For one church-based group, these discussions came to a head during my year of fieldwork. Because of increasing conflict within the church about program activities and the focus on paramilitary violence, the organization split; the majority of the staff established a new human rights NGO to carry on the program work outside the umbrella of the church, and a new board of directors took control of the original organization. For the current and former staff members I talked to, the debates surrounding the kinds of program work and political positions that the NGO should advocate were emblematic of the larger debates within the Colombian human rights community and the severe crisis this and other organizations were confronting.

For one former staff member of this group, the problems within the organization began in the 1990s as it shifted its focus from broad-based popular education human rights workshops to communities that had come under heavy attack from the Colombian army. She recalled the intense pressure to seek out the most dangerous and violent areas as sites of their human rights workshops. "One of the things that we said a lot, that [the director] said a lot, was that the closer you are to pain the more 'in solidarity' you are," she recalled. Her original work plan had been to conduct human rights education workshops in high schools around the country, emphasizing critical thinking and social awareness: "Our idea with the kids was that we were going to discover the world, so that they would find out what kind of world they were living in. When they found out what was going on in their own high school [including poverty and abuse] it was very difficult." But it was also very rewarding, as students began getting more involved with their communities and even inspiring activism among their parents. These programs were phased out, to focus on work in communities where paramilitary violence was the strongest. As a result, most of the workshops ended up being held in communities that already had received extensive human rights and political education workshops. "We lost the original flavor, the innovation, which was to reach all kinds of people, someone besides the people who were already convinced," she said. "We took refuge precisely among the people who were already convinced, who already believed in the justification that we were going to work with the poorest of the poor. The poor wouldn't do, it had to be the poorest of the poor . . . and who are the poorest? The victims of human rights violations, the relatives of the disappeared, the relatives of those massacred."

This identification with suffering was central to human rights activists who articulated their primary motivation as their emotional reaction to victims of human rights abuses. Identification with the victims was consistently expressed by activists, especially women. Many CSPP activists recalled being profoundly moved by the experience of visiting prisoners in jail and seeing their suffering. "I felt what is called pain [*dolor*] to see people in bad conditions," one woman told me. "The jail is too degrading, the conditions in which people live, in one little cell," another woman recalled. A human rights lawyer I interviewed offered the most vivid description of the emotion aroused by the victims, which led to a physical passion for human rights work. "When you feel the pain of the victim, you are infected in the skin, by the contact with this pain," he told me. "Why do we stay alive, we who work in NGOs? Because of the contact with the victims, the discourse of human rights penetrates us entirely."

Emotional identification with victims and how to define the limits of the mandate of human rights NGOs has given rise to some of the most serious divisions among human rights activists during the late 1990s.[6] The primary expression of this issue has been the debate over whether or how to classify guerrilla abuses against the populations in the areas they control (for legal scholarship on these issues, see Carrillo 1999).[7] By the late 1990s, however, professional human rights practice emphasized documenting and denouncing political violence by all powerful actors who claim political control over established territory.[8] Many activists, however, focused on the state-sponsored abuses as the one area of society they have leverage over as citizen-activists. In their view, only the state is party to human rights treaties; as the only body responsible for protecting human rights, only states should be held accountable for human rights violations. Many activists go further and believe that the repressive state is the central problem of modern society. For them, adopting international humanitarian law to criticize the guerrillas would simply fuel the government's campaign to deflect accountability for political violence. They believe that state officials would use statements censuring the guerrillas to deny the state's ultimate responsibility and to support state claims that any violence that does occur can be blamed on the guerrillas.[9] Some groups extended their argument against the use of international humanitarian law to include just war theories, claiming that repression by the state justifies violent rebellion, and human rights groups should not criticize the tactics of groups that are protesting the government's violence against the poor.[10]

The stakes are high in these debates, in terms of both gaining domestic constituencies and gaining international support. Access to financial resources can be dependent on the adoption of a professional profile. For activists, these debates also signal a shift in political identity and culture; they must decide whether or not they align themselves with radical left movements for social transformation or with an international movement that uses human rights norms to protect vulnerable citizens, establish accountability, and work for social transformation through the defense of the rule of law.

Pressure from the international community about the issue of guerrilla kidnappings brought the IHL debates to the forefront of internal NGO discussions in the mid-1990s. Jorge, a Colombian lawyer who was working with a prominent NGO at the time, recalled the important role of international funders and officials in advising Colombian NGOs on how to address violations by the guerrillas. In the early 1990s NGOs had begun bimonthly meetings with embassy officials to share their concerns and lobby for support on human rights issues. Following the FARC kidnapping of German and Swedish engineers, these diplomats urged the NGOs to make a public statement opposing the incident and to take a position against kidnapping. Jorge, who had supported efforts to include IHL in NGO lobbying, told me, "I argued that it was both a political and a legal question. It was a political question because for political legitimacy we had to do it, and a legal question because for legal standards, we had the IHL as a legal mechanism." The most important issue, in his view, was the need to maintain the support of European diplomats: "It wasn't a discussion of the law, about when the rules apply and how; it was a political argument, what are the implications of taking this position. If we wanted to engage with the diplomatic community as interlocutors, we had to take a position." The NGOs held meetings to debate the issue. According to Jorge, his colleague arguing against the use of IHL by Colombian NGOs based his position on the Hague Conventions in 1899, claiming that the conduct of hostilities allows for kidnapping as part of guerrilla warfare, given the lack of parity of weapons between the parties and their differing tactics. In 1996 the NGOs finally agreed to issue a statement condemning the kidnappings. "At stake," Jorge explained, "were the diplomatic relationships. No one doubted the benefit of having the embassies on board. They were huge pillars of support in dark times." The final declaration was read by a prominent activist who had suffered a forced disappearance in her own family, giving her greater moral authority to argue the position.

Controversy over this issue ignited again as debates about appropriate human rights activism became increasingly polarized after the definitive failure of the Pastrana administration's peace initiative and the election of right-wing President Uribe. By 2002 NGOs had been discussing their position on international humanitarian law for several yeas, debating the text of a declaration to be adopted through a consensus process in the Coordination. This document has been widely discussed during national meetings of the Coordination, as well as in regional conferences and private discussions among NGOs (including during panels at the workshop described in chapter 3). Several groups, including an organization of young lawyers, challenged the initial decision to adopt the joint position accepting the use of IHL to criticize guerrilla actions. While members of each group maintained that their positions were distinctly nuanced, they shared many central assumptions.

I spoke with one such lawyer at length so he could explain his vision of what constitutes legitimate human rights work. I met Jaime in his downtown office, a maze of cramped cubicles piled high with files, papers, and other debris from the lawyerly life. The walls were covered with international solidarity posters in many languages, invoking the rights of people to free determination in Palestine, Algeria, and Colombia. Jaime was personable, passionate, and sarcastic during our conversation. He located their work in the history of repression in Colombia, focusing on the perspective of activists persecuted by the state. The people have a right to defend themselves, he told me, and because of class relationships and the authoritarian state, the distinction between civilian and combatant was meaningless. In his view, the guerrillas were part of the spectrum of protest against the state, and the war was the result of class struggle. He claimed to be a hard-nosed realist, in touch with the realities of war that cannot be avoided through the use of paper treaties.

He first pointed out the inherent contradiction of international humanitarian law for attempting to sanitize and regulate the inherently dirty, violent business of war. Protecting the innocent is harder than such a "lovely impulse" would suggest, he told me. These conventions are victors' justice, created by states to defend themselves from insurgents and the people, who have had no hand in their creation. Jaime told me that as a lawyer, he accepted the existence of international law but not the specifics of the norms: "I can agree that there is a penal system but not agree with a law that says that if a peasant invades land, that he should be sent to jail. . . . I can't insist on a contract that commits parties that didn't sign the contract. A father can sign for his children to control them. But the Colombian state doesn't control the guerrillas."

Jaime explained that the Colombian government should not advocate that the guerrillas accept IHL because the state itself has not complied with the Geneva Conventions. "According to the first protocol, if the government creates the paramilitary force, it is required to inform other parties and take formal responsibility for them as part of their strategy," he said. "The paramilitary forces are the same as mercenary forces. They are a group created to defend the state structure, state power, state economies." He concluded that the government refused to take responsibility for paramilitary groups because the political cost would be too high, even while they benefit from paramilitary attacks against poor communities.

According to Jaime, the conditions in Colombian society—poverty, inequality, repression—justify a revolt against the system of power, which means that an insurgency against the Colombian state would be justified: "What is not easy is to recognize that in this country when people are killed because of what they think, the guerrilla is legitimate. And that the state is not legitimate, to think that it is recognized by the international community. What am I basing this on? On human rights." He went on to cite numerous factors that prove the Colombian state is not legitimate. First he claimed that 30,000 people die each year because of the conflict (a number that corresponds roughly to the total number of violent homicides each year, although only approximately 3,500 of those are considered the result of political violence by most professional human rights groups).[11] As further evidence, he listed the thousands of disappearances, the physical elimination of the UP, the more than 60 percent poverty rate, and the concentration of wealth. "To take up arms is a right that is internationally recognized. There are legitimate reasons for taking up arms. War has legitimate roots. We can't say, *violentos,* get out," he insisted. He focused on the issue of structural violence and the causes of war, "the reality of the conflict and not the butterflies of peace." "You don't have to agree with the guerrilla or with the state, but [you have to] recognize that there are legitimate conditions for war because they haven't been listened to any other way." He claimed that civilian casualties are the product of state decisions about military tactics: "You can't tell the guerrilla not to attack the police, because they are a military target. If the police put the station next to a hospital, then they [the guerrillas] have to destroy the entire town because the police make the stations super fortified." Given the disparity of resources between the standing state security forces and the guerrillas, he believed that IHL norms favor the government by prohibiting many of the common tactics of guerrilla warfare.

Like many of the military's critics of human rights standards, Jaime believed that it is impossible to distinguish civilians from combatants given the multiple ways in which all citizens are involved in the conflict, directly or indirectly. He listed as military targets anyone who pays taxes or buys war bonds, businesses who contribute taxes, members of Congress who support repressive antiterrorist legislation, the electrical system, and the president, who has long supported legalizing paramilitary groups. "Who is outside of the conflict? How can we distinguish who is part of the war and who is not? In the logic of IHL, everything is untouchable," he said. "The war involves everyone." State repression also makes everyone part of the war, by criminalizing dissent and punishing anyone who offers a critical perspective. "I don't have a rifle or a uniform," Jaime concluded, "but I can call myself *guerrillero,* as others have called me, because of what I think, what I do, what I am. I am part of the war. The state has always behaved this way, throwing people in jail, killing people, disappearing them."[12]

For Jaime and his allies, to criticize the guerrillas would be to reject the lessons of the past fifty years of Colombian history, which they recount as state repression against small farmers, in the context of a political system that has been unresponsive—or violently opposed to— efforts for peaceful change. Doña Eugenia powerfully evoked this history during the human rights workshop when she took one of the speakers to task for suggesting that guerrilla violence should be documented by human rights groups. "I want to offer a reflection on history. We have to look at our past to understand where we are today," she began, support-ing herself on the back of the chair of the person in front of her, in the measured cadence of a practiced public speaker. "We have to understand the violence, from the *comuneros* to today.[13] We never heard of interna-tional humanitarian law, when in 1948 the Liberals were tortured and killed by *chuvalitas,* tied to horses and pulled about, the fetuses pulled out of pregnant women. The guerrillas come from that time, from the Liberals because of the injustice at that time," she told the participants and then went on to list Colombia's social and structural problems, including urban unemployment, bad conditions in the cities, and the lack of democracy. "They have destroyed the UP and the people working in those organizations, [human rights activists] Jesús Valle, Hector Abad Gómez. Because we do not agree with what they are doing, because we are the opposition. The state makes its own laws. International humani-tarian law—the people don't know about that, haven't worked on that, haven't struggled over that. This is something that was invented by those who won in other epochs. Camilo [Torres] said it, what unites the people is revolutionary, what divides it is reactionary." She brought her listeners up to the present day by naming current paramilitary leaders and the U.S.-sponsored fumigation campaigns as among the injustices Colom-bians face. She was met with scattered applause as she took her seat.

VIOLENCE AGAINST GAYS AND LESBIANS AS HUMAN RIGHTS ABUSES

Even as activists struggled over identifying with victims of different per-petrators—in this case, of nonstate actors—they were confronted with new victim populations, whose claims for recognition by the human rights community required serious efforts to reframe emotional identification. Representatives of women, indigenous groups, and Afro-Colombians demanded to be considered vulnerable to particular kinds of abuses such as sexual violence and forced displacement from valuable lands and included in the human rights agenda that had previously focused on individuals targeted for participation in leftist organizing. By the late 1990s gay and lesbian activists, who reported harassment and violence because of their sexual orientation, began organizing and demanding inclusion in the human rights agenda as well. Despite the ingrained homophobia of many NGOs, by the end of the decade gay and lesbian organizations were accepted into the Coordination and their representatives given equal voice in the consensus decision-making process.

This shift has been long and slow and has meant confronting explicit and emotional homophobia. Many NGOs traced their origins to the socially conservative Catholic and Communist culture that explicitly condemned homosexuality as decadent and depraved. Diego Pérez, first director of CINEP's human rights office, recalled:

> These conceptions have led in practice to things like, at certain times people or groups of people have come to human rights NGOs, asking for help, for orientation and guidance for their defense, for example, of their rights that have been violated, from the gay community or sex workers, prostitutes. That they would even come to NGOs is very recent, and it has changed a little already, but it was very difficult for the NGOs. First, the NGOs would respond that the issue was not their responsibility, that their work was the problem of civil and political rights, the rights of people being attacked or assassinated because of their political leadership. It was very difficult to acknowledge that anyone, any citizen, could also be affected in their rights to intimacy, [that these were also] their basic rights, and that they should be assisted by the NGOs. Really what was reflected was the strength of the political conception of the left, the ideological rigidity that was there. Fortunately today this has changed because the panorama of defense of human rights has broadened to many other sectors and many other kinds of rights as well. But human rights defenders that were profoundly shaped by the left have been very rigid in their concept of rights.

While a comprehensive history of sexuality, sexual identities, and practices in Colombia has yet to be written, as in many places in Latin America men who have sexual relations with men do not identify as homosexuals and maintain public relationships with women (Lancaster 1992). A small core of gay activists began promoting gay identity and organizations through groups such as the Movement for Homosexual liberation (Movimiento para la Liberación Homosexual), active throughout the 1970s and early 1980s. The founding members included León

Zuleta, also founding member of the Amnesty International chapter in Medellín, who was expelled from the Communist Party and union movement for his sexuality and killed in suspicious circumstances in 1993, and Manuel Velandia, who is still an active voice for gay rights.

A growing Latin American gay liberation movement has explicitly adopted the organizational methods and objectives of gay groups in the United States and Europe. Several NGOs focused on gay rights have been created in Colombia. One of the best known is Colombia Diversa, which counts among its founders the son of a former president. According to its Web site, its objectives are threefold: to promote the rights of gay people, to transform the negative images of gays in Colombia, and to strengthen the gay movement politically. During a 2005 speaking tour sponsored by U.S.-based human rights and solidarity groups, Marcela characterized the group as being part of a "young" movement that began organizing only ten years ago. She related that their advocacy initially focused on issues central to the gay rights debate in the United States and Europe, such as marriage and civil union rights, AIDS, and employment discrimination. Colombia Diversa has only recently begun to concentrate on human rights violations against gays (such violence would be defined as hate crimes in the United States, but in Colombia it is linked to the political conflict). In part this is a result of the demographics of the group's membership. According to another Colombia Diversa representative, Hernán, there are "three ways to be gay in Colombia. . . . In big cities, being openly gay was not as dangerous, as people enjoyed class privilege," he said. "In small cities, you can be hidden, or the neighborhood joke. In conflictive zones, you can't do anything openly, because none of the three forces [army, paramilitary, or guerrilla] allow it." For gay activists in cities, rural violence was largely invisible.

Information management and the production of human rights reporting has been a serious problem for groups promoting gay rights. "We don't know how to do fieldwork," Marcela said, "how to document cases, what variables to examine." Hernán echoed her concern: "We need indicators to determine why people are killed, to know that they were killed because of being gay, not just because of being in the vicinity of a bombing." Colombian NGOs and international organizations including the United Nations High Commissioner for Human Rights (UNHCHR) have asked them for statistics and reporting on violence against gays, but gay rights groups have yet to be able to move "from the anecdote to statistics," Hernán said. "We just don't know how many hate assassinations there are. We just hear gossip and rumors." They were modeling their work on women's groups and studies of the impact of conflict on women.

Hernán and Marcela agree that the human rights framework will make their work "more legitimate," perceived not as an attempt to further their personal interests but as part of a larger collective struggle. They are hoping to "insert the discussion [of gay rights] into the discussion of humanitarian crisis," as a way of making what is often defined as an issue of privacy and sexuality an issue of political rights. Hernán stated, "We don't want to be tolerated, to have people put up with us, but to be seen as equals. Make people see the issue of LGBT as a human rights issue, not compassion but rights. . . . We want NGOs not to speak for us but to and with us, to speak the same language."

The international human rights organizations that Colombian human rights NGOs viewed as their primary partners were undergoing their own examinations of these issues. Amnesty International underwent a seventeen-year debate over whether to expand its mandate to treat as prisoners of conscience individuals imprisoned for homosexual acts. The long fight led to the controversial decision in 1991 in which the International Council decided to consider as prisoners of conscience persons who are imprisoned solely because of their homosexuality, including the practice of homosexual acts in private between consenting adults. Fierce debate over the issue included concern that Amnesty would alienate some of its base outside Europe and North America; its first report on antigay persecution was published in February 1994. In 1994 Human Rights Watch also modified its mandate to increase attention to the issue of abuse because of sexual orientation.

Abuses against gays in Colombia were first documented by human rights NGOs during the mid-1990s, part of widespread coverage of "social cleansing" campaigns. Vigilante groups, often formed by off-duty policemen and local business owners, targeted people deemed socially undesirable, including drug addicts, prostitutes, and gays and lesbians (the Spanish desechable—lit., "disposable"—is commonly used to describe such people). Representatives of these victim populations were not incorporated into NGOs, however, and never obtained an active voice in human rights debates.

This began to change as representatives from Colombia's NGOs saw how groups abroad were dealing with the issue during their extensive travels to Europe and the United States. There they saw progressive movements incorporating human rights, gay and lesbian groups, and antiracist platforms into their human rights practice. Many of these international counterparts had openly gay members on their staffs. Some Colombians returned from abroad with a greater awareness and acceptance of gay and lesbian issues. Daniel Garcia Peña was crucial to this process. As director of the Planeta Paz project, an umbrella group of peace and human rights organizations funded by the Norwegian government, he successfully argued that representatives of gay and lesbian groups should be included in the development of their peace platform, and he was instrumental in bringing together gay and lesbian and human rights activists. His perspective was informed by the efforts of gay and lesbian movements abroad for fuller social inclusion; Daniel had grown up in the United States during the civil rights debates of the 1970s, when his father served in the Colombian consulate, and his sister is a lesbian activist who legally married her partner in Norway. Despite significant initial resistance from both Catholic- and Communist Party–influenced organizations, gay and lesbian organizations were finally accepted into the Planeta Paz coordinating committee.

For many activists, the acceptance of gay and lesbians as colleagues and *compañeros* depended on conversion experiences in which the persecution of gays and lesbians was equated with political violence against leftist activists in an emotional process of hearing the testimony of gay activists. Daniel described one of the most dramatic transformations of a Planeta Paz staff member, Rafael, "one of the most hard-core *machista* union workers." At a workshop organized to bring activists together to develop a common platform, Rafael heard the testimony of a gay activist and "realize[d] that being persecuted for being gay was just the same as being persecuted for being a Communist. When the gay activist starting talking, he said, 'I don't expect you to understand, I don't expect you to support us, I don't expect you to want your children to be gay, I just want not to be killed, not to lose my job, not to be thrown out of my family.' When he said it that way, Rafael said, he realized it was the same thing, remembering all the problems he had with his family and work being persecuted for being a Communist."

This process has not been without problems, and many activists continue to object to and mock the inclusion of gay issues on the human rights platform. "It was really difficult at first, there were lots of jokes," Daniel recalled. The presence of gay activists at public forums, and the inclusion of their concerns in the public platform, has been a significant advance. The testimonial recounting of gay and lesbian experiences of violence and repression was central to this inclusion. Though the use of *testimonio* and *denuncia,* Colombian NGO activists could locate violence against gay men and lesbians as part of the experience of a repressive state and disapproving establishment. By focusing on the transformative experience of oppression, rather than claims to a liberatory sexual practice, gay and lesbian activists could be perceived as citizen subjects, entitled to the same claims for protection against the state as other activists. More important, it allowed gay and lesbian activists access to the spaces of activism, where they quickly began to articulate an agenda that goes far beyond the initial claims for simple protection. Activists have advanced claims for a number of rights, including employment protections, marriage, and participation in military service. Planeta Paz, a central location for articulating a progressive agenda, defines gays and lesbians as one of the "sectors" participating in political peacemaking, alongside peasants, women, indigenous and Afro-Colombian communities, environmentalists, and union organizers. They define "the [individual] body as the first territory of peace," locating demands for personal autonomy and sexual freedom alongside the peasant-based collective "peace communities" created in response to the entrenched conflict and high levels of violence in Colombia.

WHAT WE TALK ABOUT WHEN WE TALK ABOUT VIOLENCE

Categorizing violence is hard work, forcing us to deal with unsettling and troubling events, with death, suffering, and rupture. The public forums, workshops, and other official spaces of human rights work rarely acknowledge another dimension of the work: the unofficial spaces, late-night drinking sessions, hallway conversations, and seemingly casual exchanges that allow contradictory feelings to be expressed. Such conversations had been a mainstay of my own human rights practice over the years, but one such exchange I witnessed at the human rights workshop discussed in chapter 3 remains a powerful example of the contradictory ways in which such stories are recounted and shared. Exemplifying the black humor, mocking wit, and sly references to truly terrifying situations that typified many of these peripheral conversations, my fieldnotes were less than a page, jotted after a coffee break between lectures. After the first lecture, we had been divided up into small discussion groups in anticipation of the next activity but were first dismissed for the small cups of black coffee and limp pastries known as *onces* (elevens) that are served midmorning at official functions. I sat with the members of my discussion group, on plastic chairs around a small table, and after a small pause to settle into our snack, Jorge glanced at his neighbors and asked, "Have you ever been through a roadblock where they killed people?" I caught my breath at the emotional weight of the question. Jorge continued, "Thank God, that has never happened to me. Once, in Valle, they called a young guy over, he was pale and sweating, but they didn't kill him. They were going through lists, checking out who was there and pulling people aside."

There was a moment's pause, then nods around the table. The woman next to me offered her own story. Once, in Urabá, she said, "I was going with Peace Brigades International [which provides physical accompaniment to threatened activists], and they [not identified, presumably paramilitaries] stole a car full of groceries and the money we had to start a carpentry project. Because they knew what we were doing and what we had. They had guns out. Someone from Peace Brigades was hugging the driver because that is the one they were going to shoot. I was screaming in case there were some police nearby, and they, they turned the gun on me and said shut up or you'll get it, so I had to be quiet." The story had a happy ending after all—the man was released and "they" went away—and she returned to the joking style that marked the public recounting of such stories. "Afterward," she told us, "I was joking around and said, 'You guys are so pale you look like a worm, like *lombrices*.' And the Peace Brigades volunteer replied, 'You only say that because you can't see yourself.'"

A quiet woman, the one with bobbed hair who had told me earlier that this was her first human rights workshop, began to describe typical travel to her small town. "On the way," she said, "there are so many roadblocks, roadblocks put up by everyone. Even the thieves have a roadblock, and they'll steal *hasta los zapatos*, everything including your shoes." She was only beginning her tale when the workshop coordinator passed through, calling us back to our group exercise.

The sheer nonchalance of Jorge's query astonished me—have you ever been in a roadblock when they killed someone?—given the intense emotions such an experience must evoke. The tales told in response were a vivid reminder that much of the hidden work of human rights occurs outside the office, in small towns and on roads where violence is constant. The question contained an additional layer, however—of moral responsibility. If the practice of human rights work was predicated on action to prevent violence inspired by knowledge of its occurrence, this situation was the stark core of that equation. The unspoken question was, how would you react if confronted with murder in your midst? Would you bear witness silently or scream and blanch the color of a pale worm? While such calculations are impossible in the abstract, these meetings offer the incalculable solace of simply sitting at a table with those who face such equations in the course of any given day.

CHAPTER 5

The Global Imaginaries of Colombian Activists at the United Nations and Beyond

Much of human rights activism is oriented to an amorphous public sphere often referred to simply as the international community. The range of institutions and individuals that constitute the "international community," however, is often unexamined in analyses of transnational activism. Despite the rhetorical claims of politicians, Cynthia McClintock reminds us, "there is no 'international political community' similar to the 'international financial community'" in the sense of coordination within international institutions or even consensus over the meaning of central terms including human rights (McClintock 2000: 13). Much of the work to date on activists who employ the human rights frameworks has considered how international (understood as referring to U.S. and Europe-based) activists have imagined their local (understood as "third world") counterparts (Nelson 2000). Surprisingly little consideration has been given to the ways in which these "local" activists have imagined their "international" counterparts, the recipients of their urgent actions and the funders of their programs. This chapter explores the various ways in which Colombian activists imagine the international community that is the target of their activism. Some activists stress subaltern alliances, arguing that their energy should be focused on developing ties with unions, grassroots groups, and social movements in other countries. Colombians have also developed strategic partnerships with groups in other Latin American countries. However, most transnational activism remains aimed at the foreign governments of Europe and the United States and multilateral institutions made up of governmental representatives (such as the U.N. and the OAS). The United Nations Human Rights Commission, despite the controversy that resulted in its dissolution in 2006, was a privileged site for Colombian activism for more than a decade. I explore how Colombian activists successfully spurred the commission to create a new kind of human rights mechanism, an office of the UNHCHR. Colombian groups gained credibility not as victims but as professional activists, a new political identity that had only become available to activists in the past decade with the expansion of human rights funding and training programs focusing on international legal systems. Rather than view the U.N. as part of a generic "international community," these activists examined the commission as a particular location for activism—with its own rules, culture, and institutional dynamics—and this was central to their success.

I first bumped up against the global imaginaries of Colombian activists during the late 1980s. As a young volunteer and college student in Bogotá, I was constantly drawn into extended conversations about the nature of the United States and the U.S. role in the world. As a U.S. citizen, I was expected to have a commanding knowledge and articulate position on a range of issues involving U.S. policies and politics. But it was not until my housemate's sister was thrown in jail after a student protest that I realized I was also expected to be a conduit for connections into an imagined world of international activism for my new friends. Then a member of A Luchar! (lit., "to the struggle," a legal political party linked to the ELN), Sandra was tiny—our respective nicknames for each other were the dwarf and the giant, as she only reached my elbow in her customary high-heeled boots—and feisty, never shy with her opinion of my homeland. She had been thrown into a police riot tank during a student demonstration and taken to jail, my housemate breathlessly explained one day. He did not know where his sister was or in what condition. The only foreign and English-speaking person they knew, I had to help. Did I know anyone at Amnesty International? Could I get Amnesty to accept her case? The urgency of the situation—she could be tortured, even disappeared—was matched only by my helplessness. I had been a nominal member in high school, sending in enough money to earn me an Amnesty International sticker and a small red button that read "Stop Torture," which I proudly wore on my thrift-store jackets, but I had no idea how the organization functioned. I was completely at a loss, blinded by their expectations and scrabbling at any measure of connection I could conjure up.

Sandra lost several front teeth and suffered internal injuries at the hands of her police jailers, but she was eventually released. My experience as the receptacle for fantasies of global connection was just beginning, however. For the next decade, as a representative of international human rights groups, including, briefly, Human Rights Watch, and then as the Colombia analyst for WOLA, the palpable desire that "international activism" would be the salvation and a final point of justice—as well as the vocal accusations that international activism was a sham, part of an imperialist agenda, and a waste of time—were a constant refrain. Whether interviewing victims of human rights abuses in Colombia, working with activists in Washington, or conducting my more formal taped fieldwork conversations, I was constantly confronted with the frustrations and desires generated by international activism.

In part a response to the limitations and frustrations of activism at home, Colombian imaginaries of global activism are complicated and fraught with mixed emotions. As human rights activism in Colombia became more dangerous and frustrating, activism abroad became imagined as a new horizon of limitless opportunity for the solidarity and support activists no longer enjoyed in their home communities. At the same time, most Colombians were profoundly suspicious about the agendas and interests of international organizations. Transnational activism involves both opportunities and risks, for gaining symbolic and material resources as well as for losing autonomy and authenticity. Their visions of global activism included utopian and dystopian elements: a utopian imagined landscape of international solidarity with their causes; dystopian visions of corrupting international conspiracies controlled by the imperialist United States. For many activists, these visions of benefits and potential losses coexist. These global imaginaries are embedded in the same political cultures that shape these groups' domestic human rights activism; debates over how to develop international advocacy campaigns were intricately connected with Colombian-based NGOs' constant negotiations to maintain minimal consensus over their goals and strategies on this complicated terrain.

Understanding the ideas about who constitutes the global community, what international activism can achieve, and how to best mobilize international constituencies requires an examination of all the diverse locations of activism as unique localities. In her cogent article "The Global Situation," Ana Tsing argues for seeing "the global" as multiple locations, avoiding the global/local juxtaposition that has shaped much of the thinking about "globalization" during the 1990s. She argues that "we must study folk understandings of the global, and the practices within which they are intertwined, rather than representing globalization as a transcultural historical process," even while warning scholars against the dangers of "globalist fantasies" (Tsing 2000: 358). Critically examining the "folk understandings" of globalization by all the players in international activism as an imagined landscape of political potential (referred to as global imaginaries) illuminates the ways in which international activism reflects the expectations and aspirations of individuals from widely divergent political cultures. The complaints and critiques by these activists reflect the real failures of international activism to deliver promised results but also the activists' fantasies of political outcomes based on the multiple ways in which they imagine the global landscape.

The global imaginaries of activists based in Latin America, Africa, and Asia, and the ways in which these imageries shape political outcomes, remain an important site for analysis yet to be fully explored by scholars of globalization. These activists are positioned as "local," focused on domestic concerns defined by national borders, at the mercy of the more sophisticated and widely traveled "international" activists employed by multinational human rights organizations. The ways in which international activists based in Europe and the United States conceived of the objects of their activism have been extensively explored and critiqued in a number of studies (Coutin 1993; Cunningham 1995, 1999; Gorin 1993; Griffin-Nolan 1991; Hart 2001; Lorentzen 1991; Martinez 1996; Melville and Melville 1971; McLagan 2000a, 2000b; Nelson 2000; Smith 1996). The harshest of these critiques emphasize the degree to which these international activists rely on colonial imaginaries, reinforcing existing national, racial, and gender hierarchies in the guise of emancipatory alliances. All touch to differing degrees on the multiple ways in which international activism relies on and reconfigures existing ideologies of national citizenship. For many of the scholars focusing on the global imaginaries of U.S. and European activists, the activism of the "global south" remains an unexamined location of authentic political expression. New scholarship from political scientists has focused on this confrontation as the perversion of local activism in the global south. The changes imposed by international activists on their local allies are sometimes decried as the "dear cost" of activism outside their home countries, "by distorting their principles and alienating their constituencies for the sake of appealing to self-interested donors in rich nations" (Bob 2002). While this is a legitimate critique, such hand-wringing ignores the larger

issue of the inevitable evolution of activist strategies in shifting landscapes of power and opportunity over time and the range of powerful
interests beyond the "international gatekeeping" NGOs. More troubling,
this perspective erases the locality of "international activism" as a space
for anything but the corruption of the authentic local and denies local
activists' agency to redefine their own agendas as they connect with new
repertoires of political action.

My discussion here centers on the advocacy campaigns conducted at
the United Nations Human Rights Commission (the Commission). The
Commission was a central location, defined in space and time, that
brought together numerous networks of activists as they attempted to
both negotiate a common agenda and then work to promote that agenda
for the Commission members. The United Nations more broadly occupies a privileged place in the landscape of human rights, as the source of
the International Declaration of Human Rights and the most important
multilateral arbiter of disputes between states (despite ongoing debates
over the efficacy of the U.N. as a whole). Colombian activists specifically
chose the venue of the Commission as the major focus of their international activism. Their ability to view this landscape as a locality, and
work within it, allowed them to make significant progress (within the
limits of the U.N. system).

Examining the history of human rights activism at the Commission by
Colombian activists and others illuminates several aspects of how
activism nodes function. The Commission brings together multiple networks working on specific issues from a range of positions and agendas,
including governmental human rights agencies, humanitarian agency networks, solidarity committee coalitions, and the networks in each state
delegation (which includes diplomats working in Geneva and New York,
the State Department or its national equivalent, and diplomatic representatives working in the country in question). Activism at the U.N. is
shaped by the convergence of these networks, which often expand
through contact into new nodal networks. Key individuals often traveled
between networks, with the same individuals working as NGO representatives, government officials, and UN staff at different times. NGOs
such as Human Rights Watch and Amnesty International often hire former government officials to capitalize on their existing networks of informal contacts. On the other hand, government officials frustrated with
toeing the official line find greater freedom in NGO positions. To cite
only one example, when I asked an Amnesty staffer how many years she

had been attending Commission meetings, she replied that this was her first time—but she had been working with the Commission for seven years as a diplomatic representative of her Scandinavian government.

The expanded role and public failures of the United Nations in the post–cold war era has led to a number of searing critiques of U.N. action and inaction in a number of violent conflicts and human rights crises. Scholars and activists have pointed out the limitations of U.N. operations while participating in the negotiated settlements of civil wars in Central America and as major arbiters of transition governments in Cambodia and during conflicts in Africa (Lawyers Committee 1995; Mingst and Karns 1999; Righter 1995). Some of the most damning accounts concern the U.N.'s infamous failure to act in the case of the Rwandan genocide. Michael Barnett's accounts of his experience as a fellow at the U.N. desk of the State Department focuses on how bureaucratic culture in the U.N. and other governmental and supragovernmental offices shaped the possibilities for international response (Barnett 1997, 2003). Anthropologists have argued the importance of national cultural categories for understanding the actions of Canadian peacekeepers in Somalia (Razack 2000) and Fijian delegates to U.N. meetings (Riles 1998). With some exceptions (Merry 2006), despite the importance of the United Nations in the contemporary imaginary of international politics, however, there has been surprisingly little anthropological exploration of what Amitov Ghosh called the "ethnography of the future" in his 1994 article on the U.N. peacekeeping mission in Cambodia (Ghosh 1994).

In part, the paucity of anthropological studies of the United Nations reflects the ethnographic challenges of doing research in such a space, long the exclusive province of political scientists. The first challenge is physical access: to attend the meetings, I had to receive the sponsorship of an NGO accredited in the U.N. system and present the physical proof of that support (a photo ID badge) at all times while moving through the U.N. buildings in Geneva. The larger issue is a conceptual one, explored in the collection *Ethnography in Unstable Places* (Greenhouse, Mertz, and Warren 2002). The U.N. Human Rights Commission did not physically exist; it was a transient collection of shifting individuals who gathered in meeting rooms for six weeks of the year. For Colombian (and other) activists, however, the Commission was a permanent reference point in the landscape of international activism, imagined by some as an impartial arbiter of universal justice, by others as an imperialist mockery of this standard (by most, somewhere in between).

During the writing of this book, the Commission was dissolved when it became a lightning rod for debates over institutional reform of the United Nations. The Commission was critiqued by both supporters and detractors as being bureaucratic, excessively political, and ineffectual, and its inaction on widely publicized abuses, as well as the membership of abusive states as Zimbabwe, Sudan, and Saudi Arabia, substantially eroded its credibility. Also, the Bush administration escalated Republican criticism of the United Nations. After lengthy negotiations on reform of the Commission, on March 15, 2006, the General Assembly voted overwhelmingly in favor of creating a human rights council, whose forty-seven members will be elected by an absolute majority of the assembly (the United States was one of four member states to vote against the proposal).[1] Every year the council will hold at least three sessions lasting ten weeks, with the option of convening emergency meetings. The first meeting of the council was June 19, 2006; as of this writing, the implications for NGO participation are unclear.

LANDSCAPES, NETWORKS, AND EMBEDDED NODES: HOW TO TALK ABOUT ACTIVISM BEYOND BORDERS

In this chapter I use *international* as it is employed by practitioners in human rights NGOs—to describe certain kinds of work about Colombia that takes place outside the physical borders of Colombia, usually in Europe and the United States, and to describe particular organizations that do this work, most of whose headquarters are in Europe and the United States. This vocabulary is inadequate, however, and reinforces the problem by suggesting that there is a global out there, and where the local is "imagine[d] as the stopping point of global circulations[,] . . . the place where global flows are consumed, incorporated and resisted" (Tsing 2000: 338). Despite the common usage of the term that I repeat, the question remains: What makes an "international organization"? A Colombian NGO that sends representatives to the Commission in Geneva and researchers to Ecuador to study Colombian refugees or to Washington to talk with U.S. congressional staffers is considered not an "international" organization but a Colombian one. Despite Colombian NGOs' many forms of participation in "international" activism, they are understood to be less "international" than Human Rights Watch or Amnesty International, and what is at stake in this appraisal is more than an issue of scale. Designating a group "national" or "international" reflects the power and penetration—not just circulation—that is available to each group depending on where they are located in landscapes of power.

There are additional epistemological issues raised by the terms *international* and *global*. While both are employed to describe activism beyond borders, each has a different history and encompasses a distinct universe of meaning for activists. So-called international work has a long history, including its use to describe the global vision of Communist Party members from the 1880s to the present. To cite only the most obvious example, the vision of a world divided by class, not national borders, was emotionally invoked in the stirring lines of "The International." Many Colombian Communist Party activists have undertaken international educational travel through political exchange programs in Cuba, Bulgaria, and the Soviet Union. One activist I interviewed who spent a year in Bulgaria during the mid-1980s was sent with a Communist Party scholarship to learn union organizing. Another, who now teaches human rights and international humanitarian law classes as a consultant with the International Red Cross described almost a decade in Moscow during the 1980s as a student at Patrice Lumumba Peoples' Friendship University of Russia. Established in 1960 to bring students from the third world to study in Russia, the school has graduated more than 36,000 students from 100 countries. Closer to home, and united by shared language, many activists traveled to Cuba for classes, medical care, and political "vacations." Despite the disappearance of the socialist world, this history remains a living reference point for many activists.

"International work" also invokes more than a century of work among nations: the multitude of conferences, congresses, and associations at which representatives of national governments attempted to ensure the orderly development of commerce and diplomatic relations. Among the most obvious predecessors of contemporary human rights activism is the League of Nations, established after World War I. The United Nations functions clearly within this model of transborder conversations that maintain the nation-state as the locus of power in society.

Global and *globalization* came into widest usage during the post–cold war period and are employed to evoke more amorphous flows and relationships emerging from new technological connections. Here the nation-state recedes, and the borderless sphere is invoked to emphasize increasing connections among communities. The simultaneous fall of the polarized superpowers as a frame for diplomacy and the explosion of Internet and computing capabilities led many to promise a "New World Order" of limitless democracy. With the advent of the so-called war on terror, these same qualities are now often perceived as threatening and dangerous, but the emancipatory possibilities of global connections remain a powerful ideal.

Many studies of international activism have focused on activist networks, on the information flow and relationship among activists based in different countries to advance advocacy efforts for their causes. The central metaphors for this work have been the ideas of circuits, exchange, and flow to describe the political action. A central problem for this research has been how to locate these networks in specific cultural contexts. In their seminal work, Keck and Sikkink focus on networks but also stress the importance of domestic political opportunity structures, including the dynamic of "oppositions and the conflicting representations of core values around which domestic groups organize" (Keck and Sikkink 1998). *The Rise of the Network Society* (Castells 2000) brought together many lines of thinking in contemporary social science to suggest a new model for thinking about how societies are organized through networks, transformations generated by technology, and the rising role of informational flows. Castells writes, "Networks are dynamic, self-evolving structures, which, powered by information technology and communicating with the same digital language, can grow, and include all social expressions, compatible with each network's goals. Networks increase their value exponentially as they add nodes" (Castells 2000: 697). He examines as well the interconnected nodes, flexible adaptive structures, that constitute the network. More work is needed, however, on the embedded nature of networks, the activities and embodied practice in which they emerge, and on how they shape participation in and formation of network identities.

The landscape of global activism is undeniably shaped by the relationship between these institutions and the claims they stake for their own objectives and capabilities. Some scholars examining the development of transnational advocacy campaigns have focused on the binary relationship of domestic NGOs and their more powerful international counterparts (Bob 1995). International NGOs often do serve as gatekeeping institutions, selecting who among their counterparts will receive endorsements and opportunities. Yet to limit the discussion of international activism to this relationship misses the surrounding landscape of power, privilege, and opportunity. Similarly, claims by international NGOs about their ability to effect dramatic social change clearly shape the global imaginaries of the domestic organizations that hope to be the beneficiaries of such activism. When Amnesty International states it will improve the situation of prisoners of conscience through letter-writing campaigns, or even gain their freedom, activists logically expect these results and are frustrated when the process is much more complicated. At the same time, domestic activists are often extremely savvy about navigating the multiple promises and opportunities offered by international NGOs and are able to recognize and name the limitations and benefits of different agendas.

Emphasizing the complexity of the multiple terrains of transnational activism allows us "to study the landscape of circulation as well as the flow" (Tsing 2000). Here we can focus not just on physical location in geographic space but also on the relationships among institutions that channel political action, the spaces for debate and coordination, and the networks that link ongoing activism efforts. All these landscapes are complicated and shifting, involving multiple players over time. To name some of the key actors that are fundamental to my story: funding agencies and foundations that shape the programs of the organizations they finance; NGO lobbying and advocacy groups that form coalitions and network relationships; and governmental and supragovernmental bureaucracies, including the United Nations, the European Parliament, and the Organization of American States. Each of these locations is its own "locality," an internal terrain of power and relationships, histories and interests, constituencies and agendas. Much of this landscape is ephemeral, developing through the specific temporal windows of conferences, commissions, and meetings.

This focus on node and landscape to illuminate the spaces of debate and action allows us to consider how the unequal relationships of power and access shape the opportunities and results of activism. International activism encompasses a huge range of activities and relationships for Colombian activists, from the smallest and most discrete—sending an urgent action to an international network—to the largest and most amorphous—organizing big-budget international events. Almost all Colombian human rights NGOs have participated in international activism to some degree at some point. However, only those organizations that have considered the nodes and landscapes, shaping their activism to adapt to the requirements of these localities, have succeeded in expanding the activism network and pushed their human rights agenda into new realms. This process inevitably involves shaping and reshaping the message and meaning of their activism, as a result of bringing in new constituencies and publics that have their own political culture, agendas, and interests.

ALTERNATIVE GLOBAL VISIONS

The importance of the international imaginary is demonstrated by the visual landscape constructed in NGO offices, although in the decade after the fall of the Berlin Wall these international connections were almost entirely with Western Europe and the United States. With only one exception (the CCJ), all the human rights NGOs have filled their waiting rooms with international posters demonstrating their international connections. MINGA's waiting room is dominated by a huge black-and-white poster of a group of serious, racially diverse young adults from the Belgian funder 11–11–11 (named for the time and date of the end of World War I). The Seeds of Freedom Corporation (Corporación Semillas de Libertad) office is lined with posters commemorating resistance to human rights violations in Colombia (Trujillo and Sur de Bolívar), next to a poster in French advocating support for the Palestinians. In its downtown Bogotá office, ASFADDES advertises its international connections with a bulletin board filled with postcards of support from abroad and posters in English and French inviting participation in human rights events. The Lawyers' Collective's waiting room is dominated by a whimsical print from the French human rights federation Droits des Hommes. Even in the CCJ's austere waiting room, the individual cubicles are lined with international posters. The advantages to this public display of international connections are multiple. The most obvious is demonstrating and obtaining funding. The vast majority of Colombian human rights NGOs rely on foundations and grants from outside the country, with a snowballing effect: once international funding is obtained from one source, it is often easier to procure funding from other foundations. The second, and more often cited by NGO activists, is the mantle of protection that international associations are assumed to provide. Attackers will presumably think twice if a group is backed by European and U.S. supporters able to unleash a chain of political pressure and repercussions.

"The global" serves as such a powerful generator of fantasy in part because it is so unknown. In his evaluation of the Coordination, Jaime Prieto reported that less than half the participating NGOs had an "adequate" understanding of the work of their counterpart organizations. The vast majority of activists, particularly those in small towns and rural areas, never have the opportunity to travel beyond Colombia; for many, Bogotá remains an exotic destination. Despite the images gleaned from television and movies, the daily workings of power in Washington, D.C., and Brussels and other European capitals is profoundly opaque to activists as well as scholars of social movements. Many activists do not consider international activism a space for agendas, interests, and cultural formations other than their own. In their view, counterpart organizations should respond to the needs of Colombian organizations, most easily imagined as providing financial resources and political support by replying to urgent actions. These Colombian activists, again particularly those in impoverished rural areas facing daily violence and threats, are not concerned about long-term lobbying strategies but consumed with the daily tasks of survival and emergency response. If considered at all, lobbying in Washington, Brussels, and Geneva seems impossibly luxurious and difficult to consider as part of the same political project. Many such activists complain bitterly of the lack of desired support. Their imaginaries of U.S.- and European-based counterparts often wildly overestimate their funding and resources, however. For example, even activists with considerable experience lobbying abroad expressed shock at seeing the basement conference room where U.S. NGOs working on Colombia met, having imagined elaborate infrastructure and bountiful resources.[2]

Activism in Colombia also consists of complicated layers; these groups do not constitute a single "local" but multiple levels of access to resources, education, and travel. These differences are greatest between "national" groups (generally understood as Bogotá-based groups), groups in larger cities (primarily Medellín), and those in small towns and rural areas. These differences include both bureaucratic practice and political analysis; activists in small towns and rural areas are often much more attuned to the particular dynamic of violence in their areas and less willing to adjust their analyses to include national dynamics or the concerns of international counterparts. When considering international work, such activists are often profoundly critical of their "national" (Bogotá-based) counterparts as being out of touch with local realities and failing to share resources and information. For example, in Prieto's evaluation, activists' critiques included demands that the circulation of information, training, and resources from national groups to local groups should be improved. Many voiced concerns that their position as holders of privileged information desired by international counterparts was being usurped by national brokers. Similar dynamics exist in every location in the terrain of international activism: the same critiques can be heard of Washington- or Brussels-based groups by small-town solidarity groups in the United States and Europe, although such debates are invisible to Colombian groups.

While many groups critiqued the U.N. lobbying strategy devised by Colombian activists (explored at the end of this chapter), some groups developed radically different ideas about what international work should look like. They rejected the central focus on foreign governments, embassies, and multilateral organizations such as the United Nations, arguing that states will always act in their own interests. Rather than attempt to convince government representatives to bring pressure on the Colombian government (the classic mobilizing shame strategy of traditional human rights activism), these activists believed they should develop alliances with social movements in other places, focusing on solidarity among oppressed peoples. Examples frequently mentioned in interviews included unions, peasant groups, and popular organizations. Ultimately, the objective was the same: bring pressure on governments to change their abusive practices but through different means. Instead of lobbying, political pressure from grassroots groups would generate action on human rights cases. For them, the globalist imaginary of international solidarity among oppressed peoples originated in earlier Communist Party claims that the working classes of the world must unite.

There have been many initiatives to create cross-border subaltern alliances, particularly focusing on unions. Most such efforts make explicit claims to connections between U.S. consumption and Colombian production, in particular, labor practices: Coca-Cola, Drummond Coal, and the fresh-cut flower industry were three of the most prominent examples. The majority of these campaigns were brokered by U.S.-based organizations, such as the U.S. Labor Education Project and the Solidarity Center of the AFL-CIO, which produce reports on workers' rights, provide blueprints for labor activism, and organize delegations. These efforts require negotiating between the profound differences between U.S. and Colombian labor sectors and the distinct challenges facing both, such as the strong protectionist tendencies in some U.S. unions. Such campaigns are a fruitful site for future research on transnational activism.

Activists interested in developing cross-border subaltern alliances face numerous difficulties translating this vision into concrete strategies for action. In his survey of NGO activists, Jaime Prieto found that even those activists who argue for such alliances do not have concrete ideas about how to carry out promotion of "solidarity with *los pueblos*." Most grassroots movements are deeply rooted in local realities without clear counterparts in foreign organizations. By contrast, governments, embassies, and multilateral organizations such as the United Nations have explicitly designated staff to serve as counterparts for human rights NGOs and thus facilitate lobbying and advocacy, and, as part of what Sally Engle Merry (2006) calls "transnational modernity," are equipped to address human rights concerns (although not often in the ways NGOs would hope).

All foreign governments are not viewed equally by Colombian NGOs. For the majority of human rights groups that view U.S. policy in the region as a fundamental cause of violence and abuses, lobbying the U.S. government poses a number of issues. Sometimes these reflect differences over strategy, such as the focus on human rights conditions in U.S. legislation. Members of Congress interested in supporting human rights wrote into the legislation a requirement that the State Department certify progress by the Colombian government on specific human rights issues before military aid could be released. This was viewed by U.S.-based NGOs as a major victory in their lobbying efforts. However, these conditions were never enforced: President Bill Clinton waived the requirement for national security reasons, and the subsequent Bush administration consistently certified despite evidence provided by NGOs that the conditions had not been met. U.S. NGOs argued that the certification process, while flawed, kept human rights issues in the debate and allowed progress on specific cases (which was then used to justify issuing the certification). Colombian groups argued that supporting conditions created the appearance that they also would support military assistance if the government met the requirements of the conditions, a position they firmly rejected. Similarly, during and immediately after the passage of the Plan Colombia aid package in 2000, Colombian NGOs accepted funding from European governments while they largely rejected financing offered through USAID contractors even as their U.S. counterparts advocated increasing USAID funding for human rights programs. Colombian NGOs feared that accepting such money would endanger their autonomy and limit their ability to critique U.S. policy and would be used politically to justify U.S. intervention in the region.

Colombian NGOs did not simply look to Europe and the United States; they also worked to establish alliances with regional counterparts. For example, Gloria's NGO, MINGA, along with several other groups, developed work in conjunction with Ecuadoran NGOs to address the collateral damage from U.S.-sponsored counternarcotics operations. Beginning in the late 1990s, aerial spraying of chemical herbicides over thousands of hectares to destroy coca crops (known as fumigation) was conducted in southern Colombia along the border with Ecuador. The indiscriminate spraying from low-flying airplanes destroyed food and other legal crops, polluted water sources, and caused health problems in the local population.[3] While no spraying was carried out in Ecuadoran territory, wind patterns caused the herbicides to drift considerable distances over Ecuadoran territory, affecting peasant and indigenous communities along the border. Ecuadorans were concerned about "spillover" of the Colombian conflict, including Colombian refugees and the presence of Colombian armed actors in Ecuadoran territory. MINGA and other NGOs supported the creation of a binational working group to bring together Colombian and Ecuadoran activists concerned about these and other issues in order to build consensus positions. Serious differences in strategy and analysis remain, however. In one example, Ecuadorans advocated banning fumigation within five miles of the border to prevent herbicides from traveling into Ecuadoran territory. Colombians objected to such a restrictive ban, advocating a complete suspension of the fumigations in Colombian territory. They argued that the same damage being done across the border was occurring to Colombian indigenous and peasant groups. Activists also had to contend with overcoming national stereotypes. Ecuadorans frequently expressed fear of traveling in Colombia; Colombians mocked the Ecuadorans for being less sophisticated and politically savvy. Much of this binational work remains focused on traditional international lobbying, such as the joint advocacy tour conducted in the United States under the auspices of the Center for International policy, a Washington-based NGO.

ACTIVISM BEYOND COLOMBIA'S BORDERS

Colombian international activism dates to the early 1970s. At that time activism focused on raising awareness about the situation in Colombia through information exchange, public statements, and reporting. Activists recall the first evidence of international interest as an open letter sent by a group of European intellectuals to then-President Misael Pastrana (1970–74) expressing concern about political detentions. In October 1973 representatives of the InterAmerican Human Rights Commission of the OAS visited Colombia while on a Latin American tour but did not issue critical findings. That same month, the CSPP inaugurated its public activities with a press conference attended by Gabriel García Márquez, who donated literary prize money to the fledgling organization. In one of its first official actions, the CSPP sent an account of a political prisoner who had been tortured for three days to Amnesty International. Amnesty accepted the case as a prisoner of conscience and part of their urgent action campaigns. In June 1979 the Permanent Committee asked the U.N. to investigate torture in Colombia. Amnesty sent three representatives for the first official visit to Colombia in January 1980; their report was released in April to severe government criticism. President Turbay called the report vague and imprecise, based on rumor and *testimonios*, not evidence, while Justice Minister Hugo Escobar Sierra told the press that Amnesty violated Colombian sovereignty and was interfering in autonomous affairs. The Turbay administration invited the Inter-American Commission of Human Rights to return, evidently hoping its findings would contradict the Amnesty report, but the six-member delegation echoed Amnesty's conclusions by reporting serious human rights violations.

Human rights organizations also began to use international mechanisms to address abuses. NGO representatives successfully argued that a Colombian case should be heard by the U.N. Human Rights Committee. Although the Committee ruled that the groups had failed to exhaust the national legal opportunities for justice (a requirement before the Committee will rule on the substance of a case), the fact that the case had reached the Committee was considered an important advance. Later, a 1982 case of forced disappearance was ruled in favor of the plaintiffs by the InterAmerican Human Rights Commission, which was particularly important given its earlier failure to critically analyze the Colombian human rights situation.

The backbone of international activism was the Colombian exile community in Europe. While never rivaling the large numbers of Argentines and Chileans who flooded Europe during the 1970s, as the number of political detentions in Colombia grew, so did the number of Colombians abroad. While some made homes in closer Latin American countries, primarily Ecuador and Mexico, many preferred Europe. They were attracted by economic opportunities and the small but influential radical left parties that prospered in Europe; liberal political asylum laws facilitated legal immigration. Some active members of guerrilla groups became involved with the international diplomacy of armed movements that flourished in Europe during the 1970s and 1980s. Most participated in loose networks of solidarity and human rights committees that worked to publicize the situation in Colombia, collect money for Colombian organizations, and build public pressure on the Colombian government.

In many ways, Carlos, the lawyer profiled in chapter 2, typified the activities of these exiles. Alongside other Colombian exiles, he organized the Committee for Human Rights in Colombia in Spain. He recalled their early activities during an interview in his downtown Bogotá office: "We organized activities, events, and debates; offered analysis of the Colombian situation; and published pamphlets." They hoped to galvanize the Spanish public to pressure the Colombia government for release of detained activists. They also began lobbying and advocacy efforts with sympathetic leftist members of Parliament. Carlos recalled working with a Basque representative who had defended ETA (Euskadia Ta Askatasuna, Homeland and Freedom) prisoners in his law practice, as well as contacts with the socialist party and with the United Left and meetings with the Ministry of International Relations. The exile community in Europe included representatives from many of the leftist tendencies in Colombia, including guerrilla factions such as the M-19 and the EPL, labor organizers, and members of the Communist Party. For many of these activists, accustomed to clandestine political organizations in Colombia and their closed, clientalist political culture, such activities were a political education in their own right. Similar committees were established in London, Paris, New York, and Washington.

Exiles living in capital cities or in proximity to U.N. headquarters had the opportunity to learn firsthand what opportunities these international organizations presented.[4] Along with his work with the human rights committee, Carlos attended the U.N. Human Rights Commission in Geneva. For many Colombians who traveled there during the late 1980s, attending the Commission was an opportunity to meet and network with old friends in exile, establish new contacts with European solidarity and funding organizations, and educate people about their view of the Colombian situation. There was little or no effort to develop a coordinated strategy for their work at the Commission, which was largely limited to *denuncia,* angry accusations of the state's failure to prevent attacks on activists and rural communities.

Gloria's first trip to the Commission meetings in the late 1980s was typical of Colombian international activism at the time, when loose networks of activists converged around nodal events with little explicit negotiation of strategies or objectives. The World Organization against Torture had organized a seminar parallel to the Commission sessions, attended by a large delegation of Colombians, including Gloria (representing the CSPP), representatives from other human rights groups, union activists, and members of the Communist Party. Backed by inter-

national NGOs with consultative status at the U.N., the Colombians
were able to participate in the Commission through public statements.
Gloria explained:

> We managed to speak in several of the sessions with credentials from inter-
> national organizations that had status with the U.N., and we lobbied the
> diplomatic delegations. More than ask for concrete things, we wanted a
> special rapporteur [for Colombia]. What I really remember is that we did
> a lot of *denunica,* to say, look, what is going on in Colombia is this, the dirty
> war, they have assassinated so many members of the Patriotic Union, the
> people are being displaced already in the regions, paramilitarism is advanc-
> ing in different departments. We started denouncing the entire human rights
> crisis and calling attention to the fact that the issue of Colombia should be
> discussed in the United Nations. I can't tell you much more about what we
> asked for at that time because I went, and went along with the work, but
> I was just learning that the Commission existed. I wasn't prepared for the
> work.

Activists frequently used their European trips for a wide range of
activism activities: meeting with funders, public speaking tours, strategy
meetings with other activist organizations. Gloria, for example, spent several weeks after attending the seminar and the Commission traveling
through Europe on a public speaking tour supported by solidarity committees and churches. It was not until Colombian activists began to study
the Commission as a site for political action rather than simply a receptacle for denunciation that they learned to move the Commission to action.
To do so, they had to understand the evolving role of the Commission.

INTERNATIONAL ACTIVISM AT THE
UNITED NATIONS HUMAN RIGHTS COMMISSION

Human rights debates at the United Nations during the second half of
the twentieth century were indelibly shaped by the cold war and shifts in
the United Nations as a whole. The period can be summed up as one of
gradual expansion of the Commission's definition of its own mandate
and mission, expressed at the glacial pace of the U.N. and at the level of
minute changes in diplomatic language until larger debates over the U.N.
reform resulted in the reorganization of the Commission as the Council
on Human Rights in 2006. From its inception the Commission has been
one of the areas of the U.N. most receptive to nonstate participation, as
human rights abuses were by definition cases in which redress at the state
level was complicated by state responsibility. Expansion of the Com-

mission's human rights mandate was continually checked as government representatives from abusive countries used existing bureaucratic regulations to limit debate. Frustration over the inherent tension between the Commission as a space for human rights debate and as a collective of state representatives reluctant to examine their own human rights practices contributed to the dissolution of the Commission in 2006.

Until the 1960s human rights action in the United Nations was limited to drafting norms elaborating the Charter. The first and most famous was the Universal Declaration of Human Rights, passed in 1948 as a resolution of the General Assembly. Lack of treaty status made the resolution a suggestion to the signatories that was not legally binding, however. The Universal Declaration was followed by the International Covenant on Economic, Social and Cultural Rights and the International Covenant on Civil and Political Rights, which were drafted in 1954 and approved by the General Assembly in 1966. The three together are known as the International Bill of Human Rights. Originally intended to be a single document, the two covenants were split as a result of cold war politics; the United States championed civil and political rights while the Soviet Union argued for social, cultural, and economic rights. The cold war remained one of the most important factors shaping human rights activism until the fall of the Berlin Wall. The United Nations Human Rights Commission was created by the General Assembly as the primary vehicle for the discussion of human rights issues, but such debates have been profoundly hobbled from the start. As a result of a 1947 resolution, the Commission could not discuss specific complaints and could only receive voluntary reports from states.

Independence and liberation movements in Africa and Asia profoundly changed the human rights debates at the United Nations during the 1960s and 1970s. In part, this reflected the demographic expansion of the United Nations and the subsequent increase in the number of state representatives on the Commission, from eighteen in 1946 to fifty-three in 1990.[5] Over the course of the 1960s, the number of U.N. member nations almost doubled as former colonies became recognized as nation-states. These countries united in the nonaligned movement and developed into a powerful bloc interested in using human rights mechanisms to bring issues related to imperialism and colonization to U.N. debates.

The work of the Commission gradually expanded as well. In 1967 a new resolution allowed the Commission to discuss violations in particular countries. The first country-specific action was a special investigation of human rights in the Occupied Territories after the 1967 Six Day War between Israel and Syria. Soon after, South Africa became the target of censure. In 1970 the Commission was empowered to conduct confidential investigations of complaints; releasing the "Black List" of countries under discussion was seen as a kind of public pressure. In 1973 the Ad Hoc Working Group on the Situation of Human Rights in Chile was established. In 1976 the International Covenants became legally binding when the sufficient number of signatories were obtained, and committees charged with monitoring implementation of the covenants were created to review state reports and hear individual petitions (in cases in which the state had adopted an optional protocol).

The emergence of the first high-profile human rights NGO, Amnesty International, also played a key role in spurring awareness of human rights issues both at the Commission and in the public eye.[6] Amnesty also pioneered advocacy efforts at the Commission, bringing pressure on members to take a more active role in deliberating over abuses and establishing mechanisms to address them. As has been true in subsequent advocacy efforts, the results of the campaign were achieved through a combination of careful documentation, press coverage, and the serendipity of international politics. Amnesty succeeded in spurring action on torture in one of its first campaigns, which focused on Chile and Argentina.

The Commission expanded its work dramatically throughout the 1980s and early 1990s by the adoption of a number of new mechanisms, including nearly a dozen thematic mechanisms and five new conventions.[7] The Working Group on Enforced or Involuntary Disappearances, created at the request of the Economic and Social Council (ECOSOC), was the first thematic mechanism to emerge from the Commission and opened the door for additional thematic mechanisms.[8] Until 1984 the Commission considered the majority of individual countries in complex and confidential procedures. NGOs were prevented from learning anything about the resulting debates.[9] Frustration with this situation prompted the adoption of ECOSOC Resolution 1235, which allowed the creation of country-specific mechanisms, called special rapporteurs, special representatives, or independent experts.[10] Unlike the thematic mandates, which focus on reviewing individual cases and providing recommendations, such mechanisms offered an assessment of the overall situation in a given country and comparative conclusions. Country-specific mechanisms were seen as a sanction and thus were often denied entry into the country in question, forcing them to rely on outside reporting.

During the 1990s, however, a new dynamic among the member states emerged with the creation of regional and interest blocs; many of these groups have blocked Commission action.[11] While the European Union, the first bloc to be created, has been active in supporting resolutions addressing specific human rights abuses, other blocs have not been. Among the latter are the Organization of the Islamic Conference (OIC), the so-called Like Minded Group (LMG),[12] and the Non-Aligned Movement (NAM). According to one NGO analyst, increasingly "each state participates through one or more of these groupings and through which individual states are relieved of their obligation to make their positions clear and to act accordingly. . . . [T]he Commission is moving away from country specific mandates and to an emphasis on advisory services and technical cooperation" (Bauer 2001).[13]

The growing list of agenda items and participants has led to a serious time and budget crunch in the Commission. For most of the 1990s, the Commission's five-week session consisted of three daily sessions, from 10:00 A.M. to 1:00 P.M., 3:00 P.M. to 6:00 P.M., and 6:00 P.M. to 9:00 P.M. Despite these longer sessions, no permanent expansion of the budget was authorized. The budget crisis reached a head in the 2002 session, when approximately one week into the session a directive was issued from New York refusing to pay for translation fees during the evening sessions. The result was a chaotic reorganization of the agenda, including a dramatic reduction in the time allowed for NGO speakers. This generated a huge controversy among many NGO representatives, many of whom viewed the cuts as an implicit attack on the growing NGO participation in the Commission.

NGO PARTICIPATION AT THE COMMISSION

NGO participation at the Commission has expanded dramatically since the 1970s, at which time NGOs had only a very limited role (with the exception of Amnesty International). Article 71 of the U.N. Charter establishes that ECOSOC may authorize consultation with appropriate NGOs. The Conference of Non-governmental Organizations in Consultative Relationship with the United Nations (CONGO) was created in 1948. Because of the particular nature of the human rights issue—in which states are accused of malfeasance against their citizens—NGOs were seen as an important resource from the beginning. In 1986, during the U.N.'s world conference in Tehran to celebrate the twentieth anniversary of the Universal Declaration of Human Rights, CONGO organized the NGO Conference on Human Rights in Paris, which became a prototype for subsequent parallel NGO forums.

CONGO was not immune to the cold war politics that dominated U.N. activities during this period. In a publication commemorating CONGO's fiftieth anniversary, former officials recalled the difficulties of navigating political battles. Edith Ballantyne, who served as president of the Women's International League for Peace and Freedom and as president of CONGO from 1976 to 1982, wrote:

> Serving as president of CONGO sometimes felt like being caught in minefields. The minefields were the New York and Geneva "turfs," affected by the Cold War, which weighed heavily on relations among NGOs within CONGO and in their relations with the U.N. Since the early seventies, a number of leading members of CONGO had made efforts to elect a Bureau that reflected more fairly the composition of its membership. But it was "affirmative action" that finally opened the Bureau to member organizations from the Left. Political issues were often hidden behind arguments over structure, form and method of work. (CONGO 1998: 16)

One important factor in the increase in NGO participation has been the Internet, which allows access to documents from remote locations, in real time, for an infinite number of readers. Before, as the Colombian lawyers describe below, activists were required to travel to the Commission library in Geneva to study the documents and history of the Commission meetings, with the associated travel costs making U.N. participation prohibitively expensive. A vast and growing number of Web sites are now available that explain how to participate in U.N. meetings and offer guidelines and information sharing, as well as commentary on past meetings.[14]

Generalizing about NGO participation at the U.N. is difficult given the range of organizations represented, from the American Association of Retired Persons to the All India Women's Organization (both on the CONGO board from 1997 to 2000). CONGO membership has expanded dramatically, from 230 members in 1997 (an estimated 19 percent of the total 1,200 NGOs accredited to attend U.N. meetings) to 330 in 2000 (an estimated 15 percent of the total 2,000). In part this increase was due to a major change in U.N. regulations governing NGO participation. In 1996 a resolution extended accreditation to national and regional NGOs (instead of just international NGOs, as had been the case). At the same time, a number of NGOs have continued to extend accreditation to representatives of groups that are not included among the organizations with consultative status. One result has been a serious time crunch, as the number of NGOs hoping to speak increased dramatically while the time available remained the same.

The time designated for NGO participation is also used by "Gongos," government-funded nongovernmental organizations that register and attend as NGOs but speak in favor of the government. To date, no Latin American Gongos have spoken publicly, but numerous such organizations have taken the floor to discuss country-specific issues in Asia. During the 2002 session, it was very common during the NGO speaking time for an NGO representative to question why anyone would doubt the commitment of the Chinese government to human rights and rattle out statistics proving that government's concern with its population's welfare.[15]

The issue of policing NGO participation has been extremely controversial. Some observers have accused NGOs of "excessive participation," with too many opportunities to comment on Commission proceedings and too little accountability or control over the content of their comments. Government representatives and U.N. officials often view NGOs as failing to abide by the political culture of the United Nations and the unwritten rules of Commission participation. According to Jan Bauer, who writes a yearly report on the Commission meetings for Human Rights Internet, "Up to the early 1990s, it was generally understood that country situations would be addressed primarily—and in some ways even exclusively—under the agenda item reserved for that purpose (now Item 9). NGOs were expected, and in some ways required, to base statements under all other agenda items on thematic concerns (e.g. torture, arbitrary detention, the right to development) and to address the content in thematic reports and comment on the recommendations" (Bauer 1997). Between 1996 and 2002 NGOs "made every item a country item." This was in part the result of the much greater representation of smaller, national NGOs made possible by the 1996 change in ECOSOC regulations. These organizations were understandably focused on their country-specific activism, viewing the move to debate thematic issues as an effort by states to escape accountability. NGOs were also driven to present their statements because speaking before the Commission placed their concern on the international record and was a concrete achievement that could be reported to constituencies at home. Bauer has been critical of these NGO statements, which she viewed as wasting the time that could have been devoted to developing more specific mechanisms:

> The main outcome of five-minute NGO statements, especially on country situations, is to place concerns on public record (in the U.N. summary records and press releases, a one-paragraph reference). They are one of the least effective ways, however, to move the Commission to action. In general, a decision by one state or group of states to seek, or not, to take action at the Commission depends on other factors, including: (a) the publication of

a critical mass of information in the media throughout the year or during periods of evident crisis; (b) the publication of a similar mass of information in the reports of several of the thematic mechanisms; (c) submission of a critical mass of information directly to the High Commissioner for Human Rights; (d) regular NGO briefings and interventions to relevant ministries, government missions and/or members of the national legislative assembly (again, throughout the year). (Bauer 2005)

NGOs fear that more restrictive regulation of civil society participation will be exploited by governments interested in stifling dissent.

The issue of NGO participation, also a concern at the growing number of world conferences, exploded during the 2001 Durban U.N. Conference.[16] NGOs organized a large parallel conference, raising controversial issues that included the equation of Zionism with racism and the call for slavery reparations. After threatening to boycott the meetings, the United States sent a low-level delegation, then walked out of the meetings alongside the official delegation from Israel. Widely publicized as a debacle, resulting in many portrayals of NGOs as flame-throwing radicals incapable of policing themselves and of constructive behavior, Durbin has continued to mark the debate over NGO participation and spurred efforts to limit such actions.

Public discussion of NGOs as a threat that must be monitored increased after the negative press coverage of violent anarchists during the 2000 World Trade Organization protests in Seattle and the scrutiny of Muslim charity organizations after September 11, 2001. Some controversial NGOs that do have accreditation are widely rumored to be financed by abusive governments; an example is the North-South Foundation, widely alleged to be funded by Muammar Qadhafi's regime. Government delegations have periodically challenged specific NGOs' accreditation, including the Transnational Radical Party, a self-defined nonviolent organization advocating greater use of international law, and Freedom House, a U.S. Congress–funded organization monitoring civil liberties around the world.

By far the most controversial aspect of NGO participation has been the presence of representatives of armed movements using other NGOs' accreditation to gain access to the Commission. The *New York Times* has reported on the controversy over the presence of representatives of armed separatist movements at the United Nations (Olson 1998). Colombian activists are not immune to such accusations; representatives of Colombian armed groups have historically maintained a "diplomatic presence" in Europe and attended Commission meetings. M-19 members were among the first Colombians to regularly attend the meetings. Activists recall that several years ago the Colombian government representative objected to the presence of a FARC representative during the proceedings. During my fieldwork, a public debate sponsored by a local solidarity organization between the director of the CCJ and a FARC representative was publicized among the activists at the conference. The debate was attended by approximately one hundred people. Over the next several days I thought I recognized the FARC representative among those circulating at the Commission.

COLOMBIANS IN GENEVA: WHAT WAS ACHIEVED

After five years of organized lobbying, Colombian NGOs were instrumental in the creation of a new kind of human rights mechanism: an office of the High Commissioner for Human Rights in Colombia. This office was designed to monitor and report on the human rights situation and to offer advice and assistance to the Colombian government and civil society. The UNHCHR, created in 1994, was itself still a relatively new instrument to increase the international profile of human rights. While the UNHCHR's office in Colombia has been critiqued by both NGOs and the Colombian government, its reporting has been an extremely important resource for international advocacy efforts, as well as for Colombians.

Changing the Frame

The main instruments available to the Colombian NGOs were moral persuasion and political pressure to convince government representatives at the Commission that support for their initiative offered more political benefits than costs. Among the challenges faced by NGO activists was shifting the framework used to describe Colombia, from drug trafficking violence in which the government is a victim needing support to a human rights crisis for which the government is at fault. For most of the 1980s and early 1990s, the public imaginaries of Colombian violence were dominated by two ideas—that Colombia had the oldest democracy in Latin America and that it was the home of the largest and most violent drug cartels in the world. Government representatives focused on Colombian democracy and stressed the difference between Colombia, which enjoyed regular elections despite the limited political system that was a legacy of the National Front, and the military dictatorships of the

Southern Cone. Carlos, a lobbyist for the CCJ, recalled meeting with the German ambassador and several members of his staff, who told him indignantly, "Colombia is a democracy, you can't think that Colombia is like the Pinochet regime. It is a democracy that has been affected by drug trafficking violence that we have to help." The spectacular and widely publicized violence by the drug cartels masked Colombian political violence, according to the NGOs. CCJ director Gustavo told me, "The majority had a very distorted vision of what was going on in Colombia, that the problem was drug trafficking, not human rights. To change their vision was very difficult; it required a permanent presence at the Commission, and at the subcommission in August."[17]

One important strategy used by the CCJ to change the frame of the Commission was to employ the Commission's existing mechanisms to describe Colombian violence as a human rights crisis. The most significant visit in the buildup to the creation of the office was the joint visit to Colombia in October 1994 by the Commission's special rapporteur on torture and special rapporteur on summary or arbitrary executions. According to Bauer, "The effect of the reports by the secretary-general's representative and the special rapporteurs may well have been lost on the Commission had there not been a strong and reasonably well-organized NGO lobby at the Commission's 1995 session. The combined strength of the reports and the NGO effort did bring the situation in Colombia more directly into the light and enabled NGOs to secure the assistance of several government delegations" (Bauer 1995).[18]

A major shift in the campaign to raise awareness about the human rights issue occurred during a conference organized to launch the Human Rights Now! Campaign in Europe. The conference was held in Brussels at the European Parliament building and cosponsored by European NGOs; unprecedented attendance by government officials transformed the gathering from simply one more human rights conference to an event legitimating Colombian NGOs as serious and credible organizations. According to Colombian press coverage, fifteen members of the European Parliament and a twenty-person delegation from the Colombian government were present at the conference, which was covered by international media outlets including CNN.[19] Colombia's minister of defense told the representative of the U.N. Human Rights Center that Colombia should not be "punished with a black star" and put in the same category as Iran, Cuba, and Afghanistan. Activists in Europe had published two books focusing on the growth of paramilitary violence in Colombia, one focusing on rural areas (On the Hidden Path of the Dirty War) and the other, released the year of the conference, listing military officers and detailing their alleged participation with paramilitary groups *(State Terrorism in Colombia)*.[20] This conference also spurred the creation of the Colombia-Europe Coordination to facilitate lobbying and information flow.

Knowing What to Ask For

The Colombian Commission of Jurists was the first NGO to begin systematically studying work at the Commission. International advocacy had been a central part of its mandate since its creation in 1988 with substantial seed money from the Ford Foundation. The Ford Foundation was especially interested in supporting an organization that would provide credible information and a centralized strategy for international advocacy campaigns. From the beginning, the CCJ was dedicated to documenting and reporting on the human rights situation with the international community in mind; unlike other legal-focused NGOs in Colombia, such as the Lawyers' Collective, they did no casework in the Colombian judicial system.

In part because of the significant funding from Ford, the CCJ had the luxury to develop its strategy over several years, working with international experts and spending months in Europe researching the U.N. system. Visionary staff, in particular, CCJ director Gustavo Gallón, were crucial to developing the strategy. For the first several years, the CCJ helped organize conferences to occur simultaneously with the Commission meetings, such as the 1989 effort cosponsored by Pax Christi and the International Service for Human Rights with a number of Colombian bishops.[21] These meetings failed to coalesce into sustainable lobbying at the Commission. Staffing shifts and lack of institutional memory hampered the ongoing project, according to Gustavo: "People would go, but just for a week, and different people every time. So they didn't build on the work that had been done before. We started going for the whole month, and then even earlier so we could do work on Colombia."

Carlos, now CCJ's deputy director, recalled the planning for the Commission work: "We spent a long time studying the Commission, we did a lot of consultations, we spent a long time looking at old documents in libraries, at that time there was no Internet, there was no virtual access to the documents, you had to go there and look at them." They held meetings with NGO delegations from other countries with more experience at the U.N., including Salvadorans and Argentines. The CCJ undertook a study of the Commission and U.N. lobbying campaigns to compare previous cases and offer recommendations for the Colombian campaign they were planning. The study concluded that demands for a country-specific mechanism such as a special rapporteur were not politically viable but that there was precedent for the appointment of an independent expert to supervise the U.N.'s technical assistance program with the Colombian government. Carlos described the emerging strategy:

> Up to this point, no one had conducted professional human rights advocacy; people would go and have conversations with leftist NGOs. Obviously among NGOs, people believed that the Colombian situation was terribly serious, but no one really knew how [advocacy] worked among the states, what was really going on. There was no analysis of who was in what group, their coordination, their relative power. We discovered a number of things. First, that the Commission isn't a tribunal, it is a state meeting. You could read this in the documents, but you have to live it there, to realize that it is not a group that listens to people's different versions, asks for explanations and then in an impartial way decides. It is a group that listens very little, and where states' interests count for a great deal.

CCJ staff decided they needed to develop state sponsorship of their initiative. "If you don't find a patron, you can't act," Carlos told me. NGO support and pressure was not enough to move the Commission to action. The next step was to find out what specific mechanism could be employed in Colombia and how to develop political support in the Commission for such a move. Despite a seemingly entrenched, impenetrable bureaucracy, the Commission was fairly flexible in creating new mechanisms over time. The action the Commission took, however, was often limited by unspoken political considerations. The first important issue was where Colombia would be placed on the agenda of the Commission, as a country-specific discussion under item 9 or as part of the general discussion under item 3. Carlos recalled tracking different debates to understand how the agenda functioned:

> It is very important for Chile to be in a separate agenda item and not to be included in the agenda item for the general situation. The day that Chile was considered part of the general situation agenda item was considered a defeat because of the symbolism of being in one agenda item or another. . . . But there are situations that have never been their own agenda item, for example, Argentina was never its own agenda item. . . . There are a lot of contradictions, but there is a political logic having to do with the states' interests in all this.

Gustavo and other CCJ attorneys decided that their first objective should be to get Colombia on the Commission's agenda and once the debate was opened, attempt to maneuver into a more comprehensive discussion. NGO activists were unanimous in believing that Colombia should have a special rapporteur to focus on the situation, but such a measure was impossible because of the stiff resistance from Commission members. "To get on the agenda as a country for which we were asking for a rapporteur was not possible because the rapporteur signifies a political sanction against a dictatorial regime, and Colombia was not in fact a dictatorship. There is a difference between the Colombian regime and Pinochet's regime," Carlos told me. "So the important thing was to figure out how to call the attention of the international community about the situation." At that time the U.N. was providing advising services on human rights to Colombia through an agreement for technical assistance from the Center for Human Rights. So the CCJ decided to combine its politically risky demand for a special rapporteur with a request that the technical assistance be publicly supervised by the Commission by an independent expert, with a public debate over the results rather than private consulting. This request was modeled on the Commission's action on Guatemala. According to Carlos:

> Later we abandoned the idea of an expert because the technical training program ended, so we went with the idea of the rapporteur or any other mechanism for supervision because, in addition, the Commission had gone on establishing rapporteurs, independent experts, special representatives of the Commission. The important thing was the mandate, that was one of the things we discovered along the way because we had already seen that the mechanisms were flexible. That is how we got to the idea of the office. We think it is the best mechanism possible because it is better than a rapporteur because it is there permanently, and the mandate of the office is the same as a rapporteur with an additional advantage, which is the technical assistance, so this double mandate and the permanence makes it a much better mechanism. Also, it could be used to develop a human rights verification mission.

Working the System: Lobbying at the U.N.

The Colombian lobbying strategy developed by the CCJ was based on its credibility as an organization of human rights professionals. While much previous activism had focused on the spectacular performance of victimhood (such as Tibetan monks and nuns with their brilliant orange robes, the Argentine Mothers of the Plaza de Mayo wearing white grandmotherly head scarves, and Guatemalan Nobel Prize–winner Rigoberta Menchú in her Mayan dress), by the 1990s international training and funding had made "professional activist" a respectable identity. The majority of Colombian activists based their activist identity at the U.N. on being professional human rights activists rather than membership in a persecuted population or a well-known institution like the Catholic Church. Of the Colombian NGO representatives at the Commission meetings during my fieldwork in 2002, only two were directly representing victims: Gladys, from the Association of Relatives of the Detained and Disappeared, and Jaime, from an indigenous community in southern Colombia.

Lobbying required carefully calibrated emotional effects; outrage at violence still had its place. Colombians resorted periodically to public displays of protest. In 1995 activists wore yellow armbands with the word "Colombia?" in an effort to raise the question of what action the Commission was going to take on the issue of political violence in Colombia. In 1998 the Manuel Cepeda Foundation, named for the Patriotic Union senator assassinated in 1994 and run by his son from exile in France, sponsored a traveling exhibition, *The Gallery of Memory*, featuring photos of victims of state-sponsored political violence in Colombia accompanied by explanatory text. The exhibition was displayed in the hallway of the Commission during the meetings. Each year the Colombian exile community in Geneva, along with visiting activists, convene small demonstrations focusing on Colombia, waving flags and protest banners in the plaza facing the U.N. compound.

According to the mandates of professionalized human rights practice, such displays should not be too dramatic or disruptive, however, and must respect the boundaries of NGO participation to maintain credibility. The most dramatic incident involving Colombian activists occurred at the time of my fieldwork at the 2002 meetings. The presentation of the UNHCHR Office's report on Colombia, and the government's response, had been delayed for weeks because of the scheduling problems caused by the cancellation of the evening sessions. During the last week of the meetings, after a frustrating six weeks in Geneva, the chairman finally announced that the debate on Colombia would be held for one hour that afternoon. The Colombian government's position was presented by the vice president, who was responsible for the state's human rights program but was also serving as the minister of defense (following the previous minister's resignation a month earlier to protest the presidential peace plan). The NGO observation area was packed with Colombian activists as we anxiously awaited the vice president's words. As he began to speak, I noticed a young student activist with a long frizzy braid and a serious air begin walking down the aisle that divided the long row of desks seat-ing the member delegations. I had barely registered his bizarre attire—a long, loose brown robe—before he dropped the robe to the ground and held up a hand-painted sign reading "Colombian Blood!" His naked shoulders and back—all I could see as he was positioned toward the president's desk and away from the NGO observation area—were covered in red paint. There were startled gasps and some muffled laughter, and the security guards working at the metal detector outside the Commission door were called in to escort him, once again covered with the robe, out for questioning. The CCJ lawyers sitting next to me were not amused. "How irresponsible," one muttered. The CCJ reaction to this protest—made in support of the campaign that all favored—was in part based on the importance of performing professionalism.[22] To be professional required objectivity, familiarity with international law, and well-documented reporting; painting one's naked body red and parading around with a sign in protest was decidedly not professional behavior.

Much professional human rights lobbying occurred behind the scenes. The CCJ's lawyers were extremely well connected to a network of international human rights lawyers and professionals from universities, as well as diplomats and U.N. staffers. Gustavo had received a doctoral degree in France and during the 1990s became a U.N. official himself when he was appointed its Special Representative for Equatorial New Guinea, a position he filled for four years. One lawyer who had worked on the CCJ's international strategy recalled that Gustavo carried a constantly updated address book and did not hesitate to call out his contacts "full force" for strategy and networking. These were the quiet conversations and back-channel negotiations that are the hallmark of serious international diplomacy.

Professionalization entailed being a part of existing international networks of activists who were also lobbying at the Commission and included advocacy on behalf of Colombian NGOs in their meetings. Colombians asked activists representing issue-focused NGOs to include Colombia in their lobbying; labor rights groups could mention Colombian unions, or religious groups could discuss Colombian clergy killed in political violence. Throughout the 1990s an increasing number of humanitarian organizations began lobbying the Commission, focusing on the prevention of humanitarian disasters and arguing that the international community should address the political causes of such disasters. By the end of the 1990s, with Colombia defined as a major humanitarian disaster (see chapter 2), the staff of Oxfam, World Vision, and others were all including Colombia in their campaigns. Colombian representatives of indigenous communities traveled to Geneva to network with other indigenous activists. Activists with women's groups did the same, helping to organize the special rapporteur for women's 2001 trip to Colombia and using her report as a further networking and lobbying tool.

The Association of Relatives of the Detained and Disappeared, the only group of Colombian victims to consistently lobby at the U.N., built on the past experience of Fedefam, an international federation of organizations of relatives of the disappeared. Fedefam activists emphasized the case of Colombia in different situations, adopted a campaign focusing on Colombia, and sponsored an international mission to the country in 2002. ASFADDES and Fedefam activists requested joint meetings with U.N. officials responsible for addressing their issue, primarily the Working Group on Forced Disappearances and the special rapporteur for extrajudicial executions. ASFADDES gained credibility for the Colombian cause from their institutional relationship with Fedefam. In 2002 they had an additional advantage; the president of Fedefam, a representative of the Mothers of the Plaza de Mayo, was leading the U.N. lobbying delegation. The ASFADDES activist at the U.N. that year told me how much the "superstar" status of the Mothers changed the dynamic during the lobbying. "It's strange," she told me. "It's not the Mothers who request meetings, but the delegates ask to speak with them. The delegates come up and thank them for the opportunity to speak with them; that doesn't happen with anyone else. I think it is because they are so well respected, so old and well known."[23]

Much of the lobbying work of the United Nations happened in the cafeteria, known among the Colombian NGOs as La Serpiente, or the Serpent, presumably because of the S-shaped curve of the room. La Serpiente was a long room lined with glass, facing a view of Lake Geneva and the tree-covered hills on the other side of the lake. The space was more public than the Commission meeting room itself, which was policed by guards checking IDs and scanning purses and bags in an X-ray machine and required walking though a metal detector. Even entering the building required a U.N. identification card. The room was filled with low glass tables and short leather chairs, often pulled together for impromptu meetings. The cafeteria was at the far end, selling small cups of espresso and long ham sandwiches, fruit, cookies, and chocolate, next to the smoking section.

During my first trip to the Commission in 1996, I traveled from Washington for a week as a volunteer translator. In exchange for lodgings in the barren apartment of a Colombian exile, I spent my days with the Colombian delegation, translating their appeals to second-string diplomats in La Serpiente. I spent my evenings with the Colombians, singing Mexican Rancheros on the trolley through town, the Colombians shaking their head, impressed and incredulous at the trusting Swiss (there was no ticket collector on the trolleys and payment for newspapers on the street was voluntary). During that visit, the Colombian delegation was optimistic; this was the year that the agreement to create the office was announced and progress was in the air. When I returned for five weeks in 2002, the change was palpable. The Colombian activists were frustrated with what many saw as excessive focus on diplomatic frippery as violence and abuses in Colombia continued unabated.

Efforts to coordinate lobbying remained constant, developed during the early days of the CCJ's trips to Geneva. The Colombians would meet at the end of the day in one of the empty conference rooms to share the results of their day and plan strategy. The first order of business was to go around the table, making introductions. Attendance on any given day was primarily Colombian activists, some "from the regions" or smaller NGOs, and European staffers of NGOs who include Colombia in their lobbying portfolios and attend the Commission for several days. While there was no formal agenda, the meetings usually followed the same order: reports on the day's activities and then analysis from the CCJ staff. My notes from one such meeting during the 2002 session offer a typical glimpse of these discussions; country names serve as shorthand for the representatives of the official state delegation. CCJ director Gustavo began, describing meetings with France, who was a new person who claimed to be interested in the Colombia issue. He had also met with Spain, who had been sent to Geneva from the U.N. headquarters in New York City and was new to Geneva. He reported a brief conversation with the Swedish ambassador, who told him that their priority was China, maybe two or three other countries, and mentioned Colombia last. The Norwegian director of an umbrella group of Scandinavian humanitarian agencies with an office in Colombia reported a conversation with Sweden. The ASFADDES representative reported she spoke with the Argentine ambassador, who had seemed interested and wanted to talk, saying that while in the civil service in Argentina she had pushed for the convention on forced disappearances and knew about the issue. Gladys was going to try to set up meetings with others from the Latin America and Caribbean group. She told the group that the day before, she had met with Mexico, whose human rights official was María Claire de Acosta, well known to many present from her history as director of a

Mexican human rights NGO. These meetings serve as a critical space to exchange information and share strategy. Activists new to the Colombian cause have the opportunity to learn about the campaign and get coaching on advocacy if needed. These meetings also allow the CCJ to address the frequent criticism that they maintain too much control over the lobbying at the Commission by demonstrating their efforts at inclusion.

Representing All Colombians

The central element of the public face of professionalism was the consensus of the human rights community. Because professional human rights activism is a dispassionate and objective analysis of the facts according to international legal standards, all activists must agree on the diagnosis of the problem and the proposed solution. Failing to present a consensus position would seriously weaken Colombian activists' credibility. Though many human rights activists in fact had profound differences (see chapter 4), in their international lobbying they attempted to display a united front. These positions were developed during workshops organized by the Coordination. The Colombians succeeded in expanding the available mechanisms not by the dramatic enactment of an identity as human rights victims but because they convincingly enacted the representation of the consensus of human rights organizations.

According to Gustavo, the CCJ recognized the importance of establishing coalitions early in its efforts to work with the Commission. Before the Coordination, Colombian activists had organized the International Working Group to develop joint strategies for lobbying abroad. "From the first time we went to Geneva, we have worked in coalition," Gustavo told me. "We put before the group what we had seen in Geneva, because we had to do joint work, work with many difficulties. We were convinced that joint work was the only way to go, that it was not possible to carry out work with divided positions." Carlos recalled one of the first Commission meetings the CCJ attended: "We gradually encountered other Colombian NGOs, and in one of those encounters we had a terrible experience, that one of the NGOs was asking for one thing, and we were asking for something else. . . . The others asked for a rapporteur and we asked for an independent expert. . . . What we did was to try to reconcile our positions, but it was difficult, and we spent more time talking among ourselves and with other NGOs [than lobbying the Commission]." Because of this experience the CCJ organized the first "Joint Declaration" for the Commission. Subsequent annual "joint declarations," developed over months of meetings with local organizations throughout Colombia, were the single most important tool for lobbying on Colombia.

Creation of the Office in Colombia

Knowing that there was growing support among member state delegations by the mid-1990s, the Colombian government agreed to a mechanism that would deal with extrastate actors.[24] The government argued against the designation of a special rapporteur for Colombia not by denying the description of the situation in Colombia but by arguing about the causes. Like the NGO activists, the government viewed the designation of a country-specific rapporteur as a punishment and lobbied to avoid such a measure. The government saw itself as another victim of the human rights crisis. It admitted that the level of violence and human rights abuses was abysmal but denied that this was the government's fault. Instead, it claimed that the country needed the support, not the condemnation, of the international community and that it was democratically elected but trapped in a cycle of extremist violence that it did not control. Government representatives emphasized that Colombia is a democracy with regular, free, and fair elections. Historically, the country-specific mechanisms had been assigned only in cases of totalitarian regimes and dictatorships. The government used this precedent to argue that the mechanisms are not effective for investigating and monitoring human rights situations in democratic countries with terrorist groups and guerrillas. A special rapporteur would only investigate and monitor state and state agents, but according to the government, terrorist and guerrilla groups in Colombia are criminal, commit crimes against humanitarian law, are responsible for half of all the human rights violations in Colombia (kidnappings), and have an impact on the entire society. Government officials also argued that Colombia was too "complex" to be understood during one visit a year for ten days or less. Finally, they claimed that the creation of a special rapporteur for Colombia would be interpreted as a victory by the guerrillas, as a judgment against the Colombian government, and would further polarize society and weaken the government's authority.[25]

The government's proposal was to invite the High Commissioner for Human Rights to establish a permanent office in Bogotá. As a result of this negotiated agreement, the Commission chairman requested the UNHCHR to establish an office in Colombia pursuant to the invitation by the government. The decision was placed in the official records of the

1996 session of the Commission in the chairman's statement,[26] and the agreement was signed on November 26, 1996, by the Colombian minister for foreign affairs and the UNHCHR.[27]

The announcement cloaked a number of highly controversial points in the diplomatic language of the United Nations. The first issue was the nature of reporting. The NGOs argued for analytic reports, meaning that the office could make judgments about the situation and government action; the government argued for descriptive reports, which would simply list actions taken. The second controversy concerned the distribution of the reports; the government wanted the final reports to be private and restricted to only members of the Commission and U.N. staff. The final agreement stipulated analytic reporting, but nothing was to be published during the year. The final report would be given to the High Commissioner, who would then share it with the Commission and release it. The mandate of the office was wide-ranging and extensive, including advising the government, legislative branch, national bodies, civil society, and individuals, and NGOs; and receiving complaints of violations of human rights and international humanitarian law and transmitting them to national authorities.

Critiques of U.N. Lobbying

The creation of the human rights office, and its subsequent reports and actions, remain controversial. Government officials have continued to contest the findings of the office in their annual reports.[28] NGOs severely criticized the initial work of the office, claiming it was insufficiently critical of the government and focused on supporting the peace process rather than human rights. Some NGOs called for the resignation of the first director, the Spanish diplomat Almudena Masaraza. They argued that she focused on government negotiations with the guerrillas and enjoyed excessively close relationships with Colombian governmental officials and could not effectively carry out her human rights mandate. I will not explore the critiques of the office's reports and functions here. Rather, I am interested in using the critiques of international activism expressed by Colombian activists themselves to illuminate the contradictory expectations and outcomes of such efforts.

NGOs in Colombia had different visions about what lobbying before the U.N. could accomplish. Many groups understood the political dimensions of the different mechanisms but disagreed with the CCJ's decision to focus on obtaining an independent expert and, later, to negotiate the opening of the UNHCHR office. For them, the important political statement was the public censure of the Colombian government reflected in the designation of a country-specific rapporteur. For that reason, many considered the other mechanisms to be less important political statements and objected to "settling" for them.

Many activists arrived at the U.N. expecting a tribunal in which testimony of rights violations would be heard and action taken as a result of solidarity among Latin American nations. They were disillusioned when they found that the Latin American states' representatives at the Commission were unlikely to support activists' demands. Official Latin American delegations often acted to limit the Commission's action in order to prevent a mechanism from being directed at their own governments, and the delegations most likely to support action on the Colombian case have consistently been from Western Europe.[29] The role of Cuba at the Commission has been perhaps most disappointing to activists who identify with Cuba as a model of resistance to U.S. hegemony and of socialist development. The Cuban delegation has been among the most dedicated and effective in minimizing the power of the Commission and opposing efforts to expand human rights mechanisms. In part this has been a response to the relentless U.S. effort to use Commission mechanisms to focus on human rights abuses in Cuba; the United States lobbied successfully for repeated appointments of a special rapporteur for Cuba for more than ten years (Cuba has consistently denied entry to the rapporteur). Cuba has played a leadership role in the Like Minded Group, which has spearheaded many efforts to limit Commission action.

For activists who expected the U.N. to be a human rights tribunal, the Commission meetings were demoralizing, frustrating, and often incomprehensible. Many of the regional human rights representatives who had attended Commission meetings expressed such sentiments. For example, during the 2002 session, I had a conversation with an indigenous leader from southern Colombia. Sitting stiffly in molded wooden chairs after a long day of listening to speeches, slowly drinking his U.S.$10 beer under the fluorescent lights of the Swiss self-serve restaurant, he told me he regretted his decision to come: "I don't see how this makes any sense. No one speaking has any experience of human rights violations, just states and governments, and international NGOs."

Activists critiquing U.N. activism share the CCJ analysis that the Commission is a meeting of states, acting in states' interests, but come to different conclusions. For them, this reality delegitimizes the Commission as a place for authentic human rights activism. They see little point in lobbying governmental representatives who will end up acting in the best interests of their governments and ignoring the serious human rights situations presented to them. Sitting in his office in Medellín, Jaime recalled his three trips to Geneva with strong words. "It is a detestable space," he told me. "It is incredible the way people play with the tragedy of the people there." Jaime had been advocating that NGOs redirect their international efforts toward building alliances with international social movements. "Our logic is to try to build solidarity with those groups, not to depend so much on the benevolence of the governments in the European Union," he said, "although of course you need to work on that too."

Similarly, Rafael ended our interview by calling much of international human rights activism "victor's justice." After describing his twenty years as a union activist and founding member of CREDHOS, he concluded with a sweeping condemnation of the use of the human rights framework in international activism. As a lifelong Communist Party member, he was particularly disturbed by the case of Cuba at the U.N., describing the typical repression in Cuba—jailing of political dissidents—as much better than the murder of political activists in Colombia, yet U.N. action monitoring Cuba has been much more severe. "Look at the case of Cuba. To put a man in jail makes more sense than the 28,000 people killed. The Commission will never name a rapporteur to Colombia, because that would be a black mark against the government, but they do against Cuba." He also objected to the issue of international sanctions and boycotts because of human rights issues: "That is a way of rich countries using human rights to control the resources and economies of poor countries. One doesn't know how to act in terms of the *denuncias,* because they can end up being used by rich countries to control the economy. . . . The issue of human rights is a way that rich countries have found a way to impose their prices on poor countries."

Exploring the multiple sites making up the imagined international community is a central task for ethnographers of transnational activism. Colombian activists also must grapple with how to understand and work in these complicated terrains, featuring transitory and ephemeral moments for activism embedded in unequal power relations and dense networks involving governments, NGOs, and multilateral institutions. Colombian NGOs' international human rights work is not limited to European- and U.S.-based counterpart organizations, however, but also includes efforts to build alliances with regional partners. Many activists also wish to prioritize cross-border subaltern alliances with unions and social movements rather than focus on foreign governments and NGOs. Developing these desires into specific relationships and concrete strategies has proven difficult.

The Colombian NGO lobby at the United Nations is considered an example of an extremely successful NGO campaign. Longtime NGO leaders based in Geneva told me they consider the Colombians a model for nongovernmental participation at the Commission. Much of this success comes from the extraordinary resources marshaled by the Colombian Commission of Jurists. The CCJ enjoyed financial resources that allowed them to devote full-time staff to the issue, convene international conferences for guidance, and spend months living in Geneva. Their political resources included an exceptional network of international contacts and the advice of experienced human rights experts who had led previous lobbying efforts. They were perfectly positioned to develop the credibility of the Colombian NGO campaign. Establishing credibility required the performance of human rights professionalism—knowing how to work the system through a sophisticated advocacy strategy carried out in representation of a consensus NGO position. This consensus was particularly important because if the NGOs were lobbying at cross purposes, government delegates would be hesitant to back what could be viewed as partisan infighting among divided groups. Lobbying activities consisted primarily of meetings with member state delegations, U.N. officials, and international NGOs, including efforts to enlist new NGO networks to support the Colombian initiatives in their own campaigns. This campaign reflected the CCJ's ability to envision the potential for new kinds of action by the Commission and its perceptive analysis of the local rules of the game required to mobilize the Commission for action.

NGO activists' critiques of the lobbying campaign targeting the United Nations focus on the limits of such activism. They point out that such work has been restricted to a limited number of activists and is expensive and time-consuming. Many believe there is little hope for real advances at the United Nations, a body made up of representatives of states where NGOs have a restricted voice and no vote. They suggest that international activism should be redirected to international solidarity by building alliances with social movements around the world rather than pursuing legal human rights cases or lobbying the U.N. and individual governments.

Beyond the specific details of Colombians' advocacy efforts at the United Nations, this case demonstrates the importance of understanding how sites for international activism function as distinct localities, despite their ephemeral temporal and geographic qualities. Focusing on converging networks and temporary nodes can illuminate different status and power relations among institutions as widely varying groups develop joint advocacy strategies. In the Colombian case, advocacy work at the international level profoundly transformed national human rights organizations. The need for a unified lobbying position, required by the professional standard of advocacy, led to the establishment of new coalitions, workshops, and educational efforts at home. Understanding both Colombian support for and criticism of U.N. advocacy campaigns requires exploring the global imaginaries of Colombian activists. Not simply the result of the corrupting influence of international organizations, these campaigns and critiques reflect the agency and aspirations of Colombian activists.

CHAPTER 6

State Activism and the Production of Impunity

Colombian state human rights agencies have transformed the landscape of human rights activism in Colombia over the past decade even while failing to significantly improve the state's record for establishing legal responsibility for abuses and prosecuting the perpetrators. These agencies are profoundly shaped by external pressure, including U.S. and European advice and funding. In many cases staffed by former NGO activists, these agencies have opened new avenues for state activism, enabling one part of the state to marshal resources for action and leverage to influence (but not force) other areas of the state (primarily the military and judicial branches). Absent the significant redistribution of power in society and real political reforms, individual officials in such institutions are extremely limited in their ability to promote accountability.

During our afternoon interviews, Simón would often pull a bottle of rum out of a desk drawer, lean back in his chair with his feet on his desk, and reflect on the challenges of trying to build a new kind of state institution. He told me of tense negotiations with military officers in distant towns, ruminated on the accusations of betrayal issued sotto voce by former NGO colleagues, and worried about the appropriate reactions to news of threats against friends and colleagues. As the director of the Complaints Department (Sección de Quejas) of the Defensoría del Pueblo (sometimes translated as People's Defender), Simón was responsible for sifting through the thousands of cases that reached the office, deciding which to pursue and how best to press for redress. The complaints department was tucked far in the back of a cavernous brick and tile building in an old residential neighborhood in Bogotá, through a painted metal gate, past the security guard (later a metal detector) and the receptionist, across an interior parking lot, up a flight of stairs, and down a seemingly empty hallway. I visited him often as a research consultant for several international human rights organizations in 1995 and 1997, assuming (usually correctly) that he would be able to explain the political intrigue underlying the latest violent twist in the daily news. A reflective and cosmopolitan lawyer, Simón typified the varied career path of many of the first generation of state human rights bureaucrats. He had begun his career as a small-town judge, then worked for several years with a prominent NGO; after resigning from the Defensoría in the late 1990s, he spent a year traveling through India with his actress common-law wife and then began working with the United Nations.

The Defensoría, constantly in flux because of ongoing budget crises, staff changes, and general institutional uncertainty, was one of many examples of the complexities of the new state human rights institutions. Foreign governments, among them the United States, Canada, and members of the European Union, lobbied for, and funded, specific kinds of institutional changes in the Colombian state in what Sonia Cardenas calls transgovernmental activism (Cardenas 2001).[1] These agencies also instituted a new era of shifting relationships and power dynamics between governments and NGOs in the 1990s. The boomerang model of international human rights activism—local NGOs working with international NGOS and sympathetic foreign governments to bring pressure to bear against a repressive state—no longer captured the complicated dynamics between and among states and NGOs. In many cases, state officials received support from NGOs that they did not receive from official colleagues in other state capacities. Colombian NGOs trained local officials, connecting them to national and international networks, while federal prosecutors used international NGOs to bring pressure to bear on archived cases and to gain political asylum abroad when the government was unable to provide protection for their own employees.

Despite their sweeping mandates to ensure that rights are known and protected, Colombian state human rights agencies often contribute to the production of impunity.[2] Impunity is defined by absence: the lack of punishment and sanction for the perpetrator of an abuse and the failure to provide reparations for the victims. Impunity can be produced by indifference, inadequate information, or ignorance of the abuse, as well as by active obstruction of investigations and legal proceedings. Throughout the 1970s and 1980s Latin American governments often simply denied the charges when accused of human rights violations. By the 1990s government claims of indifference or ignorance were no longer politically viable positions to maintain. Foreign governments, activists galvanized by human rights reports, and international agencies specifically mandated to focus on abuses often bring significant political pressure on state authorities to address specific cases. Modern communications technologies have made access to remote areas much faster and easier. Impunity is no longer a default resulting from simple denials but must be produced through government action. By channeling concern about human rights cases into an endless loop of bureaucratic programs, state human rights agencies often serve to minimize effective action in human rights cases. In some cases, these are literally empty gestures, with committees that never meet and offices that are never staffed, with zero budget allocations or no actual programs. In other cases, staff and budget are entirely absorbed in the production of bureaucratic procedures, protocols, and physical infrastructure, only to be dismantled and reassembled with changing political winds, a new president, minister, or director. Exemplified by the expanding thicket of redundant bureaucracies, initiatives, commissions, committees, decrees, and programs, with little coordination and less institutional memory, the production of impunity is the result of a shell game of shifting responsibilities.

This morass of governmental bureaucratic inaction does, however, open opportunities for state officials to act decisively and effectively in certain human rights cases. Individual officials have been able to mobilize the symbolic resources of the state in order to develop state activism on particular cases and to serve as a critical link between civil society groups and other state institutions. These moments of opportunity are created through the fluidity of shifting bureaucracies, what Akhil Gupta has called "seizing on the fissures and ruptures, the contradictions in the policies, programs, institutions and discourses of 'the state' . . . to create possibilities for political action and activism" (Gupta 1995: 394).[3] Individual bureaucrats can act, often against the institutional imperatives of their employers, using the authority and power of the state to legitimate their actions. Simón typified this critical core of visionary officials who risk their careers—and even their lives—and are convinced that through their own actions they can reposition the relationship between state and citizen, acting through their own public service in the modern state as a guarantor of the rule of law. Like many of his former colleagues, Simón traveled among the institutional spaces of NGOs, state agencies, and international organizations and drew from a sophisticated range of sources for his ideas about cosmopolitan citizenship. The reflective voices of state human rights officials themselves offer a profound critique of the limitations and opportunities provided by the state human rights practices instituted in Colombia.

Paradoxically, state human rights agencies themselves contribute to the higher profile of human rights cases that makes the production of impunity necessary. Significant progress has been made on a number of high-profile cases in the investigatory stage by committed government prosecutors and investigators, many working in the human rights offices of the Fiscalía (the Attorney General's Office) and the Defensoría, without the institutional changes in the legal system necessary to bring the cases to a satisfactory legal resolution. Frustrated by the established inability of the Colombian legal system to adequately handle such cases, these investigators often take their evidence to international organizations, including Human Rights Watch and Amnesty International. The results of these investigations then circulate as international human rights reporting produced by nongovernmental organizations used to bring pressure on the government (Human Rights Watch 2000, 2001). Offering evidence and conclusions from state agencies adds to the legitimacy of international NGOs' claims.

Understanding the action and inaction of these agencies requires examining the specificities of the state and the history of particular institutions: how and why they are formed and in response to what political pressures and needs. This includes the complicated, and often impossible to fully trace, business of tracking funding for the state, trying to identify where the funding originates and how it is allocated. This enterprise also involves exploring the daily encounters and engagement between and among citizens and the different agencies of the state and how those encounters constitute the state. After a brief review of recent scholarship on state human rights agencies, I discuss the convoluted evolution of state human rights efforts. To illuminate how government action produces impunity, I examine the circulation of official correspondence after a large massacre, the state human rights narrative in one bureaucrat's account of violence in one region, and travel with a mixed NGO and governmental commission visiting a community after a paramilitary incursion. I conclude with the stories of officials who use their past experience as NGO activists to explain their attempts to carry out state activism on behalf of wrongly imprisoned peasants and protesters, showing the paradoxical if limited opportunities for advances in individual cases.

NEW VIEWS OF STATE AGENCIES

Colombia is not alone in the mushrooming phenomenon of state human rights agencies. Political scientists estimate that between three hundred and five hundred such institutions around the world had been created by the turn of the century, the vast majority in the 1990s (Cardenas 2001). Funded by international organizations (including the Open Society and the Ford and Rockefeller Foundations) and other governments (primarily European Union countries, Canada, and the United States), these agencies were the product of many changes in the "new world order" of the 1990s, including the post–cold war expansion of international funding for redesigning states and nation-building operations in Eastern Europe, for democratizing states in Latin America, and for the development of second-generation postcolonial states in Africa. While some scholars emphasize the ways in which globalization and neoliberal privatizations have reduced state authority and services (Hall and Biersteker 2002; Strange 1996), these agencies demonstrate an area where state functions are expanded, albeit often in contradictory ways. Through the appropriation of human rights education and documentation efforts that had previously been conducted by NGOs, these new institutions involved the conspicuous redeployment of the state as able to police its own efforts to implement a broad range of citizen rights.

Jane Collier and Shannon Speed offer one of the few anthropological approaches to this issue to date in an article on the Mexican government's use of human rights legislation to restrict the rights of the indigenous population in Chiapas. They are harshly critical of the appropriation of human rights language by state agencies: "The state government of Chiapas appears 'colonialist,' not just in imposing a literal interpretation of human rights documents on indigenous peoples, but, more importantly, in using the discourse of human rights to justify intervening in the affairs of indigenous communities whose leaders happen to displease government officials" (Collier and Speed 2000: 4). Their work draws on the traditional anthropological focus on small indigenous communities in confrontation or outright opposition to a relatively powerful national state, arguing that the human rights framework has been yet another tool appropriated by the state to enforce its hegemony. While I agree with their conclusions, in the Colombian human rights debate (as opposed to the indigenous rights debate), cultural difference is not a primary location for the deployment of state power. In my analysis I am more interested in how such agencies ensure impunity even as the struggle to assert different bureaucratic interests presents fleeting possibilities for action.

The vast majority of research on state human rights agencies has been concerned with mapping the new institutional landscape of human rights state agencies, in primarily descriptive accounts provided by practioners, legal scholars, and political scientists (Hossain 2000; Human Rights Watch 2001; Pinheiro and Baluarte 2000; Reif 2000; United Nations 1995). These accounts tend to fall into two camps: critical assessments concluding that such institutions are merely window dressing and public relations for abusive governments or laudatory accounts stressing that their existence demonstrates goodwill and progress. Neither approach has paid significant attention to analyzing the details of institutional evolution and program development. The Web site of the National Human Rights Institutions News (www.nhri.net) offers the most comprehensive survey of the expanding list of conference proceedings and reports. Cardenas has classified five kinds of national human rights bodies in her work: ombudsman offices, national human rights commissions, hybrids of the two, thematic human rights commissions (addressing specific issues or vulnerable populations), and national bodies devoted to international humanitarian law.

While generally considered domestic ("national") institutions, human rights agencies cannot be understood outside their complex relationship with transnational NGOs and other governments. Many are profoundly if not decisively shaped by what Cardenas calls transgovernmental activism—active promotion of specific institutional mandates and programs by governments (primarily the United States, Canada, and Western Europe), which include training, funding, and advising. Her work emphasizes the transnational dimension of domestic state agencies: "In principle, NHRIs [national human rights institutions] are important precisely because they serve to politicize human rights issues, or inject them into national political discourse and practice. This development is occurring in two key ways. First, NHRIs reflect how governments embed international human rights norms in domestic structures, and thereby reshape state-society relations. Second, NHRIs are forging new transgovernmental networks of human rights bureaucracies, parallel to transnational networks of governmental groups." She has focused on the role of the Canadian National Human Rights Commission, but she draws on the work of other political scientists and legal theorists who are beginning to point to the expanded role of governments in the creation of new kinds of state institutions by *other* governments (Cardenas 2001, 2003).

Ann-Marie Slaughter's influential study, *A New World Order,* for example, argues that the development of increasingly elaborate informal intergovernmental networks is playing an important role in the international exchange of information, policies, and enforcement. Though Slaughter focuses on cooperation between national judicial authorities and international and regional courts, she makes a broader argument for the role of these networks in the expansion of human rights, finance, the environment, and the fight against organized crime (Slaughter 2004).

Some state human rights agencies define their mandates exclusively in terms of transgovernmental activism. In U.S. state bureaucracies, human rights issues are treated exclusively as a foreign policy issue, and U.S. governmental human rights efforts are devoted exclusively to attempting to influence the behavior of other governments. Those issues that would be considered within the scope of human rights agencies in other countries—such as discrimination, police brutality, and state-sponsored violence—are dealt with in a range of other domestic agencies (e.g., the Department of Labor or civil rights commissions) and considered under the framework of civil rights.[4] Human rights issues are considered in terms of foreign policy debates, that is, how the United States should relate to abusive governments; the U.S. government's human rights record is assessed in terms of the degree to which the United States has participated in abuses abroad. The only U.S. state human rights agency is the Bureau of Democracy, Human Rights and Labor, which is part of the State Department, the lead federal agency charged with implementing U.S. foreign policy and representing U.S. interests abroad.[5] In contrast, Canada and many Western European countries have established national human rights commissions and ombudsman's offices to address domestic human rights concerns. These agencies, many of which were established as part of expanding welfare states of the 1960s, were designed to administer and enforce antidiscrimination legislation and as a means for the average citizen to lodge complaints and seek redress for bureaucratic unfairness, abuses, or incompetence.

Officials in these European, U.S., and Canadian agencies have been very active in promoting the establishment of governmental human rights institutions abroad as a means of addressing the human rights problems in those countries. This reflects the power dynamic of human rights agencies internationally, which flows from North America and Europe to African, Asian, and Latin American countries that presumably have greater numbers of human rights violations within their borders. This transgovernmental activism plays a critical role in establishing other such institutions in those countries, through the use of diplomatic pressure (including threats of sanctions and other punitive measures) and the provision of resources such as training and funding. As with the establishment of NGOs, the alchemy of international pressure and funding, combined with local political cultures and institutional values, has produced ambivalent and complicated organizations facing widely varying domestic situations. The ombudsman's office in El Salvador, for example, was established through the peace accords that ended the civil war there in 1991. Modeled on the Canadian ombudsman's office, the institution has been faced with significantly different challenges. Candenas notes, "The role of human rights commissions in Canada, for example, is focused on issues of equality, including pay equity and employment equity, not on the kinds of rights violations—such as disappearances, torture, and other serious violations—with which El Salvador is currently most concerned" (Cardenas 2003: 4). Elsewhere she writes:

> Highly diverse governments around the world are creating similar NHRIs largely for international reasons: international norms provide standards for national institution building, concrete forms of international assistance facilitate this process, and more diffuse international pressures (including from international economic sources) make nominal human rights improvements highly desirable. The second part of my argument is that the international origins of these national institutions leave an unintended and overlooked legacy. Despite important national differences, many NHRIs have the following paradoxical effect: they are unable to provide effective protection against human rights violations, at the same time that they create an unprecedented high demand for such protection. The ensuing institutional dynamics are far more uncertain than either unbridled optimism or cynical skepticism would suggest. (Cardenas 2001: 3)

In the case of Colombia, the human rights ombudsman's office has played precisely this contradictory role. The agency has developed official programs focusing on the rights of myriad populations—including women, indigenous people, Afro-Colombians, and children—as well as thematic issues, such as the right to a clean environment. As a result, the office has on more than one occasion issued reports and recommendations directly at odds with policy decisions by the administration or other ministries, despite having little long-term success in changing such governmental decisions. By providing educational programs as well as investigating abuses, however, particular officials have proven to be critical allies for Colombian and international NGOs.

THE PRESIDENTIAL HUMAN RIGHTS ADVISER

The Colombian state has developed one of the most complicated networks of human rights institutions anywhere in the world. A combination of constitutional mandates, congressional legislation, and executive decrees has created overlapping networks of agencies, committees, and commissions charged with educating citizens about their rights, monitoring the human rights situation, and implementing human rights policies. The first federal state human rights agency was the Presidential Special Adviser for Human Rights (Consejero Presidencial para los Derechos Humanos), created in 1987 by President Virgilio Barco as part of his peace efforts. Human rights concerns were raised by demobilizing guerrillas during the course of negotiations with the government to focus public awareness about the torture of their jailed comrades. While not a cabinet-level position, the Consejería (Special Adviser's Office) was originally housed in the presidential palace and, as the first official state human rights initiative, was awarded press attention disproportionate to the small staff. The Colombian historian and statesman Alvaro Tirado was the first such presidential adviser, and he left a significant legacy in shaping the state's human rights message. He originated the state slogan, "Human rights are everyone's obligation" *(los derechos humanos son obligación de todos),* which contributed to the first major conceptual shift of human rights—from being viewed as part of the leftist political agenda to being positioned for broader support. This slogan was also indicative of the government's efforts to relocate responsibility for political violence from state agents to society. Such efforts have been severely criticized by NGOs for diluting accountability and distracting public attention from the issue of state-sponsored violence.

Alvaro was typical of many of Colombian governmental human rights officials in his extensive education and experience. Like Simón, he began with NGO activism, continued with graduate education (most officials studied in Europe, often in France), and went on to work extensively with international human rights organizations. The curriculum vitae posted on the U.N. Web site tells part of his story. He graduated in 1968 with a law and political science degree from the University of Antioquia in his hometown of Medellín and went on to complete a doctoral degree in history in Paris. He was a founding member of the Permanent Committee for Human Rights and, according to his CV, remains a member in good standing. After serving as Special Adviser for Human Rights from November 1987 to May 1989, he worked as a consultant with the

United Nations Development Program, was appointed Colombian ambassador to Switzerland (1992–95), and was a member of the OAS Inter-American Commission on Human Rights (1992–99).

I heard some of his other stories when I met with him in his Bogotá apartment, where we sat on low white leather chairs surrounded by oversized coffee table books and small sculptures. He began by describing his consciousness of human rights as originating during the period when the National Security Law was passed by Turbay and the abuses that were committed thereafter. Alvaro told me he had been a leftist but was very careful to clarify his position; he was part of the "nationalist left" that, as he put it, "wasn't thinking about the problems of what was going on in China or the Soviet Union but rather what was happening in Colombia." He worked on the leftist magazine *Alternativa* and in the short-lived leftist movement Firmes. The first president of the Permanent Committee, Hector Abad Gómez, was a close friend and distant relative of his wife's, and Alvaro worked on Abad's campaign when he ran for mayor in the first election after the 1986 reforms that allowed for the popular election of local officials. Abad was killed during the campaign in 1987.

Shortly after Abad's assassination, President Barco called Alvaro and asked if he wanted to be the presidential adviser and organize the Consejería. He agreed to develop the office after serious misgivings. Colombia in the late 1980s was teetering on what several political scientists deemed the "edge of chaos": political and drug violence were on the increase, and the Medellín Cartel had declared war on the state, conducting a campaign of public narcoterrorism and offering a bounty for each policeman killed (Leal Buitrago and Zamosc 1990). Despite the difficulties, Alvaro told me, he did not regret his choice: "I would do it again, for several reasons. One was to see how democratic discourse was incorporated into the state. It should not be that to be a human rights defender you had to be on the left. It is an obligation of the state." Alvaro listed a number of important steps Barco took, including making paramilitary groups illegal. The most controversial issue of the time was the military. Alvaro explained, "People couldn't believe that he [Barco] was talking about human rights, of course they said that was to domesticate the army. The fact was that he introduced the human rights issue to the police and the armed forces because they were very penetrated." When I asked him to explain, he continued:

> During that time the drug traffickers were so strong, there were undoubtedly people from the police and the army connected with drug trafficking and

other things. There had to be a purge of all these people, that of course could not be done from one moment to the next, and that is why it was such a desperate situation. Even more, things like these caused people to think that we had to get rid of a number of colonels, but we saw that those who were coming up in the ranks were worse. So there needed to be policies if this was going to work—and I don't think the experience has been bad. After fifteen years the Consejería has played a good intellectual role.

Alvaro went on to describe his work with the military as discreet lobbying and discussion rather than public confrontation with abusive officers.

Like the human rights initiatives that would follow, the Consejería was poorly staffed and funded largely from abroad. During our interview, he recalled the critical role of international funding in establishing the office, especially funding from European countries, including France and Holland. The U.S. government provided money for a database project intended to track abuses. By the end of his tenure, the office had what he called "a good team" but a total staff of only fourteen people.

Then as now, the issue of human rights was viewed as extremely dangerous, contributing to Alvaro's sense of isolation: "I called people, even good people in human rights, and during the first phase they were afraid of working with me. . . . Those first months, no one wanted to work because they would be killed, or because people would accuse them of selling out by working with the state, but especially the fear, it was very hard. We created a team and an office in the presidential palace, at that time more than the actual work it was a message to the military that we had the support of the president." He described many of the frustrations of what he called "thankless work" in state human rights bureaucracies, emphasizing the emotional toll of the office: "Many of the dead were friends of mine. I even came to cry for friends of mine who were killed." He also talked about the frustration of hearing constant criticism from NGOs that he viewed as unrealistic: "People criticized so much, *dándole palo a uno*, telling you that you are covering up for the state. It pained me a lot. And it was very frustrating, because even if you do many things, in this country, with the disaster that exists, here we have to work on the medium and long term. Stopping things immediately is impossible; we are not working so things stop immediately but for something that cannot yet be seen." Finally, Alvaro credited his personal convictions as influencing his decision to leave the state system after completing his initial commitment of a year and half: "I believe in human rights internally, but I don't want to be a human rights bureaucrat, I don't want to make a career of human rights, otherwise I would have left to found my own

NGO. But I don't want that. I was there because I was convinced, in the political moment that I was there, and then I thought it was over and I left."

Before his departure Alvaro had the opportunity to work on the 1991 Constitution, then being drafted by a National Constitutional Assembly following peace talks with the M-19 and a campaign by civic movements to rewrite the national charter. He described how the Consejería played an important role in promoting the inclusion of new rights in the Constitution, and in the creation of one of the most important new human rights agencies, the Defensoría del Pueblo. Designed after careful study of the Spanish Defensoría, it was intended to be the nation's major human rights agency. The Colombian Defensoría is a "mixed" institution, combining elements of Ombudsman and Human Rights Commissions, according to Cardenas's typology of state agencies (Cardenas 2003: 783). The Defensoría has a broad mandate to educate citizens about their rights and protect them from abuse but no enforcement power. The ombudsman is elected by Congress from a field of three candidates nominated by the president; he in turn appoints regional and departmental omsbudsmen. Thematic bureaus focusing on collective rights, such as indigenous or environmental rights, operate out of the national office. In local areas, the Defensoría often works with *personeros*, a municipal ombudsman position that originated in the Spanish colonial system. Aspiring *personeros* must be approved by local councils and hold a law degree, which makes filling the position extremely difficult in many remote rural municipalities. Beginning in the mid-1980s the municipal ombudsman offices, originally designed as one of the local checks on corruption and other forms of official abuse, were increasingly charged with "human rights" oversight. With an extremely vague mandate, the actual work done by local *personeros* depends greatly on the personality and inclination of the individual official.[6]

THE ENDLESS LOOP

Following the development of the Consejería and the Defensoría, human rights programs expanded dramatically in the 1990s, including initiatives in the Interior Ministry and the Foreign Ministry (Cancellería). The judicial agencies established in the 1991 Constitution, the Fiscalía (charged with the investigation and prosecution of most crimes) and the Procuraduría (charged with investigating official misconduct), also established human rights units.[7] The vast human rights bureaucracy developed by the Ministry of Defense is discussed in the next chapter. What follows is not intended as a complete survey but a highlight of the major institutions to allow an idea of the range of programs.

In the institutional framework of the Defensoría and the existing ministries, the human rights programs of the Colombian government can appear to be an endless loop of efforts resulting in remarkably little forward motion. These programs include commissions, which bring together officials from state agencies, NGOs, and international organizations for periodic meetings on specific cases; monitoring initiatives, which focus information sharing efforts among government agencies to prevent future attacks; and the establishment of new human rights offices (such as new offices within different ministries, or addressing specific concerns). These efforts appear to exist largely to satisfy international pressure for governmental action, and they often succeed in deflecting public scrutiny. With the constant circulation of international officials (postings to diplomatic missions, international funding organizations, and the United Nations rarely exceed two years), many of the international officials view each of these programs as new initiatives without any awareness of their history.

The number of commissions convened since the mid-1990s has increased exponentially. The first major joint-government effort was Commission 1533, created by Decree 1533 of 1994, the result of negotiated peace accords between the government and the Socialist Renovation Current, a dissident wing of the ELN.[8] Commission 1533 was intended to serve as a place where NGO representatives and officials could discuss governmental human rights policies and measures to address specific incidents. A year after its founding, NGOs broke with the commission, and it was dissolved following Samper's August 1995 declaration of "internal commotion"—similar to a state of siege—after a series of massacres in Urabá.[9] In July 1996 the Samper administration created an interinstitutional governmental body, Commission 1290, to discuss the implementation of international recommendations regarding human rights. After several years during which the commission never met, there were a few sporadic meetings that did not advance beyond attempting to define logistical details. The Samper administration also created the Pressure and Follow-up Committee (Comité de Seguimiento y Impulse) to oversee high-priority cases. Since then an ever-expanding number of commissions have been created to bring together officials, NGOs, and, in many cases, international organizations to focus on specific regions (a partial list includes commissions for Urabá, Meta, Barrancabermeja,

Arauca, the Middle Magdalena Valley, and the Macizo, a mountainous region that includes parts of five southern departments).[10]

As the programs, initiatives, and commissions proliferated, new umbrella committees and directorates were established to coordinate their efforts. In 1994 the government established the National Human Rights Network, funded by the government of the Netherlands and designed to facilitate information exchange among different entities responsible for human rights in Colombia; despite millions of dollars in funding, the program was never operational.[11] Law 199 of 1995 mandated the creation of a central coordinating body within the government to create and implement a coherent national human rights policy; to my knowledge it was never implemented. Decree 0372 of 1996 created the General Administrative Special Directorate for Human Rights (Dirección General Unidad Administrativa Especial para los Derechos Humanos), which functioned within the Ministry of the Interior (formerly the Ministry of Government, later merged into the Ministry of Justice). The Directorate's mandate focused on four areas: prevention of human rights abuses, protection for human rights activists, legal support for human rights initiatives, and attention to internally displaced people. The protection programs for witnesses and victims (the Special Program for the Protection of Witnesses and Victims of Human Rights Abuses and Persons at Risk) included a division for "soft" protection—personal security precautions and relocation—and one for "hard" protection—armed bodyguards and armored cars. The Committee for the Rules and Risk Evaluation, composed of both government and NGO representatives, established the protection procedures and recommended which cases would receive priority.

In addition to the creation of new programs, the few agencies that functioned were dissolved and re-created in new institutional guises. In 1998 President Andres Pastrana dissolved the Consejería and gave the vice president's office the national mandate for establishing and implementing human rights policies. U.S. policy makers—in the process of designing a massive aid package for Colombia—heralded the move as an example of Pastrana's commitment to human rights. In fact, the office of the vice president in Colombia has been largely symbolic, with little institutional power. Many previous vice presidents have spent their terms serving as ambassadors. NGO activists criticized the vice president's lack of human rights training, his insufficient political commitment, and the conflict of interest that would exist while serving in a position simultaneously charged with politically supporting the president and designing human rights policy. In a more extreme example, during the final months of his term, Gustavo Bell simultaneously served as vice president, minister of defense, and human rights adviser.

Another round of repeating programs has been established with funding from USAID. The first Uribe administration (2002–6) established the Human Rights Observatory, which coordinates human rights programs out of the vice president's office and publishes a bilingual bulletin in English and Spanish. They have also revived the idea of a national information sharing system, now called the Early Warning System, which is designed to ensure coordinated state response to threatened attacks and is also funded by the United States; many of the officials I interviewed concluded that the system serves to warn but does not instigate a response to threats and attacks. As of July 2002 the most comprehensive document outlining Colombia's multiple state human rights agencies was the Planning Department Comprehensive Review (Conpes), which contained over forty pages of programs and events but no analysis of how much of this effort was actually being implemented. These endless loops, parallel institutional structures, and bureaucratic mazes severely complicate efforts by both domestic activists and international agencies to engage with Colombian officials on human rights issues.

THE PRODUCTION OF IMPUNITY

The higher profile of human rights campaigns in the post–cold war period created increased demands for accountability, such as the civic letter-writing campaigns of Amnesty International, the rulings and declarations of international bodies such as the U.N. and the OAS, and foreign governments' insistence on reform as a condition of assistance. Human rights programs became an established part of the agenda of international development programs and a central element of "democratization" efforts around the world. The speed and geographic reach of new technologies have made the global public more aware of such abuses than during any other time in history. These campaigns to mobilize shame did spur governments to action but often not in the ways activists intended. While the focus of most of this international activism was on accountability and bringing the perpetrators of human rights violations to justice, instead the result was often a growing number of human rights programs without an accompanying increase in prosecutions of abusers.

By channeling this activism into the endless circulation and exchange of information in these institutions, state human rights agencies contributed to the production of impunity.

The officials from foreign governments (the U.S. Congress, the U.S. and Canadian embassies, and European Union programs) and international organizations (the U.N. or funding programs) all expressed frustration with the multiplicity of agencies and programs. One U.N. official described his meetings with the Colombian government as spinning his wheels because of "lack of traction." Each encounter appeared to start from zero, with different officials attending each meeting, no written record of agreements, and no follow-up.

Some officials from within the Colombian government confessed similar concerns to me during interviews. Sonia, who worked in the Department of Planning, told me, "We realized that the efforts were too isolated, all the different organizations, the Defensoría, the Foreign Ministry, the Ministry of the Interior, the Ministry of Defense, the Police. Everyone had their own human rights programs. Here at Planning we learned about the programs because they all sent programs for funding, and they were all very similar programs. . . . The overlap is remarkable." While some had differing mandates and responsibilities, she admitted, the majority focused their human rights program on the same thing: human rights education. "They should work together if they are doing the same kind of thing—human rights education. But no. Each one publishes their own little pamphlets, each one does their own thing. Why? Because that is the state [eso es el estado]. They duplicate the efforts, basically it is a problem of training—of everyone doing the same kind of training in human rights." According to Sonia, the Department of Planning has attempted to reduce replicated efforts, holding yet more meetings to coordinate funding and programs, but she admitted that the issues "have yet to be resolved."

The production of impunity is in part a result of reprisals against state officials. Investigating human rights abuses is often extremely dangerous work, and state officials are rightly concerned that they will fall prey to abusers anxious to avoid detection. While no comprehensive tally exists, a number of human rights officials have been threatened and attacked, and a significant number have been killed because of their activism on human rights cases. In its report on the Attorney General's Human Rights Unit, Human Rights Watch quoted the Bogotá daily El Tiempo, which found that 196 Unit staff had received serious death threats in a twenty-one-month period from 2000 and 2001; the report went on to list at least 19 judicial investigators and prosecutors who had been killed since 1998 as a result of their work (Human Rights Watch 2002: 11). The report concluded that the attorney general had largely ignored the safety issue for his staff, and in fact made them more vulnerable.

The lack of money and staff has also prevented the institutional development of state human rights agencies. Despite the sweeping mandates outlined in human rights policy, the budgets and staff of state human rights agencies are pitifully small. To cite only two examples, only thirty-five prosecutors were assigned by the Attorney General's Office to handle hundreds of the most complex human rights cases, most involving multiple victims and perpetrators. The vice president's human rights bureaucracies have never had more than thirty people on staff, despite being required to cover the entire country.

Human rights agencies, chronically underfunded, are often the first to suffer budget cuts. During the height of the Samper administration's expansion of new human rights programs, I interviewed a number of officials about their budget problems for a report on the situation of human rights defenders published by a Washington-based NGO (Tate 1997). "This is supposed to be the year of human rights, and Samper is killing us by cutting the budget," *defensor* José Fernando Castro Caicedo told me in 1997. "I'm not sure if it is retaliation for our criticism of his administration, but we requested U.S.$6 million for next year, and we got U.S.$400,000. When we asked the people at the Planning Administration if human rights were a priority or not, they said no. So you see the contradiction between what he says and what his administration does" (quoted in Tate 1997: 34). The directors of several smaller programs told me their budget problems were so severe that they could not carry out their daily work. In one case, an agreement with the Colombian Red Cross to provide humanitarian support to threatened people needing immediate protection had yet to be signed, and the aid remained undelivered for months; the delay was explained by several officials as the result of the fact that Ministry of the Interior's human rights office lacked money for basic office supplies, including paper for official correspondence.

As a result of the critical role of transgovernmental activism in the creation of state human rights agencies and the lack of domestic governmental funding, many state agencies have turned to applying for international funding from foreign governments and international foundations. In many instances, informal lobbying with the international diplomatic corps has been central to channeling funding to specific projects.[12] One official I interviewed repeatedly had worked in various state human rights agencies for his entire career, beginning with the Consejería in 1994, only to find that political changes in the bureaucratic structure reduced his access to the diplomatic corps and thus funding for his programs. He had begun his human rights career lobbying the Colombian Congress about human rights legislation, went on to work on cases before the Organization of American States, the commissions created to investigate the largest massacres, and finally moved on to policy. At the time we had coffee in a downtown Dunkin' Donuts across the street from the rebuilt Palace of Justice, he complained that his leverage at work had declined considerably. Before, he could speak directly with the vice president. "Sometimes he paid attention to me," he said, "sometimes he didn't, but it was a connection to someone who had decision-making power." Now he had to channel his communication through another level of program directors. He could also no longer speak directly to representatives of the international diplomatic corps: "Before, I could take advantage of the energy of the international community. I could use the meetings to ask for funding for small projects or develop interest in particular projects, like the peace communities. For example, I asked for money for the witness protection program, because the Fiscalía didn't have one. It wasn't much money, $60,000 to $80,000 [in U.S. dollars]. We used it to protect a lot of people, and it meant that we had very good relations with the Fiscalia. But I don't know what has happened to that now."

A woman who also began her human rights career with the Consejería, told me of the first educational campaigns following the 1991 Constitution to teach people about their new rights: "We worked on empowering the local people, like teaching people about the role of the *personeros,* the local human rights committees. We worked to strengthen local organizations, black and indigenous organizations." The program was funded by the Dutch embassy under its technical assistance program.[13] The French government funded the publicity campaigns on human rights education, including human rights fairs and a train that followed the old train route from Bogotá to the Atlantic Coast, stopping for two-day cultural fairs in small towns along the rails. "We had videos and documents that we would pass out, about human rights, and we would set up quick consulting on human rights complaints," she explained. Among their cultural activities, they held national and international conferences on human rights, published books about the issue, and supported civil society groups. After leaving the Consejería, she worked on the human rights program of the Procuraduría; at the time of our interview, she was working with a U.S.-based consulting firm that had been contracted by USAID to administer the U.S.-funded human rights program by delivering grants and training to Colombian NGOs and governmental agencies.

This pattern of funding has a number of unintended consequences, including the development of a more porous relationship between NGOs and certain state agencies. Highly trained human rights professionals circulate between NGOs, state agencies, and international institutions, while the same bodies fund all three. State agencies cannot help but develop the same funding dynamic as NGOs, becoming project driven and tailoring their programs to the funding interests of foreign governments and international agencies. As a result, governmental agencies become subjects to the classic critiques of externally funded NGOs. Their accountability is no longer to their constituencies—citizens—but to foreign governments and agencies. Such funding is often unsustainable, subject to the whims and passions of the funding source. In the final twist, their competition becomes NGOs, as state agencies apply to the same sources of funding for many similar kinds of projects.

FROM THE GOVERNMENT'S FILES: THE CHENGUE CASE

The Vice President's Human Rights Program file on the Chengue case exemplified how international concern was channeled into a seemingly endless circulation of letters and faxes while exchanging remarkably little actual information. The massacre happened in a small town in Sucre on the Atlantic Coast where dozens of people were killed with machetes and stones on January 17, 2001. Several factors contributed to the prominence of the massacre. The first was the dramatic story and brutality of the killing, conducted by hand after the perpetrators dragged the victims from their homes during the night. Prior to the massacre, local residents had repeatedly requested government protection.[14] The killings were also covered extensively in the *Washington Post. Post* correspondent Scott Wilson told me months later over coffee in a chic Bogotá coffee shop that the interviews he conducted with survivors of this and other massacres in nearby towns, some in still-bloodstained surroundings, had profoundly affected him. Local military commanders and paramilitary death squads were implicated in the massacre; military forces in the region were under the command of navy Admiral General Rodrigo Quiñonoz, who had been trailing accusations of participation in massacres in the regions where he served since the early 1990s. The official human rights file on the Chengue case was a thick collection of faded press clippings, fuzzy copies, and official government documents.

As I flipped through the file in the sunny courtyard of the Vice President's Human Rights Program, I was struck by the way in which the documents represented the modern circulation of human rights information. Rather than address the details of the case itself, or the progress of the legal investigation, the file was primarily correspondence between and among governmental offices and NGO activists stating concern about the case. The paperwork included domestic communication loops, from Colombian NGOs and among state agencies; and transnational communication loops, including inquiries from international NGOs and governmental missives from one governmental representative to another.

The first layers in the file involved domestic circulation between governmental agencies. It contained public press sources and alternative media from the Internet; rather than appear to have access to privileged state secrets, the minimal details provided in official documents suggested that newspaper reporting might offer them much-needed information about the case. The first paper was an official letter from the vice president's office regarding "Case 11391," requesting information from the Fiscalía and Procuraduría. That was followed by a yellowing newspaper clipping about the investigation involving Quiñonez in the case; the printout of an email urgent action announcing the assassination of a prosecutor investigating the case from Equipo Nizkor, a human rights group focused on distributing information about Latin America via the Internet; and a copy of a Peace Brigades biweekly update with a note about the case. The response to the first letter summarized progress on the case: the United Self-Defense Forces of Colombia, the nation's largest paramilitary group, was responsible for the massacre. The letter named Rodrigo Antiono Mercado Pelufo, alias "cadena," and those under his control as the individuals who carried out the killings and concluded that the investigation was still in preliminary stages, with no arrests made.

Transnational communication included both state-to-state exchanges and letters from NGO activists and international organizations concerned about the case. Again, none of these exchanges contained anything beyond minimal details; most seemed dedicated to raising the profile of the case itself rather than a genuine effort to illuminate the details of state action. One layer of the file contained a letter to the vice president from the foreign affairs director of the Foreign Ministry along with a communiqué from the World Organization Against Torture listing the Chengue case (and the case of immigrant children on a hunger strike in

Spain). Urgent action letters from Spain, the United States, Switzerland, and Austria, in English and Spanish, were stacked in the file. Following them was a letter to the Canadian ambassador from the vice president's office in response to his inquiries about the case, describing the vice president's trip to the region and the issue of the assassination of the mayor of Juradó, also under investigation; a fax from the embassy lay under the letter. A fax from the Colombian embassy in Washington reported that it had received a letter from Amnesty International's office in Washington and the response from the vice president's office. The final pile contained a fax from the president's office with a copy of the letter from the Chicago Religious Leadership Network on Latin America; urgent actions from Finland, England, Germany, and Colombian human rights organizations; a request for information from the Colombian embassy in England; a few more newspaper clippings; and more urgent actions.

Aside from the newspaper articles, the only document that demonstrated any familiarity with the specific details of the region and the case was a letter from the captain of a counterguerrilla battalion of the Colombian army. In it, the captain shifts the burden of proof from law enforcement agencies to human rights agencies and activists. His insistence that local officials provide proof of wrongdoing to military offices could be read as a threat, as military collaboration with paramilitary forces in the region was well known. Dated approximately four months after the massacre and directed to the municipal human rights ombudsman (personero) from the area, the letter informs him that the few peasants who remained in the area were able to harvest their crops without problems (sin contratiempos), thanks to the presence of the troops from the battalion, and that while no civilians remain in Chengue, the area is known as a corridor traversed by the bandoleros of the FARC. The captain instructs the personero to send witnesses and anyone with a human rights complaint to the Human Rights office of the battalion. These offices, explored in detail in chapter 7, were created in the mid-1990s as part of the military's public relations campaign and on the battalion level function within the psychological warfare division. By insisting that anyone concerned with human rights abuses "expand their testimony" to military officers could be read—and probably would be read—as an effort to intimidate such witnesses into silence in a region where previous complaints have been met with reprisals and credible evidence suggests ongoing military involvement in human rights crimes. "Finally," the letter continues, "given your closeness to the rural areas, respectfully we request that you inform us if guerrilla camps exist or not with the object of preventing them from continuing to commit crimes [*delinquiendo*] and in general abusing the civilian population." With this request, the military attempts to convert the municipal ombudsman into a military informant, making him responsible for the quality of military intelligence in the region. The letter was also sent to the Procuraduría, the Defensoría, the vice president, and the United Nations.

Missing from the government's file on the Chengue case were any specific notes from meetings held to discuss the case and assign responsibilities, or any direct communication with the community. Letters reference the vice president's trip to the region but offer no details of what he witnessed or specific measures the government intends to take in the case.

The Chengue investigation remains ongoing; to date no arrests have been made. Yolanda Paternina, a prosecutor working on the case, reported death threats; she was killed in front of her home on August 29, 2003, after arresting three men allegedly involved in the massacre. A witness in the case, one of the survivors of the massacre, and three judicial investigators involved in the case were later also killed. General Quiñonez was appointed military attaché to Israel, one of Colombia's largest weapons suppliers. A political officer at the Colombian embassy in Washington assured me that this was certainly a harsh punishment for the general, whom she described as a real *tropero*, only happy when out in the field directing troops. According to a Reuters news story, his visa to the United States was revoked because of "suspected links to drug trafficking" (Webb 2002). He has yet to be tried.

THE STATE HUMAN RIGHTS NARRATIVE
AND THE STORY OF A MASSACRE

President Alvaro Uribe, first elected in 2002, dissolved the Office of the Presidential Adviser for Human Rights and replaced it with the Vice President's Human Rights Program. USAID had made the office a centerpiece of its $20 million human rights program, unaware that the vice president rarely influenced policy. The USAID moneys funded educational programs, conferences, and a newsletter (produced in English and Spanish, presumably in order to present the Colombian government's human rights advances to the U.S. Congress).

The program was housed in a restored rowhouse in the old colonial section of downtown Bogotá, several blocks behind the presidential palace and Congress. Like the NGO offices, there was no sign to alert passersby of the office's purpose; from the street, the only thing differentiating the house from its neighbors was a slightly more recent paint job. I knocked on the shuttered wooden door, which opened to reveal only a sliver of uniformed (and armed) guard, asking me why I was there. Impressed enough by my *gringa* appearance and claim of an appointment, he allowed me to pass into the hallway to the receptionist, who in turn offered me a plastic badge in exchange for my driver's license and told me to take a seat on one of the wooden chairs beside a tall doorway. The walls in the small waiting area were lined with cheaply printed posters in English advertising a truth commission in Indonesia. I could see the typical layout of many colonial buildings through the half-open door: the first floor had offices open to a square-tiled courtyard atrium, which was filled with small tables and seated officials drinking coffee; on the second floor above us, the offices lined an open passageway overlooking the courtyard below.

I had expected the interview to be canceled, because the night before, in an emergency nine o'clock press conference, President Pastrana had finally declared an end to the peace talks with the guerrillas. The negotiations had been the centerpiece of his administration and had taken place in the "despeje" (demilitarized zone), five municipalities in southern Colombia (described in the media as an area the size of Switzerland) where the government had withdrawn military and police presence and allowed the FARC free rein. Now the security forces were in the process of retaking the region, and human rights officials were concerned that violence would escalate. I decided to go to the scheduled interview anyway, as waiting rooms often offered rich fieldwork opportunities. To my surprise, Iván, the director of cases for the Vice President's Human Rights Program, was happy to talk to me.

Iván ushered me into his corner office. He was dressed in the uniform of a midlevel state official, pink shirt and blue tie and a big watch with small separate faces telling the time zones across the world. A single shelf of the bookcase behind him held a row of books and government publications leaning sidewise or piled on top of each other, and there were two small piles of papers on a table behind him. With the exception of a leather binder on top of a large manila envelope, his desk was empty of any paper, holding only a precisely arranged laptop, desk lamp, and cell phone. To begin our interview, he leaned back in his chair, put his hands behind his head, shook his head with a satisfied grin, and said, "This country is chaos, let me tell you."

He began with a brief discussion of the disintegrated peace talks—how there had been a contingency plan since the January crisis, how the

FARC had left the zone and the paramilitaries were surrounding it, but that nothing out of the ordinary seemed to be happening. Then, in response to my first general questions, he began explaining his work as "director of cases." Most of the "on the ground" work was carried out in a committee—Commission for Pressure and Follow-up—set up to organize officials from different governmental agencies to follow up specific cases. The commission dealt only with serious, highly publicized cases, including some instances of mass displacement and specific massacres. It organized periodic monitoring trips because, Iván said, "we want to have a much clearer sense of what was going on in the region, the dynamics associated with the different objectives of the armed actors."

Iván used the case of La Gabarra to make his point, saying it was typical and "very illuminating." Coincidentally, it was the same series of massacres that led to the dismissal of General Alberto Silva Bravo (discussed below). The La Gabarra case was summarized in the Vice President's Observatory on Human Rights in Colombia, a glossy four-page newsletter funded by USAID:

> The first episodes of this case took place on 23 May 1999 in La Gabarra municipal district, municipality of Tibú, department of North Santander, with the death of six people, the kidnapping of 21, and the setting up of illegal roadblocks. Mass murders, kidnappings, and disappearances occurred again in the area about a month later. This prompted the migration of people to urban areas and to Venezuela. Fact-finding missions for the return of displaced population confirmed that members of the United Self-Defense Groups of Colombia were present in the area, and the government raised the alarm. On 20 August a new massacre claimed more victims and provoked further population displacement. Over 130 people died and hundreds were forced to leave their homes in 1999. Another 26 people were killed in January this year. The commander of the Army Brigade stationed in the locality, the commander of North Santander Police Department and the head of the regional DAS district were transferred from their posts, on the grounds of alleged omission. The President of the Republic, exercising his discretionary powers, dismissed the V Brigade commander through decree 1710 of 1st September 1999. (Human Rights Observatory 2000: 4)

The newsletter went on to report that arrest warrants had been issued for paramilitary leaders and that eight "private individuals" had been arrested. There is no discussion of events prior to May 1999; the government "raised the alarm" (as opposed to taking preventive action) only after the first series of killings. The language used is dispassionate and detached and in the passive voice. No perpetrators are named; the paramilitaries are not mentioned.

Iván began by describing the political history of the region, a frontier zone along the border with Venezuela with a strong guerrilla tradition. Filo Gringo, a neighboring *vereda* that got its name from the foreign oil workers passing through, had long been a sanctuary for the ELN; the area included the alleged home base of Cura Pérez, the Spanish ex-priest who had been the group's most senior commander until his death from hepatitis in 1998. The FARC also had a presence in the region, in addition to a few scattered remnants of the EPL. "There is petroleum, and a lot of coca. It's a commercialization zone for coca, meaning that the coca is manufactured into cocaine and sent up the Atlantic Coast," he told me. "You start to see the entire paramilitary dynamic—it is a very complicated situation," literally, such a big situation—"when they started all the massacres." Yet for Iván, the story of La Gabarra did not start with the massacre but the arrival of the guerrillas.

As he spoke, his cell phone rang. The tune of the ringer was the Lone Ranger theme song. He leaned back in his chair, addressed the phone in rushed low voice, then turned the phone off.

"Mapiripán, Puerto Elvira, Chengue"—he rattled off the names of small towns around the country that had become synonymous with the massacres that had happened there. "These were all cases of special interest. When you do the follow-up, you learn things."

He explained to me the things he had learned about La Gabarra. The first massacre was of a family that had the largest cocaine laboratory in the zone. "It was the first thing the *paras* did to take control of the laboratory. Because the family had decided to keep paying tribute to the guerrillas so they could keep working." In the second case, the paramilitary commander ordered the detention of two people. "I interviewed one of them, and he told me that when they got there, the *paras* told them, we know that you are guerrilla collaborators. They said that they were not; the *paras* said, we know that some of your friends are guerrilla informants, but we are going to spare your lives if you get all the *comerciantes* together and tell them to work with us and not the guerrillas."

Iván asked me if I understood how the drug trade worked and began to draw a small diagram on a sheet of paper. "There is a chain . . . small laboratories, peasant owned, to *comerciantes*," drawing an arrow up from the circle representing the small peasant. I had traveled through coca-producing regions examining the impact of U.S. counternarcotics strategies and had seen the examples from his makeshift diagram: the small laboratories were usually shacks where peasant farmers make coca paste using weedwackers to chop the coca leaves and a mixture of gasoline and sulfuric acid to distill the alkaloid powder. *Comerciantes,* the generic Spanish word for commercial trader or businessman, was widely used to describe the intermediary drug traffickers responsible for buying coca paste from farmers and selling it to traffickers who process cocaine.

Iván returned to the details of La Gabarra. "The paramilitaries called together all the *comerciantes* and told them, you are going to work with us from now on. The AUC told them, you are going to pay the peasants a certain rate, so much for the kilo of coca paste, more than the guerrillas, so that it created terrible instability in the zone." At each point in the chain, he explained to me, the FARC charged a percentage, from the production, the sale, the distribution. "The *comerciantes* decided to work with the FARC, they don't obey the AUC's order, so there is an AUC massacre in the zone. After that, the AUC dominates, they fill the entire chain, of sale, processing, and distribution of drugs." Paramilitary control was facilitated by the geography of the region—one river and one road reaching many remote rural communities. "The second step," Iván continued, "was how to break the FARC's communication system. That was when they had the third massacre, killing the guys who run the boats, the *lancheros.*"

The lesson of the story was that this massacre was not a human rights abuse, the murder of defenseless peasants by a repressive state. This was a struggle between lawless bandits to control drug traffickers. He denied that the paramilitaries' purpose was political. The object of their violence was not to destroy the social base of the ELN, although that did occur. Their intention was "to occupy all the territory where drugs are, and the border." Because of the paramilitary attacks, including two additional massacres, the inhabitants fled for neighboring towns. "See how on the ground you get a different view," he concluded. His story of this massacre assumed that I would be familiar with the NGO *denuncias,* which focused on the paramilitary relationship with the local army and police commanders and almost completely elided the presence of the guerrillas and the role of the drug trade in the local economy. In his retelling of the massacre, these were the major causal factors. The state was completely absent; there was no mention of local officials or the security forces.

Yet he went on to announce the lessons of this massacre, returning, albeit reluctantly, to the official bureaucratic human rights narrative. "First, these were massacres foretold, *masacres anunciadas,*" he said, paraphrasing the title of a famous García Márquez short story, "Chronicle of a Death Foretold," often invoked in discussions of Colombian violence. "Independent of whether or not they had this dynamic—the guerrillas, the drug trade—the state has a duty to guarantee the safety of the population." "Second," he said, "it appeared there was a tolerance [*convivencia*] by state officials of paramilitary groups."

He ended his account there, but I asked explicitly for more details. The issue of state connections to paramilitary groups was the single most contentious issue for human rights officials. Carefully couching his response in the passive voice, he explained, "It is known that there are thirty military, police, and civilian *autodefensas* detained. It appears there was *convivencia* with the security forces. And the massacres were foretold, by social NGOs and even state agencies. There was even a commander, the president asked a general to resign, General Bravo Silva." He went on to describe the state-sponsored commissions established to investigate rural violence (described in detail below).

His narrative omitted entirely any supporting evidence for his vague conclusion that the massacres had been foretold or that the state was involved. In his version, there was no local population in the town, no state agencies, no civil society, no NGOs, no organizations or officials at any level, such as neighborhood associations, local assemblies, mayors, schoolteachers, policemen, or army commanders. There were drug producers and traffickers, guerrillas and paramilitaries but no one outside the cycle of criminality. The criminalization of general populations served to reduce their claim to rights; who would protest the massacre of drug trafficking guerrillas by paramilitaries? In legal terms, committing criminal acts does not limit the full range of rights to which individuals are entitled, but for rights claims to resonate and gain political legitimacy, the innocence of the victim is a crucial point. Criminals are widely viewed by the public as well as government officials as forfeiting their rights by their actions; human rights activists are often accused of defending the rights of bandits (Caldeira 2000).

The narrative of criminalization—that victims of violence are criminals who deserve what they get because only the innocent have rights— was a common tactic used by governmental spokesmen to generalize blame, and to generalize responsibility for violence, particularly when discussing drug-producing regions such as southern Colombia and, now, the border region with Venezuela. When questioned, Iván revealed that there were other organizations, including state agencies, that had intervened, but the process and substance of those interventions were omitted. His account located violence as simply existing in the world outside the law, taking place in an area of illegal economy (drug trafficking) and illegal political groups (guerrillas), completely disconnected from the realm of the rule of law and state institutions.

THE GOVERNMENT IN ACTION

Commissions established after violent acts are a major form of government action on human rights cases. When I was interviewing a young lawyer in charge of the early warning system for the Defensoría in Barranca, he mentioned a *comisión mixta*—made up of both NGO and government representatives—temporarily convened to visit a displaced community currently camped out in Las Brisas, a small hamlet about an hour outside of town. "Just show up, and if there is room in the truck we'll take you," he replied when I asked if I could tag along. I did, and ended up wedged on a bench in the back of a covered pickup the next morning. I took stock of my fellow travelers. There were a number of NGO activists, including Patricia from the Popular Feminine Organization, Ricardo from the Regional Human Rights Corporation, and several others I did not recognize. The state representatives included Daniel, a lawyer from the vice president's office, and the regional *defensor* and his aide; though I did not know it at the time, the local military commander would attend the commission meeting as well. Daniel had arrived on the 6:00 A.M. flight from Bogotá on one of his periodic visits to the region; he seemed on edge. By contrast, the regional *defensor* joked with the NGO activists. He was well known in the region; a decade before, he had been one of the most high profile human rights activists in the town. He had begun his career as a labor lawyer and had been a founding member and president of CREDHOS in the late 1980s. After death threats and the murder of his bodyguard and several colleagues, he fled the region, spending more than a decade in Central America working with the United Nations. His acceptance of the government posting was a profound surprise to many, given his radical politics, but his rhetoric seemed only slightly dampened from earlier days. Many speculated about how long he would last in the job, given his well-known confrontations with the military commanders in the region.

The explanations of what had happened, exactly, to cause the one hundred plus families to flee from their community a week before were confusing. It was not until several weeks later that I heard the apparently definitive version. The paramilitaries arrived demanding a "tax" payment from anyone working in the area. One of the fishermen refused; his body was found several days later. In the meantime, the paramilitaries had returned, demanding more money, and when that was not forthcoming insisted that the dead man's son accompany them. Family members, warned of the possible incursion, gathered around him; in the confusion (riot, or defensive action, depending on who was telling the story), one of the paramilitaries was killed. Now the entire community had fled, setting up camp with friends and relatives, afraid of reprisals. Soldiers from the local battalion had also set up camp among them, occupying the nearby school as their base. We were there to "assess" the situation, in the hope that a long-term solution—ideally, returning to their houses—could be found. The NGO representatives' major concern was the presence of the army. Taking over people's homes and yards was in violation of international law, which mandates the separation of civilian and military spaces. They had met with the local military commander to discuss "part of the agreement with the community that they would not settle [*meterse*] in the houses," Patricia told me.

Outside of town, we traveled for ten minutes down an "improved" road, made of packed dirt sprayed with one of the region's most abundant resources, unrefined crude oil, to keep down the dust and soften the ride. Peeking out through the truck's smudged windows, I saw the small wooden shacks typical of the region; families had crowded together under tarps and in the small buildings. We passed several shacks with young soldiers napping in hammocks or smoking cigarettes nonchalantly in the yard, their machine guns set beside them in the dirt.

There were no written notes or records of the conversations from the commission's investigation, including the meeting with the community. In fact, there was no documentation of any part of the process of government involvement in this case in evidence during any part of the commission's travels and meetings. There were no notes from previous meetings, no official record of conversations with the community or among the state agencies and NGOs that participated. There was no registry of the community members' concerns or collection of the press coverage of the event—a significant issue, as community members alleged military officers had made misleading and possibly dangerous statements to the press. No notes would be taken during the meeting, and after its conclusion, there was no official record of the community representative's statements or the reaction by officials. Given the usual emphasis on paperwork in government transactions, the absence was notable and served to demonstrate the transient and flexible nature of the commission's work, which could be represented later in multiple ways by participants without the counterbalance of a paper trail.

The truck finally came to a stop before a cement patio covered with a zinc roof, bordered by a small store on one side—simply shelves nailed to the outside wall of the building, lined with small tubes of toothpaste, bottles of *aguardiente,* shampoo and dishwashing soap, bags of rice and pasta—and a pool table covered in dirty plastic on the other. The members of the *commisión mixta* settled into green and red plastic lawn chairs, set in a wide semicircle facing an empty packed-dirt yard. As we sat, a few men, wiry muscle clad in the tattered threadbare shirts and shorts of the rural poor, arrived on ancient, gearless bicycles. Slowly, the circle was completed as a small crowd of presumably displaced *campesinos* tentatively approached.

Patricia began the meeting by standing and greeting the crowd, telling them that we had assembled as part of a larger amorphous commission that was following the events. NGO representatives and officials all frequently referred to the "process"—the events causing the displacement, current circumstances, and the official efforts to resolve the situation. Details of the process—who participated, prior commitments made—were left unelaborated, and no documentation to support any of the claims being made was ever produced.

Daniel stood to give his name, leaning slightly against a wooden roof support, thin and formal in his suit and tie. He began with the classic phrases of consolation: "We lament these events and express solidarity with the family of the victim"—a short, serious woman who stood emotionless but clearly acknowledged by the crowd—"and with you." He continued with the stock phrases of government bureaucrats everywhere: "We are here to offer support and help to the community, to express to you the intention of following the situation as much as circumstances permit." And to spread the blame: "The Ministry of the Interior has taken up in a much more direct way the management of this situation, but they could not be here today. Please understand that we have many limitations that do not allow us to do adequately address your situation."

The final general welcome, from one of the NGO representatives, was met by silence from the crowd. We sat in silence for what seemed like an hour as the crowd shifted, eyes down. Finally, a middle-aged woman stepped forward. As a state employee herself—the local schoolteacher—she assumed the authority to speak for the community. She spoke quietly and simply: "What we feel is fear. Now, surrounded by the army, to a certain extent we feel secure. But outside, there is more fear. We are worried about how we will settle again in our town after what has happened. We need to be satisfied that security is not lacking."

As the crowd had gathered, the military authorities had arrived, and they now stood behind the pool table in full military regalia. The colonel stepped forward, pledging in a long speech that security for the community would be provided until it was no longer needed. The rest of the halting discussion focused on the issue of security, and for the *campesinos* in the crowd, security meant not being alone. "We are in a state of *nerviosismo*," one older man explained, "they [the paramilitaries] had a death, a *baja*, and this pains them, makes us more vulnerable. If we go out, there could be reprisals. Here we count on security, but only here. People have to travel to search for food, to work in agriculture or fishing. We are blanketed by fear, *temor que nos acobia*." After the schoolteacher agreed that security was all right "while they [the military] are here," the older man added, "It is a long-term problem. The months go by, and the organizations that accompany us begin to leave."

After listening to these and other speakers, whose main thrust was not concern about military occupation of their homes but about what might happen when the soldiers left, Daniel suggested to the crowd that perhaps frequent patrols could be coordinated with the base. In response, the acting mayor raised another fear about the military: how they manage information. He told the commission that the local newspaper, the *Vanguardia Liberal,* and other media had reported that the community had been displaced by the guerrillas. "It wasn't like that," the mayor said. "It was voluntarily because of fear [*voluntariamente por miedo*]." Other tales reported as coming from military officials were that the dead man had been a drug trafficker and that the region was a drug trafficking shipment zone. "This isn't like that, this is a poor region," the mayor said. "Such talk just makes our problems larger. Military people need to be honest in their communication." The widow nodded silently.

The *defensor* told the crowd that as a member of the Committee on Displacement, he could submit a *derecho de petición* (official request for government action) and demand that the colonel submit a correction to the newspapers. If the colonel did not do this he could be charged with violating the community's fundamental rights. Another NGO representative offered a third version, also reportedly published as a quote from the colonel, who allegedly said that the people did not want to leave their homes but were pressured to do so by the very institutions claiming to help them, several of which were represented on the commission: the Defensoría, NGOs, the U.N. Refugee Agency, and the Catholic Social Welfare Agency.

Daniel shifted, seeming to acknowledge the civilian agencies' apparent powerlessness to affect the military institutions, and asked the crowd: "What can we do with the security forces? We know that unfortunately some military officers, what they do is put people at worse risk. We can request that their work be better in terms of the national attitude to these organizations. We can talk to them, but we don't have much influence. But we can make the suggestion that they have tended to make irresponsible declarations."

Finally, one of the NGO representatives brought up the issue of the army occupying people's houses. We have asked them not to do this, he told the crowd, because it increases peoples' risks, and it constitutes a violation of international humanitarian law: they cook there, they sleep there. We could designate a specific area for them, someone suggested. Patricia replied with an argument from international law: the army should not occupy the houses, because it makes them a target. Daniel told me later that he was tired of the politically motivated agenda of the NGOs. Their concerns were getting the military to end their occupation of local homes and schools, but according to the government officials, the soldiers had no place to live. The third speaker from the crowd, one of the nameless men clutching their baseball caps in their clasped hands, a gesture of respect unrecognized by the officials, said of the soldiers, "They are only human, and they need a place to cook, a place to wash." During the meeting, however, Daniel repeated the NGOs' concern. "As the NGO representative said," he told the group, "it is a violation of international humanitarian law, and we will talk to the security forces."

The discussion ended with what other government agencies, not represented on the commission, must do, and with the voicing of palpable concerns about future violence from the crowd. According to the members of the community gathered before us, speaking softly and reluctantly, no one from the attorney general's office had interviewed the displaced families. This meant that there was no investigation into the presence of paramilitary groups. But there had been no threats, only rumors, someone offered from the crowd, rumors that they would burn down the houses, that they were going to go from house to house. Rumors, one man said softly, that sometimes become reality. Daniel asked if anyone had seen any of the "groups," here or there, or heard rumors of them, but was met only with silence. Finally the schoolteacher explained, "We don't know the people in this town [meaning the area where the displaced peasants had settled], maybe a few but not all of them." She left unsaid the excuse: how would we know who is from what group or the other? How could we say those words out loud? At no time during the course of the meeting was there any overt mention of an investigation, of actual perpetrators.

Daniel concluded the gathering by telling the other commission members that he would be unable to attend the next meeting on the agenda, the Committee for the Displaced, because he had other commitments. To the crowd, he said, "Be watchful so that more events do not occur. We cannot be here next Thursday, but we will continue to accompany you. The Interior Ministry is very capable"—not the ministry where he worked but one that had sent no representatives to the commission—"and has greater ability to support you more effectively. We thank you for your time, and your words, and we hope that things will be better."

There were numerous representatives of the state present at the commission, each positioned differently in relation to the state writ large. The *defensor* positioned himself as the protector of the population from the abusive power of the state, threatening to sue the local military commander for his careless slander in the newspaper. The military, occupying the land and houses, was a contradictory presence, offering security but also a sense of unarticulated threats and contributing to misunderstandings about the nature of the conflict and the community. Other state agencies, such as the Ministry of the Interior and the Fiscalía, were conjured up in their absence as precisely the powerful players whose intervention could resolve the assembled crowd's concerns; their powers and authority were invoked as the necessary but unavailable corrective to the multiple problematic situations.

Daniel, a national human rights bureaucrat, offered excuses as to his own powerlessness before other, more powerful state agents (the military) and shifted responsibility to absent parties (the Ministry of the Interior). No one in the meeting suggested that the source of the threats against the community—paramilitary groups widely believed to be working with at least the tacit support of local military commanders—be addressed. Daniel's role in the production of impunity was ambiguous, however, as he did attempt to react to the local community's expressions of concern about how to negotiate the issue of security and achieve a delicate compromise with the military forces in the area.

This ambiguity is the most intriguing characteristic of the bureaucrats I spoke to, and opens the door to the greatest opportunity for activism within the state. Many of the officials involved in the Colombian governmental human rights bureaucracies are undoubtedly merely concerned with punching the clock, with preserving their paychecks by performing the least institutionally disruptive tasks and avoiding any pretense of productivity. But in the vast majority of the interviews I conducted—limited to a largely preselected group of officials well known to the human rights community and self-selecting in their willingness to talk to me—they offered nuanced reflections about the limitations of their institutional positioning and their individual willingness to embrace the risks inherent in human rights activism. They also offered examples of the complicated daily choice of which battles to wage and the toll of the constant calculations of situational ethics.

Daniel, a career bureaucrat clearly unwilling to risk the few advantages of his position, had offered me such reflections when we first met, by chance, in the downtown office of the Vice President's Human Rights Program several months before. He had allowed me to flip through and take notes from the file described above to find out what, if any, government follow-up had occurred with the Chengue case. Working through my chain of contacts at the vice president's office, I met him when I approached his fabric-lined cubicle, in back of one of the long offices lining the first-floor courtyard, after he was recommended as the "official in charge" of the case. I could hear his insistent tone, arguing on the phone, before he wandered out to shake my hand. As I explained my project at one of the small tables in the common area, he eyed me slyly over a cigarette, and so began a series of conversations that lasted over the next several months.

Daniel was a lawyer, one of many in cheap suits and polyester ties filling the offices of the Vice President's Office on Human Rights. He answered my questions with wry good humor and a reflective bent that I was eager to exploit; I asked if my initial inquiries could segue into a full interview. He acquiesced, and I learned the details of his early career. He had spent the last fifteen years working at the Consejería (now the Vice President's Office on Human Rights). He began as a messenger delivering papers to other government offices while going to law school and was then hired to work on staff as part of the agency's evolving projects.

He had first worked in the National Human Rights Network, designed to link the *personería* offices throughout the country with computer technology and training paid for by the Netherlands in the mid-1990s. He spent his time traveling throughout the country, installing computers and telling people about the program, but despite his efforts it never got off the ground. "The agencies were too jealous of each other to want to share information," Daniel told me with a shake of his head. "The idea was that the *personeros* could send information to security forces if bad things were happening," an earlier version of the "early warning system" being developed through the Defensoría with USAID funding. "I don't know how the people in power made the decisions, but it never worked out. It was a bad investment all around."

In his current job with the Vice President's Human Rights Program, Daniel was charged with one thematic issue—paramilitarism—and more than five geographic regions spread throughout the country, each with its own complicated dynamics, most of which were new to him. "Some staff have left," he told me, presumably after the Uribe administration arrived in August 2002, "and so everyone got assigned new regions." He gets about twenty communiqués a week, including *tramites* (official paperwork) and *denuncias,* and spends a lot of time traveling to meetings and setting up "verification" missions to document the situation of communities at risk or under attack. Most of these meetings and missions involve a wide range of bureaucratic players, including international organizations (Christian Aid, Save the Children, the U.N. Human Rights Office, and the World Food Program, to name a few), local NGOs, local government officials, other national agencies (including the Defensoría and the Ministry of the Interior), military authorities, and others.

He viewed these commissions as critical for the government to realize what is happening on the ground. "It's very important to be in the zone, to realize what the facts are, because the press accounts are so far from the truth." Now, he told me, the commissions have been temporarily suspended for an internal evaluation process, because there has been "a lot of criticism," and they are trying to figure out how to make them "more concrete." So for the past six months he had only traveled to "coordinate" but not "accompany," meaning he would meet with other officials but not community members.

Like the NGO critics of the government, Daniel voiced frustration with the constant turnover and the rhetoric without action of the successive administrations he had worked under: "There are changes every time there is a new government. They have an idea of what they want to do with the human rights program, each of the four administrations since Barco—he created the Consejería office. The result is always the same; the administrations never pass from rhetoric to doing what needs to be done. They don't do anything. They don't take the recommendations seriously."

Over time, he told me, the relationship between the government and the NGOs had changed: "Seven or eight years ago, it was a complicated thing. Now they listen, participate, let you talk. In Barranca, two years ago the NGOs wouldn't sit down with the military for anything in the world; now they do. They criticize the military a lot, and often the military deserves it. But the military listens. But that doesn't translate into changes." He paused, reflecting briefly on his own struggles with local military commanders. "It is very frustrating, you work and work, but there are no results." Despite his forays into dangerous territory, he told me he was not afraid. "Here in Bogotá you live like a prince. In the regions the situation is very dramatic. You are vulnerable to every side."

After offering his opinion about worsening guerrilla violence and the growing authoritarian presence of the paramilitaries, he concluded by simply voicing his frustration with the entrenched violence. "You can't dare to think what would be better, a peace process strengthened with international monitoring, or total war that in five years would end all of this," he told me. "You think that here, there is nothing that can be done. As a human rights defender, you want things to be fixed through dialogue, but you see that it would be very hard. There are very poor zones, and people tell you of all their complicated problems. Some say, 'Before we lived in poverty but in peace, but now we live in poverty but in war, surrounded by so much wealth.' This country deserves better luck. People in the regions expect the world of us." He paused. "It is a sad situation."

FROM NGOS INTO THE STATE: FOCUSING ON THE POSSIBILITIES

Many state officials who began their careers with NGOs frequently expressed their frustration with the state system, but they also stressed the opportunities presented by working with the state. All the officials I spoke with took pains to explain how their current jobs were simply a new incarnation of their commitment to human rights and offered specific examples of the opportunities that their positioning within the state offered them to improve the situation of certain victims or advance the investigation of specific cases. Juan Méndez, an Argentine lawyer with a long and distinguished career in human rights that included serving as director of Human Rights Watch/Americas, spoke of the unique progress bureaucrats in these institutions were able to achieve:

> For some reason only in Colombia, these institutions are created and take on a life of their own. For example, when we were looking at the massacres in the late 1980s, they had done some incredibly good fact-finding, done by the Procuraduría, because some member of the police or the military participated in the massacre. . . . That was a real difference between Colombia and other countries in the same or similar situations. People had a different sense of their duty. In other countries, if you were trying to research human rights

cases, people didn't want to talk to you, they thought you were coming to investigate them and what they were doing, and they would try to hide. They would always defend the state agents involved in wrongdoing, arguing that they were just carrying out their duties. In Latin America, this was one of the worst problems in terms of human rights. But in Colombia, things were different; this was not the right way to describe the situation. The Colombians have a sense of their duties, and they exercise them.

One of the lawyers I interviewed, now working with the United Nations, was reflexive and defensive as he described his migration from NGOs to various staff positions with the Defensoría. It began, he told me, with the realization that "you could do something from within the state." The new institutions were being created, and many *compañeros* decided that they would give this part of the state a chance, carefully distinguishing between the institutions that supported the administration and these new agencies. "We didn't go to work there as infiltrators. We didn't have any commitment to any actor or political force. We were trying to position human rights work within the state. There were changes, imperceptible but important to those of us who lived it." He recalled stiff resistance from the military, which "always accused [them] of being the political arm of the subversives," but he stressed the importance of the fact that these agencies were embracing human rights from within the state. "For some, particularly the military, the issue never stopped being part of the subversion's game. But within the state, the issue was taking hold." He listed a few of the human rights initiatives of the time, calling them "*focos* within the state," using the phrase made famous by Che Guevara to describe the vanguard of revolution. For Alonso, part of the appeal was being able to work in conflict areas where abuses were a major issue. He also began working in the human rights education workshops for the military and the police. He explained:

> The military started their own human rights offices, and when you were traveling in different parts of the country you would be in the battalion, and find that there was a human rights official who was your counterpart, who was someone you could talk to, usually an official from intelligence. But that was good. Of course, the only thing they did was respond to letters and urgent actions from NGOs about possible disappearances and torture, but it was good to have them in that job. . . . It was good [*muy rico*] to see these changes. You look now, and you think that it has always been this way, and that is not true. It took a lot of work. It took a lot of work to convince the military that the Defensoría was part of the state, that we are the state just like you, that we are equal. . . .
>
> The state is much more comfortable. You have the backing of a structure

that gives you status—and image, guarantees as a public servant. If I hadn't been wearing the vest of the Defensoría, I wouldn't have gone into many of the areas where I worked, many areas, because the vest gives you more security. While I was working and traveling, I ran into many actors, the guerrillas—the ELN, the FARC, the EPL—and the *autodefensas*. If I had gone as an NGO, I probably would have been killed, by the *paras* in Catatumbo, or some other place.

Many people take the role of a public servant [*funcionario*]. They are just waiting for the paycheck at the end of the month, and to do any extra work is to give yourself away [*regalarse*]. I can think of two examples. One day after work there was a march on [one of Bogotá's central avenues], and I joined it because I always liked getting involved in that kind of thing. There were teachers who were being loaded into a police van. I went to them [the police] and said they had to tell me where they were going to take them. The police didn't want to, so I got my ID from the Defensoría and said that I was an official, and to prevent any human rights violations, they had to tell me what was going on. They still didn't want to. By that time a crowd had gathered. I had to get up on a curb and give a speech about how they weren't going to be able to disappear or torture anyone. As the police drove the van away, I got in a taxi and followed them, all the way to the station. I was able to talk to them, make sure they were all OK, and then through a written memorandum [*acta escrita*], I got the police to release them to me. I didn't get home until 2:30 that morning. The next day I went into work, and I gave them the memorandum and told them what had happened. They said, you are an official from 8:00 A.M. to 6:00 P.M. What you did was outside your job.

It is a different dynamic — they told me at the Defensoría I shouldn't have done these things, but I believe that a human rights defender doesn't have a schedule [*horario*].

A woman who also went from NGO activism to giving human rights workshops to the military with the Defensoría, recounted similar frustrations, and hopes, for her work in the Colombian state. She was one of the staff people brought on to work in the Ministry of the Interior, transformed since my last visit four years before. Previously, I had wandered at will through a warren of dingy offices, several filled with what appeared to be haphazardly stacked abandoned furniture. This new world—the product of USAID funding—was brightly lit and shiny, full of yellow and blue signs. The name of the program, with the presidential seal, was etched in glass in the door, and access was carefully policed by several layers of administrative vigilance. The room was filled with a blue loveseat against one wall, three chairs with a small table between them against the other, between them a metal detector and two private guards, one in the black and yellow puffy jacket of a messenger, the other in the blue psuedopolice uniform. A plastic evergreen garland blinked Christmas lights over the receptionist's window, and the door to the office area was wrapped by a wide red and gold ribbon with a bow, tied as if the door was one side of a huge package.

I never got a chance to interview the director, who was leaving for vacation the next day and politely dodged my requests for a meeting when I would run into him at conferences and public events. Instead, I spent the morning talking to his assistant, who recognized me from my days with the NGOs; she told me of her first activist work, on behalf of a family friend who had been disappeared by the military, and then about her more than a decade spent working with NGOs.

Like Alonso, she recalled the accusations of betrayal facing NGO activists who chose to work with the state. They called us "the NGO traitors," she told me,

> [for] going to work for the enemy state. But it was nice to get away from the anxiety of the NGOs, [when we would] know things were happening, people were being detained, but not being able to do anything about it. To work in a place where we did have the power to go and visit people who were detained, to find out what happened with people, to be able to talk directly with the public forces. If you knew what was happening in some village, you could say, we know that you are flying over these areas. You can do what you need to do, but you have to take care of the civilian population.

She first worked in the complaints department but soon grew bored with the repetitive job. "I was sick of it," she explained. "I was working on too many complaints, all I did was fill out the forms, repeating the same story fifteen hundred times, that the armed forces did this and that." So she began working on human rights training for military officers. Her greatest pride were the specific cases in which she was able to ensure the release of individuals wrongly detained by the military.

> And we got people out, we got eight people released. I even got a peasant released by a colonel, now a general. At the time, he was the colonel in charge of the mobile brigades. And in a base in Sumapaz the head of the brigade had detained a peasant who had nine children. The guy wouldn't let him go. He had him for three weeks. I talked to the colonel. I said, "Look, we can solve this two ways, you can hand over the peasant to us, or we can start a disciplinary proceeding. The head of the brigade already has committed a lot of abuses that we could charge him with; it will be a big problem for him, a big problem for you." I kept thinking of all those kids, and I knew that if the peasant was going to get out alive we had to settle it amicably, *a las buenas*. So he said, "OK, let me see what I can do." The camp was twenty-four hours away by foot, in the Bogotá district but very remote. He

called me the next day and said, "Well, we can do it." I said, "I'm not going
out there to pick him up. You have to set it up to hand him over to the priest
who is there." He said he would, Friday at eleven o'clock. That morning
he called—the weather is terrible, the helicopter can't land, can I have a
few more hours? By two o'clock, we decided. And he did hand the guy over
to the priest. And that was that. I mean, what would I get with a disciplinary
case with the Inspector General that would never go anywhere?

There were also painful cases, terrible cases, where we didn't get people
out. There was the case of the 17th Brigade. The Defensoría knew about
it but didn't do anything. There were eleven guys, ex-guerrillas I think, and
the brigade had them and made them work for them [as informants], with
a quota system — so many heads a month, turn in so many people, so many
cadavers, every month. It was terrible. But they never got them out of there.
Later they were named in a massacre, but no one would get them out. They
had no way out of there.

In part because of frustration with state inaction in this case, she left her
position to return to work with NGOs for several years; further frustration with those working conditions led her back to her current state job.

Traditionally, academic and policy debates about the state in Colombia
have focused on extremes; the state is weak and in partial collapse, or the
state is repressive and authoritarian. I have attempted to sidestep these
debates by focusing on the daily drama of the state, how bureaucracies
are built or wither through the regular exchanges with citizens about
services and constant negotiations with competing agencies for resources.
Furthermore, these polarizing extremes ignore the shifts in power and
opportunity and the influences that shape institutional evolution. However, the pressure brought to bear by international funders and individual
officials cannot overcome the larger limitations of state inaction and the
relative powerlessness of these agencies. More like the Chimera, the
mythical monster cobbled together with the parts of a lion, dragon, and
goat, than a monolithic, coherent entity, the vast differences among
Colombia state institutions must be understood in the context of the history and perspectives of the officials who shape their daily practice.

State human rights agencies are in part an additional example of the
unintended consequences of human rights activism. International pressure for government action on human rights cases has increased but in
most cases without having an impact on the broader power structures
that produced the abuses. One high-ranking U.N. representative who
had worked extensively with Colombian human rights officials was pes-
simistic in his assessment of their overall impact. Dedicated and highly

trained human rights officials, many of them former NGO activists, have been able to harness the authority of the state to respond in certain cases, providing a critical service to some victims. However, this representative concluded: "Of course, at some point it seems like the creation of institutions is a game, because all the offices that were created and all the committees and commissions over and over again. In the end, the results are disheartening as well. There is a lot of initial work that is done. For a fact-finder like me it is wonder, it is beautiful to find the information. But in terms of breaking the cycle of impunity, it does not work. There is no closure. As the investigations go forward, there is always some interruption, a short circuit."

Proliferating state human rights agencies, through the creation of endless bureaucratic loops incapable of prompting significant political reforms, end up primarily engaged in the production of impunity. By siphoning off the human rights funding and resources offered by the foreign governments and international agencies, these state bureaucracies become another mechanism through which perpetrators of political violence evade public scrutiny and sanction.

CHAPTER 7

Human Rights and the Colombian Military's War Stories

Since the late 1990s the Colombian military has developed a proactive human rights strategy of its own that has included publishing human rights reports, hosting conferences, and establishing a network of battalion-level human rights offices. This does not mean, however, that they accept the human rights arguments of NGOs or of government investigators pressing for investigations of specific allegations. The Colombian officers I interviewed saw these human rights claims as part of a politically motivated war against them, an orchestrated campaign in favor of the guerrillas. For the military, human rights discourse is part of the battlefield. The military's attempts to harness the power of human rights—by gaining access to international legitimacy and funding—has meant that it has proactively attempted to fit human rights ideas into existing military conceptions of the state and society. First, military officers used human rights arguments, focusing on due process, to defend themselves from accusations of misconduct. They claimed that by launching allegations into the public sphere, instead of processing them through the judicial system, human rights NGOs were violating the officers' rights to defend themselves. More recently, a new generation of colonels has incorporated human rights—understood as the nonabusive treatment of local populations—into the traditional military doctrine dealing with civic-military relations, psychological operations, and civic action.

Colonel Vargas was the first Colombian officer to guide me through his vision of the Colombian conflict and the role of human rights in the military's strategy. I first met Colonel Vargas as we both stood in the scanty shade outside a meeting hall in a small, sweltering town on the Magdalena River. An internationally known women's association, one of the most outspoken on human rights issues in the region, was reopening one of its local programs, which had been closed for a year after paramilitary death threats. A slew of human rights activists and local government officials had traveled to the town for the day in a show of solidarity. Unlike the military officers I had seen at other human rights–themed events (or even some of his military colleagues at this one), Colonel Vargas did not stand glowering in the back, arms crossed on his chest in thinly veiled hostility, but moved through the crowd like a politician. He smiled, shook hands, called out the names of local women leaders in greeting, and stood close to the government human rights officials from Bogotá. He was the embodiment of the new military—modern, professional, humanitarian—even while the epitome of the old. Under periodic investigation since the early 1990s for his alleged involvement in the creation of paramilitary networks in a neighboring region, the colonel now headed the military's community-outreach efforts. We spoke at length, in the final months of his special posting as a "community liaison officer" for a pilot program in one of the most conflictive regions of Colombia, and then again months later at his new posting as commander of a counterguerrilla battalion in another combat zone. His vision exemplified the new thinking by the Colombian military about human rights: instead of simply dismissing human rights as politically motivated propaganda, they were willing to try to use this weapon for themselves.

During our initial meeting, Colonel Vargas invited me to interview him so that I could have a better understanding of his programs. Several weeks later I sat for almost two hours with him in a concrete room on the base, empty except for the desk shoved in one corner, a loud but ineffectual air conditioner, and an assortment of religious and tourism posters. My tape recorder shared a barren desktop with a wooden in-box holding nothing but a pistol. He did not comment on my brief introduction to my research but instead started talking with the tumbling rush of a true believer. In his stories, I heard the themes that would be repeated by almost all the military men who talked with me. Raised in a lower-middle-class family, he was filled from youth with the love of pageantry and military glamour and had lived surrounded by military institutions (schools, housing, hospitals) in a military life. He was hopeful that Colombia could fulfill its destiny as a true paradise, strident in the need for reforms to end social inequality, and dismissive of corrupt politicians who cared nothing for the country except to line their own pockets and save their own skins. But the colonel and the other officers I interviewed also insisted that they are human rights defenders. We are the victims of guerrilla slander, which is the source of the investigations against us, they told me. Colombians have too many rights, while the military is denied the rights that would allow them to win the war. These officers believe that human rights will help them win the war by bringing the local population to their side.

Changing military attitudes toward human rights reflect the international acceptance of human rights in the early 1990s, particularly by the U.S. military, and is a response to the increasing legitimacy of Colombian nongovernmental human rights groups. Central to military positioning on human rights is the ongoing debate within the Colombian military, and its U.S. military supporters, about the appropriate legal framework for counterinsurgency warfare and the role of the military in defining national security policy. The analysis of the role of the military in human rights presented here does not address its role in perpetrating or preventing political violence but rather focuses on the institutional history of the Colombian military and the ways in which officers understand their position in Colombian society. I begin with the conversations I had with military officers, their positioning in Colombian society, and their relationships with their U.S. counterparts. After exploring shifting military attitudes toward human rights, I conclude by examining military human rights training programs and reporting.

NO ONE TALKS TO THE COLONELS

The first step in my interviews was the simple realization that many officers wanted to talk. In part, this willingness to talk depended on rank. Noncommissioned officers (NCOs) were often reluctant, even when interviews were approved, to express any opinion. Midlevel career officers would speak with me if their commanding officers authorized the interview. But the colonels I approached were overwhelmingly enthusiastic about the opportunity to sit down with a *gringa* anthropologist and a tape recorder. In all but a few battalions (those located on the same bases as the five Division Commands), those I met with were the highest-ranking officers on the base, accustomed to holding ultimate authority and to being expansive in their opinions. I did experience the logistical problems caused by the fact that these officers were involved in fighting an ongoing "internal conflict"; combat operations in nearby towns delayed and caused the cancellation of some interviews.

The colonels and their military colleagues were anxious to tell their side of the story because they felt misunderstood. Blamed for their inability to contain the relentless violence that has plagued Colombian political life for the past century, military officers describe themselves as the exploited scapegoats of a corrupt political class and an oblivious society that did not provide them with the resources they required. Unlike other armed forces in Latin America, Colombia's military does not represent, and is not made up of, the elite. In interviews with members of the Colombian business class, the military was seen as ineffective, uncultured, and bumbling. While we sipped small cups of Colombian coffee in the paneled conference room of Colombia's embassy in Washington, one high-ranking diplomat acknowledged that the Colombian military lacked social support. In the United States, he told me, you would find military officers, generals, at important state dinners, but not in Colombia. "No officers are members of the Jockey Club [Bogotá's most elite social club]. They are considered *medio lobo*—the best translation is, I think, 'kitsch,'" he said. "In Colombia, they are not socially important. People are embarrassed if their daughters marry a military officer."

The military does, however, provide a vehicle for the upward mobility of the lower middle class, families who had the means to support sons in primary and secondary public schools but without the capital for university or the initiative for private entrepreneurship. The military officer corps consists largely of the sons of the lower middle class. The cost of military academies puts them out of reach of the poor and lower classes; students are not charged tuition but must pay for their uniforms and equipment themselves, a substantial financial burden (adding up to several thousand dollars) in a country where the minimum wage hovers around U.S.$170 a month. For many generations of the large Catholic families typical of rural Colombia, sons were destined to be "the soldier or the priest." In contrast, wealthy families avoid obligatory military service and send their sons to the country's private universities or abroad.

For many career officers and NCOs, the military offers an attractive opportunity for lifetime employment. For most of those who joined during the 1970s, combat remained relatively rare for a country in the midst of an "internal conflict," and many mentioned "job security" as the primary motivation for their military vocation. "The majority of men who join the institution do so because of the stable social level it provides," one sergeant with fifteen years' experience told me. "You get medical insurance, a steady paycheck; you get paid vacations, credit, social security. There are a lot of benefits, besides being called to join because you want to be a good citizen."

Yet alienation from both the political elite and wider Colombian society is a constant theme among military officers.[1] For most of the conflict's forty years, the vast majority of combat and large-scale political violence has remained rural, even as the country has urbanized.[2] The hallmarks of prosperous, stable countries (regular elections and a flourishing economy) have been largely unaffected by the violence. Many military officers I spoke with felt that the majority of Colombians did not even acknowledge the violence faced by the military because it did not touch their lives. "We are at war, not just now but forever. It is just that the people didn't recognize it before, but we have always been in a defensive attitude and we have maintained ourselves in a permanent war," one major told me, noting that the escalation of kidnapping in the past several years had changed some people's awareness. "Before, people didn't pay attention to the conflict because the conflict hadn't come into the urban areas as much." This sentiment was echoed by a counterguerrilla officer who had been wounded and watched soldiers under his command die in combat. "Other people don't have any idea of what the armed forces are doing and that, yes, we are at war. The common people, maybe they keep working normally because nothing has been done to them; they have never been wounded."

TALKING TO GRINGOS

Military officers also welcomed the opportunity to speak with me because I am American. Like its civilian Colombian compatriots, the Colombian military has an intense and ambivalent relationship with the United States. The United States has been the primary model and ally for the Colombian military for the second half of the twentieth century.[3] This relationship began in earnest with Colombia's provision of a battalion to fight alongside the United States during the Korean War, the only Latin American country to do so. In the context of the ongoing domestic "unrest" of La Violencia, the decision to send troops was viewed by some as pandering to the United States and a convenient means for the Conservative president to rid the corps of Liberal officers, but it undoubtedly left a lasting legacy. Exposed to the U.S. army's weaponry, training and structure, the Colombians excelled on the battlefield and returned with a new vision of a professional military, including new ideas of military command structure, doctrine, intelligence, and communications. These lessons were widely taught in the reinstituted military academies and ushered in a new era of close ties with the United States (Blair Trujillo 1999; Tovar and Franky 2001; Valencia Tovar and Villalobos Barradas 1993). Throughout the late 1950s and early 1960s, there was "extensive collaboration effort between [the] U.S. and Colombia in developing the latter's internal security apparatus" (Rempe 2002: 4).

The U.S. military apparatus was central in defining Colombian military doctrine throughout the cold war, as it did throughout Latin America. Based on a paradigm that became widely known as the National Security Doctrine and taught by the United States to allied militaries, this counterinsurgency doctrine had a fundamental role in shaping Colombian military doctrine and operational response to the guerrillas.[4] The National Security Doctrine focused on internal threats and unconventional warfare, in which asymmetrical forces fighting as proxies for the superpowers waged war primarily off the battlefield, through sabotage, psychological operations, and guerrilla attacks. This doctrine served as the foundation for Colombian counterinsurgency strategies as the military struggled to counteract a range of guerrilla forces that formed in the 1960s and 1970s (McClintock 1992; Rempe 2002).

Prior to and following their experience in the Korean War, a cohort of officers saw high levels of poverty and inequality as the central issue in counterinsurgency warfare—what became known as the "sociology school" of counterinsurgency. These officers insisted that military campaigns alone could not address the problems facing Colombia but that civilian politicians had to commit to long-term, sustained development and education programs and psychological operations carried out so that the peasants knew of the plans to improve their situation (Vargas Velásquez 1992, 2002). Viewed as too critical of civilian politicians, the proponents of this school were quickly replaced with adherents of the less-intensive strategy of containment.

The containment strategy, also developed by U.S. military analysts, recommended that given a cost-benefit analysis of the scale of military operations required to eliminate small guerrilla forces, the latter be allowed to operate relatively freely in remote rural areas. During the 1970s, U.S. military attention was largely turned elsewhere and the Colombian military left to its own devices. The Colombian military focused on administrative perks and privileges, developing an extensive bureaucratic apparatus that remains in place to this day (e.g., a very high logistical to combat soldier ratio of 6:1, compared to the international average of 3:1). Thus a career in the military was seen as a relatively safe and stable livelihood. According to Richani, "The low-intensity conflict has allowed the military to develop an institutional setup that was relatively comfortable within the context of a civil war" (Richani 2002: 182).

The end of the cold war and subsequent efforts to redefine national security and the "New World Order" profoundly challenged the Colombian military's articulation of its mission. After the fall of the Communist republics that provided the ideological model for the armed Colombian left, government and military officials attempted to portray the guerrillas as "dinosaurs," outmoded beasts headed for extinction. Paradoxically, the majority of military spokesmen insisted that the Communist menace lived on as a powerful organizing force behind human rights activism and the "political war" against the military. In the more than a decade since the fall of the Berlin Wall, the FARC has dramatically expanded its military strength, financed in large part through criminal activities.

In the post–cold war era, the U.S. military was engaged in its own soul-searching as the leadership attempted to redefine the military mission and engaged in spirited debates about the military's role in peacekeeping and humanitarian missions, counterterrorism, immigration and border control, and counternarcotics operations. Drug trafficking had been declared a national security threat by the United States in 1988, and the Pentagon was made the lead agency in international counternarcotics operations; the militarized, zero-tolerance approach of U.S. policy makers made counternarcotics operations the justification for expanding (rather than reducing) U.S. military presence in Latin America in the 1990s. The Colombian military had been highly resistant to accepting a counternarcotics mission; instead, it continued to view its only adversary as the guerrillas, to the extent that the armed forces illegally diverted U.S. counternarcotics assistance for a counterinsurgency offensive in 1991. These events, the general perception of the military as corrupt and ineffective, and a highly publicized purge of the National Police by charismatic police chief José Rosso Serrano led the vast majority of U.S. military assistance to be channeled to the Colombian police until the late 1990s, exacerbating existing institutional rivalry. Throughout this time the military leadership promoted the view that the guerrillas were simply an extension of the international narcotics trade, in an effort to gain access to U.S. assistance that continued to be limited by law to counternarcotics operations. U.S. Secretary of Defense William Cohen announced a new military-to-military cooperation agreement in December 1998,

the same year the United States began training Colombian army counternarcotics battalions prior to Clinton's massive aid package. Called
emergency supplemental funding, Plan Colombia began funneling more
than $1 billion a year to Colombia in 2000, making it the third largest
recipient of U.S. military assistance in the world, after Israel and Egypt.[5]

As U.S. officials increased their relationships with the Colombian military in the late 1990s, its officers were expected to interact with a widen-
ing circle of Americans, including journalists, civilian politicians, and
human rights activists. Throughout the 1980s and 1990s Colombia had
been home to a long-standing corps of journalists covering the drug trade
and other issues of interest to a U.S. audience; one freelancer told me he
left the country after four years because he couldn't stand doing another
cycle of "Medellín gang rehab, violent emerald warlords, and forgotten
war victims" features. During the late 1990s, U.S. coverage expanded,
with the *New York Times, Washington Post,* and *Los Angeles Times* all
relocating their Latin America or Andes bureaus to Bogotá. An expanding corps of freelance war correspondents also arrived (Cotts 2001).[6]
Congressional representatives and staff, State Department personnel, and
other interested agency employees also made regular trips through
Colombia to inspect U.S.-financed programs.

Human rights activists increased their research trips to Colombia as
well. The major human rights groups (including Amnesty International,
Human Rights Watch, and, on a much smaller scale, WOLA) had conducted periodic research missions to Colombia and published regular
reports for more than a decade. However, in U.S. policy debates
Colombia had long been considered a drug policy issue, not a human
rights issue, and was a low priority. With the Clinton aid package, attention to human rights issues in Colombia significantly increased in the
U.S. debate. In one of the first major expressions of interest among
NGOs that previously had not focused on Colombia, in January 1997 I
helped organize a delegation of NGO leaders from Washington. The
group included the director of WOLA, a senior associate from the Center
for International Policy, and the deputy director of the Latin America
Working Group; all went on to make Colombia advocacy and activism a
major focus. Modeled on delegation work developed more than a decade
earlier during the height of U.S.-based activism against U.S. military aid
to Central America, standard procedure for this and subsequent delegations involved meeting with military officials to confront them—armed
with published human rights reports and the details of specific cases—
with the contradictions between their stated goals and the reality of

human rights abuses. Such encounters were intended to probe the Colombian military's understanding and acceptance of human rights norms and the action on specific cases.

In February 2000, with a delegation that consisted of two members of Congress and six congressional staffers, I participated in two such meetings. WOLA sponsored the delegation, which meant covering the costs through special fund-raising, organizing the itinerary, and leading the actual trip; as the WOLA Colombia analyst, I organized much of the trip and acted as the group's leader in Colombia. During two day-trips outside Bogotá, one to a "Peace Community" in San José de Apartadó, Urabá, and the other to examine illicit narcotics issues in Puerto Asís, Putumayo, we met with local military commanders. In each region, the commanders greeted us with a carefully honed message about human rights, offering a defensive message about their role as "true human rights defenders" and anticipating what were by then well-known criticisms of the military's human rights performance. Seated in wide circles at times almost shouting distance apart, the delegation watched during the stiff, formal speeches of military commanders describing the complexity of threats in their region, their respect for human rights, and their profound support of the local population. The members of Congress, in carefully couched remarks, offered their respect and appreciation for the military mission while expressing concern about reported cases of military abuse. Mindful of my future research, I tried to stay as inconspicuous as possible in the background during this carefully orchestrated performance of official human rights activism.

In Puerto Asís, the U.S. ambassador and a large entourage joined the delegation for a day, so for security reasons we were confined to a large school auditorium, surrounded by pacing security officials with bomb-sniffing dogs. The peasants—and the military commanders—had to come to us. In the Putumayo region, long a FARC stronghold, the paramilitaries had gone on a major offensive several years before, establishing almost total control in the small-town centers over the course of three years. The United States had made this region the centerpiece of its counternarcotics strategy, called the "Push into Southern Colombia." It was here that the U.S.-funded and trained counternarcotics army battalions were being set up, and allegations of military collusion with paramilitary forces had caused serious concern at the embassy and among the commanders anticipating training and support. The commanders, slumped like the rest of us at uncomfortable student desks, blamed the allegations on the drug traffickers, who stood to profit if U.S. operations failed.

"There is distortion, slander, damage to the image of the work that we are doing," the commander told us. "That is natural because it is in the interest of those who oppose the process begun by the state government for a 'Putumayo without coca' [the slogan of the government's campaign]." They insisted that legal standards were followed: "We follow a process, if there is a death in combat, with the *fiscal* [the prosecutor charged with investigating crimes]." They were anxious that we appreciate their efforts, describing in detail combat operations against the paramilitary—whom they referred as *antisociales*—and guerrilla forces. "Last year, aggressive operations against the paramilitaries killed nine *antisociales,* captured twelve, and turned them in to the Fiscalía. We also captured weapons," the commander reported. Having heard accusations that the army was favorably disposed to the paramilitaries, he explained, "The reasons we appear to focus on the guerrillas is proportional; they have more troops. Also, the guerrillas fight the army, while the *autodefensas* avoid combat with the army." Emphatically, he declared that they had "no relation, couldn't even think of it," with the paramilitaries. "Our attitude is clear and transparent on the issue of human rights, not only that we should respect them, but that it's our moral obligation to protect them."

In Urabá, which we traveled to over the explicit and vehement objections of the U.S. embassy staff, we flew into Apartadó and then traveled in a rented bus to the headquarters of the 17th Brigade. This region had a long history of both guerrilla and paramilitary presence. The fighting between the two groups had prompted several local communities, with the support of the Catholic Church and a number of NGOs, to declare themselves completely off-limits to all armed actors, including the army; these were the Peace Communities referred to above. The communities had been hard hit by paramilitary attacks; at the time of our visit, community leaders told us that nearly one hundred people, almost 10 percent of the residents, had been killed since their founding in 1997. Local commanders viewed the refusal of the communities to allow them to patrol their lands as a direct affront, and contradictory to the community's requests for support. While insisting that the 17th Brigade remained "ever vigilant," the commander declared that the "the Constitution doesn't specifiy areas where we can't go" and that they want to "offer the communities all possible security." He attacked the communities' claim of neutrality, alleging that the guerrillas have entered and infiltrated them. The commanders defended themselves against allegations of military collusion with paramilitary forces, stating, "Our policy is to fight against the self-defense forces. We are very clear that any tie represents jail time, as required by Colombian law. Some had such ties, and they are now in jail." The human rights reports are part of a campaign against them, they said. "To call them paramilitaries is to discredit us, part of a campaign to discredit us that subversive organizations are carrying out against military organizations."

These military officers knew that the stakes were high: according to the so-called Leahy Amendment, added to foreign aid law in 1997, military units whose members have committed gross human rights violations with impunity cannot receive U.S. aid or training. U.S.-based human rights NGOs have insisted that the law is not being fully implemented. However, several battalions, including one in the Putumayo region and the 17th Brigade, have been suspended from scheduled assistance because of concern about their human rights records.

DEFENSIVE POSTURE:
THE LEGAL WAR AGAINST THE MILITARY

Many Colombian military officers believe that NGO human rights activism that documents and denounces military abuses is an aspect of the political and legal war against the military. For them, "human rights" were simply the facade of the armed Communist left, cloaking the political war of the guerrillas in the acceptable language of international law. Active duty and retired officers bitterly recall the high-profile cases of military officers dismissed from duty because of alleged involvement in human rights abuses, offering them as examples not of military wrongdoing but of the diabolical success of the Communist-inspired guerrillas and their naive international allies. When designing my interview strategy, I had considered attempting to find these vocal critics of human rights activism. First among them was General Alvaro Velandia Hurtado. The highlights of his case were reported in the "Milestones" section of *Time* magazine on September 25, 1995: "DISMISSED. ALVARO VELANDIA HURTADO, brigadier general and commander of Colombia's Third Army brigade; from the armed forces by President Ernesto Samper, under pressure from human-rights groups, for approving the 'disappearance' and murder of a member of the M-19 guerrilla group in 1987; in Bogotá. Velandia's discharge, recommended by the attorney general's office in July after a four-year investigation, makes him the highest ranking officer removed from the Colombian military for alleged human-rights abuses" (*Time* 1995).[7]

I had followed the case for years as it wound through the Colombian judicial system. A rare combination of factors, including an incredibly dedicated (and photogenic) family led by the victim's sister, Yanette Bautista (later head of ASFADDES), a pledge to support human rights by beleaguered president Ernesto Samper, and critically positioned committed governmental prosecutors, led to the unprecedented outcome. Living in Bogotá in 1994 and 1995, I was a passing acquaintance of Yanette and her nephew, and as a consultant for Human Rights Watch I had worked with and befriended the brother of the senior government prosecutor, a government human rights official in his own right (Yanette, her nephew, and the prosecutor would be forced to flee the country as a result of the case). It would have been relatively easy for me to find out where now-retired General Velandia spent his days. But I decided that to target officers involved in human rights abuse cases would unfairly slant my findings; they would of course be predisposed to speak out against NGOs. I was interested in finding out the mainstream institutional views on human rights in the military. Rather than attempt to find specific officers involved in well-known cases, I would simply work my way through my military contacts.

And so I found my way to Velandia's office, not because he was an anomaly, but because he was one of the most insightful analysts of the Colombian conflict and military, according to retired General Adolfo Clavijo, president of the Association of Retired Generals and Admirals, professor, and writer. I had arrived at Clavijo's door more comfortable in my performance of ethnographic empathy than I had been in my initial interviews (Robben 1995), and for several hours in his university office our conversation ranged over his early years in the service, the history of the Colombian conflict, and his opinions on current events. Like his colleagues, General Clavijo viewed NGOs as part of the extreme left, attempting to discredit the military by spreading lies. His views were not a surprise to me, for I had already read *Shearing the Wolf: The Unknown Dimensions of the Colombian Internal Conflict,* a book published by the association and coauthored by Clavijo in 2002. A searing and detailed critique of human rights activism, the book asserts that Marxist Communist ideology is unified and strong, underpinning the armed subversion, nongovernmental groups in Colombia, and their international allies, as well as shaping the human rights reporting from the U.N., the OAS, and the U.S. State Department. He ended our interview by conducting a short interview of his own. He asked about my experience in Colombia and my interest in the military, to which I responded with stories of my early days studying at the National University. I restricted my comments to the few general observations that both truthfully represented my personal opinions and reflected the Colombian consensus (e.g., Colombia is a wonderful and complicated country that is wildly misrepresented abroad; U.S. counternarcotics policies are ridiculous and misdirected). After pronouncing me one of the most *simpática* (nice, friendly) *gringas* he had ever met, he told me I must speak with General Velandia and sent me on my way with the general's phone number.

I met Velandia in a sunny midtown office that occupied a large, open room on the upper floor of an aparment building. Velandia was then serving as the president of Interlanza, the Association of Colombian Lanzeros, or Rangers (the United States established a ranger school in Colombia in the mid-1950s). Interlanza includes among its membership active duty ranger officers as well as retired soldiers and organizes events and forums. At the time of our interview, Velandia also served as the director of communications of *Acore,* a newspaper whose mission, according to the masthead, is to "express the thinking of the Retired Officials of the Military Forces of Colombia."

The very picture of a distinguished gentleman, with coiffed silver hair, wearing an elegant pale blue shirt and matching tie, Velandia began our interview by announcing that he was going to tape my interview with him. I nodded from my seat at a narrow table in front of his desk, where I faced a panoramic view of the hills with my back to the room. He had been misquoted in the past and wanted to prevent any possible future misunderstandings, he explained. Throughout our conversation, the two tape recorders, his and mine, lay on the table. He would occasionally reach down and stop the tape—once to take a phone call from a recently promoted general ("They often call me for advice," he explained) and once to ask how old I was, then to comment, "You have beautiful eyes, a lovely voice." He pointed to my neck, "a scratch as if from a kiss." His eyes were bright and wide, unblinking with the importance of what he had to tell me. To collect my thoughts and break his gaze, I had to look down at my notebook and pretend to write. He was focused and solicitous, served by a stream of young women throughout our interview, offering more tea or copies of his recent articles. The unspoken details of his dismissal and the Bautista case hung in the air; the closest I came to inquiring about it was asking if anything "complicated" had ever happened to him while in the service. He replied with a story of an ambush in Arauca in which eight of his soldiers died.

While speaking with me, Velandia emphasized the war. Colombia was a country at war that had not defeated its guerrilla forces "for the same reasons the U.S. lost in Vietnam, that the Russians lost in Afghanistan."

During my interviews, Colombian military officers often mentioned the war in Vietnam, as an example of U.S. failure—discrediting U.S. advice and demands—and as an excuse for and an example of the difficulties of counterinsurgency warfare. "War is very difficult to understand unless you are within [*metido*] the war," he told me. "When you are within the war, you try to protect yourself, and anything that moves is your enemy. That is why the North American soldiers saw those hamlets that they went to as enemies, and because they suffered wounded and dead soldiers, they saw enemies everywhere. Who understands this? Only someone who has been to war. Otherwise you don't. Everyone says, you shouldn't kill people. If I am sitting at a desk, I don't understand why people get killed. But if I am with my wounded people, and a civilian crosses my path, I think that he is my enemy." As for human rights, he began the interview by dismissing them out of hand. The guerrillas, funded by the drug traffickers, had used the peace talks and amnesties to get their leaders out of jail, to build up their ranks to escalate the fighting. "That was when the NGOs began to directly manage the issue, influencing foreign governments and international organizations. For example, the U.S. State Department; for example, the American embassy in Bogotá." They were all influenced by the guerrillas? I asked. Of course, he replied. "You can see their reports are copies of guerrilla reports, the NGO reports, the International Red Cross, the United Nations, the OAS. They started denouncing things, and because no one here believed them they went abroad and then came back with the same reports in foreign languages and starting applying pressure with these *denuncias,* and to generate an ambience of mistrust in terms of international relations with Colombia. They started calling Colombia a country that violates human rights and said that the military has a backward view [*concepción cuadriculada*], that they don't see what is going on, that human rights are constantly violated."

While particularly bitter and vehement, Velandia's views are representative of the opinion throughout the military that human rights cases denounced internationally are part of a guerrilla conspiracy. Even active duty commanders trying to impress U.S. audiences with their professionalism express such views. On April 10, 2003, during a U.S. Army conference held in a congressional office building on Capitol Hill, Brigadier General José Arturo Camelo, executive director of the Defense Ministry's Judge Advocate General's Office, called human rights groups "friends of subversives" and accused them of waging a "legal war" against the military. In his remarks, intended to demonstrate the human rights reforms of the Colombian military, he claimed that the work of Colombian human rights NGOs were part of a larger guerrilla strategy (Tate 2003). Similarly, in a January 2003 speech at the Pentagon, the head of the Colombian Armed Forces, General Carlos Ospina Ovalle, told the public that most allegations of human rights abuses by the Colombian military are false and politically motivated. "The FARC has political friends outside Colombia, and they try to show us as abusers," Ospina said. "Honest people around the world know that we are serving our people well" (quoted in Kelly 2003).

THE FIRST INSTITUTIONAL RESPONSE: THE COLOMBIAN MILITARY AS VICTIM OF HUMAN RIGHTS VIOLATIONS

Even while remaining critical of NGO human rights activism, a new generation of military officers realized that they could no longer simply dismiss human rights accusations as guerrilla slander. This was particularly true as the United States began increasing its funding and training programs, which had human rights vetting requirements attached by Congress. NGO reports began to have real consequences in the career advancement of Colombian officers, with the denial of visas to travel to Europe and training by U.S. Special Forces teams. The Colombian military began to portray itself as a victim of human rights violations. With no due process or day in court, the military argued, these accusations were wrongly destroying the careers of innocent patriots and even contributing to failure on the battlefield, as officers remained in the barracks for fear of engendering allegations any time they engaged in combat operations.

This new attitude was demonstrated by Colonel Gómez, a highly praised commander who distanced himself from Clavijo's critique. "General Clavijo is a very special man. I am a friend of his, and know that he is a thinker and intellectually curious. He is a dean at the Military University, he has written many things, so he has a critical attitude," he said with a rueful laugh. "But he retired at least ten years ago and sees the situation very differently. You know, everyone describes the party according to how they did on the dance floor." He smiled as he obliquely referred to the fact that the generation of retired generals who now make a living advising politicians and writing newspaper editorials were widely seen as incompetent, responsible for letting the war drag on with little to show for it except a bloated military bureaucracy. Also unspoken was the assertion that these new colonels were a different breed of soldier. I learned that Colonel Gómez and his battalion were in fact being publicly praised for their work when I accidentally arrived twenty-four hours before the president's "surprise" arrival for a security council meeting. In between preparatory meetings, the colonel offered his reflections, standing under a mango tree in the searing midday heat of Colombia's Caribbean coast as I held my tape recorder under his chin.

This battalion had been chosen for a presidential visit because, according to the press, they had recently foiled a planned guerrilla attack. They were also to be praised because of their implementation of a controversial new national security program, the "Million Friends" Network, set up to allow the military to pay wide networks of covert informants. At the time, during the first months of the program, the thwarted attack was seen as a replicable success worthy of publicity; the evening news was also featuring "Reward Mondays," in which hooded informants received stacks of cash (the show was later suspended because of criticism of the program). The colonel, lithe and friendly, with a quick wit and clipped mustache, was responsible for security and organizing the visit. The battalion grounds were in top shape; the trim lawns were lined with whitewashed stones and small signs printed with inspirational slogans such as "Only the victorious deserve to live" (*Solo los vencerdores merece vivir*). My presence and questions appeared to elicit little but intellectual curiosity. Neither threatened nor threatening, he was simply pausing for reflections in the midst of a very busy day.

Earlier in our conversation, when I asked Colonel Gómez what he thought about human rights, he emphasized the institutional learning process. "Because the issue has a lot of international weight, the army in particular has learned a lot. There have been seminars, special training courses, conferences, visits to the units, a human rights office. At the military school where cadets are training, at the weapons courses, the issue is now part of the curriculum, incorporated into the academic plan, into all of the courses that we do, from the level of cadets to generals. In all the courses there are some class hours for human rights. The issue *ya es nuestro* [now belongs to us]."

In his account of the first military human rights offices, General José Manual Bonnett Locarno (Ret.) emphasized this proactive vision of the military leadership, who saw that they needed to organize against NGO human rights activism. First as the inspector general of the army and then as commander in chief of the armed forces, General Bonnett oversaw the creation of military human rights offices, the organization of conferences, and the publication of materials. Though he taught at a downtown university, General Bonnett remembered traveling to human rights events. "Forums were held all over the country, national forums were held, I went to world forums on human rights. . . . The big effort was in 1993 or '94, when they created the offices, trained people, sent people to study and learn . . . [because] the commanders became aware that this was a weapon that was being used against us by the Communists and this weapon had to be fought. We had to counteract [*contrarrestar*] this weapon."

The first Colombian military human rights office was established in the Ministry of Defense in 1994, part of a growing governmental human rights infrastructure established by President Samper following the reforms of the 1991 Constitution. Staffed largely by civilians, the office first attempted to break through entrenched resistance to anything having to do with "human rights" among military staff. The first director of the office was Pilar Gaitán, a petite blond with an impressive résumé of graduate degrees and human rights studies, with the careful makeup and substantial gold jewelry common to Colombian professional upper-middle-class women. Her father had been a general and the minister of defense; she had worked on Samper's campaign and was a college class-mate of Samper's campaign manager and then minister of defense, Fernando Botero. NGO activists speculated that she had been chosen for the position not only because of her academic training and family con-nections but also because of her previous experience with military mis-treatment. During the mass arrests of December 1979, following the National Security Statute and the M-19 robbery of the Canton Norte, like thousands of other students Gaitán had been detained for several days in a military battalion, interrogated, and possibly tortured. Over small cups of coffee in her Bogotá apartment, she spoke low and fast of her early days running the Defense Ministry's human rights office:

> In 1994 human rights was a much stigmatized issue. But President Samper decided to make human rights a global effort across the board in all the ministries. For the first time, the military, through then–Minister of Defense Botero, decided to open a human rights office. The office was supposed to promote the issues of human rights and international humanitarian law. When we started, the issue was practically forbidden. It was seen as a pro-guerrilla stance, provoking not just annoyance but outright hostility. We decided to focus on training, and let other people handle the accusations [*denuncias*] of human rights violations.

Her voice quickened as she recalled the difficulties of the early days; at several points in our conversation she cast me a harried glance and asked for additional assurance that particular comments would remain off the record. "They thought I was evil, that I was going to take their eyes out [*sacarles los ojos a todos*], investigate everything about them, and it wasn't like that," she told me. "So we started emphasizing that they should have their rights respected too, ensure that they have due process guarantees and the right to a fair defense for military officers accused of human rights violations. That is how we started being able to win a little ground."

In the mid-1990s military officers as victims became a central narrative in the military reaction to human rights activism, taking on increased importance as the military faced political and battlefield defeats. Officers chafed under the civilian leadership of President Samper, who became an international pariah after DEA agents revealed that he accepted Cali Cartel contributions to his campaign. Coup rumors periodically flared, and the flamboyantly outspoken head of the army, General Harold Bedoya, was forced to resign after a showdown with Samper over proposed negotiations with the guerrillas in July 1997. His replacement, General Bonnett, was widely viewed as inept. One U.S. embassy official referred to Bonnett and his staff as the "Apple Dumpling Gang" and judged the military "pathetic" (quoted in Kirk 2003: 188).

The relationship between the United States and Colombian military forces was generally tense during this period as well. U.S. aid was restricted to counternarcotics operations, which the vast majority of Colombian military officers emphatically did not view as their mission. Until the 2000 Clinton aid package, almost all U.S. military aid to Colombia was channeled to the National Police, an institutional rival of the army that enjoyed a stellar international reputation thanks to successful operations against the major cartels and an internal purge (as well as the close friendship between Police Chief José Rosso Serrano and key Republican congressional staff). U.S. military training courses involving human rights and U.S. legislation requiring human rights vetting for foreign militaries receiving U.S. assistance put the issue of human rights front and center for the Colombian military. For almost all of 1997, the armed forces did not receive the minimal U.S. aid appropriated for them because Joint Chief of Staff General Bonnett refused to sign the memorandum agreeing to submit his forces to human rights screening as required by the Leahy Amendment.

Militarily, the armed forces were struggling as well. Throughout the mid-1990s the FARC adopted the strategy of a standing army rather than the guerrilla warfare tactics of previous years and conducted a series of attacks on military outposts that resulted in humiliating defeats for the armed forces. Through criminal activity, primarily kidnapping and the "taxing" of narcotics production and shipping, the FARC had doubled its troop numbers and bought increasingly sophisticated weaponry, while the ELN regularly made headlines by bombing the oil pipelines responsible for one-third of Colombia's tax revenue. The FARC took soldiers and police as captives, at one point holding more than four hundred as "prisoners of war." Many were held for more than four years; at this writing the FARC is still holding at least forty soldiers. The FARC also kidnapped a series of politicians and other public figures in an attempt to build pressure for an exchange of captured soldiers and kidnapped public figures for jailed FARC leaders. Public perceptions of military incompetence, and pressure from civilian leadership to produce better battlefield results, put the military on the defensive.

Confronted with discontent at home and human rights accusations abroad, officers focused on the violations of their rights—the rights to a fair trial, defense counsel, to face their accusers, and to know the evidence against them. According to this logic, human rights *denuncias* were responsible for the military defeats: having no recourse against these unfair allegations, officers would avoid any combat operations in order to escape being demoted, jailed, or fired as a result of unjust charges of misconduct. This fear even had a medical diagnosis; it became known as the Procuraduría syndrome, after the oversight agency created by the 1991 Constitution to investigate allegations of official misconduct. Military officers complained of being *empapelado,* literally, papered over, by complaints and investigations of allegations of misconduct.

Standing under the mango tree, Colonel Gómez agreed that human rights had been "perverted" *(desviado)* by the army's enemies. He went on to explain how the guerrillas make it appear that the army is guilty of their misdeeds: "For example, when they do something, they put on the uniform, our uniform, and they go and mistreat the population. They kill an entire family or torture someone, and they say, this was the army. At the end of two or three years, they will manage to demonstrate that the army wasn't responsible, but the general is already detained, the sergeant is already in jail. He has already spent four or five years in jail for a crime he didn't commit."

The Internet has played a critical role in this circulation of accusations. It provides universal and indefinite access to information; anyone with a computer with a modem and a phone line can post and download *denuncias,* and they remain in cyberspace indefinitely. By giving these unsubstantiated claims a longer life and greater reach and putting them instantaneously into the homes of activists around the world, the Internet creates a parallel system for judgment, entirely outside the jurisdiction and requirements of the formal legal process. By becoming the subject of international Internet activism, military officers felt they had little or no recourse.

My first military interview ended with such a story. Colonel Vargas remained conscious that allegations against him from almost a decade ago continue to circulate via the Web. When he was a captain assigned to a rural mountain ridge stronghold of the ELN in the early 1990s, he was one of the military officers accused of abuses during a major campaign by Colombian and international human rights NGOs. In a detailed report published in Spanish and a fifty-six-page summary published in English, then-Captain Vargas and others were accused of creating a para-military network that killed hundreds of peasants and local community leaders and forced 4,000 people (of a total population of 14,000) to flee their homes. According to the NGO report, this paramilitary network was an example of the Colombian military counterinsurgency strategy employed throughout the country. Captain Vargas was also accused of forcing local children to walk ahead of patrolling troops; according to the report, two children were killed and one wounded when they stepped on land mines.

When asked about his time stationed in that now-notorious area, Colonel Vargas launched into an elaborate explanation of how the local guerrilla commander organized a *montaje,* a slander campaign, against him. He ended the story by acknowledging how the Internet keeps these accusations in circulation:

> If you go on the Internet, there it says human rights violations in Colombia are so terrible, we are going to tell you about some cases. It will say Capt. X in X town . . . used innocent children leaving the schoolhouse as human shields, and as a result two were wounded, two were killed. And the truth is, if you go there and asked what happened in 1991, it is because they [the guerrillas] tricked the NGOs. . . . These terrorists in the FARC and the ELN have specialized groups for this. I should bring a lawsuit, a lawsuit against Amnesty [International] and the others, and see if we can clear this up, but there is no time. But if some day there is a serious problem I will have to take this seriously and demonstrate to the world what happened.[8]

HUMAN RIGHTS AS PSYCHOLOGICAL OPERATIONS

Colonel Gómez had ended our brief interview under the mango tree by describing human rights as a "combat multiplier." Despite the "perverting" of the issue for political gain by the guerrillas and their supporters, according to Colonel Gómez and other forwarding-thinking officers, the essence of human rights—understood as respect for the physical integrity of the civilian population—could help the military win the war. "If the issue is handled well," he told me, "it can be a combat multiplier; it is a trust multiplier." This did not mean an end to violence; he believed that human rights activists would have to acknowledge that "combat is legal" during wartime: "During combat people are killed, people are wounded, but just because there is combat there doesn't have to be lawsuits." The critical issue is legitimacy, which engenders support from the population, meaning that the military will be more successful on the battlefield. This support can be gained through the deployment of human rights. "If I abusively grab someone and take them and mistreat them, this doesn't help anything, not our institutional image, not the combat itself. It makes anything we are trying to do illegitimate," he told me. "Human rights is what gives us legitimacy."

The first military officer to link psychological operations, civic action, and human rights as part of the same spectrum of counterinsurgency operations was Colonel Vargas, in my first military interview. Sitting in his damp concrete office, he listed in numbing detail all the programs and plans the army had developed for working with poor neighborhoods, students, and local community organizations: street paving, fixing sports clubs, health brigades, cultural activities, children's recreational programs, "soldier for a day" and "girls of iron" programs for high school students. These were not charity programs offered to improve the lot of the region's many desperately poor families. These programs were seen as central to the military's recapture of a "strategic area," that is, an area viewed as essentially under the control of the guerrillas for the past two decades. "The general idea is that the army is involved in everything, in all the community association meetings, in the neighborhoods, so that the self-defense forces and the FARC and ELN terrorists, there are still a few, can't settle there. It means that the *state* is there," he told me. "This is the primary objective, that legitimacy returns and that the people genuinely believe in their institutions, believe in their military forces." He went on to say that similar efforts were being started in other conflictive areas and that this new strategy is being expanded through the military:

> I have taken classes in Bogotá; it is called community support class, classes in community development, civic affairs, where we have learned that the best way to win the war is to win the trust and the support of the civilian population. In addition, we are in the midst of an internal campaign among

the officers, the soldiers, and the noncommissioned officers to improve the attitude and treatment of the civilian population, because the only way to win the war is to win the hearts and minds of the people, helping them and creating a team of the community and the military forces against all the violent actors, against all the terrorists.

"Winning hearts and minds" is a phrase that became famous in the U.S.-sponsored counterinsurgency campaigns of the Vietnam War. Shorthand for what is technically known as psychological operations, or psyops, and linked to civic action, the phrase points to the centrality of civilian support for successful war efforts.[9] Psyops, which includes all propaganda related to war efforts, have a long history but did not develop into their current form until technological advances allowed for mass communication and the cold war emphasis on unconventional warfare drove military planners to focus on counterinsurgency.[10] Psyops include an extremely wide range of activities, "affect[ing] not only military targets but political, economic, or social structures within the target area," and can include "deceptive methods" used in the "plan[ning] and execution of truth projection activities." Standard psyops include leafleting battlefields with messages urging opponents to surrender and the radio and television broadcast of propaganda in enemy-controlled territory. Both these tactics have been widely used by U.S. forces.[11]

No Colombian military psychological operations doctrine materials are available, but it is safe to assume that its doctrine is largely based on U.S. military doctrine. Colombians make up one of the largest number of officers of any country in Latin America trained by the United States at the Western Hemisphere Institute for Security Cooperation (formerly the School of the Americas), more than ten thousand Colombians in the past decade. Psyops and military intelligence are among the classes taken by these Colombian officers. The only currently available document that discusses Colombian psyops doctrine is a report dated 1985 that explains it relies heavily on U.S. training.[12]

The incorporation of human rights programs into pysops has long been part of U.S. military training, particularly for their Latin American allies. While U.S. troops had been receiving minimal training in the rules of law since the 1950s (training that was expanded in 1974, six years after the My Lai massacre), the U.S. commander in chief issued the first written directives on human rights training in 1990 (Vickers 2000). The U.S. role in training Latin American militaries at the School of the Americas received a great deal of attention because graduates were linked to human rights abuses in their home countries; as a result, expanded human rights training was instituted.[13] The anthropologist Lesley Gill demonstrates graphically the limitations of this training in her ethnographic encounters with U.S. and Latin American officers participating in this training (Gill 2004).[14]

The U.S. military began putting human rights pressure on its Colombian military allies in the late 1990s, during efforts to expand military assistance from the Colombian National Police to the armed forces. Legislation requiring that any units receiving such assistance pass human rights screening prompted significant resistance in 1997, when General Bonnet as commander in chief refused to sign an agreement pledging cooperation. He continues to complain of Washington using human rights as a "political weapon." Colombian military compliance was encouraged by linking human rights vetting with military perks such as international training missions; Colombian military officers were routinely treated to a trip to Disney World during their U.S. training, for example. Elite training in the United States is also seen as crucial for career advancement. The cancellation of visas by the German and U.S. governments because of human rights issues has been bitterly decried by the Colombian military leadership.[15]

Following the pilot project set up in the Ministry of Defense in 1994, each service branch (Army, Navy, Air Force) set up a national human rights office and then gradually opened human rights offices in each battalion, to a total of 115 by 2000 (Fuerzas Militares de Colombia 2000). These offices are staffed by a combination of military personnel, civilians, and members of the "administrative corps," civilian professionals who receive minimum military training and wear uniforms but do not command troops. On the battalion level, Colombian military human rights offices are located in or closely linked to the S-5 (Psychological Operations) structure. The offices are shared and in some cases staffed by a single noncommissioned officer. I spent an hour talking with one such NCO in his cramped, crowded office in a conflictive area of southern Colombia. He recalled that when he enlisted, in 1987, "there were confrontations, but nothing like there is now." He joined, over the objections of his mother, who had been the victim of police abuse and had watched the army destroy her small town in the partisan violence of the 1950s.

As the human rights NCO and leader of the Integration Committee, Sergeant Muñoz coordinates intelligence operations, plans special events, and directs the "girls of iron" and "boy ranger" programs. These community outreach programs feature local children's clubs run out of the military base, consisting primarily of camouflage face painting and assistance in such civic-military activities as literacy campaigns but also include some basic military training. Sergeant Muñoz recalled:

> My training in psychological operations really opened my eyes to how we are fighting the war in Colombia, and how it should be fought. Before, we just focused on combat. But three, five years ago, it became a political war. The subversion is going through different stages. First was a guerrilla war. Then there was the war of the masses, with the large-scale attacks on towns. Then the Bolivarian Movement [the FARC's clandestine political movement, launched in 2000]. They started the political war just recently, with their spokesmen in Germany, in Europe, saying good things about the FARC, making the army seem like the bad guys. Then, when the peace talks broke off, in Europe they stopped seeing the FARC like a guerrilla group and say that they are a terrorist group. They [the foreign governments] made them close down their offices abroad.
>
> So we have to do what they do. We take testimony and photos and write reports. We sent them abroad, to NATO, to the United Nations, to the Defensoría. They started messing things up, and we took advantage of the situation. That is when we created the S-5 with human rights. The S-5 has always existed, but it was never very important; they never paid much attention to it. Until now. Now they are paying a lot of attention to human rights, because the guerrilla was really getting to us. Now we have training courses, courses on human rights.

The sergeant went on to explain that through human rights training, treatment of soldiers in the army had dramatically improved. He described conscripts as the first to experience the brutality of the army and the first to benefit from their new human rights programs: "The new officers have changed their mentality. Before, they would beat us a lot. Human rights didn't exist. Treatment of the soldiers was a big problem in many of the units; they said that the one who screamed the most would get beat the hardest. They would make people spend two weeks in the *calabozo* [a small pit dug in the ground to hold prisoners] or spend ten days buried up to your neck. Now they call that torture, but before it was just punishment." Mistreatment of conscripts is still a significant problem for the armed forces. In a February 19, 2006, cover story titled "Torture in the Army," the Colombian newsweekly *Semana* revealed dramatic testimony of official abuse of twenty-one new soldiers during training, including beatings, burnings, and rape. In the resulting scandal, the army chief of staff was forced to resign, and the inspector general opened a wide-ranging investigation into the events. Periodic reports of suicides among conscripts have also raised concern about the abuse of soldiers.

According to Sergeant Muñoz, one reason the conscripts abused the civilian population was that they themselves had been abused. In his account, the reforms that followed the development of military human rights training programs and psyops improved the military's treatment of its soldiers, who then were better able to respect the people they encountered during their field operations. This in turn improved the army's combat record, as the army's historic inability to defeat the guerrillas was explained by its abuse of the population, a problem resolved through this new human rights program: "The way we were trained was what created our consciousness as soldiers. Because we were treated so badly, we were resentful, angry, and we got our vengeance in public order duties. That was before the psychological operations started. When we arrived at a farm, we would destroy everything, destroy the fruit trees and the vegetables, kill the farm animals. We would steal everything, and we would get rid of the peasants with our rifle butts [*a patadas*]. Now we have learned about civic-military relations."

Sergeant Muñoz concluded by predicting that human rights would help the Colombian military win the war. He based his assumption on the theory of guerrilla warfare advanced by the Chinese Communist ideologue who developed the theory of prolonged popular war. "According to the book by Mao Zedong, there are rules of war," he told me, "and the army that has the civilian population on its side has won 90 percent of the war. That was why we were losing against the guerrillas." Human rights—understood as not mistreating the peasant population—would help the military win their hearts and minds, and thus the war.

MILITARY HUMAN RIGHTS TRAINING

The Colombian military offers human rights training to interested civilians as well as to its soldiers. I saw an example of the outreach for their educational program in an ad that appeared in *El Tiempo* announcing open inscription for the human rights correspondence course offered by the 5th Brigade and Oracle University.[16] This correspondence course was one of the ways the military was proudly demonstrating increased competence in human rights; hundreds of soldiers (and interested civilians) had taken the class, and I wanted to see what exactly was being taught. I had first heard of the course several years before, while working in Washington. An enthusiastic young captain requested a meeting with me and, once sitting in my office, eagerly announced his plans to design a human rights course. He was with the 5th Brigade, based in the eastern city of Bucaramanga near the border with Venezuela, and had received special dispensation to attend Columbia University's School for International Policy and then return to design a human rights correspondence course. During the time of his visit to my office, however, the 5th Brigade was involved in the growing scandal surrounding the La Gabarra massacre (see chapter 6). Dozens, possibly hundreds of people had been massacred over the course of several weeks in the small towns under their jurisdiction. Human rights NGOs told the press that they believed local military and police commanders had collaborated with the paramilitary perpetrators. In an interview published in *El Tiempo*, the commander of the 5th Brigade, General Alberto Bravo Silva, had in return accused the NGOs of being guerrilla supporters. As the captain enthusiastically explained how this course would improve soldiers' understanding of their rights and obligations under international law, I interrupted him. What about your commanding officer, General Bravo Silva? I asked. Hasn't he been accused of human rights abuses? Hasn't he accused human rights defenders of being guerrillas? The captain paused. "Well," he explained, "we maintain a clear division of labor." (General Bravo Silva, along with two regional police commanders, was relieved of his command by President Pastrana on August 30, 1999; on January 19, 2002, the Procuraduría officially closed the case against him.) Given this history, I was eager to see the contents—and results—of the young captain's efforts.

Even armed with the telephone number, it was not easy to find the human rights office of a brigade in a major city. After several confusing calls, during which my inquiries were met with puzzled sighs and then blank silence by the women on the other end of the phone, I finally reached an officer who acknowledged working in the human rights section and scheduled an appointment. In the snarled traffic worsened by an afternoon of steady, sooty rain, I spent more than an hour en route to the battalion from my apartment. Passing through several military checkpoints, I reached the human rights office located at the far end of a several-acre compound, housed in one of several identical rows of low brick office buildings. The front area housed the psychological operations program, staffed by a long-haired teenage girl gazing blankly at a computer seated next to a teenage boy in fatigues. Maps on the wall showed the location of different illegal armed groups; a map of the southern state of Meta indicated the different FARC fronts with black circles. A map of a city, probably Bogotá, showed different militia units of the FARC and the ELN; neither map showed any paramilitary presence. The human rights office was at the back of the room, in a small recessed cubicle. After carefully reading my letter of presentation from New York University and asking several times for me to explain my project, the major staffing the office agreed to talk.

The major, a slightly chubby, dark-skinned mestizo, was first hesitant but gradually warmed to my questions. He began by explaining that the focus of his work was education, protection, and *denuncias*. "Education includes the seminars, courses, and academies on human rights," while the protection program was aimed at protecting soldiers from "problems, misunderstandings, . . . situations that cause doubt about the position of the institution." He was especially eager to explain the kinds of *denuncias* they made: "We don't just teach classes to our men about human rights. We also denounce actions by terrorist groups, the AUC and the FARC. In my jurisdiction, Cundinamarca [the state surrounding Bogotá], the main terrorist group is the FARC, followed by the AUC." He swiveled the computer screen over to my side of his desk; I was sitting in a broken office chair, low to the ground and missing the back. The major had pulled the chair up to face his wooden desk, the desktop entirely obscured by piles of papers. On the ancient computer screen bearing the luminescent green script of the 1980s were tables filled with numbers. "There were 343 terrorist actions in Cundinamarca so far this year. We don't separate them out by perpetrator, because to us, a perpetrator is a perpetrator. But here [he pointed to another table] there are more violations by the FARC than by the AUC. We denounce terrorist actions with the *denuncias* that you see here." He picked up a pile of paper-clipped documents from his desk, long legal-sized sheets of Colombian official papers; each was stamped "Fiscalía de la Nación," and the top paper was dated about two weeks earlier. He read a section, his finger on the page; it was a report that a small bomb had gone off on the Transmilenio, Bogotá's new trolley line. "This is clearly a violation," he told me. "They are trying to get the civilian population involved in the war. They don't care who falls. So what we do is keep the statistics, denounce specific cases, and try to *judicilizarlos* [set up formal cases in the legal system] so the cases are resolved [*no quedan en la impunidad*]." Rather than investigate allegations of military misconduct, according to the major, the human rights office collected case histories of abuses by illegal armed actors. The Colombian military's human rights offices became one more reporting agency.

"Who do you denounce them to, on a national level?" I asked him.

"We denounce them before the Fiscalía," he answered; I did not point out that the report he showed me had come from the Fiscalía. "Before the Defensoría del Pueblo, and to the Red Cross. Of course, that is not a *denuncia*," he clarified, "because they are neutral, they are a completely neutral institution, it is just so they know what is going on." His implication was that the aforementioned Colombian legal institutions were not neutral but partisan players in the conflict. "On an international level we compile texts, pamphlets, and books about all the *denuncias*. For no cost, we sent them to the international community, to embassies, with the aim of showing them the goals of these groups, what these *bandoleros* and terrorists are trying to achieve."

"What is your human rights training?" I asked him, interested in the career path that brought him to this office cubicle.

"I took the basic human rights course," he told me, presumably the 5th Brigade human rights correspondence course that he now administers, and was now studying in a certificate *(diplomado)* program. Serving in this office was just another in a series of military postings.

I asked him to explain the human rights course, and he enthusiastically complied. "When we started the human rights course, there were one hundred people, that was last year. Now there are more than one thousand enrolled. They have to pass an exam." Anyone can take the class, not just the military. "We decided to offer the course because unfortunately some universities haven't taken up [*asumido*] the issue the way they need to. . . . The idea is that people who graduate and get the certificate then create human rights promotion groups, as volunteers, to give classes on human rights to soldiers, to high schools. We want human rights to be everywhere, to be in families and all sectors of society. People just talk about human rights in terms of the conflict, but we don't agree, we think that human rights should be about everything in society."

The idea of human rights as the responsibility of all citizens is expressed early and often in the introduction to the online curriculum of the correspondence course. The first paragraph states that the 1991 Constitution "expressly determined that it is the duty of every person to respect the human rights of others and not abuse their own rights, and so to defend and educate others [*difundir*] about Human Rights." The introduction goes on: "The work of education [*promoción*], protection, and defense of human rights concern us all: State and Civil Society. That is why a frank and permanent dialogue about this issue [*problemática*] with the different sectors of society and, in particular, with international and national nongovernmental organizations is of primordial importance." The course puts human rights squarely in the center of the "hemispheric and universal agenda," alongside "drug trafficking, the environment, immigration, and free trade." The course itself is divided into twelve modules, neatly framed in legalistic terms: ethics and military conduct; history of human rights; the 1991 Constitution; human rights protection agencies in Colombia; international humanitarian law; the U.N, the OAS, NGOs, the European Union, the international criminal court; internal displacement; and the InterAmerican system. Students are graded on the completion of worksheets, a test, and a three-page essay; soldiers participating in the course can forgo the essay if they spend eight hours teaching human rights or international humanitarian law to lower-ranking personnel.

The major explained how the human rights course had clarified the confusion over different international norms. "People sometimes confuse human rights and international humanitarian law but that has changed a lot, gotten a lot better," he told me. "The quality of instruction in human rights is getting much better." According to his enrollment lists, soldiers of all ranks (250 scholarships were available to low-ranking soldiers) were taking the course as part of much-publicized "professionalization" efforts throughout the army.

HUMAN RIGHTS REPORTING OF THE COLOMBIAN MILITARY

To find out how the military's human rights reports are produced, I spent several hours in the army's national human rights office, housed at one end of a long hallway in the Ministry of Defense. Much of that time I spent perched on the edge of a folding chair, sipping sweet coffee and waiting for the arrival of the captain in charge while three civilian lawyers wandered from one cubicle to another carrying faxes and stacks of paper. I attempted small talk with one of the office administrators, a soft-spoken man who admitted that working with the military was "hard, sometimes," but declined to give any details other than the frequent turnover. His last boss was now teaching at Fort Benning, in Georgia, he told me. The new boss had been there a while, almost nine months, but it had taken him a while to get the feel of the office. The office responded to all the complaints it received but mainly dealt with cases of mistreatment of soldiers; the more serious human rights cases are the jurisdiction of the Fiscalía and the Procuraduría. Reading over his shoulder, I could see that the top letter on a stack at least two feet high was from an NGO, asking the office how it was planning to address the "paramilitary situation."

When the captain finally arrived, he led me to a small glassed-in room at the back of the office. His desktop was bare, and a nearly empty book-shelf behind him contained only a few books on international law lean-ing against several plastic binders. With piercing green eyes, the pale beige skin of centuries of racial mixing, and the rapid slur of the Caribbean, he told me he was a lawyer from the Atlantic Coast, part of the "administrative corps, not 100 percent military but one of the people who work with the military, professionals like lawyers, doctors, den-tists." "We don't go out to the battalions," he explained, "except when we are going to the *revista* [inspection], and we don't command troops." He and his colleagues in the administrative corps had received three and half months of military training at the Military Academy.

"This office deals with coordination of all the human rights offices of all the units, divisions, and brigades. We provide the institutional response to any concerns; we are the bridge between the state and units regarding everything having to do with human rights," he told me. This included coordinating the 5th Brigade human rights training course. Like his NGO and civilian counterparts, he complained that human rights programs struggled with limited resources. "We have to keep presenting projects to see if we can get more funding. We present joint projects with the Ministry of Defense. We get a little something for our projects. We also organize conferences on human rights." Finally, he told me, the of-fice does public relations and investigative work. "We meet with NGOs, investigators like yourself, providing neutral information about the con-flict. We answer *derechos de petición*, we meet with community mem-bers, and we carry out inspections."

When I asked him for an example, he told me of one recent massacre that he had investigated. "You know the case of Alaska, the *vereda* in Buga, where twenty-seven people were killed last year by paramilitaries, in October, in the jurisdiction of the Palacé Battalion?" he asked me. "According to information from the NGOs, there was collaboration between the *autodefensas* and the Palacé Battalion. We went to carry out the *revista* a month ago, and we found that the Procuraduría had deter-mined there was no evidence and so they closed the case, that there was no connection. . . . We could prove that the troops from the Palacé Battalion were out on operations and were not involved at all."

It was not until nearly the end of the interview that the captain explained to me how he had gotten this job. Before coming to Bogotá, he worked in Cali as a military legal adviser on human rights issues for the Palacé Battalion, the one allegedly involved in the massacre. "I came to this job because the commanders trusted me, from the work that I did

with the Third Division [which has the Palacé Battalion under its juris-
diction]. I was at the Third Division when the incident with the Palacé
Battalion happened, as their legal advisor," he told me. "And we showed,
with the judicial investigators [*agentes de control*], that there was no involvement by the Palacé Battalion." The captain viewed his past involvement with the suspects in the case as an advantage; he knew them and
the way that they worked, so obviously they could be guilty of no
wrongdoing. This is one example of the conflict of interest in military
investigations of human rights abuses often criticized by NGOs. Officers
directly implicated in cases are often charged with investigating them; until the 1999 reform of the military penal code, commanding officers also
served as the judges in cases involving officers under their jurisdiction.

Inspections like the one described by the captain are rarely published
in the military's human rights reports, even those cases with favorable
outcomes for the accused officers. Instead, their human rights reports
focus on abuses by the "illegal armed actors," primarily the guerrillas.
These reports have developed their own genre and style, featuring bold
type, glossy paper, and color photographs, generally displaying higher
production values than NGO reports. Funding from the U.S. government
for the Ministry of Defense pays for translation and publication of these
reports into English as part of the military's public relations campaigns.
Photos can generally be classified into two categories. The first are posed
portraits of human rights events sponsored by the military, often panels
of military officers and governmental and NGO human rights experts.
The other, and more prevalent, category is graphic examples of violations: crying children in front of bombed-out buildings; bandaged victims
of land mines; mutilated bodies displayed on the ground. These publications are in fact much more graphic than government or NGO publications, probably in part because of the cost of color reproduction. But
those NGO publications that do feature photos, primarily those of
Amnesty International, employ a broader spectrum of images: graphic
portraits of mutilated bodies but also marches, protests, and portraits of
individual activists.

The Colombian Ministry of Defense has also received training from
the Rendon Group (TRG), a powerful Washington public relations firm.
As part of the U.S. aid package, for the previous several years TRG was
given a contract to work with the Colombian military to refine its "message."[17] Because the U.S. government agencies are prohibited from
directing propaganda at the U.S. public, these campaigns have been

directed to European and Colombian audiences. According to a TRG senior representative, their objective in Europe has been to change the understanding of the nature of the FARC, and its membership, from revolutionary peasant organization to terrorist group. In Colombia, TRG has focused on efforts to make the Colombians view the military as trustworthy and effective.

Colombian military human rights reports rarely discuss paramilitary abuses, instead focusing almost exclusively on guerrilla violence. During a visit to a battalion in the Magadalena River port town of Puerto Berrío, I asked one of the human rights officers why their reports featured only guerrilla attacks. We were standing on the battalion's veranda, overlooking a wide vista of river and banana trees; the battalion was housed in a former hotel, built at the turn of the century when paddleboat travel on the river was the quickest route from Bogotá to the Atlantic Ocean. He flipped through a glossy magazine, page after page of pictures of crumbled buildings, houses reduced to rubble, and crying children. This report was on bomb attacks of towns, he told me; the *autodefensas* don't carry out such attacks. When I asked him if his office had any reports featuring statistics on the incidents that involved the *autodefensas,* he squirmed briefly and promised he would look into it.

Despite this professional training of the Colombian military, much of its reporting fails to accurately employ the language of international human rights legal standards. When I asked the captain from the Atlantic Coast if he had reports that found evidence of collaboration between paramilitary groups and the army, he handed me a report titled "Bojaya: FARC Genocide." The Bojaya incident had received extensive press coverage in May 2001 when more than 118 civilians were killed after a FARC bomb destroyed the church where they sought refuge during combat between the paramilitaries and the guerrillas. I was particularly interested in the use of the word *genocide* and asked the captain why they had described the attack as an act of genocide rather than a war crime. "Because it was clearly genocide, an attempt to exterminate the population," he told me. "Look at how many were killed compared to how many people lived in that town. The attack against the population was clearly because of the FARC's lack of responsibility and of the *autodefensas'* [lack of responsibility] too."

"But genocide has a limited definition in international law, that you are completely trying to exterminate a group for racial or religious reasons," I said, wondering how this incident fit the standard definition of genocide.[18] He repeated the definition after me, nodding in agreement. "Do you think the FARC is fighting on religious or ethnic grounds?" I asked.

"It could have been on ethnic grounds, it could have been," he told me.

I could barely keep my disbelief from my voice as I asked, "You think the FARC is attacking people on ethnic grounds?"

He paused. "Or on political grounds. They are attacking people on political grounds, a political war against the entire Colombian population."

"Bojaya: FARC Genocide" is one example of the frequent misuse of the legal terminology of international human rights norms by the Colombian military in an apparent effort to make its claims more dramatic. Combat in which soldiers are killed is called a massacre; guerrilla attacks against government offices in small towns, which often kill numerous civilians because of the use of inaccurate weapons such as homemade cylinder bombs and car bombs, is called genocide. These reports are distributed internationally as part of the military's public relations campaigns and argue graphically and through descriptions of guerrilla attacks on soldiers and civilians that the Colombian military—and Colombian society as a whole—is the victim of abuses.

The problem for many military human rights officers is excessive documentation, in the form of requests for military backup in potentially threatened areas. Military officers complain of limited resources squandered in responding to people "crying wolf." One possible solution, often mentioned in the recommendations of NGO human rights reports, was the creation of an "early warning system" that would allow the military to respond to prioritized, confirmed threats. Through the U.S. aid package, millions of U.S. dollars had been spent attempting to design and implement such a system. I asked how the early warning system was functioning. "That is at another level, the early warning system through the Defensoría, those are the warnings that come from above," the major administering the human rights correspondence course explained to me. "We have to respond, but we get tons—many, many early warnings, all these warnings are a problem for us." His tone was resigned. "We have to respond to each alert. It costs a lot of money, to move a helicopter, to move troops, it requires a lot of resources. The Defensoría sends us alerts, but there are many people who don't go through the Defensoría system. If the *personero* from a town sends us an alert, we can't ignore it, we can't respond to one alert instead of another. So the system is saturated. Saturated. We can't tell people that we will say yes to one and no to another." When I asked him if he could establish priorities, he simply shook his head. "It is tremendous, tremendous. People are always telling us that they are going to take over this population or that population, we have to evaluate to see if it is true or not." "Look," he pulled one of the stacks of papers from his desk, and waved it in my face. "Look how they accumulate."

By adopting human rights language in military doctrine and positioning itself as the victim of human rights violations, the Colombian military has profoundly altered the political landscape of Colombian human rights activism. Military officers present a fundamentally different vision of human rights in order to counter NGO claims. NGOs focus on accountability and civilian oversight of the armed forces, promoting investigations of allegations of abuse and legal reforms to limit military powers. Their fundamental vision is that of defending individuals against a repressive state, working to protect space for political opposition, social protest, and dissent. The military continues to reject this activism as a politically motivated campaign against them and in support of the guerrillas. In its local human rights offices, the military has incorporated human rights programs into psychological operations and civic action campaigns aimed at increasing civilian support for military efforts. The military's human rights programs fail to acknowledge, much less address, the profound contradictions facing the armed forces as a body that claims to be producing human rights documentation and is officially charged with defending the state from insurgent violence and safeguarding the well-being of civilians while frequently being charged with human rights abuses. While NGO reporting is focused on galvanizing other activists and the international community to bring pressure to bear on the Colombian government to address political violence, the Colombian military is part of the state that is being pressured to respond. Underlying these programs are the assumptions that neutrality is not possible in the context of a guerrilla war, that all dissent and opposition necessarily supports the insurgent struggle against the state, and that minimizing mistreatment of local populations by state security forces is a means of increasing civilian support for the military. Taken from guerrilla warfare and U.S. counterinsurgency doctrine that views civilian support as a critical component of military campaigns, these programs aim to "win the hearts and minds" of local people rather than protect rights.

Conclusion

The Politics of Human Rights Knowledge

When I began my human rights activism as a nineteen-year-old intern at CINEP in downtown Bogotá, what I learned about violence in Colombia was literally a revelation. The blurry photocopied accounts of torture, killings, and massacres revealed a new world of violence to me. Months before, I had spent *semana santa,* the national holiday week before Easter, traveling through the small hamlets and villages between Cartagena, my then home, and Montería, capital of Córdoba, Colombia's northwesternmost state. My guide was a young medical student who offered sporadic medical care to the homeless children who gathered at the free lunch program where I volunteered. He later confessed that he first assumed I was another tourist trying to get high (many of the street kids sold pot and other drugs), but we slowly became friends, and he offered to show me the place where he had been raised. He was a local celebrity, the first to go to college, and as we traveled along the marshy dirt roads lined by thatched wooden houses, shacks really, we were greeted by cries of *Doctor!* and he was offered bottles of honey and strings of live chickens in exchange for his second-year medical school advice. Jose told me he was the illegitimate son of the Indian maid and one of the region's largest landowners. Denied his father's name and fortune but offered college tuition, he dreamed of returning a respectable doctor. Jose offered me the stories of his youth, stories I would later recognize in *One Hundred Years of Solitude,* which was based on García Márquez's childhood in similar villages a few hundred miles down the same road. I was proudly introduced to the last man to remember seeing a jaguar; when only a child, he had come to settle in the jungle with a machete and the clothes on his back. We traveled through Planeta Rica, Rich Planet, his hometown's improbable name, and Cienega de Oro, Golden Swamp, and Puerto Escondido, Hidden Port.

I was caught in the romance of unfamiliar rural life and blind to the daily implications of the poverty that surrounded us, requesting an additional bowl of water to rinse out my hair without thinking of the two-hour round trip to the nearest river. The undertow of violence and danger was even more opaque. I petulantly complained that *I* was not afraid, I did not understand why there were places he did not take me. One night, in a small wooden house that had belonged to his grandmother, he slept with a machete next to his hammock. When the dogs began to bark in the darkness, he clutched the blade behind him as he ventured out. Just someone lost on the road, he said when he returned a few minutes later, the dogs silent. Later he told me the man had asked directions to the house of a rich cattle rancher down the road; the rancher had been killed that very night.

Six months later, under the fluorescent lights of CINEP's downtown office, I read of other killings that had happened along those dirt roads the weeks prior to and after my visit. People gathered at a storefront, at a young boy's birthday party, workers on a lunch break; the massacres became known by place-name while the names of the dead were forgotten: El Tomate, la Mejor Esquina, Honduras, and La Negra. This was a new Colombia that was revealed to me. More than a new language, customs, *aguardiente,* and dancing, this was an education in the landscape of violence, a new geography of people and places defined by violent acts. That is the place where twenty were killed; that is the curve in the road where the bodies are thrown; that is the corner where he was last seen alive. Her boyfriend was found three years later, the body burned almost beyond recognition. She was killed crossing the street in front of the office by a man on a moped who was never caught. He survived the attack by crawling, shot, behind the table at the bar.

Like many other gringo political tourists before me, I felt consumed by this new knowledge. Arriving back in the United States five days before the 1989 U.S. invasion of Panama, I was undoubtedly insufferable in my attempts to forcibly educate my family and former high school classmates, home for the holidays in the middle of their sophomore year in college. I did not know what to do with my new knowledge, so I operated on the only model that I knew, that of transformative witness. While my lectures may have seemed an individual pathology to the unsuspecting acquaintances subjected to them, I was in fact drawing on the theory of knowledge that undergirds much of contemporary human rights activism. In this paradigm, knowledge transforms us, changing both our internal selves and our relations in the world, and brings with it the responsibility to bear witness to that knowledge in the world. I was engaged in attempting to mobilize shame, theirs and my own, as citizens in the newly proclaimed only remaining world superpower.

REVEALING THE PUBLIC SECRET

It took me many years of working in Colombia to realize that there was another level of human rights work, the object of which was to reveal not what was undiscovered but what was already known. For those who lived their lives immersed and surrounded in stories of violence and the machinations of politics—including villagers in conflict zones but also many journalists, embassy personnel, and policy makers—the violence revealed in human rights reporting was well known even as it was denied. In this register, human rights activism served to make public what was known but cannot be said, transforming the public secret into the public transcript.

Michael Taussig describes the public secret, what is widely known but cannot be publicly stated, as a fundamental dimension of political life, particularly in regard to politics and war. The public secret, he writes, is "an arm of statecraft and wise government" (Taussig 1999: 69). His first insight into the nature of the public secret came in Colombia in the early 1980s, during the rise of paramilitary operations and official counterinsurgency campaigns, when "people dared not state the obvious."

> We all "knew" this [collusion between death squads and the military], and they "knew" we "knew," but there was no way it could be easily articulated, certainly not on the ground, face-to-face. Such "smoke screens" are surely long known to mankind, but this "long knowness" is itself an intrinsic part of knowing what not to know. . . . Such is the labor of the negative, as when it is pointed out that something may be obvious, but needs stating in order to be obvious. For example, the public secret. Knowing it is essential to its power, equal to its denial. (Taussig 1999: 6)

James Scott describes the public transcript as the shared discourses of hegemony that define the interactions between the powerful and the oppressed and generally fill the public sphere (Scott 1992). His work focuses on uncovering the hidden transcripts, the alternative discussions of power and revenge elaborated by subalterns outside the public eye. Here I am more interested in tracing the shifts and evolution of the ethical dimensions of the public transcript as a fruitful site for examining social transformation and power.

From this angle, human rights activism is an effort to bring certain public secrets into the public transcript, to make what is known but denied part of the general discussions about the nature and cause of violence and possible solutions. For NGO activists, the public secret is the role of state agents in violent repression and the strong ties between paramilitary forces and military commanders in many regions. For state human rights officials, the public secret is the powerlessness of state agencies in many regions of the country, outgunned and overrun by powerful illegal armed groups. For military officers, the public secret is the toll of the guerrilla attacks. Of course, some of these secrets are more public than others, and each of these accounts highlights certain elements while eliding, and in some cases denying, others.

The efforts to expand the public transcript are not limited to Latin American activists but constitute a central dimension of much political advocacy. Teresa Whitfield includes one account of such an effort in her study of the murder of four Jesuit priests and their housekeeper and her daughter by members of the Salvadorean military trained by the United States during the 1989 military offensive of the Farabundo Martí National Liberation Front in San Salvador. Activists had insisted for more than a decade that U.S. military assistance and training in El Salvador should be suspended, but policy makers led by President Reagan continued to supply the Salvadorean military with aid and training, until the Jesuit murders made the public secret of abuse by the armed forces part of the public transcript. She opens her chapter on the changes in U.S. policy following the murder and its investigation pushed by members of the U.S. Congress with the words of a congressional staffer, who reflects on his own experience of the public secret:

"Congress is a funny place," mused one senior foreign policy aide in 1991. "People go on for years, tacitly agreeing to ignore certain realities—in this case the realities of the Salvadoran military—and then something like the Jesuit case happens that makes it impossible to ignore them any longer. It seems to cause a sea-change in what people know, but it isn't really, it is more a sea-change in the politics of that knowledge. Unlike the intelligence community with its 'need-to-know,' Congress works on a 'need-not-to-know' basis. It was politically useful for a variety of reasons to have El Salvador under Duarte as a democracy. You operate as if this is realistic and you are unaware of what is happening until something happens that brings you face to face with what you knew all the time." (Whitfield 1995: 159)

THE TRUJILLO REPORT ENTERS THE PUBLIC TRANSCRIPT

The incident that first crystallized my thinking about the efforts to transform public secrets into a public transcript was the Trujillo Commission (see chapter 1). This commission was created in 1994 with representatives from NGOs, civilian state human rights agencies, and the military to investigate the torture, murder, and disappearance of more than one hundred people in Trujillo, Valle, in the early 1990s; the commission's final report implicated drug traffickers and local military commanders in the crimes. I spent several hours talking about the commission with Manuel, who described his work on the commission as "one of the most important experiences of [his] life."[1] I had first met him during my early years in Colombia as an intern, when he was a lawyer for one of the large NGOs. Fifteen years later, he had gone through many incarnations: he joined the Defensoría's legal team, taught law, returned to the NGOs to direct a documentation project, and finally worked in the federal court system. By the time of our interview, seven years had passed since the commission had been convened, but the feelings—fear, tension, pride, and even amusement at many of the internal squabbles—seemed fresh.

Manuel began by acknowledging the massacres as a public secret. "I didn't want to work on the commission," he told me. "The massacres had affected me deeply. I refused to know, I didn't want to know anything about the massacre." Refusing to know what he already knew reflected the danger the commission represented. As Taussig writes, even the appearance of knowledge can be dangerous; people "know they must not know" (Taussig 1999: 131). "I thought it was very dangerous, dangerous physically because the drug traffickers were still in control of the northern Valle," Manuel told me, "and politically dangerous because of the implications of a failure." Manuel knew that possession of this knowledge was dangerous, a threat to his physical safety because of the possibility of reprisals by those found responsible for the violence. He also feared a more amorphous, existential threat: what would happen to Colombian society should this known violence fail to be translated into a public transcript.

The entire Trujillo Commission was organized to result in the public acknowledgment of what was known but denied. In its report the commission declared its official mission was to be an "investigative commission," to "clarify the doubtful aspects of the events, pronounce regarding the responsibility of the State and the alleged authors, and formulate recommendations about compensation for the victims" (Comisión de Investigación 1995: preface). To outside observers, the purpose of the commission appeared to be to discover what exactly had happened to the many people who had disappeared from their small hamlets, or whose bodies had washed ashore on the bank of the Cauca River. Manuel revealed that this reading missed the essential point of the commission: by the time it was established, the events of the cases had been well documented and publicized during the previous investigations by Colombian judicial agencies for the court cases (which had been dismissed by the military tribunal) and the NGOs' investigations for their reports. Everyone knew what had happened at Trujillo, but the events were officially denied. "For the commission, the facts of the case had already been established, the investigation part was almost all done," Manuel said. "What we had to do was the analysis of the evidence, not so much gather more proof but figure out what it meant."

Initially, none of the participants were confident that a consensus position could be produced; they believed that the drive to keep the secrets was too strong. Manuel believed that the commission was set up for failure from the beginning: "Everyone expected the commission to fail. On each side people had a team waiting outside the deliberations, ready to write a document when the consensus failed and there was a majority document—they were ready to write their dissenting positions. . . . People wanted it to fail."

Several critical factors made the production of a new public transcript possible, however. The new state human rights institutions established by the 1991 Constitution were one important element. For the newly created Defensoría, the commission was a chance to demonstrate that the agency would not simply produce posters about human rights education but could serve a critical function mediating between human rights victims and the investigative bodies charged with bringing such cases to justice. When given a chance to design the working structure of the commission, the *defensor* made consensus building a priority. Manuel explained:

> The *defensor* saw it as an opportunity and really supported it in a very impressive way. He gave the commission a lot of autonomy, in terms of how the secretary-general was able to work, but a lot of support, in terms of infrastructure. They hired a team of really good lawyers. We had a secretary, a messenger. He established clear rules of the game. There was a three-part

structure, of NGOs, control organisms, and government organisms. We had general meetings and established everything by consensus. The first part was the accumulation of all the information, all the *expedientes,* the court files. The work was divided into three subcommissions, working on the penal case, the civil case, and the international response. We were two months working on this, all the time, full time, discussing the case.

The critical task of the commission was thus to produce a consensus interpretation of what had happened in Trujillo. Key individuals among the NGO and the state human rights agency representatives were committed to producing this consensus, Manuel recalled: "They were good lawyers and liked good debates, but they weren't people who would fight just to fight. They were people who would support a consensus. They didn't have a warrior personality. [The most radical member], you had to have him on a leash, because every once in a while he would get up and say, this isn't working, this is worthless, and you had to call him back and calm him down." The commission became an environment where what was known could be spoken and debated; the central issue was not whether the state was responsible but to what degree state responsibility could be publicly reported. Manuel concluded: "People compromised, even [the most radical NGOs], because to get as far as we did was unthinkable. For them to recognize state responsibility, and get the important recommendations as part of the commission, was unthinkable. It was a huge triumph. And the cost of splitting the commission, of its failure, was too high."

The first major debate over evidence involved the acceptance of the witness's testimony; Daniel Arcila had been a civilian participant in several of the most brutal murders, but he had been declared mentally incompetent by the government's forensic medicine agency, and the military representatives argued his testimony was inadmissible. According to Manuel, "The NGOs contributed a lot. [NGO lawyer] Omar did the analysis of the evidence, the credibility of the testimony of the informant Daniel [*analisis probatorio*]." The commission made a consensus decision to admit Arcila's testimony.

Establishing the public significance of the violence in Trujillo was accomplished through the design of the commission process, which was not essentially an investigative one but rather a deliberative one. Given the previous investigations by Colombian judicial agencies for the court cases and the NGO studies for their reports, much of the key evidence had already been produced by the time the commission convened. The consensus process meant that there could be no dissenting opinions when the final report was produced. The commission was a closed universe of debate in which the political costs of refusing to participate were greater than the costs of admitting what was already widely known—that military officers working with local drug traffickers were responsible for the violence. Manuel told me:

> Our trick was to make it a process of constant deliberation, a permanent debate among all the agencies [*instancias*] working on the commission. Everyone participated. People talked and cursed each other out and everything. What happened was that the military representatives, who came in talking really hard-line, ended up being displaced—they lost standing in the commission compared to the civilian agencies, who won more space as the debate went on.
>
> By the time everything reached the final stage, everything was really tied up [*amarrado*]. There were a lot of debates and disagreements, as is natural, but the real debates were about the degree of responsibility of the state, and who would be included in the universe of the victims. In the final report, there were only 35 covered [in detail], from the three biggest incidents, but there were more than 200 other victims that weren't included, because there was less direct evidence, there were newer incidents, and because they were going to be included in the later investigations. Everyone accepted the truth of the facts of the case; the issue was the degree of responsibility of the state, how far it went. The *defensor* ceded on that point. It could have gone a lot further, much further, in terms of the involvement of the army. But he settled on the commander of the Third Brigade. But they could have included the police, the higher army commanders, because the evidence was there. But if it had been included, the consensus of the commission would have been broken. The people would have dropped out.

By emphasizing the need for consensus, the commission underscored the importance of the public transcript as a hegemonic discourse. Without agreement from all the participants in the commission process—the government, the military, NGOs—the result would simply be another partisan claim that could be dismissed. The commission reached the limits of what would be accepted into the public transcript, however. The subcommission addressing the international response was the one group that failed to produce a consensus position by the end of the commission's work. The NGOs lobbied for an international tribunal to increase awareness about the case, but the government representatives refused to allow any further reporting. "They felt like they had lost, that we scored a goal against them [*le metieron un gol*]. We wanted a follow-up commission about the recommendations, but the government wouldn't agree," Manuel told me. In issuing its report, the commission had gone as far as it could go, revealed as much as could be publicly known.

This view of human rights work as attempting to shift the public transcript about violence was reflected in the attitude of Alvaro Tirado, the first presidential adviser for human rights, when we spoke in his Bogotá apartment. When he described his approach to human rights work with the military, his attitude initially confused me. He told me that his strategy had been to first approach military officers in closed-door meetings, informing them of the problems with their behavior and warning them that further abuses would be publicly investigated. "Other people wanted a confrontational thing," he told me, "that I just talked to the press and *said what everyone knew,* that there were military officers involved in this, but that would have made the work impossible. We were trying to do the work" (my emphasis). Still consumed with a vision of human rights work as revealing the unknown, I was fixated on his apparently tautological position that to publicly say what everyone already knew would prevent him from doing human rights work. Wasn't human rights work making the unknown known? If everyone knew what was going on, why would saying such a thing publicly be so dangerous? How could making public statements about human rights abuses prevent the accomplishment of human rights work? In his account, he stressed the fruits of his consensus approach, the many military officers forced out through existing military protocol because of abuses, the importance of the president's backing, and the general difficulties he faced. Alvaro's view—a view not shared by many in the NGO community—was that the most important aspect of his job was to strive for a new public consensus about human rights work, even if this required not confronting the perpetrators of abuse.

PUBLIC TRANSCRIPTS AND UNINTENDED CONSEQUENCES

The importance of the public transcripts about violence contributes to one kind of unintended consequence of human rights activism: the ways in which groups alter their practices of violence to avoid having them categorized as human rights violations.[2] By bringing this violence to public attention and debates, human rights activism does not result in the reduction of violence but forces new and shifting forms of violence that are designed to avoid the scrutiny of analysts and observes. NGO activists in Colombia point to two major examples: the dramatic increase in violence by paramilitary groups in the mid-1990s and the new kinds of violence practiced by paramilitaries at the turn of the twenty-first century.

While definitively proving causality is difficult (perhaps impossible given the lack of objective sources on the military), many NGO activists are convinced that the dramatic decrease during the 1990s in human rights violations directly attributable to the Colombian military was the result of the corresponding rise in paramilitary violence (CCJ 2002; Sánchez and Meertens 2001). The increasing profile of NGOs activism and the growing pressure from their U.S. military counterparts to demonstrate a clean human rights record through such mechanisms as the Leahy Amendment made the Colombian military deeply concerned about allegations of violence. While paramilitary groups in Colombia are the product of numerous factors (most notably the vast resources available from the illegal drug trade), the tacit support of their operations by military officials concerned about their human rights record certainly appears to have facilitated paramilitary expansion in many areas.

During the late 1990s, paramilitary leaders themselves became increasingly concerned about their political status under the tutelage of their spokesman, Carlos Castaño. Paramilitary troops in many regions had received training in international humanitarian law from the International Red Cross; ICRC representatives in rural regions told me that paramilitary leaders had been very receptive to this training. Paramilitary documents circulating on the Internet began discussing the need to obey human rights standards, and the paramilitaries' Web page links to pages of communiqués on human rights issues from paramilitary "political advisers." This rhetoric has translated into changes in practice but not the changes desired by NGO activists. Violence has not been substantially reduced, simply reconfigured to escape categorization as human rights violations. One small-town councilman told me of being summoned by a local commander and warned that the paramilitaries had learned how to avoid human rights scrutiny. Because a massacre is defined as four or more individuals killed in a single act (the same time and place), paramilitary groups kill their targets one by one, scattering the bodies in different places or holding the bodies for several days. Human rights groups have responded with a new category for such deaths: multiple homicides. Such a term does not have the emotional impact of *massacre,* however. In their public statements, paramilitary leaders—and some government spokesmen—point to the decline in the number of massacres as progress while ignoring the fact that the total number of violent homicides remains the same. Similarly, in areas where paramilitary forces used to force inhabitants to abandon their land and homes to consolidate paramilitary control, they now prevent people from traveling from the region (called "confinement" by human rights groups). Difficult to quantify and assess, such measures avoid the public scrutiny made possible by human rights categories.

WHAT DO HUMAN RIGHTS DO?
LIMITATIONS AND CRITIQUES

Human rights is an international category, established at the lofty level of international treaties and multilateral agreements, shepherded through international conferences by diplomats and bureaucrats at the United Nations and in governmental conference halls around the world. Claiming this framework can give activists a piece of this international action, an opening (albeit small and tenuous) for wedging a claim for international attention and a fragile hope for international response. Of the limited number of international frameworks available in the public transcripts to fit Colombia—humanitarian crisis, drug war, war on terror—the human rights framework allowed activists to locate Colombia on the international agenda and focus on their primary concern, political violence. By taking their claims to the United Nations Commission on Human Rights and the U.S. Congress, activists could participate in policy debates otherwise closed to them. To participate in these debates, activists must choose between the only slots available for Colombia, a weak state victim of drug trafficking and organized crime, or an authoritarian repressive state.

Many activists, however, continued to see human rights as a problematic category for their political activism because it erased some of their major concerns. Professional human rights practice does not allow for the full expression of their political beliefs and agendas, confined to the limits of acceptable diplomacy and dispassionately based on the bloodless standards of international law. There is no room to argue for social change and the transformation of the world order, against inequality and the misuse of power, for autonomy and independence.

Activists were painfully aware of the contradictions and limitations they faced in their discussions, and at times bitter debates, over whether to embrace professional human rights practice and how to pursue international advocacy campaigns. As Merry writes:

> This is the paradox of making human rights in the vernacular: in order to be accepted, they have to be tailored to the local context and resonate with the local cultural framework. However, in order to be part of the human rights system, they must emphasize individualism, autonomy, choice, bodily integrity and equality, ideas embedded in the legal documents that constitute

human rights law. These core values of the human rights system endure even as the ideas are translated. Whether this is the most effective approach to diminishing violence against women or promoting global social justice is still an open question. It is certainly an important part of the expansion of a modernist view of the individual and society embedded in the global north. (Merry 2005: 221)

Many activists attempt to strike a delicate balance by modeling an ideal legal standard in which individual perpetrators can be named and brought to justice but also indicting institutions and organizations for the collective violence they inflict as a matter of course.

Anthropologists, with the discipline's focus on culture, process, and power, are especially well suited to examine these dynamics. The first generation of anthropologists that examined human rights issues focused on the tensions between universal claims and cultural relativism, however (Engle 2001; Messer 1993). During the 1990s, anthropologists began focusing on human rights activism itself. One line of scholarship considering the issue of cultural meaning in human rights activism has focused on critiquing the production of human rights knowledge as a misrecognition of local realities by international human rights organizations. (Martinez 1996; Wilson 1997, 2000). These scholars have contributed to a more nuanced analysis of local violences and the encounter between local communities and international human rights production. My work is one of a growing body of ethnographies of rights activism that focus on the cultural dimensions of the deployment of human rights frameworks. Merry has focused on the transnational spaces where women's rights are codified and on local campaigns in India, Hong Kong, Fiji, and Hawaii that make various forms of violence and discrimination against women an issue of women's rights (Merry 2005). Lori Allen explores human rights, humanitarian, and nationalist discourses among Palestinians (Allen 2006). Lesley Gill's work on U.S. military human rights training for Latin American armed forces is the first anthropological consideration of the military's attempt to contain the meaning of human rights activism (Gill 2004). Each of these scholars focuses his or her analysis on how different political actors remake universal human rights into forms that resonate and mobilize in a range of localities.

Some critics point to the limitations of the kind of knowledge about violence that is produced through human rights reporting (Martínez 1999; Wilson 1997). Like all forms of legal documentation, human rights reporting does not address the issue of why violence happens but accountability for specific acts: who has committed them. This model of accountability also limits the production of knowledge about resistance and agency, critical sites for understanding how violence affects local populations, often minimized in human rights reporting on victimhood. Greg Grandin, a historian who also worked on the Commission for Historical Clarification in Guatemala (CEH), summarized the paradox this way:

> It would be unrealistic to expect the CEH to resolve a debate that has long perplexed historians, yet the conflict between "agency" and "structure" speaks directly to the issue of responsibility. Who is to be held accountable for the atrocities that took place in Guatemala if history is to blame? The CEH, which drew on social analysis to explain the context but used established jurisprudence to investigate specific violations, was careful to avoid this trap: the causes of the war may have had deep historical roots, yet the violations the CEH was charged with investigating had individual authors. Nevertheless, the question remains: If history is not to be repeated, what is it in history that could have been different? (Grandin 2000: 402–3)

Academics are not the only ones to identify and reflect on these limitations on human rights practice. As we sat in a small-town office, one NGO activist attempted to answer Grandin's question—what could have been different?—as he reflected on the past twenty years of work with small peasant organizations attempting to carve out a living and a social fabric in the hamlets and villages that lined the Magdalena River Valley. A normally unflagging optimist, Dario confessed that he occasionally despaired while watching the paramilitary forces take over the region where he had been born and raised. The problem with the dirty war, he told me, is that they had killed all the best ones, the leaders. There had been good leaders, people with a different vision, who had tried to do politics in a different way in the small towns that dotted the plains in the valley:

> Our problem was the conception of human rights. We just focused on the military, on state responsibility. We didn't see that behind the faces of the *militares* were the *caciques*, the political bosses. We reported the facts without judging who makes those facts happen. It is the same now, people talk about the paramilitaries, denounce the military. But who talks about the mayor, the council, what happens with that? It has taken a long time to realize the social and economic support for the paramilitaries. We didn't think it would happen, didn't think about the political project beyond the *denuncia* of the events.

Dario's laments reflected one piece of the tension over how to classify violence and delineate responsibility. Activists and human rights professionals from all positions ruminated on these contradictions, on what was gained and what was lost, as they adopted specific categories to classify the violence that surrounded them.

Other critics of human rights practice argue that it produces certain kinds of depoliticized subjects. While such analyses rightly point to the limits of the political subjectivities produced through legal categories, they fail to consider the extreme heterogeneity of the kinds of claims made under the rubric of rights, from imperial powers' rights to invade other countries to disenfranchised minorities' rights disallowed by the state. Such claims demonstrate the importance of examining the context and ideological content of human rights claims without assuming a single monolithic meaning. Here, I have explored one corner of the complicated international landscape of rights claims through an examination of the evolving set of claims made by three groups of human rights professionals. They share some common elements of a rights practice. All have been pushed to transform their rights claims through an often contentious and contested engagement with the international community. All employ tactics from an established repertoire of rights activism, centered on the public reporting of certain violence acts. But these actors are engaged in radically different ideological projects, and to reduce their activism to simply the production of a particular kind of neoliberal subjectivity misses the richness and complicated political field this activism embodies. Such assumptions also miss the broader spectrum of political practices to which much nongovernmental human rights activism is attached; they focus on the production of legal documentation, the tip of the iceberg. The less visible realms of political activism are much more difficult to map and more ephemeral than the paper trail of international legal activism. This activism constitutes a much more complicated and contested terrain of political identities and subjectitivies, with deep histories in local fields where multiple identities are performed and mobilized in different ways at different moments. Even participants in this activism often lack consensus about the goals of their activism, the kinds of identities they ultimately imagine they are promoting, and their aspirations for future political regimes (Merry 2005; Tsing 2005). These spaces are some of the most important for considering the issues presented by any kind of political action in the twenty-first century.

HUMAN RIGHTS ACTIVISM AND THE WAR ON TERROR

Like all ethnographies, this project has been transformed by events that I could not have imagined when I began or controlled while in the field.

The most transformative of these occurred before I even left for Bogotá, while sitting in my Washington apartment preparing for my comprehensive exams and making my final travel plans. On September 11, 2001, I watched the smoke billowing above the horizon to the west from my bedroom window, what I would soon find out was the result of the Al Qaeda attack on the Pentagon. With the rest of the country, I sat transfixed over the next week, uncertain of the meaning of the events unfolding before me.

In many ways, those attacks made my project seem even more urgent. The nation—through the voices of journalists and analysts—was engaged in the collective, public, and explicit process of categorizing an act of violence to make it socially legible, to justify and ensure certain public policy choices. The long reach of the war on terror has led to dramatic shifts in policies in the United States and abroad and been the justification for two invasions. As I left for Bogotá, none of the questions about the meaning of these events had been resolved. The historical assessment of these events remains an ongoing debate, but the shape of how these events and their public labeling have changed the context for all international activism has become sharper.

Among my former colleagues, there was immediate despair. Debates that many in the human rights community believed decisively settled years ago were revived. U.S. senior statesmen advocated torture and even selective assassination by the U.S. government. Basic civil liberties and due process guarantees were eroded through antiterrorism legislation. Human rights and humanitarian concerns were immediately banished as important foreign policy concerns. The United States, the world's only superpower, was at war. The post–cold war moment was over.

Colombia was integrated into the war on terror. The United States had labeled Colombian guerrilla groups terrorist organizations years before; on September 10, 2001, the paramilitaries were added to the list. After the 9/11 attacks the State Department coordinator for counterterrorism, Francis X. Taylor, told reporters, referring to Colombian paramilitary groups, "They will receive the same treatment as any other terrorist group, in terms of our interest in pursuing them and putting an end to their terrorist activities." Colombian groups were compared to Bin Laden, and the country named the Latin American front line for the war on terror. For Colombian human rights defenders, the war on terror had many implications. U.S. military assistance to Colombia, long focused on counternarcotics operations, was broadened to "counterterror," opening the door for U.S. support of counterinsurgency campaigns. Colombian

President Alvaro Uribe, a central Bush ally elected on a hard-line platform during my fieldwork, built up the military, passed antiterrorism legislation, and denounced human rights work. In a June 17, 2004, press
conference, he condemned Amnesty International for "legitimizing terrorists." Colombian military officials pointed to the U.S. treatment of
prisoners at Guantanamo Bay to justify their own military tribunals and
long pretrial detentions. U.S. attention had shifted to the Middle East,
and the crowd of journalists and policy makers who had flooded
Colombia turned their attention elsewhere.

But in many ways the situation in Colombia remained the same. The
Al Qaeda attacks occurred before I began my official research, and of
course much of what I discuss occurred after the attacks. I have not
included an analysis of how the war on terror has changed human rights
activism in Colombia, focusing instead on history and activism to the end
of the 1990s. People in Colombia did not feel the shift so dramatically;
most continue their activism largely as before even as the political terrain
continues to evolve. Government-supported demobilization of paramilitary fighters, without a corresponding dismantling of paramilitary power
structures, is remapping the landscape of violence and power; guerrillas
expand their operations into new areas of the country as drug production
routes shift with innovations in trafficking techniques. The conflict continues, its internal dynamic independent of the label applied by U.S. policy makers.

Among the biggest changes were the limits in the international connections crucial to human rights activism. The United Nations Human
Rights Commission meeting I attended in spring 2002, the first since
the attacks, was preoccupied with terrorism, reframing the debates on
human rights standards. Governments from around the world voiced
their support for repressive measures. In the United States, interest in
Colombia declined dramatically as policy makers and the media focused
on the Middle East. In the months following the attacks, one of my freelance journalist friends told me that in the moments he learned of the
attacks, his first thought was for family and friends in New York. His
second was, well, there goes this story. Like many of his colleagues, he
ended up reporting from Baghdad; I saw other familiar faces reporting
from Afghanistan, Iraq, and Washington. Coverage of Colombia in
mainstream U.S. newspapers, minimal in the best of times, was replaced
by the Middle East. Colombian activists and officials were still attempting to figure out their new place in the global order and U.S. priority list.

The war on terror also changed the ending I had imagined writing.

Over the years as I was developing my proposal and preparing to carry out my fieldwork, I had developed a narrative arc I imagined would be the shape of my story. Despite the dedicated efforts of human rights groups, political violence in Colombia had only worsened over the previous decade, appearing more chronic and entrenched. The imagined ending of my story was the international accomplishments of Colombian human rights activists, who had succeeded in raising international awareness of Colombia as a human rights crisis, spurring the U.N. Commission on Human Rights to take the unprecedented step of opening an office in Colombia. Their international advocacy campaigns had been a model for other NGOs from other countries interested in similar efforts. In true American style, I searched for a "happy ending"—this was going to be it. With the advent of the war on terror, those accomplishments had been dramatically reduced, as the window of political opportunity for human rights organizing slammed shut. Despite the universal appeal of happy endings, I have attempted to hear the dissenting voices, to explore these moments of reversal, division, and uncertainty. To understand where we have been to more fully understand the debates and setbacks of the present.

Most important, the story is not over. I have chosen to focus on the neatest bookends of this story: the development of human rights institutions—NGO, state, and military—in the long decade between the end of the cold war and the war on terror. Each generation defines its political struggles according to the repertoire of political imaginaries at hand or invented, despite their limitations and contradictions. Fr. Bartolomé de Las Casas argued for better treatment of the Indians by defending their Catholic souls; the citizens of the modern nation-state take up the cry of human rights. I offer one piece of that story, but it is beyond my talents to imagine here what the next rallying cry will be.

Notes

1. A large number of scholars have have examined how rights activism was translated into the vernacular of U.S. political culture by solidarity groups that employed the human rights framework (e.g., Coutin 1993; Coy 1997; Cunningham 1995, 1999; Lorentzen 1991; Nelson 2000; Smith 1996). Some scholars have described the ways in which differences in national political cultures can limit opportunities for transnational organizing (Cortright and Pagnucco 1997), the importance of networks (Keck and Sikkink 1998; Kriesberg 1997; Smith 1997; Risse, Ropp, and Sikkink 1999), and how the Catholic Church (and other denominations to a lesser degree) has had a central structural role in supporting transnational activism and has been an important resource for symbolic action (Berryman 1984; Byrsk 1994; Loveman 1998). An important subset of scholars has examined how the genre of testimonial literature is used during activism with varying results. This genre emerged as an attempt to translate the experience of human rights violations and activism across national borders and within national cultures and to construct a new reader-subject relationship; it has been central to organizing responses to human rights abuses in Central America and the Southern Cone from the 1970s and 1980s to the present (Beverley 1989, 1991; Beverley and Zimmerman 1990; Harlow 1992; Yudice 1991), in part as a result of growing interest in representing the voice of the subaltern (Spivak 1988). Purporting to tell the collective story of oppressed groups, these narratives focused on the experience of human rights violations and in some cases resistance (Menchú 1983; Partnoy 1986; Timerman 1981). U.S. activists also produced memoirs in the testimonial genre that explored these themes (Gorin 1993; Griffin-Nolan 1991; Melville and Melville 1971). Many of these narratives were performed during speaking tours and public events featuring U.S. and Latin Ameri-

can activists, a site that has yet to be sufficiently theorized for the Latin American case (McLagan 2000a, 2000b). David Stoll's (2000) criticism that the details of Menchú's testimonial are false and his broader accusation that the left misrepresents the collective claims of Latin Americans highlight the importance of exploring the cultural meaning of human rights activism for the activists and community members involved in the production of human rights claims (Arias 2001; Nelson 2001; Warren 2000). While his confrontational style and simplistic arguments have prevented the most productive exploration of these issues, Stoll demonstrated the importance of exploring the issue of agency and multiple political registers in activism. In my analysis, I attempt to demonstrate how activists create meaning through their human rights practice and are often profoundly aware of the limits and contradictions of their work as they struggle to articulate a response to violence with the existing repertoire of activism.

2. The emergence of the first high-profile human rights NGO, Amnesty International, spurred awareness of human rights issues by governments, the public, and the United Nations. Amnesty was founded in London in 1961 by Peter Benneson, a leftist British barrister, with the support of Eric Baker, a prominent Quaker antinuclear activist, and Louis Bloom-Cooper, a lawyer. The organization's first campaign was for the release of "prisoners of conscience," which they defined as any person physically restrained from expressing an opinion that does not condone violence. All campaigning was to be ideologically balanced, with each Amnesty group adopting one prisoner from the West, one from the East, and one from the developing world. This mandate was expanded to advocating fair trials and an end to torture for all detained people. By the end of the 1970s Amnesty had approximately 15,000 members in over one hundred countries, although the majority of their members were upper-middle-class professionals in Europe and the United States.

Amnesty produced much more reporting on Latin America than on the Soviet Union and Warsaw Pact allies during the 1970s and 1980s, despite the attempt to maintain ideological balance in the cases of detainees they adopted. According to researchers, this was due to both methodological and strategic concerns. Amnesty's mandate required obtaining official permission to travel; clandestine missions during which researchers masqueraded as tourists or journalists were forbidden. This requirement made research trips to the Soviet Union practically impossible during this period (Human Rights Watch staff members, then Helsinki Watch, traveled clandestinely to obtain their information). Latin American governments often granted Amnesty permission, probably for several reasons. As leaders of non-superpower countries, the military juntas were paradoxically anxious to receive international legitimacy and recognition and eager to prove to the world their transparency. As U.S. allies, military leaders also probably did not fear the consequences; declassified U.S. embassy cables have revealed that U.S. officials assured Latin American officials of continued U.S. military and economic aid despite their repressive tactics. Regardless of the methodological difficulties, researchers were concerned that publicity on the cases in the Soviet Union would result in reprisals against prisoners rather than their release. As a result of this combination of factors, early Amnesty research focused on the Southern Cone dictatorships, primarily in Chile, Uruguay, and Argentina. In

October 1977 Amnesty International received the Nobel Peace Prize. Its membership peaked in the late 1990s, but it remains one of the most important transnational human rights organizations.

3. A comprehensive history of human rights activism in Latin America, and the relationship among national groups, has yet to be written. Before 1960 there was only one organization in the Southern Cone explicitly concerned with human rights: the Liga Argentina por los Derechos del Hombre (Argentine League for the Rights of Man), established in 1937 in response to political participation after the military coup of Uriburu in 1930 and with unofficial links to the Communist Party. During dictator General Alfredo Stroessner's thirty-five-year rule, the Paraguayan human rights community remained relatively small and focused on specific cases. In Brazil, language differences prevented much exchange with activists in other parts of the continent. Brazil's massive nongovernmental documentation project *Nunca Mais,* supported by the Catholic Church, was a model for later efforts to investigate governmental repression. Chilean activists formed the most immediate human rights groups after the overthrow of the democratically elected socialist Salvador Allende on September 11, 1973. Over the course of the Pinochet regime, several generations of human rights groups emerged, first directly supported by the Catholic Church, then family members of victims, and finally groups organized by political parties. The most well known of these groups was Vicaría de la Solidaridad (Vicariate of Solidarity), founded in 1975. Important factors in the creation of Chilean groups were the support of the Catholic Church and preexisting transnational and national social and political networks linking religious leaders, progressive students, and academics and other professionals (Loveman 1998: 490). Despite sharing Chile's democratic political culture and institutions, Uruguay developed the smallest organizations in number and size, in part because theirs was a largely secular society in which the Catholic Church had little moral authority or means to channel resources to victims of repression. With over 50 percent of the population living in Montevideo and the military galvanized to fight the Tupamaro insurgency, almost all facets of Uruguayan life were militarized at the time of the coup. Prior legal restrictions meant that much of the repression occurred in a legal framework; Uruguay had fewer disappearances but the highest concentration of political prisoners anywhere in the world. Following the defeat of the generals' constitutional amendment in 1980, Servicio Paz y Justicia (SERPAJ-Uruguay) was created in 1981; its efforts were severely limited by the lack of an institutional channel through which international funds could be received (Loveman 1998: 506). In Argentina the Catholic Church displayed an ambivalent attitude toward the military government, and the country lacked the embedded activist networks found in Chile. Because of abuses and the erosion of legal rights as a result of precoup counterinsurgency efforts against Montoneros, three human rights groups were established before the 1976 coup, with ecumenical church leaders playing a critical role in all three. SERPAJ, founded in 1974, focused on local aid and popular education. As a result of frustration with SERPAJ's minimal political action, the Movimiento Ecumenico por los Derechos Humanos (Ecumenical Movement for Human Rights) was founded in February 1976 through a combination of personal networks and external resources and

supported by Dakonia, a Swedish NGO. The Asemblea Permanete por los Derechos Humanos, whose focus is documentation, was formed by individual professionals as an alternative to the Liga because of its Communist sympathies. These
groups have received little scholarly attention, which has been focused on the
Madres de la Plaza de Mayo, and they were hampered by lack of support from
the church, lack of financial and political resources, and persecution (including
bombings and disappearances) and never reached the level of development of
Chilean groups (Fruhling 1988: 162). After the coup a new social identity
emerged, family member of the disappeared, resulting in the creation of three
new human rights groups 1976 and 1977: the Madres (Mothers), the Abuelas
(Grandmothers), and the Familiares (Family Members) of the disappeared. However, the vast majority of family members of the disappeared did not participate
in human rights organizing. For analysis of the Argentine experience, see Brysk
1994; Loveman 1998; Keck and Sikkink 1998; Taylor 1997. According to one
senior human rights researcher, Argentina "seeded the continent" with experienced activists and lawyers in exile who went on to assist with establishing
human rights groups. The important role of Southern Cone groups in shaping
human rights practice was also a result of timing; Argentina began the transition
to democracy in 1982 and thus initiated debates over amnesty, investigations,
and reparations well before other countries.

   4. The countries that experienced significant insurgencies (Guatemala, El Salvador and Peru) provide interesting counterexamples, but none has been considered a significant model for the Colombian NGO activists I discuss here. In part
this is a result of racism, which viewed the whiter and more European Southern
Cone countries as higher status. The worst years of Central American violence
occurred during the 1980s, when the transition to democracy was already well
established farther south. The exile population was generally much less educated, rural, and primarily destined for the United States. The Peruvian case is
slightly more complicated. In many ways Peru's patterns of political violence
throughout the 1980s and 1990s were similar to those in Colombia, but the differences were significant enough to shape a very different kind of human rights
community. Like Colombia, Peru suffered from a long-running insurgency, with
massive violence and displacement. Unlike Colombia, Peru has a large indigenous
population (from 30 to 60 percent, depending on how it is measured) and is more
rural and impoverished. Also unlike in Colombia, the Peruvian military has been
very involved in politics, with numerous coups and military juntas from 1968 to
1980. While Colombia was the only Latin American country to avoid a debt crisis in the 1980s, Peru suffered from severe economic turbulence and hyperinflation in the 1980s; while Colombia was home to the world's most sophisticated
drug traffickers, much of the coca used to make the cocaine they trafficked was
grown in Peru (and its neighbor Bolivia). While Peru's MRTA was similar to
Colombia's nationalist Marxist guerrillas (e.g., ELN and M-19), the most powerful guerrilla group in Peru was the neo-Maoist Shining Path, which viewed civil
society, including human rights leaders, as competition and subjected it to violent
attacks. According to the 2003 Peruvian Truth and Reconciliation Commission,
69,280 people died or disappeared during the counterinsurgency campaigns
(22,507 were fully identified as dead, 46,773 as disappearances). The Shining

Path was held directly responsible for the death of 12,561 people, a little more than half the victims identified as dead; approximately one-third of the dead were killed by government security forces. After the Shining Path was largely defeated, Peru experienced a crisis of democracy, with Fujimori staging an *autogolpe* (lit., "self-coup," in which the president seizes control of all branches of government) in 1992, dissolving Congress and severely weakening the judiciary and other democratic institutions. During the 1990s, more than 20,000 were imprisoned under antiterrorism legislation, and the administration was plagued by corruption scandals.

Like in Colombia, the Peruvian human rights movement had its origins in the left (Hinojosa 1998; Roberts 1998). Also like in Colombia, the Catholic Church played an important role but was not as central as Chile's Vicaria de Solidaridad because of a much stronger conservative tendency within the national hierarchy. While the Peruvians looked to the Argentine Madres for inspiration, the vast class differences between the primarily urban and middle-class Madres and the indigenous poor family members of the disappeared in Peru complicated their alliance. The primary force behind much human rights organizing in the country was the Central Coordinadora, which has been held up as a model by international supporters, according to the movement supporter and historian Coletta Youngers. She also concluded, however, that the same political and socioeconomic homogeneity that served as a foundation for the Coordinadora's cohesiveness also meant that there was little diversity among the participants, particularly the leadership (Youngers 2003).

Peru enjoyed a relatively high profile within the international community, with extensive links through the Catholic Church (whereas Colombia was a net exporter of priests, many U.S. congregations sent missionaries to Peru). In contrast to its policy toward Central America, the U.S. government actively supported human rights in Peru; by the late 1980s officials went on record expressing concern to counterparts in the Peruvian government about the safety of human rights activists. In part this was result of the Peruvian groups' clear condemnation of guerrilla violence, which allowed more support from governments and international institutions. One of the most important differences between Colombian and Peruvian human rights groups was the Peruvians' categorical rejection of revolutionary violence as a result of the Shining Path's brutality and targeting of civil society. To do so, they adopted international humanitarian law, which establishes the limits of conduct during warfare and the obligations of warring parties toward civilians and protected populations.

5. One example is the use of the Alien Tort Claims Act to bring cases against human rights violators in the United States. The first case tried under the act was brought by activists supporting the family of Joelito Filartiga, who had been tortured and killed in 1976 by a Paraguayan policeman who had moved to the United States and was living in Brooklyn (White 2004).

6. Beginning in the 1970s, U.S. activists were also able to draw on the human rights rhetoric of the U.S. government. By far the most visible escalation of human rights rhetoric from the U.S. government occurred under President Jimmy Carter. During his 1976 inaugural address, President Carter stated that human rights should play a central role in U.S. foreign policy and that "our moral sense

dictates a . . . preference for those societies which share with us an abiding respect for individual rights" (quoted in Korey 1998: 187). Carter articulated a vision shared by the vast majority of U.S. officials who are human rights supporters—as an extension of the "American values of freedom, liberty, and independence, a particular *American* mission to the world" (Korey 1998: 183; emphasis added). In addition to his rhetorical commitment to human rights, Cater appointed former NGO staffers to key newly created human rights positions, which focused on the role of human rights in U.S. foreign policy (Schoultz 1985).

7. The quotations in this paragraph are taken from my notes on Jackson's presentation, "The Humanitarian Adjective: A Weapon of Mass Distraction," at the Watson Institute for International Studies, Brown University, Humanitarian and Human Rights Workshop, October 9, 2003.

8. Arturo Carrillo pointed out that *contando muertos* could be more accurately translated as "counting corpses." I have opted for employing a degree of poetic license and use the phrase "counting the dead."

1. MAPPING THE ETERNAL CRISIS

1. Colombia's most significant fiscal crisis in a century occurred in the late 1990s, when unemployment almost doubled and the number of people living in poverty rose to 55 percent; economic growth reached a record low of -4.5 percent in 1999. The financial crisis has spurred budget cuts in government agencies and, some argue, has exacerbated violence, but Colombia remains significantly wealthier than many other Latin American countries.

2. A comprehensive discussion of violence statistics can be found in Gonzalo Sánchez's introduction to the edited volume *Violence in Colombia, 1990–2000* (Bergquist, Peñaranda, and Sánchez 2001). The 2002 figures were found on the U.S. Department of State Web site (http://travel.state.gov/travel/colombia.html) and are based on figures provided by the Colombian government.

3. Colombia's long-running conflict is noteworthy given the political changes that have occurred over the past twenty years throughout the continent. In the rest of Latin America, military dictatorships (in Brazil and the Southern Cone) have given way to electoral democracies, and civil wars have ended in peace accords (in Central America) or the guerrillas' defeat (in Peru). It is not my intention to suggest that these processes have been painless, or complete. I list them here as comparisons with Colombia's continuing civil conflict. Despite the fact that these developments have been largely partial and highly flawed, they demonstrate political transitions and, most important, reductions in political violence that have yet to be experienced in Colombia. The results of these processes of so-called democratization are often ambiguous. Levels of common crime have skyrocketed, to such a degree that San Salvador and other areas have periodically made the front pages on the continent with higher per capita murder rates than Colombia. This increase in criminality and especially the drug trade (also occurring in Mexico, Brazil, and other Latin American countries) has been called the "Colombianization" of the region.

4. Colombia has also been home to the continent's only indigenous guerrilla group, the Quintin Lame Armed Movement (MAQL); unlike other Colombian

insurgencies, however, its goals focused on protection of indigenous communities rather than overthrowing the state. A small group that was active in Cauca, the home of Colombia's largest—and most organized—indigenous group, the Nasa Paez, the MAQL was "established as a multiethnic organization in which indigenous fighters, peasants, urban militias and mestizo intellectuals were all seen as equal members" (Rappaport 2005: 70). The group was named for Manuel Quintin Lame, a Nasa sharecropper instrumental in organizing indigenous communities during the first half of the twentieth century. The MAQL demobilized during Gaviria's peace initiative in 1991; many of its members went on to found the Fundación Sol y Tierra.

5. Sally Engle Merry has a thoughtful discussion of the conceptions of culture in the debates on women's rights and suggests that a more productive stance is to view culture as "unbounded, contested, and connected to relations of power, as the product of historical influences rather than evolutionary change" (Merry 2006: 15). She goes on to cite Comaroff and Comaroff, "who suggest interrogating the 'production, in imaginative and material practice, of those compound political, economic, and cultural forms by means of which human beings create community and locality and identity, especially on evanescent terrains; by means of which, in the face of material and moral constraint, they fabricate social realities and power relations and impose themselves on their lived environments; by means of which space and time are made and remade, and the boundaries of the local and global are actualized' (1999: 296)."

6. The 1886 Constitution also ended literacy requirements for male voters in national elections and restored the preeminence of the Roman Catholic Church, including control over public school curricula. In the period immediately following, known as the Regeneration, Liberal political participation was limited, while the economy flourished with the increase in coffee exports. The early twentieth century was a time of relative tranquillity for Colombia, beginning with the dictatorship of pragmatic Conservative Rafael Reyes, who minimized conflict by integrating Liberals into his government.

7. Until 1903 Panama was a department of Colombia. The U.S. decision to build the transoceanic canal there, after attempts through Nicaragua failed, led to the creation of an independent country with almost a third of its national territory (the canal zone) controlled by the United States. Panamanian independence was bitterly controversial in Colombia. The United States softened the blow with a multimillion-dollar payment ushering in a period of expansive growth known as the "Dance of the Millions."

8. During the period known as the Liberal Republic (1930–46), which began with the administration of moderate Liberal Enrique Olaya Herrera (1930–34), Liberals began removing Conservatives from political offices. The Liberal Party was itself split, however, when Gaitán formed UNIR in 1933. He championed the cause of urban and rural workers and drew members from the newly created Communist Party as well as many Liberals. Gaitán and the Communist Party united behind the administration of Alfonso Lopéz Pumarejo (1934–38), whose "Revolution on the March" abolished literacy requirements for suffrage, centralized state power, and promised land reform. Despite this relatively tepid reformist platform, the right wing of the Liberal Party, led by Eduardo Santos,

opposed the president as too extreme. Conservatives, led by Laureano Gómez, abstained from elections and denounced electoral reforms as partisan, anti-Catholic, and socialistic; with no representatives in Congress, Conservatives declared the government illegitimate.

9. Many developed well-known nicknames; among the most famous was El Condor in Valle del Cauca; his evolution from mild-mannered cheese salesman and Conservative Party lackey to paid assassin was the subject of the Colombian classic novel *Condores no entierran todos los días* and the movie of the same name.

10. The study of rural banditry has emphasized the role of bandit groups in state building and, following Hobsbawm, social banditry as a form of premodern rebellion (Hobsbawm 1959, 1969). Much of this work explores banditry's importance in the expansion of capitalism into new areas as a link between rural populations and the market economy. Much of the research in Latin America has debated the degree to which bandits can be considered oppositional political actors (Blok 1972; Joseph 1990, 1991; Sánchez and Meertens 2001; Slatta 1991). In recent work, authors move away from banditry as a category because it suggests that these actors function entirely outside the law, losing their complex relationship with the state. Gallant suggests "military entrepreneur" as "a category of men who take up arms and who wield violence or the threat of violence as their stock in trade" and focuses on their flexible role within the state, including at times working as proxies for state agents (Gallant 1999: 27).

11. The Conservative Party had no significant presence in the 2002 election, which was won by an independent and former Liberal, Alvaro Uribe. By his reelection in 2006 (possible because of a constitutional amendment to allow reelection), the two major contenders were incumbent Uribe and the Polo Democrático (Democratic Left) candidate, Carlos Gaviria, with Liberal Party boss Horacio Serpa a distant third.

12. Pushed by Communist leaders and ideologues, including the lawyer José Alvéar Restrepo, the guerrillas began articulating an organizational structure and political platform. This organizing experience remained an important point of reference for later human rights groups; one of the most important legal aid groups bears the name José Alvéar Restrepo Lawyers' Collective. In their first national conference, held in Boyacá in August 1952, representatives from almost all the country's most important guerrilla fronts issued the First Law of the Plains (Llano), creating a national guerrilla command structure. Two years later, on June 18, 1953, a guerrilla assembly adopted the Second Law of the Plains (Law Organizing the Revolution on the Eastern Plains of Colombia), 224 articles envisioning the extension of the revolution to the entire country and the installation of a popular government.

13. Senior military officers continue to view the civilian checks on their counterinsurgency campaigns as the reason guerrilla violence grew in the 1980s and 1990s and often mention the early near-defeat of the ELN as an example.

14. The M-19's attempts to co-opt the internal control of other political groups (including ANAPO and the Firmes coalition) failed. The Dominican embassy takeover was viewed as a dramatic success, with the M-19 leaders escaping to Cuba with a million-dollar ransom. The theft of Colombian military weapons

had more serious results, however: the Turbay government unleashed a wave of repression, including arrests and torture.

15. See the Web page of Fundación País Libre: www.paislibre.org.co.

16. Pax Christi Netherlands, *The Kidnapping Industry in Colombia* (Utrecht, 2001), 35.

17. See Nazih Richani, *Systems of Violence: The Political Economy of War and Peace in Colombia* (Albany: SUNY Press, 2002). There is great debate over these figures. Some place the FARC's total earning as high as 900 million or a billion dollars a year, though this seems highly improbable given the size of the Colombian economy, the total illegal export earnings and the position of the FARC in the overall illegal economy.

18. Marc Chernick, "Negotiating Peace Amid Multiple Forms of Violence: The Protracted Search for a Settlement to the Armed Conflicts in Colombia," *Comparative Peace Processes in Latin America,* ed. Cynthia Arnson (Stanford: Stanford University Press and Woodrow Wilson Center Press, 1999); Gustavo García Arenas and Mónica Roesel, eds., *Las verdaderas intenciones de las FARC.* (Santafé de Bogotá: Corporación Observatorio para la Paz: 1999). For an earlier record of FARC positions during negotiations in the 1980s, see Jacobo Arenas, *Correspondencia secreta del proceso de paz* (Bogotá: Editoral La Abeja Negra, 1989).

19. Scholars have been divided on the legacy of Rojas Pinilla's administration, some focusing on his dictatorship and others stressing his populism. His primary failure may have been the partial peace instituted by the halfhearted amnesties he offered. Violent eviction of peasant squatters in the second half of his government and the ongoing guerrilla resistance proved a prescient model for the periodic waves of government repression, guerrilla violence, and tentative rapprochement characterizing Colombian political life for the next five decades.

20. U.S.-assisted operations resulted in the killing of Pablo Escobar in 1993 and the jailing of the heads of the Cali Cartel. The contradictory alliances made during counternarcotics operations often paired the interests of competing drug traffickers with law enforcement officials; the clearest example was the PEPES. United under the leadership of Fidel Castaño, later a major paramilitary leader, the PEPES included "Colombian state officials, business leaders, the Cali Cartel and survivors of the Moncada and Galeano clans" (Bowden 2001). The PEPES were responsible for a number of bombings as well as numerous murders of people associated with the Medellín Cartel.

21. The word *extraditables* is derived from *extradition*. The U.S. government actively pursued the extradition of many Colombian drug traffickers, believing that the U.S. justice system was less vulnerable to corruption; the process has been extremely controversial in Colombia. Some Colombian analysts have argued that extradition violates sovereignty (particularly for cases of drug trafficking, which involve crimes in both countries); drug traffickers often used appeals to sovereignty as well as violence to protest extradition cases against them. Pablo Escobar was famously reported to have said, better a tomb in Colombia than a jail cell in the United States.

22. During twenty-five years of state-sponsored agrarian reform, only approximately 900,000 hectares were redistributed; by 1988 Colombia had one

of the worst ratios of land inequality in the world. As measured by the World Bank, the Gini Coefficient for land in Colombia was .86, with 0.0 being perfect equality and 1.0 representing complete inequality of land distribution. For comparison: Brazil (0.85), Peru (0.91), Korea (0.35), (Taiwan 0.45). See Marcelo Giugale, Olivier Lafourcade, and Connie Luff, eds., *Colombia: The Economic Foundation of Peace* (Washington, D.C.: World Bank, 2003), 490.

23. For greater detail on the history of paramilitaries, see Mauricio Romero, *Paramilitares y autodefensas, 1982–2003* (Bogotá: IEPRI, 2003); Francisco Cubides, "Los paramilitares y su estrategia," in *Reconocer la Guerra para construir la paz,* ed. Malcolm Deas and Maria Victoria Llorente (Bogotá: Grupo Editoral Norma, 1999); Carlos Medina Gallego, *Autodefensas, paramilitares y narcotráfico en Colombia: Origen, desarrollo y consolidación. El caso "Puerto Boyacá"* (Bogotá: Editorial Documentos Periodísticos, 1990).

24. See Michael McClintock, *Instruments of Statecraft: U.S. Guerrilla Warfare, Counterinsurgency, and Counterterrorism, 1940–1990* (New York: Pantheon Books, 1992), 222–23.

25. Washington Office on Latin America, *Losing Ground: Colombian Human Rights Defenders under Attack* (Washington, D.C.: WOLA, 1997). Human Rights Watch, *Colombia's Killer Networks* (New York: Human Rights Watch, 1996). See also Office of the High Commissioner for Human Rights in Colombia, *Report of the High Commission for Human Rights on the Situation of Human Rights in Colombia* (Geneva: U.N. Human Rights Commission, 2000), 24.

26. For more detail on the drug trafficking and paramilitary groups in Colombia, see Alonso Salazar, *La parábola de Pablo: Auge y caída de un gran capo del narcotráfico* (Bogotá: Editorial Planeta, 2001); Robin Kirk, *More Terrible than Death: Massacres, Drugs and America's War in Colombia* (New York: Public Affairs, 2003), 108–9; Alvaro Camacho, "Narcotráfico y violencias en Colombia" (paper presented at the symposium "Análisis histórico del narcotráfico en Colombia," Museo Nacional, Bogotá, October 30, 2003).

27. Mapiripán, a port town with about 1,000 inhabitants on the Guaviare River, was a major site of coca paste sales and a longtime FARC stronghold. The massacre was one of the most brutal and high profile in recent history. From July 15 through July 20, 1997, gunmen from the AUC took control of Mapiripán, killed at least forty people, and threatened others. The exact death toll was never established, as many of the bodies were dismembered and thrown into a nearby river. Following a lengthy investigation, a military court sentenced General Jaime Uscategui to forty months in jail for dereliction of duty because he failed to respond to repeated requests for action by local authorities and his own subordinates. One of the military officers who requested assistance, Colonel Hernan Orozco, was himself investigated for misconduct as a result of his public testimony in the case; he received a sentence of thirty-eight months in jail and now lives in Miami. In an interview with Colombian news media, paramilitary drug lord Carlos Castaño promised "many more Mapiripáns," signaling that the attack was a hallmark of the paramilitary's new offensive strategy targeting the civilian population in strategic drug trafficking routes and areas with historic guerrilla presence.

28. Jorge 40 went on to attribute the participation of women in combat to romantic jealousy: "Of course many women who won't give up carrying a gun do so because of jealousy; they are not going to let their men get away with anything." Isabel Bolaños is one example of a woman limited to the traditional gender role within the paramilitary organizational structure. Originally linked to peasant organizations and guerrilla groups including the EPL, she admitted to working closely with Castaño in development projects throughout the late 1990s before her capture in 1999, when she was charged with various paramilitary crimes. Bolaños's life history was included in *Las mujeres en la guerra*, a collection of testimonies by Patricia Lara (Bogotá: Editorial Planeta, 2000). It is also likely that she was the woman identified as Rosa in Alma Guillermo Prieto's article in the *New York Review of Books*, "Our War in Colombia" (April 30, 2000).

29. Among the reports on violence against women are those by Radhika Coomaraswamy, U.N. Special Rapporteur for Violence against Women, following her visit to Colombia in 2001 and Amnesty International, *Colombia: Violence against Women: Scarred Bodies, Hidden Crimes,* AI Index: AMR 23/048/2004.

30. Much of the information presented here about the history of Trujillo comes from *El poder y la sangre* (The Power and the Blood), by the Colombian historian Adolfo Atehortúa. The author and the history of the book itself deserve comment as both are instructive about the complications of writing about Colombian violence. From Cali, Atehortúa dedicates the book to his father and his father's murderers: "killed before I knew him, *assassinado a piedra* [killed by stoning] coming home from a Conservative rally in 1960; to his killers, drunken liberals, whom I forgave as a child." In the introduction we learn that the book began as a joint research project with political science master's students from Javariana University in Cali in 1989. The authors worked closely with Father Tiberio Fernandez, whose death was a central factor in the creation of the Trujillo Commission. The growing violence in the region paralyzed their research and generated a crisis of representation for the authors: "We had to ask ourselves how to present the text, as a *testimonio* or as an academic analysis" (Atehortúa 1995: ix). The book combines the two formats, ending each analytic chapter with testimonies from the interviews and oral histories.

31. The town that was to become Trujillo was founded by Leonardo Salazar and his friends, who created the first local government council, a "junta pobladora," or settlers' junta. While his family owned a small plot in neighboring Riofrio, Salazar bought the hacienda La Esnada (then only a *claro*, lit., "clearing," a place in the jungle sparsely planted with food crops), divided it into lots, and installed his brother and several other acquaintances. The settlement, known as La Esnada and officially founded in September 1922, counted almost 500 inhabitants by the end of 1923. Rumor had it that Salazar recruited from among newly released criminals and prostitutes to fill the available land. Ensuring property rights required constant attention to political favors channeled through clientalist networks connecting local voters with the national politicians positioned to assist them, and newer arrivals found a champion in the Liberal politician Ernesto Pedraza. Land claim disputes led to drawn out court battles, in which Conservative Salazar supported large landowners' efforts to secure titles while Liberal Pedraza promoted the rights of smaller peasant farmers.

Partisan divisions flared as the parties vied to secure the growing public works budgets for their own patronage networks. Residents asserted their independence in 1929, complaining of ongoing electoral fraud when they attempted to vote in Riofrio, the municipal capital. With a letter threatening protests of "more than a thousand men willing to fight for their rights and spill their blood if it is necessary," a commission traveled to Cali to argue for the creation of a new independent municipality (quoted in Atehortúa 1995: 59). The official designation of the new municipality of Trujillo on April 9, 1930, did nothing to settle the constant political intrigue, however. Conflict in Trujillo began in earnest in December 31, 1931. Local politicians had been united by efforts to ensure the municipality's independence; with administrative autonomy secure, long-percolating divisions erupted over voting rights. Conservatives attempted to purge Liberals from the voting lists, claiming they were registered to vote in other municipalities, and the Conservative majority on the voting board *(jurado)* agreed. Liberals announced they were defending their rights; Conservatives denounced an unruly mob attempting to subvert the process. When Liberals won the next local elections, Conservatives complained Liberal police did not allow their participation, but internal divisions among Liberals soon brought Conservatives back to power.

In Trujillo the Liberal Party split; the president appointed a new mayor without consulting local party activists. Conservatives, boycotting congressional races, focused on the local council elections; in Trujillo Conservatives went as far as financing dissident Liberals to encourage divisions (Atehortúa 1995: 113). Political violence gained ground as a campaign tactic, with an attempted dynamite attack at the hotel housing the mayor. Liberal boss Pedraza found his power base threatened by party leaders from Cali, with his supporters more interested in pragmatic defense of their interests than the party line. A Supreme Court decision on land claims favoring Salazar's allies positioned him as the exclusive dealer in Trujillo land titles. Pedraza then accused him of conspiracy against poor farmers, and the conflict escalated. In 1935 Pedraza survived an assassination attempt and stepped back from politics. In a bitter editorial, he lamented, "In the Liberal Party there is no doctrine: there are regional *caciques* who offer employment and they run roughshod over *[arrastran]* everyone" (quoted in Atehortúa 1995: 129). Salazar, in the meantime, developed a new tactic for his wealthy clients—occupying settled land, then selling it to preselected buyers as *baldío* (empty land that could be claimed) at a low price.

The tone of local debates has been conserved by the local newspaper, which favored the Liberals. An editorial complained in February 1936, "Every week we hear those claiming to be the representatives of God on earth giving the most unjust and vulgar sermons against the government and the Liberal elements that defend them" (quoted in Atehortúa 1995: 119). The week before, the bishop had denounced government persecution of Catholics and declared all laws passed by Congress illegitimate because of the lack of Conservative representation. The newspaper also published rumors of secret Conservative meetings at which party activists planned the assassination of anyone caught on the roads who did not support them and promised revenge in kind: "If this is the evil *[infame]* way that they want to make our homes weep, we will also make the tears flow in their houses." Conservative leaders in turn accused Liberals of harboring more than one million false voting cards *(cédulas)*, a continuing rallying cry used to discredit the government.

Conservatives came to power in Trujillo in 1941 as the Liberal split allowed Conservatives to gain control of the council and Conservative José Rios was appointed mayor. The same dynamic brought Conservatives back to the Casa Rosada (Colombia's presidential home) in 1946, when Gaitán split the Liberal vote with the official candidate and Conservative Mariano Ospina Peréz won the plurality (1946–50). The Conservatives' campaign, orchestrated by radical Conservative Alvaro Gomez, focused on retaliation for the Liberal persecution of Conservative peasants during the Olaya Herrera administration.

During La Violencia, Liberals complained of unjustified detentions, fines, and political persecution. The *guardia civil* (national police) expanded their power, now acting on their own with the tacit approval of the mayor, and the number of reported murders skyrocketed from an average of one a year to more than forty-three. (Atehortúa wrote in a footnote that these figures are at best indicatives of patterns, because most murders were not reported or investigated.) Liberal leaders resigned in protest from the national government, and military officers were appointed as governors and mayors in many parts of the country as part of national security measures. Liberals won control of the Trujillo council in 1949 but were forced to flee. Conservative Leonardo Espinosa, Trujillo's up-and-coming *gamonal*, led an armed attack against Liberal headquarters, giving them two weeks to leave town. After a bomb was left in the building a month later, they did.

In October 1949 President Ospina named a well-known *pájaro* supporter governor of Valle. *Párajaros* began attacking towns in an effort to "*conservatizar* [make conservative] the entire western mountain chain, town by town" (quoted in Atehortúa 1995: 162). One witness to these attacks was Pedro Antonio Marín, a young traveling salesman who was selling his wares in Ceilán, across the Cauca River from Trujillo. He described how in April 1948 the town was taken over by four hundred Conservatives, "armed with machine guns, rifles and carbines," in revenge for the prior detention and murder of a Conservative politician. "The world was undone with fear, courage was a lost cry before so many men . . . and so finally, I lost my goods in La Primavera" (quoted in Atehortúa 1995: 163). Marín fled south with hundreds of other Liberal families, seeking refuge in remote mountains and jungles. They would eventually join thousands of other Liberals and Communists in makeshift rural communities, united in shifting alliances to face the persecution of government-backed Conservatives. Marín, alias Manuel Marulanda and nicknamed Tiro Fijo (Sure Shot), went on to become the maximum commander of the Revolutionary Armed Forces of Colombia and the country's oldest guerrilla leader. As of this writing, he remains the head of the FARC leadership.

During the military dictatorship that followed La Violencia, General Rojas Pinilla appointed a governor known to be under the political thumb of Conservative power broker Leonardo Espinosa, who by 1960 consolidated his rule over Trujillo—control that began with his attacks driving Liberals out of town. His Liberal competition, Ernesto Pedraza, by then unable to unite the Liberals, was assassinated on January 31, 1960. From 1946 to 1963 Trujillo had twenty-one military mayors, primarily low-ranking and poorly trained sergeants (Conservative politician Rios regained the mayoral office briefly in 1953).

Trujillense political life was dominated by violent conflict within the Conservative Party, with selective assassinations coming to rival campaigning as a means of consolidating support. Espinosa had cemented his power by exchanging votes for a road paving project linking Trujillo to Riofrio and through continued support for "his" mayor; his status as a power boss reached such renown that he was a model for Cali writer Gustavo Alvarez Gardeazabel's 1987 novel, *The Last Gamonal*. By the end of the 1970s Espinosa's stranglehold on politics in Trujillo was challenged by the Giraldo family, who used their national connections to escalate the local political dramas. After the Giraldos won control of the council in the 1978 election, political violence between the factions escalated. Espinosa survived an assassination attempt, and a military mayor was named in 1979. The violence only got worse, however. On June 16 a Giraldo brother and council member was killed. A curfew was declared, but the growing list of victims included local politicians, community leaders, and politically uninvolved bystanders. Regional papers, including *El País* of Cali, published editorials calling for "peace accords" between the rival factions, to no avail. Despite the appointment of a second military mayor, the assassinations culminated in the January 8, 1980, fatal shooting of Espinosa. The assassination of civic leaders continued; they were viewed as possible competition despite the Giraldo family's unrivaled political power.

32. Like many of their radical compatriots, the ELN attempted to build a rural power base. Atehortúa presents a rather utopian view of ELN activities in the region: "They won the appreciation of vast sectors of the peasantry with actions the state never took: promoting community organizations, helping with [the] harvest, advice and meetings to improve production and guarantee transport, collective work brigades to build bridges and open trails, equitably distributing water, educating children, and little by little beginning the administration of justice. *Guerrilleros* got rid of miscreants and ne'er-do-wells, resolved conflicts, controlled the use of alcohol, and improved the conduct of husbands in their homes" (Atehortúa 1995: 275).

33. Perpetrator testimony was crucial to documenting a number of major human rights cases. Most perpetrators appeared before NGOs and government agencies out of fear of becoming targets themselves for knowing too much. During my work with human rights organizations, I had the opportunity to interview several paramilitaries: an assassin who claimed to work with the military in Meta, a military officer who participated in the death squads in Barrancabermaja, and a woman who was the treasurer for a paramilitary group in Putumayo. All offered details of their crimes in the hope of obtaining protection.

34. Daniel Arcila's testimony was challenged, however, by government officials, who had him evaluated by the forensic psychology branch of Medicina Legal (Department of Forensic Medicine) and declared mentally incompetent. Arcila returned to Trujillo before the commission was convened and was last seen in the central plaza on May 5, 1991, surrounded by a group of armed men; he is presumed dead.

35. A public order judge acquitted the five men accused of the crimes, includ-

ing two paramilitaries, two local landowners, and Major Urueña. The ruling was upheld on appeal. The military conducted its own investigation and acquitted Urueña; he was promoted to colonel.

36. The commission included the *defensor,* the *fiscal* or a delegate, the *procurador* or a delegate, a member of the Senate Human Rights Commission, a member of the House Human Rights Commission, the minister of government or a delegate, the minister of the exterior or a delegate, the defense minister or a delegate, the presidential adviser for human rights or a delegate, an Administrative Department of Security delegate, the National Police inspector general, the armed forces inspector general, and representatives of the Conferencia Episcopal, the Colombian Red Cross, Justice and Peace, a delegate of ASFADDES, the CCJ (then Andean Commission of Jurists Colombian Section), the Lawyers' Collective, and the CSPP.

37. Each year in March the U.S. Congress issues a "certification" that countries are taking appropriate measures to combat illicit narcotics production and trafficking. The process is highly politicized; when Colombia was decertified, analysts pointed out that Mexico had a worse record than Colombia but would not be decertified for political reasons.

38. Debates have continued unabated over how to appropriately respond to what were now being labeled complex humanitarian emergencies and complex political emergencies, and how to implement humanitarian principles and whether or not to endorse military interventions in the name of humanitarianism, including if and how to incorporate human rights activism into humanitarian assistance programs (Rieff 2002). In some cases, ignoring issues of accountability has led to humanitarian operations that assist perpetrators of abuses; the most famous example occurred after the genocide in Rwanda: in the refugee camps in Zaire militias involved in the genocide received food and medical treatment, as well as free rein to organize military operations (Gourevitch 1998). In other cases efforts to address local structures of power have backfired spectacularly, such as the U.S. military intervention in Somalia and Haiti. The "production" of humanitarian crises has been the subject of a number of new critiques, particularly following the roundly criticized experiences of international organizations in the Balkans and Central Africa (de Waal 1997).

39. The single major event that triggered humanitarian interest in Colombia was the massive displacements in 1997 of Afro-Colombian communities. More than 10,000 people, including more than 7,000 from one town, fled paramilitary incursions in the largest single incident of forced displacement in Colombia. They settled in makeshift camps in Turbo and Apartado, which were initially funded by emergency money from the British embassy. A journalist friend covering these events recounted that a European diplomatic official told him he was inspired to help because the people "really looked like refugees," referring to press photos of long lines of poor and malnourished Afro-Colombians, a visual reference that could have been taken anywhere in Africa. The scale of the displacement and the image of thousands of Afro-Colombians arriving in the already overburdened urban centers inspired headlines such as "Colombia: Latin America's Rwanda." Aid workers believe that in part because of the international response, no incidents of forced displacement on a similar scale have occurred since. According to

a priest who has worked in the Choco region for more than twenty years, "The government calculated that the displaced were going to disperse. They even offered them bus fare to wherever they wanted to go. But the church supported them so they could stay and demand the right to return and their other rights from the government. . . . The scorched earth policy was too politically costly. After that, in the region, they used a different strategy, with different orders. The paramilitaries arrived and carried out selective assassinations, not massacres. They killed many people, but one by one. They only told two communities that they all had to leave." However, there remain many areas in which several hundred people or more will seek shelter in local sports stadiums or government offices during times of conflict.

40. The ICRC began its work in 1969 with prison visits. In 1980 it established a permanent mission in the capital and the first field offices in Villavicencio and Bucaramanga. With its expansion in the mid-1990s, the ICRC more than doubled its staff; by 1998 it had a budget of almost $13 million.

41. Created in 1979, the Project Counseling Service (PCS) is made up of the Danish Refugee Council (DRC), the Norwegian Refugee Council (NRC), Action by Churches Together (ACT/NL), Swiss Interchurch Aid (HEKS), and the Canadian agency Inter Pares (IP). PCS works in Peru, Central America, Mexico, and Colombia.

42. *Constitución Política de Colombia,* 1991, 29; my translation.

43. Other major international organizations that opened programs focusing on peace efforts in Colombia include the International Crisis Group, which had a Bogotá office from 1998 to 2003, and the Center for International Policy, which hosted a meeting between U.S. policy makers and FARC representatives in Mexico City in 1999.

44. Francisco Santos, a member of the prominent Santos family (which boasts a former president and the owner of Colombia's leading paper, *El Tiempo*), became director of País Libre. As vice president during the Uribe administration (2002–6) he was charged with designing and implementing state human rights policy. In the early 1990s País Libre collected more than a million signatures in a successful campaign for a proposed law increasing the penalties for kidnapping, which was passed in 1993. The organization also supported compensation by the state to those who gave information to the authorities that led to the liberation of kidnapped persons or to the capture of those involved.

45. País Libre also joined with Redepaz, the CCJ, ASFADDES, and other NGOs in a campaign for legislation that would make forced disappearance a criminal offense, something they had not been able to achieve despite a decade-long struggle. The absence of legal status for this offense resulted in a series of legal problems for the families, in addition to making prosecution of perpetrators, generally state agents, impossible. The diplomatic corps, especially ambassadors from the European Community and the U.N. Office of the High Commissioner for Human Rights in Colombia, were very supportive of these lobbying efforts.

46. The planners intended that the Assembly become a permanent body to channel the participation of civil society; it continued to meet periodically but with a much lower profile during the pro-war Uribe administration.

2. SOLIDARITY WITH OUR CLASS BROTHERS

1. *Doña* is a Spanish term of respect typically employed to designate a powerful elder. Eugenia's colleagues used this term, and I have chosen to do so also as a sign of her position in the human rights community.

2. The political persecution of the left by government forces has a much longer history, but I begin with the kinds of violence registered as human rights violations.

3. I do not mean to suggest that NGOs are controlled by leftist parties, or even that members/leaders remain active members of leftist parties. This is a common allegation made by the Colombian right, including the extreme right-wing newspaper columnist Plinio Apuleyo Mendoza, as well as the Colombian military (see chapter 3). This view is simply factually wrong, and while my argument of the influence of the left on NGOs may be used by those who hold this view, it is certainly not my intention to strengthen their viewpoint.

4. The history of liberation theology, and the final assessment of its ultimate role in the church, is still being written. Even as it was first developed, the doctrine generated significant controversy, especially over its use of Marxism and the political activism it encouraged; a 1984 statement from the Congregation for the Doctrine of the Faith, a powerful doctrinal watchdog group, condemned "false liberationism." Early writing by practitioners and sympathetic scholars emphasized liberation theology's utopian promise, the extreme poverty and inequality in the region, and the brutal repression of its leadership and members (Berryman 1984; Gutierrez 1971; Lernoux 1980, 1989). More recent scholars have a soberer assessment of the results of liberation theology, examining in detail the severe political, personal, and communal crises its practice generated for certain communities. Critics have also focused on liberation theology's neglect of ritual and the hierarchical role of church leadership, rather than the "base communities" it claimed to generate, in directing activism (Burdick and Hewitt 2000; Levy 2000; Nagle 1997).

5. Four of the ELN's most influential members, including their maximum commander who was known as "El Cura Pérez" (Pérez the Priest), were Spanish priests who came to Colombia as part of the radical Catholic Worker movement.

6. Earlier attempts at rural education, such as radio schools and programs to strengthen rural community planning organizations (*juntas de acción comunal,* developed nationwide beginning in 1958), also laid the groundwork for later consciousness-raising efforts.

7. Doctors and other medical professionals have had a particularly high profile role in progressive organizations in part because of their awareness of structural poverty and rural inequality. Beginning in 1950, all doctors and dentists are required to serve a "rural year" in order to receive their licenses to practice medicine. By practicing medicine in remote underserved areas, doctors gain valuable experience but also come into contact with the radically different challenges facing rural areas.

8. The legal category "political prisoner" denotes people who are detained and accused of "political crimes"—breaking laws because of their membership in an illegal political group or for political ends. They are not necessarily innocent

of criminal acts (murder, kidnapping, bombings, drug trafficking, etc), but because of their membership in a political group or their political ends they are not put into the category "criminals." In daily use, however, these categories are slippery and contested, with deep divisions over which individuals can claim the status of political prisoner. I have chosen to use the phrase "political prisoner" where the groups themselves use it.

9. President Julio Cesar Turbay (1978–82), when questioned about political prisoners in Colombia during a state visit to Europe, told the press, "I am the only political prisoner in Colombia." Omaira Montoya was a pregnant biologist detained with Mauricio Trujillo by the army in 1977 in Barranquilla; while he was tortured and later found alive, Montoya never reappeared. She is described by ASFADDES as the victim of the first "forced disappearance" in Colombia. A leftist militant, she had links to the ELN.

10. Opus Dei is an extremely conservative Catholic order founded in Spain in 1928 that was very influential in opposing later reforms within the church hierarchy, in particular liberation theology.

11. According to Castañeda, dependency theory linked Marxism and nationalism, arguing that the economies of Latin America were conditioned to the economies of "developed" nations, and had emerged in part as a response to the failure of modernization theory, popular in the 1950s (which argued that Latin America was simply behind and as their economies caught up to the developed West, economic growth would generate social change that would make possible more "developed" politics). Castañeda writes, "In a nutshell, this perspective posited the virtual neocolonial status of the hemisphere, the dysfunctional nature of capitalism in the region and the consequent historical impotence of the local business classes, the lack of democratic channels for reform, and the inviability of any form of nonsocialist development" (Casteñada 1993: 71). Among the prominent practioners were André Gunder Frank and Fernando Henrique Cardoso.

12. Joan Manuel Serrat is a Spanish singer, part of the Nova cançó movement in Catalonia, whose music was banned during the Franco dictatorship. He went into exile briefly in Mexico in 1974, staying there until Franco's death in 1975. Silvio Rodriguez and Pablo Milanés are Cuban folksingers and part of the Nueva trova movement of political folksinging that emerged after the Cuban Revolution. The Chilean poet Pablo Neruda won the Nobel Prize and supported revolutionary causes. The Uruguayan writer Mario Benedetti was forced into exile from 1973 to 1985. The Spanish poet Miguel Hernández died after being imprisoned by the Franco regime; his poetry deals with his experiences of poverty and the tragedy of the Spanish Civil War. Other important cultural imports during this time included the Nueva canción movement in Chile such as the music of Victor Jarra, who was famously tortured to death by the Pinochet regime; Violeta Parra; and Mercedes Sosa.

13. Playa Girón is the Cuban name for the beach where the U.S.-sponsored unsuccessful invasion of Cuba landed in 1963.

14. According to one founding member of CREDHOS, "The 1980s were when the violence arrived in Barranca. The displaced arrived, in the barrio Progreso, toward the east, people who were displaced from Puerto Una, Puerto Boyacá. The majority of the displaced people were the social base of the FARC. The

ELN wasn't as strong, they had been in Arauca and then arrived in this area later. Puerto Boyaca had ten Communist local town council representatives [concejales], Puerto Berrío had five Communist concejales; it was clearly a social base of the FARC. Then in 1984–85 the Belisario Betancur peace process created the UP, and there were all the killings of the UP."

15. Manuel Gustavo Chacón was a trade unionist killed on January 15, 1988; naval intelligence together with the paramilitary death squad MAS were implicated in his death. Public buildings in Barrancabermeja and an ELN front operating in the region were named after him.

16. DFID is the British state international aid agency, the equivalent of USAID.

17. Enver Hoxha was prime minister of Albania from 1944 until his death in 1985; Josip Broz ruled Yugoslavia as Marshall Tito from 1945 until his death in 1980.

18. While the relationship between guerrillas and social movements throughout Latin America remains a largely unwritten history, there were significant differences between the Colombian guerrillas and other guerrilla organizations elsewhere in the region. For example, the Shining Path in Peru was completely hostile to non-guerrilla-controlled grassroots organizations, viewing them as bourgeois elements to be destroyed. In El Salvador, the guerrillas adopted a strategy allowing significantly more distance between their leadership and civilian social movements, emphasizing different strategies (political organization, military offensives) at different times (Wood 2003).

19. While twentieth-century activists have generally grouped rights into two categories, civil and political rights and economic, social, and cultural rights, the linkages between different kinds of rights have varied over time. For example, Lynn Hunt's insightful collection of documents from the French Revolution demonstrates that civil and political rights were considered separate throughout the eighteenth century (Hunt 1996). The historian Kenneth Cmiel pointed out that as a consequence, women obtained the right to own property (a civil right) long before being granted the right to vote (a political right) (Cmiel 2004: 5).

20. Drug traffickers also actively attempted to highjack the human rights discourse for themselves. In repeated public statements, Pablo Escobar and others declared that they were the victims of human rights violations and politically motivated persecution by the state.

3. HUMAN RIGHTS AND THE PRACTICE OF POLITICS

1. While I discuss the changes that occurred in human rights activism in terms of the "1990s," I am referring to the long decade after the cold war and before the war on terror, roughly dating from the end of the 1980s until the early 2000s. Even these dates are approximate, and this gives a somewhat artificial sense of more complete closure than actually existed at the time. I do not mean to suggest that there were radical changes overnight. Also, the chronology of new organizations does not uniformly map onto this divide: the Colombian Commission of Jurists, for example, was established in 1988. However, my general point about the differences in activism between the two major periods of human rights

activism within the changes in the general political landscape makes the distinction useful.

2. In an earlier publication, *This Is Not My Church* (Esta iglesia no es mia), Vargas targets liberation theology and Catholic activists while explaining that human rights activism by NGOs "is how Colombia [became] the victim of the worst kind of activity by terrorist groups operating as Communist subversive groups—they openly express this in their documents—that with the drug cartels seek . . . to impose this totalitarian political system. . . . [They promote] the cultivation, processing, and trafficking of illegal drugs, [and] systematically dedicate themselves to the extermination of all Colombians opposing their nefarious project" (Vargas M. 1999: 15). Plinio Apuleyo Mendoza wrote the preface. The book contains little independent scholarship or analysis; the bulk of the text consists of blocks of quoted texts from the writers themselves framed by Vargas's shrill commentary.

3. The director of the CCJ, Gustavo Gallón, sued Manuel Vicente Peña for "false and dishonest accusations with the clear intention of damaging the legitimate activity carried out by the CCJ in the defense and promotion of human rights" and Fernando Vargas of VIDA for "presenting to the InterAmerican Human Rights Commission documentation that included as evidence Pena's false accusations." Peña countersued Gustavo for being an "apologist for drug trafficking, terrorism, and subversion." The attorney general ruled against Gustavo and the CCJ in 1997 (*El Tiempo*, "Comisión de Juristas pierde proceso penal," March 14, 1997).

4. The letter was published in *El Tiempo*, November 13, 1992, and republished in *This Is Not My Church*. In it, Apuleyo Mendoza wrote that Justice and Peace had published "scandalously false information, such as asserting that in El Carmen, groups belonging to hitman gangs based in Medellín operated in El Carmen." He went on to claim that El Carmen had been under the control of the ELN for twenty-five years, the peasants rebelled, then were attacked by the ELN and accused by Justice and Peace of being paramilitary supporters for not belonging to the ELN. Plinio Apuleyo Mendoza is by far the most prominent of these writers. Born in 1932, he studied in Paris at the Sorbonne, has written award-winning fiction, and enjoys a well-publicized friendship with Gabriel García Márquez. He (described on the book jacket as a "former guerrilla and one of the founders of the Cuban press agency Prensa Latina") is also coauthor— with Cuban Carlos Alberto Montaner and Peruvian Alvaro Vargas Llosa, son of the novelist Mario Vargas Llosa—of *The Guide to the Latin American Idiot*. According to a review of the book in the summer 1997 issue of *Foreign Policy*, "Few targets are spared as the authors take on the totalitarian illusions of Latin America's revolutionary left, the long love affair with the Cuban Revolution, liberation theology (in a chapter mischievously called 'Rifles and Cassocks'), and good old Yankeephobia. Exaggerated, even unfair at times, this book nevertheless provides a rollicking good read." The book was also glowingly reviewed by the *Weekly Standard* and reportedly was a best-seller in Latin America.

5. Eduardo Umaña was a prominent human rights lawyer who began his career in the 1970s, was a founding member of the José Alvéar Restrepo Lawyers' Collective, and mentored several generations of young lawyers and

activists. He was assassinated in his office on April 28, 1998, by three people posing as journalists, probably in retaliation for his work on human rights cases.

6. One important difference with other NGOs was their international focus; their strategy at the United Nations is discussed in detail in chapter 5.

7. The Ford Foundation has been a critical force in developing human rights activism around the world. Its history of supporting human rights groups began in Latin America, after many of its partners were persecuted by the military juntas that came to power in the 1960s and 1970s. The foundation had begun establishing field offices in Latin America in 1961. Its initial programs were devoted to financing state institutions and planning ministries, but the foundation quickly began major investment initiatives in universities. Following the military coups in Brazil and the Southern Cone, these university programs were disrupted; many graduate programs were forced to close, and numerous professors with long-standing ties to the foundation were fired or jailed or fled the country. The foundation responded with a two-pronged approach, establishing grant programs to fund academics fleeing their home countries and creating new independent research institutions for those who remained in "internal exile." Convinced of the need for NGOs and checks on repressive governmental power, the foundation in 1976 approved a special appropriation of $500,000 for "a new effort to advance human rights and intellectual freedom," which opened the door for the much more extensive human rights programs that followed (Carmichael 2002: 251). During a major revision in the foundation's priorities in 1981, "human rights and social justice" was established as one of six major themes, with "governance and public policy" one of the five principal units of the foundation's Program Division. While comprehensive data on the details of the Ford Foundation's human rights funding are unavailable, the foundation has given more than U.S.$200 million for international human rights funding over the past twenty-five years. One of the most important elements of their funding has been their commitment to "flagship organizations." For example, Human Rights Watch and the Lawyers Committee for Human Rights (now Human Rights First) have both received annual Ford Foundation grants since their founding in 1978. Of the international divisions, the Latin America bureau has devoted proportionally greater amounts to human rights issues. To date, the foundation's focus has been almost exclusively civil and political rights for a broad range of groups, including NGOs targeting specific populations and providing legal services, as well as academic programs.

8. In 1999 a third office was established in Washington, and the Coordination became the Colombia-Europe-U.S. Coordination.

9. In practice, the coalition of OIDHACO organizations and the London Accord are often almost completely the same. Both continued to meet as of 2007.

10. One example of such a commission is described in detail in chapter 6.

11. *Personeros* were appointed until the 1991 Constitution; following those reforms, candidates were appointed by mayors and then elected by town councils.

12. Horacio Serpa is a senior statesman in the Liberal Party who has held several cabinet positions and was until August 2004 the Colombian ambassador to the United Nations. He began his career as a member of Congress closely tied to Barranca.

13. This view was largely supported by the evidence from ongoing violence in postconflict Central American societies. In some areas of El Salvador and Guatemala, despite negotiated settlements with guerrilla groups and hundreds of millions of dollars in international assistance, violence in the postwar period was higher than it had been during the previous decade.

14. Rodrigo was referring to the recently released book *My Confession,* in which the Colombian journalist Mauricio Arangueren Molina transcribed extensive interviews with the paramilitary leader Carlos Castaño. Many activists were reluctant to read it, for fear of legitimizing the paramilitary project. Others expressed distaste for the narrative itself, in which Castaño admitted to—and justified—having participated in numerous political murders.

15. These policies were implemented by the Gaviria administration. The reduction in protectionist tariffs resulted in a dramatic rise in imports. Many Colombian activists blame these policies for increasing unemployment in Colombia and for the severe economic crisis of the late 1990s.

16. Switching between common terms for the paramilitary forces was common. People often used the word *autodefensas*—the name claimed by the forces themselves, and used by the government—but then slipped into the shorthand *paras. Paramilitares* was used to make clear the connection between the forces and the military.

4. THE EMOTIONAL POLITICS OF ACTIVISM IN THE 1990S

1. These insights have borne fruit in the work of scholars examining activism in a number of contexts (Brysk 2000; Conklin 1997; Cortright and Pagnucco 1997; Coutin 1993, 1995; Cunningham 1995, 1999; Loveman 1998; McLagan 2000a, 2000b; Smith 1996; Stephen 1995; Warren 1998).

2. The official criteria for consideration as a martyr by the Catholic Church was established in the mid-1700s as a believer who dies for the faith, whose killer is provoked by a profession of faith and motivated by a hatred of the faith; martyrdom requires a witness and the victim's refusal to recant. While other theologians, including Thomas Aquinas, argued that dying for the common good could be sufficient sacrifice to be considered a martyr, the official Catholic definition continues to require evidence of being killed for one's faith. The pope recognized Salvadoran Archbishop Oscar Romero, shot while saying mass as a result of his opposition to the military, as a martyr but refused public support of other religious activists killed as a result of their political activities.

3. Many activists, however, refused to accept this level of sacrifice and left the church, their political activities, and or the country as the level of reprisals intensified. David Stoll, among others, is highly critical of radical Catholics' role in encouraging activists to continue with dangerous political activities and views the increase in Protestant and Evangelical religious membership as in part a result of Christians seeking a less dangerous church home (Stoll 1993, 2000).

4. Peterson writes extensively about the role of martyrdom in the construction of activist identities in El Salvador. For example: "The courage necessary to fulfill the demands of this understanding of Christianity is made possible by convictions that first the true believers cannot escape martyrdom and second that

persecution demonstrates true belief" (Peterson 1997: 126). This is particularly true in the case of "potential martyrs," activists who continue with high-risk activism, whom she described as understanding their cause not as a conscious choice but as an integral element of their identity, surpassing the need even for individual safety or survival: "A 'true' Christian, they seek not to escape suffering but to confront it and grasp it, to incorporate it into an overarching belief structure; end of the story is no longer personal agony or death but rather the realization of the ultimate goal for which suffering is borne. Progressive Catholic theology presents this goal in terms of a fuller, even eternal, life for both martyrs and the communities for whom they sacrifice. This conviction that suffering serves a positive end is central to the interpretive framework that makes political violence meaningful" (Peterson 1997: 133).

5. The "sacred heart of Jesus" is an iconic picture of Jesus in the Catholic Church; he is portrayed with his hands outstretched, and his heart, circled in thorns and glowing in a radiant light, is pictured outside his body in front of his chest. The image is traditionally hung in Colombian homes.

6. The discussion of justifications of political violence by groups attempting to register protest or overthrow the state has been indelibly changed since the Al Qaeda attacks of September 11, 2001. In this discussion, I am not attempting to justify or reject different positions but to understand the political logic and resonance of these positions as an important element in how activists positioned themselves as morally motivated political actors engaged in ongoing struggles over how to maintain, expand, and control the meaning of their activism.

7. The other major debate over how to classify violent acts by actors has focused on paramilitary groups. For some NGOs, these groups are simply the facade of the Colombian government, and they classify paramilitary violence as part of the state counterinsurgency strategy. Other groups maintain that drug trafficking profits and collusion with regional economic elites have given some paramilitary groups in certain areas of the country a degree of autonomy from government control.

8. This debate was not an issue for the early decades of the human rights movement in Latin America. IHL was never part of the work of the human rights groups that developed in response to the Southern Cone military dictatorships. While urban guerrilla forces did commit selective violent acts, including bombings and kidnappings, they developed negligible military strength and were quickly crushed by overwhelming counterinsurgency campaigns. The Nicaraguan Contras (the right-wing force backed by the United States in their attempt to overthrow the Socialist Sandinista government) were the first nonstate actors whose abuses were documented by Human Rights Watch and the Washington Office on Latin America. HRW documented abuses by the Farabundo Martí National Liberation Front (FMLN) of El Salvador, most notably in its campaign to assassinate mayors in areas supporting the army. The FMLN publicly accepted the jurisdiction of IHL over their operations and promised to end the campaign; Mexico and European governments granted FMLN representatives significant political recognition, and their international diplomacy was critical during the eventual peace talks. In Guatemala, the insurgency was largely crushed in the 1980s by the overwhelming force of the military's counterinsurgency program;

the Clarification Commission found guerrillas responsible for less than 3 percent of human rights violations. In 1992 Amnesty International adopted a policy to begin receiving cases of abuses committed by insurgent forces.

The Peruvian human rights community, in contrast, was the first to fully embrace the use of IHL to criticize the guerrillas. They began in response to the violence of the Shining Path, which completely rejected international rights standards. Further, the Shining Path viewed social movements and civil society organizations, including human rights groups, as competition and routinely attempted to infiltrate them, sent death threats to activists, and even assassinated community leaders. The human rights community's decision in the early 1990s to adopt IHL as the framework for criticizing guerrilla abuses followed significant debate. Their insistence on using specific legal terms (IHL instead of human rights) and presenting credible documentation was interpreted by some critics as "as wishy-washy and as a means of avoiding a direct condemnation of [the Shining Path]" (Youngers 2003: 276). In addition to concerns about the public relations impact of this decision, there were concerns about how the human rights community should respond to attacks against state agents. For example, policemen, often posted alone in remote provinces, are legitimate military targets, according to IHL, but in practice were abandoned by the state to their fate. The peasant self-defense squads *(rondas campesinas)* were also considered legitimate objects of attack under the Geneva Conventions. Despite these legal considerations, Peruvian groups were careful to adopt all victims of political violence regardless of perpetrator. They made a practice of sending condolence letters to the family members of police killed by the Shining Path or the MRTA and in many cases provided more assistance to victims of guerrilla violence than did the Peruvian government. According to one veteran of the Peruvian human rights movement, "We decided to denounce each and every crime committed by Shining Path with the same energy and conviction with which we denounced violations by the state. In addition, differentiating ourselves from most Latin American human rights groups, we broke with the idea of neutrality. . . . We felt solidarity with civil society's desire to defeat the Shining Path and we supported legitimate efforts by the state to accomplish this goal" (quoted in Youngers 2003: 438) .

As a result, they were careful not to champion the rights of guerrilla collaborators, defining their mission as to "protect and support innocent victims," in a policy adopted in 1987 at a national meeting of human rights groups. After the massive detentions following the antiterrorism legislation, they launched the "in the name of the innocent" campaign (estimated at approximately one-third of the nearly 22,000 people detained). The Shining Path fielded its own lawyers. One unintended outcome of this policy was that human rights activists became de facto judge and jury, with their adoption of particular cases often influencing the outcomes (detainees not represented by human rights lawyers were assumed guilty). Rejection of guerrilla violence also made Peruvian activists more supportive of democracy and ending the war. While Colombian groups focused on "humanizing the war" through the use of international humanitarian law, Peruvians realized that negotiation with the Shining Path was impossible, resulting in greater support for democracy and state-sponsored initiatives.

9. There have been significant shifts in the debate over IHL in Colombia

over the past two decades. During the 1970s, many guerrilla groups advocated the IHL framework while the military opposed it, with both sides assuming that accepting IHL would concede belligerent status to the guerrillas. Legal debates over the issue focused on the nature of the guerrillas and the conflict, specifically, whether the Colombian situation constituted a civil war in which armed groups had the capacity to replace the state. During this period, there was almost no focus on the content of the Convention and the minimum standards for the conduct of warfare, and little interest on the part of NGOs to intercede in the debate. By the 1990s the growing acceptance of IHL norms contributed to the Colombian government's support, particularly among the new staff at state human rights agencies. In 1996 Congress passed a law ratifying the Geneva Protocols, and the military began including IHL in its human rights programs and advocacy, despite some ongoing internal disputes. The guerrillas began to reject calls for adherence to IHL, viewing it as a tool of the government; in public statements, guerrilla spokesmen called international law bourgeois and capitalist and said it had nothing to do with them.

10. Discussion of what kinds of events justify warfare has a long history in philosophy (for a classic exploration of these debates, see Walzer 2000).

11. The figure 30,000 deaths a year in the conflict is not generally accepted. According to the Colombian Commission of Jurists, during the late 1990s, deaths resulting from the internal conflict (including deaths in combat, political assassinations, and deaths of civilians in combat operations) averaged about 3,500 a year, 15 to 20 percent of the total number of violent deaths, which averaged between 25,000 and 30,000 a year. Some activists argued that all violent deaths should be considered a result of the conflict, because the murder rate would presumably be lower with a functional state.

12. He offered an alternative humanitarian accord that would include a prisoner exchange between the guerrillas and the state and an agreement that neither the army nor the guerrillas would kill people but would detain them. Both sides would reject the use of indiscriminate weapons if there is no military or police presence in an area. In his description of a future accord, he commented, "The guerrillas have the right to detain people to find out if they have money for extortion; the state taxes and the guerrilla extort." Finally, he argued that the focus on child soldiers (usually recruited by the FARC and an increasing object of international funding and programs) should be redirected to children in poverty.

13. The Comunero Revolt was a diffuse but widespread popular rebellion between 1780 and 1781 against taxes imposed by the colonial Spanish government in what was the Viceroyalty of New Granada; the revolt was led by Manuela Beltrán in Socorro, Norte de Santander, and spread to other regions.

5. ACTIVISTS AT THE UNITED NATIONS AND BEYOND

1. Several reports presented options for reforming the Commission; a December 2004 report from the High Level Panel on Threats, Challenges and Change recommended universal membership and a yearly report on human rights throughout the world. A March 2005 report by U.N. Secretary-General Kofi Annan, "In Larger Freedom," called for dissolving the Commission and replac-

ing it with a smaller, permanent Human Rights Council (instead of the six-month annual meeting of the Commission), with its membership restricted to countries with good human rights records.

2. In an additional example of the complicated power dynamics of such international landscapes, one veteran activist commented, after observing the dreary basement meeting room, "You would never guess that these NGOs are more powerful than the government of Canada!"

3. These claims were disputed by U.S. and Colombian governmental officials. Allegations of the health impact of fumigation remained the most controversial claim; officials argued that no causality could be proven between the chemicals used in fumigation and the reported cases of ill health.

4. Travel to Geneva continues to serve as a practice that strengthens networks of exiles. Colombian human rights activists sought asylum in Western Europe throughout the 1990s, and international conferences and travel served as an opportunity to plan new events and for ad hoc reunions among friends and colleagues.

5. When established in 1946, the Commission had 18 member states. Membership was increased to 21 in 1961, to 32 in 1966, and to 43 in 1979; the final increase was to 53 in 1990.

6. Human Rights Watch was not a significant player at U.N. debates until much later and did not focus on Latin America until the late 1980s. HRW's first focus was the Soviet bloc; its original name was Helsinki Watch, after the Conference on Security and Cooperation in Europe, created in July 1973 and formalized in the Helsinki Final Act, adopted on August 1, 1975. The Helsinki Process included series of follow-up meetings to address issues, and Soviet dissidents began to establish NGOs to monitor compliance with the agreement. Helsinki Watch was established in the United States in February 1979, chaired by Robert Bernstein (a publisher and chair of Fund for Free Expression) and directed by Jeri Laber. The Ford Foundation gave the organization a two-year grant totaling U.S.$400,000 to create the Committee, with a mandate to establish liaison with watch groups in other countries or functioning in exile and to encourage the formation of such committees, gather documentation, and conduct media outreach (Korey 1998: 238). Americas Watch was established in 1985, and additional geographic and thematic divisions followed. HRW did not get U.N. consultative status until 1990, in part reportedly because of then-director Aryeh Nier's scorn for the U.N., which he viewed as ineffective.

7. Special Rapporteur on Religious Intolerance (1986); Special Rapporteur on the Use of Mercenaries as a Means of Impeding the Exercise of the Right of People to Self Determination (1987); Special Rapporteur on the Sale of Children, Child Prostitution and Child Pornography (1990), Working Group on Arbitrary Detention (1991); Special Rapporteur on Freedom of Opinion and Expression (1993); Special Rapporteur on Racism, Racial Discrimination and Xenophobia (1993); and Special Rapporteur on Violence against Women (1994). The treaties include the Covenant on Civil and Political Rights, 1976; the Covenant on Economic, Social and Cultural Rights, 1990; the Convention on the Elimination of All Forms of Racial Discrimination, 1969; the Convention on the Elimination of all Forms of Discrimination against Women (CEDAW), 1981; the Convention against Torture and Other Cruel, Inhuman or Degrading Treatment, adopted

1984, in force 1987; Convention on the Rights on the Child, adopted 1989, in force 1990.

8. The Dutch lawyer and academic Theo van Boven, who was appointed director of the Division on Human Rights in 1978, took an activist view of his position and encouraged the Commission to request authorization of a special rapporteur to examine the problem of arbitrary and extrajudicial executions. S. Amos Wako, a Kenyan legal expert, was appointed special rapporteur in 1982. The special rapporteur for torture was created in 1985, and Dutch expert and outgoing chair of the Commission, Peter Kooijmans, was appointed; he was replaced in 1993 by Nigel Rodley of Amnesty International.

9. The military junta in Greece and the murder of political dissidents by Idi Amin in Uganda were among the first cases to be considered under this procedure; from 1978 to 1984, twenty-eight cases were opened, with almost no concrete results.

10. During the 1980s, country-specific mandates were created for Afghanistan, Guatemala, Equatorial Guinea, and Iran; in the 1990s, for Iraq, Cuba, Haiti, El Salvador, Myanmar (Burma), Yugoslavia, Somalia, Cambodia, Sudan, Rwanda, Burundi, and Zaire.

11. A separate but related issue is the controversy over the election of abusive states to membership on the Commission. Among the most notable offenders: Bahrain, China, Saudi Arabia, and Pakistan in the Asia group; Cuba and Venezuela in the Latin America and Caribbean Group; Algeria in the African Group; and Russia in the Eastern European Group. For the first time, the United States was denied a seat on the Commission in 2002.

12. The Like-Minded Group includes Bangladesh, Bhutan, China, Cuba, Egypt, India, Indonesia, Libya, Nepal, Pakistan, Philippines, Saudi Arabia, Sri Lanka, Sudan, Syria, and Vietnam and has been one of the most vocal and effective blocs preventing Commission action and arguing for the reduction of the use of human rights mechanisms.

13. During the 2002 session, European Union efforts to promote action on country-specific matters were vigorously opposed by other state blocs. Examples include the the union's leadership on a resolution about the situation in Chechnya. Muslim countries and the OIC initially supported the measure but voted against it in protest of EU activism. The Special Rapporteur for Equatorial Guinea lost its mandate because of the actions of the African bloc, the Special Rapporteur on Sudan was maintained only with a one-vote margin, a resolution on Zimbabwe failed, and the mandate of the Special Representative on Iran was discontinued; all were EU initiatives. The focus on Israel and the Occupied Territories has also come to consume a disproportionate amount of time; a total of eight resolutions and decisions were adopted on this issue, including Lebanese detainees in Israel, Syrian Golan, and Israeli settlements.

14. There are a number of Web sites devoted to the issue of NGO participation at the United Nations, including the Global Policy Forum, which promotes greater participation at the United Nations (www.globalpolicy.org/ngos/index .htm); and NGO Watch, which critiques the lack of accountability and political bias of NGOs (www.ngowatch.org/). There are extensive sites maintained by the United Nations itself (http://www.un.org/partners/civil_society/home.htm).

15. In one example I witnessed, by Dr. Jianhua Li, deputy director of the research department for the China Society for Human Rights Studies, he began: "I'd like to share with you my feelings toward the criticisms of China's human rights record. Countries accusing China's human rights violations happen to be those which waged wars against China and massively violated the human rights of the Chinese people in history." He went on to mention that Chinese people enjoy greater rights and freedoms and economic prosperity than ever before. Another document circulating during the Commission, left on the tables outside the meeting room, was a photocopied booklet with a deep purple cover and the intriguing title, "The Gloomy Side of Amnesty International: On the Wicked Calumny and Foul Report against Eyadema's Regime," by Ehoue Eric Fiokou-Toulan, described as a founding member of the Togolese branch of Amnesty International. The booklet chronicles the author's growing conviction that Amnesty International is actively plotting the overthrow of the Togolese government through its human rights reports. He described one of the reports as a "heinous plot against Togo, published on May 5, 1999, under the title *Togo: State of Terror*." (Quoted passages taken from my notes.)

16. In 2001 the United Nations World Conference against Racism, Racial Discrimination, Xenophobia and Related Intolerance (WCAR) was held in Durban, South Africa. It was the third U.N. conference on racism following the World Conference to Combat Racism and Racial Discrimination in 1978 and the Second World Conference to Combat Racism and Racial Discrimination in 1983. More recently, U.N. events have been held on related issues, including the World Conferences on Human Rights (Vienna, 1993), Women (Beijing, 1995) and Social Development (Copenhagen, 1995). Other major U.N. conferences and follow-up meetings have focused on the environment (Rio and Rio plus Five) and housing (Cairo and Cairo plus Five).

17. According to Arturo Carrillo, who worked as a lawyer with the CCJ's international program during this period, the subcommission played a critical role as "a kind of think tank within the broader system." CCJ lawyers had their first contact with U.N. system experts when they went to the subcommission in 1994, and it was the first part of the U.N. system to produce a resolution on Colombia. The subcommission's subsequently decided not do country-specific work but elevated the status of the CCJ in the universe of NGOs working at the U.N. "It was a very elite club, the crème de la crème, the people who got the sub-commission to move on a country issue," according to Carrillo.

18. This was not the first visit by U.N. human rights delegates to Colombia. Between 1987 and 1989 three delegates traveled to Colombia: the special rapporteur on torture, the working group on disappearances, and the special rapporteur on arbitrary executions. In addition, the secretary-general's representative on internally displaced persons visited Colombia in June 1994; his report led the way to opening an office of the High Commissioner for Refugees in Colombia, albeit with a very limited mandate.

19. The government delegation included Minister of Defense Fernando Botero Zea, High Commissioner for Peace Carlos Holmes, Presidential Human Rights Adviser Carlos Vicente de Roux, all three cabinet-level positions. ("Un eco necesario: Conferencia de Bruselas," *Colombia Hoy,* no. 132 [March 1995]: 18–20).

20. Nationaal Centrum voor Ontwikkelingssamenwerking (National Center for Development Cooperation), *El terrorismo de estado en Colombia* (State Terrorism in Colombia) (Brussels: Ediciones NCOS, 1992); and *Tras los pasos perdidos de la Guerra Sucia* (On the Hidden Path of the Dirty War) (Brussels: Ediciones NCOS, 1995).

21. International Service for Human Rights played a critical role in assisting NGOs with lobbying strategies at the Commission. It offered a training course for activists, which CCJ staff attended. The organization had a number of connections to Colombia; CCJ director Gustavo Gallón was a member of the board (the director, Adrian Claude Zoeller, was married to a Colombian). International Service for Human Rights and other Geneva-based NGOs were a small but crucial network for Latin American activists interested in lobbying the Commission.

22. In part, their concern was over the issue of accreditation. The young man represented a Colombian NGO without official status before the U.N. and had gained access to the meetings through sponsorship from another organization (as had the majority of activists there), whose directors later denied any knowledge of his planned protest. As his sponsoring organization, they faced investigation and possible censure from the United Nations.

23. The ASFADDES representative present in Geneva during my fieldwork also criticized NGO lobbying at the U.N. She said that a different person from her organization is sent each year, making institutional learning almost impossible; because of complaints about this system, ASFADDES will be instituting a several-year term. Although international travel is generally considered a high-status perk, she told me that she herself found the experience very difficult and frustrating, with limited opportunities to speak and difficulty getting meetings with member states' representatives, and she did not want to return.

24. The Office of the United Nations High Commissioner for Human Rights in Bogotá was largely a result of NGO lobbying but was created with the permission of the Colombian government. In part, the government realized that there was growing concern about Colombia in the Commission. A serious corruption scandal had weakened the Samper government and the legitimacy of the Colombian government. Samper felt personally and politically vulnerable, under investigation by Colombia's Congress and denied a U.S. visa (among other things, this measure forced him to apply for a special transit visa to attend the U.N. General Assembly meetings in New York). He had also pledged more action on human rights. Like the activists, the Colombian government shared the view that assigning a country-specific rapporteur was essentially a critique of the government. In an effort to prevent such an appointment, the Colombian government sent two letters to the Special Procedures Branch of the Center for Human Rights. Among other things, the letter requested regular follow-up visits of thematic rapporteurs who had traveled to Colombia, and an invitation to the special rapporteur on the independence of judges and lawyers, committed to establishing a committee to follow-up on U.N. recommendations, and announced new reforms of the Military Penal Code.

25. These arguments did have weight within the Commission. One example was the changes made to the conclusions presented in the report of the Special Rapporteur for Arbitrary Executions in his 1996 report. While the first draft

strongly recommended a rapporteur, the final text urges establishment of a "mechanism through the office of the High Commissioner" (Baur 1997).

26. The full text of the Chairman's Statement (April 1996): "The Commission on Human Rights requests the High Commissioner for Human Rights to proceed, upon the initiative of the Government of Colombia and the identification of adequate sources of financing, to establish at the earliest possible date a permanent office in Colombia with the mandate to assist the Colombian authorities in developing policies and programs for the promotion and protection of human rights and to observe violations of human rights in the country, making analytical reports to the High Commissioner; requests, likewise, the High Commissioner to report to the Commission at its fifty-third session on the setting up of the office and on the activities carried out by it in implementing the above indicated mandate."

27. The agreement, originally intended for a period of seventeen months, has been repeatedly extended and is still in force as of this writing in 2007. The staff of the office has been repeatedly expanded, and field offices have been opened in Medellín and Cali.

28. The government has released substantial response documents—over ninety pages—listing their objections to the reports submitted by the office.

29. This is not always the case; Latin American reformist human rights officials do sometimes work to strengthen NGO claims, particularly following reform efforts in their own countries. During the 2002 session, for example, Maria Claire de Acosta, the Mexican human rights ombudsperson of the Fox administration, expressed support of Colombian NGOs at lobbying meetings with them. Similarly, an Argentine official who had been involved in the drafting of the legislation addressing disappearances expressed support during lobbying by ASFADDES. Previously, officials from the Southern Cone countries had rejected all such efforts even in the postdictatorship period.

6. STATES AND THE PRODUCTION OF IMPUNITY

1. Other examples are the human rights agencies established in postconflict situations or by transitional governments, such as in El Salvador or South Africa; the degree to which those political transformations succeeded in redistributing power is currently the subject of great debate, as is the significance of the state human rights agencies in those and similar contexts.

2. Here I was inspired by Michael Herzfeld's concept of the social production of indifference in his landmark study of Greek bureaucracies. Herzfeld described the "social production of indifference" by government officials, concluding that indifference was an active response that contributed to the construction of social identity (Herzfeld 1992, 1997).

3. Gupta also makes important observations about the difference between national bureaucracies and local structures, challenging "Western notions of boundary between state and society" in the more fluid relationships between public servant and private citizen in small rural communities (Gupta 1995: 384). The roles of the relationships of Colombian local human rights officials, including municipal ombudsmen, to national bureaucratic structures and NGOs offer

fruitful ground to explore these issues in future research but are beyond the scope of this project.

4. To explore why these issues are considered in a domestic civil rights framework rather than an international human rights framework in the United States is beyond the scope of this project; for the most comprehensive introduction to these issues to date, see Carol Anderson's history of how African American leaders defined their struggle with the civil rights, rather than human rights, framework (Anderson 2003).

5. The agency was created in October 1977, as the Bureau of Human Rights and Humanitarian Affairs, by congressional mandate, in response to the emphasis on human rights articulated by President Carter. The office was staffed with career Foreign Service Officers, and the first leaders were political appointees active in the civil rights movement; the first assistant secretary of state for human rights and humanitarian affairs, Patricia Derian had been a founder of the Mississippi Civil Liberties Union. The agency faced numerous obstacles, including "highly conflictive relationship with other bureaus of the State Department" (Drezner 2000: 774). With only twenty staff members in 1979, President Ronald Reagan took further steps to weaken the bureau (Drezner 2000; Hartmann 2001; Schoultz 1985). President Clinton changed the name to the Bureau of Democracy, Human Rights and Labor (DHL) and shifted the mandate in 1998. DHL's major mission is human rights reporting on the human rights records of other countries, purportedly in order to assess the advisability of U.S. assistance. Each March, by congressional mandate, the DHL must produce hundreds of pages addressing a growing range of human rights issues in almost every country in the world; the 2004 report was 5,000 pages long and covered 194 countries. Embassy human rights officers draft the reports, which then are revised by DHL staff in Washington. The human rights reports produced by the office were often accused of political bias, particularly during Reagan's highly ideological administration. During the 1980s and early 1990s, the U.S.-based human rights group Lawyer's Committee for Human Rights published critical evaluations and counterreports. The office also supports the establishment of human rights programs abroad through USAID-funded programs. Since Plan Colombia, the State Department has held periodic congressionally mandated meetings with Washington-based NGOs to determine if the Colombian government is making progress on a series of specific human rights issues, a requirement for the delivery of military aid.

6. The U.N. Office of the High Commissioner for Human Rights in Colombia completed a study and evaluation of *personeros* in 2001. It found numerous problems with the existing program, including the lack of a clear mandate, poor training (particularly in rural areas), and the wide variation in commitment and capacity, depending on the region and the individual.

7. The highest profile of these was the Human Rights Unit of the Fiscalía, which investigated the major human rights cases until almost all the approximately thirty-five prosecutors were forced to flee the country because of death threats. Though restaffed and expanded, the limitations of the Unit made it extremely difficult to keep up with the number of cases. The Unit was funded with a specific line item in the U.S. aid package to Colombia, but there were numerous complaints about the kind of aid supplied (such as noncompatible

computers and sophisticated forensic analysis equipment that Colombians were unable to use) and the extreme delays in delivery. The *fiscal* appointed by President Uribe radically changed the profile of the Unit. He announced publicly that he considered its focus on paramilitary cases politically motivated and ordered that it instead concentrate on guerrilla abuses (Human Rights Watch 2002).

8. According to the terms of the agreement, the special adviser for human rights held a forum to analyze proposals put forward by the CRS during the negotiations, with the eventual aim of reaching consensus on specific policies. This process resulted in a joint government-NGO commission with four working groups: peace policies, international humanitarian law, impunity, and protection of human rights.

9. NGO representatives said that the commission could not continue given the circumstances, and it ceased to function. In a joint NGO statement, they described the government's attitude as a "180-degree turn" and said, "Previous government statements in support of human rights have been put off or subordinated to policies stemming from the state of internal commotion." According to NGOs, these discussions initially provided fruitful space for dialogue and produced a series of recommendations reached by consensus. However, among the serious problems the process faced was the fact that many of the government representatives lacked sufficient political authority and support to make decisions and implement reforms. One month after the rupture of Commission 1533, on September 28, 1995, an ad hoc coalition of human rights groups sent a letter to Samper stressing escalation of attacks against human rights activists and requesting governmental action. On November 16, 1995, twenty-four NGO representatives met with the president and the special adviser, Carlos Vicente de Roux; according to those who were present, Samper used the occasion to repeat his campaign promises.

10. Officials I interviewed agreed that the commissions have varied widely in their outcome, and no comprehensive evaluation of these commissions had been carried out, in part because of the difficulty of establishing criteria. One government official who has participated in a number of such commissions told me, "The level of agreement and closeness between the state and civil society is very difficult. In trying to evaluate the different commissions, each one has its own dynamic, and there are lot of factors that have to be taken into account. . . . [T]here is little progress because there is not consensus within the Commission. The primary problem is between the state [which resolves its own internal differences] and civil society."

11. The network was administered by the Consejería, and was supposed to connect the following institutions: the Prosecutor General's Office, the Attorney General's Office, the Public Defender's Office, the Ministry of Defense, the Forensic Medicine Institute, Administrative Department of Security, the National Army, and the Ministry of Foreign Affairs.

12. This is not only true in Colombia, of course: I heard from one U.S. military officer that the $2 million grant from the United States to the Colombian military to pay for the expansion of the Colombian military justice system was the result of a cocktail party conversation between a U.S. general and a Senate staffer.

13. She noted that the government-sponsored workshops worked closely with local committees established with the support of local governments and NGOs (see chapter 2). She said, "We did local workshops on the national level. Of course we couldn't cover 100 percent of the country, but we had priority zones, the ones that had the most need of government support, and we worked with local authorities—that is, when the local human rights committees still existed. There were more than two hundred." She described the workshops as "training in human rights, in the technical part, about the international human rights system, about human rights in the Constitution, human rights instruments and how to use them." Afterward, she explained, "we would do a workshop on the diagnosis of the human rights situation in that local area and what would be the most useful human rights instruments to address the issues . . . in that area. We talked about both civil and political rights, [as well as] social, cultural, and economic rights. We focused on the instruments that were required for that local area."

14. Chengue residents had written to the local military authorities and to Colombia's president, Andres Pastrana, in April 2000 and again in October 2000, asking the government for protection because paramilitary groups had threatened them. A local military commander had responded on December 1 that the military did not have enough troops to protect all the areas under threat. Six of the men who signed the letters to the government were among those killed on January 17.

7. HUMAN RIGHTS AND MILITARY WAR STORIES

1. For more on the institutional history of the military, see chapter 1.

2. By "large-scale political violence," I am referring primarily to massacres and forced displacement involving large numbers of people; high-profile political assassinations have taken place in central urban areas, including Bogotá, Medellín, and Cali.

3. Early Colombian military doctrine was modeled on European, primarily Prussian, military doctrine, taught through a series of military missions from the Chilean and Swiss militaries.

4. What has come to be called National Security Doctrine is not an official military doctrine codified in military documents (as psychological warfare doctrine is, for example) but the general vision of national security that prevailed during the cold war and was reflected in the yearly National Security Strategy documents presented by the president.

5. Since the initial "emergency supplemental," the U.S. has continued to provide approximately $700 million annually to Colombia through annual aid packages, referred to as Plan Colombia. Following the attacks on September 11, 2001, Colombia has dropped in the rankings of international aid but remains the largest non–Middle Eastern recipient of U.S. assistance.

6. With the 2001 attacks in the United States, the expanding "war on terror," and the subsequent reduction of international coverage of Latin America, many of these freelancers have relocated, to the United States or to the Middle East.

7. General Velandia's discharge from the army was overturned by a ruling of

the Concejo de Estado issued on May 23, 2002, and made public on July 4, 2002. This ruling found that General Velandia had not been properly notified of the original ruling; Colombian law requires that the discharged person must be informed personally of the decision, and General Velandia had reportedly gone into hiding at the time of the decision. Despite the fact that the ruling did not question his responsibility in the matter and that the Colombian judicial system had found that in similar cases the requirement of personal notification did not apply, the Uribe administration announced they intended to pay General Velandia hundreds of thousands of dollars in missed pay, covering the time since his dismissal. See Amnesty International, "Colombia: Violadores de los derechos humanos deben ser destituidos y enjuiciados," AMR 23/70/02/s, July 9, 2002.

8. I entered Colonel Vargas's real name in Google and found that he is listed in several places. Most prominently, he is quoted in current press articles on the Colombian military's efforts. He is correct, however, that his name appears with allegations of human rights abuses. He is mentioned in the text of a Human Rights Watch report, and the incident with the children and the land mines is mentioned in Colonel Vargas's entry in a list of "notorious Colombian graduates of the School of the Americas."

9. The Joint Doctrine for Psychological Operations, dated July 1996, is the most recent official document to lay out basic definition of psychological operations to be carried out by the U.S. military and taught as official doctrine to its allies: "The purpose of psychological operations ("psyops") is to induce or reinforce foreign attitudes and behavior favorable to the originator's objectives. . . . [These] operations [are] planned to convey selected information and indicators to foreign audiences to influence their emotions, motives, objective reasoning, and ultimately the behavior of foreign governments, organizations, groups, and individuals." Foreign Internal Defense—what the U.S. military calls internal conflicts like those in Colombia—can use psyops to influence a number of specific "targets." For those operations targeting the civilian population, the goal is to "gain, preserve, and strengthen civilian support for the HN [host nation] government and its counterinsurgency programs." Civic action (CA), community development programs sponsored by military forces that rely heavily on psyops, is defined by U.S. military doctrine as "the linchpin of the military role in national development." "The overall objective of CA in counterinsurgency is to mobilize and motivate civilians to assist the government and military forces. The operations are directed at eliminating or reducing military, political, economic or sociological problems. Close and continuous psychological operations support is needed to maximize the effect of CA" (Department of the Navy and Department of the Army, *Doctrine for Joint Psychological Operations,* Joint Pub. 3–53, 1996; available at dtic.mil/doctrine/jel/new_pubs/jp3_53. pdf).

10. During the cold war, the U.S. military leadership viewed the Soviets as consummate experts of pysops and emphasized the importance of counteracting their efforts through a number of proxy conflicts. The first Office of Chief of Psychological Warfare was opened in 1951, followed the next year by the creation of the Psychological Warfare Center at Fort Bragg, North Carolina. Part of wider efforts to expand U.S. capabilities in "unconventional warfare," the center continues to be linked to the Army Special Forces, which is also housed at Fort

Bragg. Of current U.S. military doctrine, unconventional warfare doctrine, including psyops, is only a small part of the larger military apparatus that remains focused on conventional war threats. Conventional warfare doctrine addresses combating an advancing, standing army. Unconventional warfare, on the other hand, encompasses counterinsurgency warfare and a range of activities that are called Military Operations Other than War (MOOTW). MOOTW includes peacekeeping, humanitarian, counternarcotics, and foreign internal defense operations. The Special Forces infrastructure remains outside the command structure of the larger army, isolated from other services, and controversial among the military hierarchy in the degree to which it is seen to be operating on its own terms.

11. A separate issue is the degree to which psyops doctrine actually encourages the use of violence and counterterror as a means of "gaining civilian support." A principal architect of U.S. psyops and civic action doctrine, General Edward Lansdale, advocated a broad range of strategies, including threats and mutilation of enemy corpses. He proudly told of using local legends in his successful 1950s campaign against the Huk rebellion in the Philippines. According to his own testimony, he would ambush rebel patrols, killing at least one of them, then drain the body of blood, make two puncture wounds in the neck, and leave the body on the trail for local villagers to find. During U.S. counterinsurgency efforts in Vietnam, where General Lansdale also played a central role, in "Operation Black Eye," a printed paper eye was left on the bodies of assassinated Vietcong; the printed eyes were widely distributed to suspected Vietcong leaders. In 1984, a CIA Spanish-language manual was distributed to U.S.-sponsored Contra fighters for use against the Nicaraguan Sandinista government. Titled "Psychological Operations in Guerrilla Warfare," the manual made headlines in 1984, after it was leaked to U.S. journalists, for advocating assassination in a section titled "Selective Use of Violence for Propagandistic Effects," which read: "It is possible to neutralize carefully selected and planned targets, such as court judges, judges, police and State Security officials, CDS chiefs, etc. For psychological purposes it is necessary to take extreme precautions, and it is absolutely necessary to gather together the population affected, so that they will be present, take part in the act, and formulate accusation against the oppressor." Congressional hearings absolved the CIA of institutional responsibility. Interestingly, in his 1985 year-end report, Colonel Richard Downie refers to the material in these manuals being incorporated into Colombian psyops manuals. In 1997 manuals were made public that had made reference to using torture and other practices technically illegal for U.S. forces; these manuals had been used until the early 1990s for training Latin American military forces at the School of the Americas (Latin American Working Group 1997). Since the 9/11 attacks, the debate on legitimate uses of torture has been reopened.

12. In his end-of-mission report, Colonel Downie (later the director of the Western Hemisphere Institute for Security Cooperations and then an instructor at the National Defense University) wrote about his year in Colombia as psychological operations staff officer. He begins his report by noting, "Colombian Psyop Doctrine, until recently, had been based on US Psyop material written in 1974. This doctrine applied mainly to how US type Psyop units provided Psyop assis-

tance to foriegn nations. . . . A draft Colombian Pysop manual oriented toward the Colombian-specific situation is forthcoming. This manual is based on actual Colombian Psyop experiences in counter-guerrilla warfare, the CIA Psyop manual written for Nicaraguan Anti-Sandanista guerrillas and Psyop reference manuals from other countries. . . . Unlike US policy, the Colombians legally can, and do, direct Psyop toward their own troops and toward their civilian population. Psyop aimed at both these groups is designed to garner approval and support for the military and its policies, and respect for the *institutions* of democracy" (original emphasis).

13. An extensive campaign drawing attention to these issues flourished among opponents of U.S. military assistance to Latin American militaries during the 1980s and 1990s and remains active (Gill 2004).

14. Gill offers a compelling description of how the training offered by the U.S. military fits into the global reach of U.S. hegemony, and the sometimes conflictive relationships between Latin American students and their U.S. teachers. Unfortunately, she does not provide an institutional history of such programs in the military or examine the historic institutional differences among the Latin American militaries that participate (Gill 2004).

15. However, U.S. military and civilian leadership is also ambivalent, and in some instances reluctant, about the adoption of human rights standards. U.S. military personnel are on record as rejecting human rights monitoring using the same due process arguments as their Colombian counterparts. Military personnel told reporters from Amnesty International that tracking military officers receiving U.S. training for human rights performance following their training was "illegal" and "'unconstitutional'—principally in violating military students' 'privacy.'" In a 2002 report on the state of the Colombian army, published by the U.S. Army War College, a retired U.S. military officer and current liaison between the Colombian and U.S. militaries devotes space to a broad dismissal of human rights reports (Marks 2001). He focuses on Human Rights Watch's 2001 report documenting links between paramilitaries and the Colombian military, calling it "slanderous." He acknowledges in a footnote that he bases this conclusion on conversations with the accused generals; according to the HRW authors of the report, he never contacted them to discuss evidence in the case. In another instance, during the question-and-answer period of a February 2003 special seminar at George Washington University, a man who identified himself as a State Department AID desk officer for Colombia said that "Amnesty International gets its information from the FARC."

16. "Oracle University" is listed across the bottom of the ad in English; despite requests for further information from the military and Web searches, I could not obtain any additional information about the university.

17. The Rendon Group's Web site opens with the slogan "Information as an element of power" and describes itself as "working closely with the office of the [Colombian] Minister of Defense." Its statement continues: "TRG created and implemented a training program focused on assisting the Ministry in its effort to communicate internationally relative to its fight against narcotics trafficking. TRG deployed a full-time three-person training team to Colombia, staffed by experts in message development and dissemination, strategic communications

planning, and media event planning. The TRG in-country staff worked closely with counterparts in the Colombian Army, Navy, Air Force and National Police. Specialized training was also provided for media spokespersons. As a result of TRG's efforts, the Colombian Ministry of Defense created a special communications unit to coordinate information dissemination to the media from the combined public security forces." The work of TRG has been widely covered by the progressive media after it received more than $60 million in contracts with the U.S. government for public relations efforts, many related to U.S. policy in the Middle East, over the past decade. The founder, John Rendon, was called "one of the most powerful men in Washington" in a November 17, 2005, story by James Bamford, "The Man Who Sold the War," in *Rolling Stone*.

18. The most complete history of the term *genocide* is Samantha Power's *"A Problem from Hell": America and the Age of Genocide* (New York: Basic Books, 2003).

CONCLUSION

1. This section is largely based on my interview with Manuel, because of the clarity of his reflections; during the course of my fieldwork, I interviewed at least nine members of the Trujillo Commission, representing civil society organizations and state human rights agencies. I was unable to locate the military representatives.

2. Other scholars of human rights activism have pointed out the unintended consequences of such efforts in other places. In the case of international activism against secret tribunals in Guatemala, for example, "human rights intervention can first empower local actors and then, once particularly egregious forms of public execution are dissolved and international attention wanes[,] . . . inhibit traditional forms of justice to not only undermine legal practices and ideals, but also allow extra-judicial assassinations to continue" (Schirmer 1997: 182). Merry documents how efforts to promote women's rights in India foments religious violence there (by nurturing Hindu efforts to repress Muslim communities) and ethnic nationalism in Fiji (as native Fijians attempt to revive the village practice of bulubulu, used to move rape cases out of the legal system and as part of new nationalist politics by native Fijians against Indo Fijians) (Merry 2005).

Selected Bibliography

Abella, Arturo. 2000. *Laureano Gómez*. Bogotá: Planeta.

Abrams, Phillip. 1998. "Notes on the Difficulty of Studying the State." *Journal of Historical Sociology* 1 (1): 58–89.

Abu-Lughod, Lila. 1990. "The Romance of Resistance." *American Ethnologist* 17 (1): 41–55.

Alameda Ospina, Raúl, and Eduardo Sarmiento Palacio. 1999. *La guerra y la paz en la segunda mitad del siglo XX en Colombia*. Colección Controversia. Bogotá: Ecoe Ediciones.

Alape, Arturo. 1972. *Las muertes de Tirofijo*. n.p.: Ediciones Abejon Mono.

———. 1989. *Tirofijo: Las vidas de Pedro Antonio Marín, Manuel Marulanda Vélez*. Colección Documento. Bogotá: Planeta.

———. 1994. *Tirofijo: Los sueños y las montañas, 1964–1984*. Bogotá: Planeta.

———. 1999. *La Paz, La Violencia: Testigos de excepción*. Bogotá: Planeta.

Aldana, Walter, ed. 1998. *Conflictos regionales: Atlántico y Pacífico*. Bogotá: Fescol.

Allen, Lori. "The Polyvalent Politics of Martyr Commemorations in the Palestinian Intifada." *History and Memory* 18 (2): 107–38.

Alonso, Ana María. 1994. "Politics of Space, Time and Substance: State Formation, Nationalism, and Ethnicity." *Annual Review of Anthropology* 23: 379–405.

Alonso, Carlos. 1998. *The Burden of Modernity: The Rhetoric of Cultural Discourse in Spanish America*. New York: Oxford University Press.

Alto Comisionado para la Paz. 2006. "Cuadros resumen." www.altocomision adoparalapaz.gov.co/desmovilizaciones/2004/index-resumen.htm.

Altorki, Soraya, and Camila Fawzi El-Solh, eds. 1988. *Arab Women in the Field: Studying Your Own Society*. Syracuse, NY: Syracuse University Press.

Alvarez, Sonia. 1997. "Reweaving the Fabric of Collective Action: Social Movements and Challenges to 'Actually Existing Democracy' in Brazil." In *Between Resistance and Revolution: Cultural Politics and Social Protest,* edited by R. G. Fox and O. Starn. New Brunswick, NJ: Rutgers University Press.

Alvarez, Sonia, Evelina Dagnino, and Arturo Escobar, eds. 1998. *Cultural Politics, Politics of Culture: Re-visioning Latin American Social Movements.* Boulder, CO: Westview Press.

Alvarez Gardeazabel, Gustavo. 1987. *El último gamonal.* Bogotá: Tercer Mundo.

Americas Watch. 1994. *Estado de guerra, violencia política y contrainsurgencia en Colombia.* Bogotá: Tercer Mundo.

Americas Watch Committee (U.S.) and Human Rights Watch. 1992. *Political Murder and Reform in Colombia: The Violence Continues. An Americas Watch Report.* New York: Human Rights Watch.

Amnesty International. 2000. "Protection of Human Rights Defenders in Colombia: One Step Forward, Three Steps Back." www.amnestyusa.org/countries/colombia/document.do?id=5F75DD0B0D63E50F802568C70036F56D.

Anderson, Benedict. 1991. *Imagined Communities: Reflections on the Origin and Spread of Nationalism.* New York: Verso.

Anderson, Carol. 2003. *Eyes off the Prize: The United Nations and the African American Struggle for Human Rights, 1944–1955.* Cambridge: Cambridge University Press.

Angel, Gabriel. 2000. *La luna del forense.* Bogotá: Ediciones Magdalena Medio.

An-Na'Im, Abdullahi Ahmed, ed. 1992. *Human Rights in Cross-Cultural Perspectives: A Quest for Consensus.* Philadelphia: University of Pennsylvania Press.

Appadurai, Arjun. 1991. "Global Ethnoscapes: Notes and Queries for a Transnational Anthropology." In *Recapturing Anthropology: Working in the Present,* edited by R. G. Fox. Santa Fe, NM: School of American Research Press.

———. 1997. *Modernity at Large: Cultural Dimensions of Globalization.* Minneapolis: University of Minnesota Press.

———. 2000. "Grassroots Globalization and the Research Imagination." *Public Culture* 12 (1): 1–19.

Aranguren Molina, Mauricio. 2001. *Mi confesión: Carlos Castaño revela sus secretos.* Bogotá: Editorial Oveja Negra.

Arenas, Jacobo. 1985. *Cese el fuego: Una historia política de las FARC.* Bogotá: Editorial Oveja Negra.

———. 2000. *Diario de la resistencia de Marquetalia.* Bogotá: FARC.

Aretxaga, Begona. 1997. *Shattering Silence: Women, Nationalism, and Political Subjectivity in Northern Ireland.* Princeton, NJ: Princeton University Press.

Arias, Arturo, ed. 2001. *The Rigoberta Menchú Controversy.* Minneapolis: University of Minnesota Press.

Arocha, Jaime. 1998. "Inclusion of Afro-Colombians: Unreachable National Goal?" *Latin American Perspectives* 25 (3): 70–89.

Arnson, Cynthia. 1993. *Crossroads: Congress, the President, and Central America, 1976–1993.* Philadelphia: University of Pennsylvania Press.

———. 1999. *Comparative Peace Processes in Latin America.* Washington, DC: Woodrow Wilson Center Press.

Arrieta, Carlos Gustavo. 1991. *Narcotráfico en Colombia: Dimensiones políticas, económicas, jurídicas e internacionales.* 2d ed. Bogotá: Ediciones Uniandes/Tercer Mundo.

Asad, Talal. 2004. "What Do Human Rights Do? An Anthropological Enquiry." *Theory and Event.* http://muse.jhu.edu/journals/theory and event/voo4/4.4asad .html.

Association of Retired Generals and Admirals. 2001. *Esquilando el lobo.* Botgotá: Association of Retired Generals and Admirals.

Atehortúa, Adolfo. 1995. *El poder y la sangre: Las historias de Trujillo.* Bogotá: CINEP.

Barnett, Michael N. 1997. "The U.N. Security Council, Indifference, and Genocide in Rwanda." *Cultural Anthropology* 12 (4): 551–78.

———. 2003. *Eyewitness to a Genocide: The United Nations and Rwanda.* Ithaca, NY: Cornell University Press.

Bauer, Jan. 1995–2003. Reports on United Nations Commission on Human Rights, Fifty-third Session through Fifty-ninth Session. Human Rights Internet, www.hri.ca/uninfo/hrbodies/unchr.shtml.

Behar, Ruth. 1993. *Translated Woman: Crossing the Border with Esperanza's Story.* Boston: Beacon Press.

Bejarano, Ana Maria, and Eduardo Pizarro Leongómez. 2002. *From "Restricted" to "Besieged": The Changing Nature of the Limits to Democracy in Colombia.* Working Paper no. 296. Notre Dame, IN: Kellogg Center for Human Rights, University of Notre Dame.

Bell, Linda, Andrew Nathan, and Illan Peleg, eds. 2001. *Negotiating Culture and Human Rights.* New York: Columbia University Press.

Bergman, Susan, ed. 1996 *Martyrs: Contemporary Writers on Modern Lives of Faith.* San Francisco: HarperSanFrancisco.

Bergquist, Charles W., Ricardo Peñaranda, and Gonzalo Sánchez, eds. 1992. *Violence in Colombia: The Contemporary Crisis in Historical Perspective.* Wilmington, DE: Scholastic Resources.

———. 2001. *Violence in Colombia, 1990–2000: Waging War and Negotiating Peace.* Wilmington, DE: Scholastic Resources.

Berryman, Philip. 1984. *The Religious Roots of Rebellion: Christians in Central American Revolutions.* New York: Orbis Books.

Beverley, John. 1989. "The Margin at the Center: On Testimonio." *Modern Fiction Studies* 35 (1): 11–28.

———.1991. "'Through All things Modern': Second Thoughts on Testimonio." *Boundary* 2 18 (2): 1–21.

Beverley, John, and Marc Zimmerman. 1990. *Literature and Politics in the Central American Revolutions.* Austin: University of Texas Press.

Bickford, Louis. 2000. "Preserving Memory: The Past and the Human Rights Movement in Chile." Paper presented at the 22d International Congress of the Latin American Studies Association, Miami, FL.

Blair Trujillo, Elsa. 1993. *Las fuerzas armadas: Una mirada civil.* Colección Sociedad y Conflicto. Bogotá: CINEP.

———. 1999. *Conflicto armada y militares en Colombia: Cultos, símbolos e imaginarios.* Medellín: Editoriales Universidad de Antioquia.

Blok, Anton. 1972. "The Peasant and the Brigand: Social Banditry Reconsidered." *Comparative Studies in Society and History* 14 (4): 494–503.

Bob, Clifford. 2001. "Marketing Rebellion: Insurgent Groups, International Media, and NGO Support." *International Politics* 38 (3): 311–34.

———. 2002. "Merchants of Morality." *Foreign Policy* 129 (March–April): 36–45.

Bourdieu, Pierre. 1977. *Outline of a Theory of Practice.* Cambridge: Cambridge University Press.

Bowden, Mark. 2001. *Killing Pablo: The Hunt for the World's Greatest Outlaw.* New York: Atlantic Monthly Press.

Braun, Herbert. 1985. *The Assassination of Gaitán: Public Life and Urban Violence in Colombia.* Madison: University of Wisconsin Press.

———. 1994. *Our Guerrillas, Our Sidewalks: A Journey into the Violence of Colombia.* Niwot: University Press of Colorado.

Brenner, Arthur, and Bruce Cambell, eds. 2000. *Death Squads in Global Perspective: Murder with Deniability.* New York: St. Martin's Press.

Broderick, Walter J. 1975. *Camilo Torres: A Biography of the Priest-Guerrillero.* New York: Doubleday.

———. 2000. *El guerrillero invisible.* Bogotá: Intermedio Editores.

Brown, Wendy. 2004. " 'The Most We Can Hope For . . .': Human Rights and the Politics of Fatalism." *South Atlantic Quarterly* 103 (2–3): 451–63.

Brown, Widney. 2001. "Human Rights Watch: An Overview." In *NGOs and Human Rights: Promise and Performance,* edited by Claude E. Welch Jr. Philadelphia: University of Pennsylvania Press.

Brysk, Alison. 1994. *The Politics of Human Rights in Argentina: Protest, Change, and Democratization.* Stanford: Stanford University Press.

———. 2000. *From Tribal Village to Global Village: Indian Rights and International Relations in Latin America.* Stanford: Stanford University Press.

Burdick, John, and W. E. Hewitt, eds. 2000. *The Church at the Grassroots in Latin America: Perspectives on Thirty Years of Activism.* Westport, CT: Praeger.

Buruma, Ian. 1994. *The Wages of Guilt: Memories of War in Germany and Japan.* New York: Farrar, Straus and Giroux.

Bushnell, David. 1993. *The Making of Modern Colombia: A Nation in Spite of Itself.* Berkeley: University of California Press.

Caldeira, Teresa. 2000. *City of Walls: Crime, Segregation, and Citizenship in São Paulo.* Berkeley: University of California Press.

Calhoun, Craig. 1991. "Problem of Identity in Collective Action." In *Macro-Micro Linkages in Sociology,* edited by J. Huber. Newbury Park, CA: Sage.

Canadian Lawyers for Human Rights (CLHR). 1994. "Human Rights Ombudspersons: A Comparative and International Analysis." Ottowa: CLHR.

Cardenas, Sonia. 2001. "Adaptive States: The Proliferation of National Human Rights Institutions." Car Center for Human Rights Policy Working Paper (T-01–04).

———. 2003. "Transgovernmental Activism: Canada's Role in Promoting National Human Rights Commissions." *Human Rights Quarterly* 25: 775–90.

Carmichael, William. 2001. "The Role of the Ford Foundation." In *NGOs and Human Rights: Promise and Performance,* edited by Claude E. Welch Jr. Philadelphia: University of Pennsylvania Press.

Carrigan, Ana. 1993. *The Palace of Justice: A Colombian Tragedy.* New York: Four Walls Eight Windows.

Carrillo, Arturo. 1999. "Hors de Logique: Contemporary Issues in International Humanitarian Law as Applied to Internal Armed Conflict." *American University International Law Review* 15: 1–150.

Carroll, Leah. 1999a. "Mixed Signals: Violent Democratization and the 'Combination of All Forms of Struggle' in Colombia." Manuscript.

———. 1999b. "Palm Workers, Patrons, and Political Violence in Colombia: A Window of Opportunity for the Left Despite Trade Liberalization." *Political Power and Social Theory* 13: 149–200.

Castañeda, Jorge. 1993. *Utopia Unarmed: The Latin American Left after the Cold War.* New York: Alfred A. Knopf.

Castells, Manuel. 2000. *The Rise of the Network Society.* Oxford: Blackwell.

Certeau, Michel de. 1984. *The Practice of Everyday Life.* Berkeley: University of California Press.

Chatfield, Charles. 1997. "Intergovernmental and Nongovernmental Associations to 1945." In *Transnational Social Movements and Global Politics: Solidarity beyond the State,* edited by J. Smith, C. Charfield, and R. Pagnucco. Syracuse, NY: Syracuse University Press.

Chernick, Marc. 2005. "Economic Resources and Internal Armed Conflicts: Lessons from the Colombian Case." In *Rethinking the Economics of War: The Intersection of Need, Creed, and Greed,* edited by C. J. Arnson and I. W. Zartman. Washington, DC: Woodrow Wilson Center/Johns Hopkins University Press.

Clark, Ann Marie. 2001. *Diplomacy of Conscience: Amnesty International and Changing Human Rights Norms.* Princeton, NJ: Princeton University Press.

Cmiel, Kenneth. 1999. "The Emergence of Human Rights Politics in the United States." *Journal of American History* 86 (3): 1231–50.

———. 2004. "The Recent History of Human Rights." *American Historical Review* 109 (1): 117–35.

CODHES. 2003. "La otra guerra: Destierro y repoblamiento: Informe sobre desplazamiento forzado, conflicto armado y derechos humanos en el 2002." *CODHES Informa* (44): 1–11.

Cohen, Stanley. 2001. *States of Denial: Knowing about Atrocities and Suffering.* Cambridge: Polity.

Colburn, Forrest. 1994. *The Vogue of Revolution in Poor Countries.* Princeton, NJ: Princeton University Press.

Collier, Jane, and Shannon Speed. 2000. "Limiting Indigenous Autonomy: The State Government's Use of Human Rights." *Human Rights Quarterly* 22: 877–905.

Comaroff, Jean, and John L. Comaroff. 1999. "Occult Economies and the Violence of Abstraction: Notes from the South African Postcolony." *American Ethnologist* 26: 279–303.

Comisión Colombiana de Juristas (CCJ). 1995. *Colombia, derechos humanos y derecho humanitario: 1994*. Bogotá: CCJ.

—. 1996. *Colombia, derechos humanos y derecho humanitario: 1995*. Bogotá: CCJ.

—. 1997. *Colombia, derechos humanos y derecho humanitario: 1996*. Bogotá: CCJ.

—. 2000. *Colombia, derechos humanos y derecho humanitario: 1999*. Bogotá: CCJ.

—. 2002. *Colombia, derechos humanos y derecho humanitario: 2001*. Bogotá: CCJ.

—. 2005. *El deber de la memoria: Informe sobre el año 2004*. Bogotá: CCJ.

Comisión de Investigación de los Sucesos Violentos de Trujillo. 1995. *Caso 11,007 de la Comisión Interamericana de Derechos Humanos informe final*. Bogotá: Consejería Presidencial para los Derechos Humanos.

CONGO. 1998. *Congo at Fifty: A Reaffirmation of Commitment*. New York: CONGO.

Cortright, David, and Ron Pagnucco. 1997. "Limits to Transnationalism: The 1980s Freeze Campaign." In *Transnational Social Movements and Global Politics: Solidarity beyond the State*, edited by J. Smith, C. Charfield, and R. Pagnucco. Syracuse, NY: Syracuse University Press.

Cott, Donna Lee Van. 2000. *The Friendly Liquidation of the Past: The Politics of Diversity in Latin America*. Pittsburgh: University of Pittsburgh Press.

Cotts, Cynthia. 2001. "Let's All Go to Bogotá." *Village Voice*, March 2.

Coutin, Susan Bibler. 1993. *The Culture of Protest: Religious Activism and the U.S. Sanctuary Movement*. Boulder, CO: Westview Press.

—. 1995. "Smugglers or Samaritans in Tucson, Arizona: Producing and Contesting Legal Truth." *American Ethnologist* 22 (3): 549–39.

Cox, Larry. 2000. "Reflections of Human Rights at the Century's End." *Human Rights Dialogue of the Carnegie Council on Ethics and International Affairs* 2 (1). www.cceia.org/resources/publications/dialogue/2_01/articles/603.html.

Coy, Patrick. 1997. "Cooperative Accompaniment and Peace Brigades International in Sri Lanka." In *Transnational Social Movements and Global Politics: Solidarity beyond the State*, edited by J. Smith, C. Charfield, and R. Pagnucco. Syracuse, NY: Syracuse University Press.

Crawford, Neta. 2002. *Argument and Change in World Politics: Ethics, Decolonialization, and Humanitarian Intervention*. Cambridge: Cambridge University Press.

Cunningham, Hilary. 1995. *God and Cesar at the Rio Grande: Sanctuary and the Politics of Religion*. Minneapolis: University of Minnesota Press.

—. 1999. "The Ethnography of Transnational Social Activism: Understanding the Global as Local Practice." *American Ethnologist* 26 (3): 583–604.

Das, Veena, Arthur Kleinman, Mamphela Ramphele, and Pamela Reynolds. 2000. *Violence and Subjectivity*. Berkeley: University of California Press.

Das, Veena, Arthur Kleinman, Margaret Lock, Mamphela Ramphele, and Pamela Reynolds, eds. 2001. *Remaking a World: Violence, Social Suffering, and Recovery*. Berkeley: University of California Press.

Dávila, Andrés. 1998. *El juego del poder: Historia, armas y votos.* Bogotá: Ediciones Uniandes.

———. 1999. "Ejército regular, conflictos irregulares: La institución militar en los últimos quince años." In *Reconocer la guerra para construir la paz,* edited by M. V. Llorente and M. D. Deas. Bogotá: CEREC/Ediciones Uniandes/ Grupo Editorial Norma.

Deas, Malcolm D., and Fernando Gaitán Daza. 1995. *Dos ensayos especulativos sobre la violencia en Colombia.* Bogotá: Fonade.

Deas, Malcolm D., and Carlos Ossa Escobar. 1994. *El gobierno Barco: Política, economía y desarrollo social en Colombia, 1986–1990.* Bogotá: Fedesarrollo/Fondo Cultural Cafetero.

De Francisco, Gonzálo. 1999. "La fuerza pública y la estrategia para enfrentar el fenómeno guerrillero." In *Reconocer la guerra para construir la paz,* edited by M. V. Llorente and M. D. Deas. Bogotá: CEREC/Ediciones Uniandes/Grupo Editorial Norma.

DeMars, William. 1997. "Contending Neutralities: Humanitarian Organizations and War in the Horn of Africa." In *Transnational Social Movements and Global Politics: Solidarity beyond the State,* edited by J. Smith, C. Charfield, and R. Pagnucco. Syracuse, NY: Syracuse University Press.

de Waal, Alex. 1997. *Famine Crimes: Politics and the Disaster Relief Industry in Africa.* London: African Rights and the International African Institute with Indiana University Press.

Donnelly, Jack. 1993. *International Human Rights.* Boulder, CO: Westview Press.

Drezner, Daniel. 2000. "Ideas, Bureaucratic Politics, and the Crafting of Foreign Policy." *American Journal of Political Science* 44 (4): 733–49.

Dudley, Steve. 2004. *Walking Ghosts: Guerrilla Politics and Murder in Colombia.* New York: Routledge.

Echandía Castilla, Camilo. 1999. *El conflicto armado y las manifestaciones de violencia en las regiones de Colombia.* Bogotá: Presidencia de la República de Colombia.

Engle, Karen. 2001. "From Skepticism to Embrace: Human Rights and the American Anthropological Association from 1947–1999." *Human Rights Quarterly* 23 (3): 536–59.

Escobar, Arturo. 1992. "Culture, Practice and Politics: Anthropology and the Study of Social Movements." *Critique of Anthropology* 12 (4): 395–432.

———. 1995. *Encountering Development.* Princeton, NJ: Princeton University Press.

Escobar, Cristina. 2002. "Clientalism and Citizenship: The Limits of Democratic Reforms in Sucre, Colombia." *Latin American Perspectives* 29 (5): 20–47.

Ewig, Christina. 1999. "The Strengths and Limits of the NGO Women's Movement Model: Shaping Nicaragua's Democratic Institutions." *Latin American Research Review* 34 (3): 75–102.

Farmer, Paul. 1992. *AIDS and Accusation: Haiti and the Geography of Blame.* Berkeley: University of California Press.

Felstiner, William, Richard Abel, and Austin Sarat. 1980. "The Emergence and Transformation of Disputes." *Law & Society Review* 15 (3–4): 631–54.

Fisher, William F. 1997. "Doing Good? The Politics and Antipolitics of NGO Practices." *Annual Review of Anthropology* 26: 439–64.

Fox, Jonathon. 2000. "Assessing Binational Civil Society Coalitions: Lessons from the Mexico-U.S. Experience." Paper presented at the annual meeting of the Latin American Studies Association, Miami, FL.

Fox, Richard. 1997. "Passage from India." In *Between Resistance and Revolution: Cultural Politics and Social Protest,* edited by R. Fox and O. Starn. New Brunswick, NJ: Rutgers University Press.

Fox, Richard, and Orin Starn, eds. 1997. *Between Resistance and Revolution: Cultural Politics and Social Protest.* New Brunswick, NJ: Rutgers University Press.

Freire, Paulo. 1990. *Pedagogy of the Oppressed.* Translated by M. B. Ramos. New York: Continuum.

Fruhling, Hugo. 1988. "Organismos no gubernamentales de derechos humanos en el paso del autorianismo a la democracia en Chile." In *Una puerta que se abre.* Santiago, Chile: Imprenta la Unión.

Fuerzas Militares de Colombia. 2000. *Fuerzas Militares de Colombia y los derechos humanos.* Bogotá: Fuerzas Militares de Colombia.

Gallant, Thomas. 1999. "Brigandage, Piracy, Capitalism and State-Formation: Transnational Crime from a Historical World-Systems Perspective." In *States and Illegal Practices,* edited by J. M. Heyman. New York: Berg.

Gallón, Gustavo. 1979. *Quince años de estado de sitio en Colombia: 1958–1978.* Bogotá: Editorial America Latina.

Gamson, William. 1975. *The Strategy of Social Protest.* Homewood, IL: Dorsey Press.

Garcia, Clara Ines. 1996. *Uraba: Region, actores y conflicto.* Bogotá: Instituto de Estudios Regionales, Universidad de Antioquia.

Ghosh, Amitav. 1994. "The Global Reservation: Notes toward an Ethnography of International Peacekeeping." *Cultural Anthropology* 9 (3): 412–22.

Gill, Lesley. 2004. *The School of the Americas: Military Training and Political Violence in the Americas.* Durham, NC: Duke University Press.

Giraldo, Javier. 1996. *Colombia: The Genocidal Democracy.* Boston: Common Courage Press.

Giugale, Marcelo, Olivier Lafourcade, and Connie Luff, eds. *Colombia: The Economic Foundation of Peace.* Washington, DC: World Bank.

Global Policy Forum. 2000. "NGO Status at the U.N." www.globalpolicy.org/ngos/ngo-un/info/status.htm.

González, Fernán. 1977. *Partidos políticos y poder eclesiástico: Reseña histórica, 1810–1930.* Bogotá: CINEP.

González Arias, José. 1992. *El estigma de las repúblicas independientes, 1955–1965.* Bogotá: CINEP.

González Arias, José Jairo, and Elsy Marulanda Alvarez. 1990. *Historias de frontera: Colonización y guerras en el Sumapaz.* Bogotá: CINEP.

Goodwin, Jeff. 2001. *No Other Way Out: States and Revolutionary Movements, 1945–1991.* Cambridge: Cambridge University Press.

Goodwin, Jeff, James Jasper, and Francesca Polletta. 2001. "Introduction: Why Emotions Matter." In *Passionate Politics: Emotions and Social Movements,* edited by J. Goodwin, J. Jasper, and F. Polletta. Chicago: University of Chicago Press.

Gorin, Joe. 1993. *Choose Love: A Jewish Buddhist Human Rights Activist in Central America*. Berkeley, CA: Parallax Press.

Goring, Ruth. 2003. "Executing Justice: Which Side Are We On? An Interview with Colombian Human Rights Activist Padre Javier Giraldo, S.J." *PRISM Magazine*, July–August. www.derechos.org/nizkor/colombia/doc/giraldo1 .html. Accessed February 18, 2004.

Gourevitch, Philip. 1998. *We Wish to Inform You That Tomorrow We Will Be Killed with Our Families: Stories from Rwanda*. New York: Farrar, Straus and Giroux.

Grabe, Vera. 2000. *Razones de vida*. Bogotá: Planeta.

Grandin, Gregory. 2000. "Chronicles of a Guatemalan Genocide Foretold: Violence, Trauma, and the Limits to Historical Inquiry." *Nepantla: Views from the South* 1 (2): 391–412.

Green, Linda. 1999. *Fear as a Way of Life: Mayan Widows in Rural Guatemala*. New York: Columbia University Press.

Greenhouse, Carol J., Elizabeth Mertz, and Kay B. Warren. 2002. *Ethnography in Unstable Places: Everyday Lives in Contexts of Dramatic Political Change*. Durham, NC: Duke University Press.

Griffin-Nolan, Ed. 1991. *Witness for Peace: A Story of Resistance*. Louisville, KY: Westminster/John Knox Press.

Gugelberger, Georg, ed. 1996. *The Real Thing: Testimonial Discourse and Latin America*. Durham, NC: Duke University Press.

Gupta, Akhil. 1995. "Blurred Boundaries: The Discourse of Corruption, the Culture of Politics and the Imagined State." *American Ethnologist* 22 (2): 375–402.

Gupta, Akhil, and James Ferguson. 1992. "Beyond 'Culture': Space, Identity, and the Politics of Difference." *Cultural Anthropology* 7 (1): 6–23.

———, eds. 1997. *Anthropological Locations: Boundaries and Grounds of a Field Science*. Berkeley: University of California Press.

Gusterson, Hugh. 1997. "Studying up Revisited." *Political and Legal Anthropology Review* 20 (1): 114–19.

———. 2000. *Nuclear Rites*. Berkeley: University of California Press.

Gutiérrez, Gustavo. 1988. *A Theology of Liberation: History, Politics, and Salvation*. New York: Orbis.

Guzman Bouvard, Marguerite. 1994. *Revolutionizing Motherhood: The Mothers of the Plaza de Mayo*. Boulder, CO: Scholarly Resources.

Hale, Charles. 1994. *Resistance and Contradiction: Miskitu Indians and the Nicaraguan State, 1894–1987*. Stanford: Stanford University Press.

———. 1999. "Travel Warning: Elite Appropriations of Hybridity, Mestizaje, Antiracism, Equality, and Other Progressive-Sounding Discourses in Highland Guatemala." *Journal of American Folklore* 112 (445): 297–315.

Hall, Rodney, and Thomas Biersteker, eds. 2002. *The Emergence of Private Authority in Global Governance*. Cambridge: Cambridge University Press.

Hall, Stuart. 1991a. "The Local and the Global: Globalization and Ethnicity." In

Culture, Globalization, and the World System, edited by A. King. Minneapolis: University of Minnesota Press.

———. 1991b. "Old and New Identities." In *Culture, Globalization, and the World System*, edited by A. King. Minneapolis: University of Minnesota Press.

Harlow, Barbara. 1992. *Barred: Women, Writing, and Political Detention*. Hanover, NH: Wesleyan University Press/University Press of New England.

Hart, Stephan. 2001. *Cultural Dilemmas of Progressive Politics: Styles of Engagement among Grassroots Activists*. Chicago: University of Chicago Press.

Hartlyn, John. 1988. *The Politics of Coalition Rule in Colombia*. New York: Cambridge University Press.

———. 1989. "Colombia: The Politics of Violence and Accommodation." In *Democracy in Developing Countries: Latin America*, edited by L. Diamond, J. J. Linz, and S. M. Lipset. Boulder, CO: Lynne Rienner.

Hartmann, Hauke. 2001. "U.S. Human Rights Policy under Carter and Reagan, 1977–1981." *Human Rights Quarterly* 23 (2): 402–30.

Haugaard, Lisa. 1997. "Declassified Army and CIA Manuals Used in Latin America: An Analysis of Their Content." Latin America Working Group, Washington, DC. www.lawg.org/misc/Publications-manuals.htm.

Hayner, Priscilla. 2001. *Unspeakable Truths: Confronting State Terror and Atrocity*. New York: Routledge.

Helg, Aline. 1987. *La educación en Colombia, 1918–1957: Una historia social, económica y política*. Bogota: CEREC.

Herzfeld, Michael. 1992. *The Social Production of Indifference: Exploring the Symbolic Roots of Western Bureaucracy*. Chicago: University of Chicago Press.

———. 1997. *Cultural Intimacy: Social Poetics in the Nation-State*. New York: Routledge.

Heyman, Josiah McC. 1995. "Putting Power in the Anthropology of Bureaucracy: The Immigration and Naturalization Service at the Mexico–United States Border." *Current Anthropology* 36 (2): 261–88.

Hinojosa, Ivan. 1998. "On Poor Relations and the Nouveau Riche: Shining Path and the Radical Peruvian Left." In *Shining and Other Paths*, edited by S. Stern. Durham, NC: Duke University Press.

Hobsbawm, Eric J. 1959. *Primitive Rebels: Studies in Archaic Forms of Social Movement in the Nineteenth and Twentieth Centuries*. Manchester: Manchester University Press.

———. 1969. *Bandits*. New York: Delacorte.

Hobsbawm, Eric J., and Terence O. Ranger. 1983. *The Invention of Tradition*. Cambridge: Cambridge University Press.

Hochschild, Adam. 1999. *King Leopold's Ghost: A Story of Greed, Terror, and Heroism in Colonial Africa*. New York: Mariner Books.

———. 2005. *Bury the Chains: Prophets and Rebels in the Fight to Free an Empire's Slaves*. New York: Houghton Mifflin.

Holston, James, and Teresa Caldeira. 1996. "Cities and Citzenship." *Public Culture* 8: 187–204.

Hopgood, Stephen. 2006. *Keepers of the Flame: Understanding Amnesty International.* Ithaca, NY: Cornell University Press.

Hossain, Kamel. 2001. *Human Rights Commissions and Ombudsman Offices: National Experiences throughout the World.* London: Brill.

Hoyos, Diana, and Marcela Ceballos. 2004. *Electoral Behaviour Trends and Decentralisation in Colombia's Municipalities, 1988–2000.* Crisis States Centre, Working Paper no. 57. London: London School of Economics.

Human Rights Observatory. 2000. *Bulletin.* Bogotá: Vice President's Human Rights Office.

Human Rights Watch. 1990. *The "Drug War" in Colombia.* New York: Human Rights Watch.

———. 1992. *Political Murder and Reform in Colombia: The Violence Continues.* New York: Human Rights Watch.

———. 1993. *State of War: Political Violence and Counterinsurgency in Colombia.* New York: Human Rights Watch.

———. 1994. *Generation under Fire: Children and Violence in Colombia.* New York: Human Rights Watch.

———. 1997. *Human Rights Watch World Report 1996.* New York: Human Rights Watch.

———. 1998. *War without Quarter: Colombia and International Humanitarian Law.* New York: Human Rights Watch.

———. 2000. *Ties That Bind: Colombia and Military-Paramilitary Links.* New York: Human Rights Watch.

———. 2001a. *Protectors or Pretenders? Government Human Rights Commissions in Africa.* New York: Human Rights Watch.

———. 2001b. *"The Sixth Division": Military-Paramilitary Ties and U.S. Policy in Colombia.* New York: Human Rights Watch.

———. 2002. *A Wrong Turn: The Record of the Attorney General's Office.* New York: Human Rights Watch.

———. 2003. *You'll Learn Not to Cry: Child Combatants in Colombia.* New York: Human Rights Watch.

Human Rights Watch/Americas. 1996. *Colombia's Killer Networks.* New York: Human Rights Watch.

Hunt, Lynn. 1996. *The French Revolution and Human Rights: A Brief Documentary History.* Bedford: Bedford/St. Martin's Press.

Ignatieff, Michael. 1999. "Human Rights: The Midlife Crisis." *New York Review of Books,* May 20, 58–62.

———. 2001. *Human Rights as Politics and Idolatry.* Princeton, NJ: Princeton University Press.

Inter-Church Committee on Human Rights in Latin America (ICCHRLA). 1997. *One Step Forward, Three Steps Back: Human Rights in Colombia under the Samper Government.* Toronto: ICCHRLA. www.web.net/~icchrla/Colombia/Pol-1Forward3Back-Oct97.htm.

Isacson, Adam. 2002. "Firm Hand, Large Heart." In *Human Rights Dialogue,* ser. 2, no. 8. New York: Carnegie Council on Ethics and Foreign Policy. www.cceia.org/resources/publications/dialogue/index.html.

Ishay, Micheline, ed. 1997. *The Human Rights Reader: Major Political Essays,*

Speeches and Documents from the Bible to the Present. New York: Routledge.

Jackson, Jean. 2003. "The Crisis in Colombia: Consequences for Indigenous Peoples." American Anthropological Association Committee for Human Rights. www.aaanet.org/committees/cfhr/rpt_crisis_in_colombia.htm.

Jameson, Fredric. 1991. *Postmodernism, or the Cultural Logic of Late Capitalism*. London: Methuen.

Jaramillo, Jaime Eduardo, Fernando Cubides, and Leonidas Mora. 1986. *Colonización, coca y guerrilla*. Bogotá: Universidad Nacional de Colombia.

Jeffery, Neil, and Tara Carr. 2004. *The Impact of War on Afro-Colombians: A Community under Seige*. Washington, DC: U.S. Office on Colombia.

Jelin, Elizabeth, and Eric Hershberg, eds. 1996. *Constructing Democracy: Human Rights, Citizenship, and Society in Latin America*. Boulder, CO: Westview Press.

Jenkins, Craig, and Bert Klandermans, eds. 1995. *Politics of Social Protest*. Minneapolis: University of Minnesota Press.

Joseph, Gilbert M. 1990. "On the Trail of Latin American Bandits: A Reexamination of Peasant Resistance." *Latin American Research Review* 25 (3): 7–53.

———. 1991. "'Resocializing' Latin American Banditry: A Reply." *Latin American Research Review* 26 (1): 161–74.

Joseph, Gilbert, and Daniel Nugent, eds. 1994. *Everyday Forms of State Formation: Revolution and the Negotiation of Rule in Modern Mexico*. Durham, NC: Duke University Press.

Joseph, May. 1999. *Nomadic Identities: The Performance of Citizenship*. Minneapolis: University of Minnesota Press.

Kearney, Michael. 1992. "The Local and the Global: The Anthropology of Globalization and Transnationalism." *Annual Review of Anthropology* 24: 547–65.

Keck, Margaret, and Kathryn Sikkink. 1998. *Activists beyond Borders: Advocacy Networks in International Politics*. Ithaca, NY: Cornell University Press.

Kelly, Matt. 2003. "Colombia General Denies Rights Violation." Associated Press, January 28.

King, Anthony D., ed. 1997. *Culture, Globalization and the World-System: Contemporary Conditions for the Representation of Identity*. Minneapolis: University of Minnesota Press.

Kirk, Robin. 1993. *Feeding the Tiger: Colombia's Internally Displaced People*. Washington, DC: U.S. Committee for Refugees.

———. 2003. *More Terrible than Death: Massacres, Drugs and America's War in Colombia*. New York: Public Affairs.

Kline, Harvey F. 1995. *Colombia: Democracy under Assault*. 2d ed. Nations of the Modern World, Latin America. Boulder, CO: Westview Press.

———. 1999. *State Building and Conflict Resolution in Colombia, 1986–1994*. Tuscaloosa: University of Alabama Press.

Klinghoffer, Arthur Jay, and Judith Apter. 2002. *International Citizens' Tribunals: Mobilizing Public Opinion to Advance Human Rights*. New York: Palgrave.

Korey, William. 1998. *NGOs and the Universal Declaration of Human Rights: A Curious Grapevine.* New York: St. Martin's Press.

Kriesberg, Louis. 1997. "Social Movements and Global Transformation." In *Transnational Social Movements and Global Politics: Solidarity beyond the State,* edited by J. Smith, C. Charfield, and R. Pagnucco. Syracuse, NY: Syracuse University Press.

Lakoff, George. 1999. "Metaphorical Thought in Foreign Policy: Why Strategic Framing Matters." Manuscript.

Lancaster, Roger N. 1992. *Life Is Hard: Machismo, Danger, and the Intimacy of Power in Nicaragua.* Berkeley: University of California Press.

Landazábal Reyes, Fernando. 1966. *Política y táctica de la guerra revolucionaria.* Bogotá: Editorial Pax.

———. 1975. *Factores de violencia.* Colección Tribuna Libre. Bogotá: Tercer Mundo.

———. 1985. *El precio de la paz.* Bogotá: Planeta.

———. 1987. *La integración nacional.* Colección Documento. Bogotá: Planeta.

———. 1988. *Colombia, sus problemas y soluciones.* Bogotá: Planeta.

———. 1993. *El equilibrio de poder.* Bogotá: Plaza and Janes.

———. 1997. *La hora de la reflexión.* Bogotá: Editorial Temis.

Langer, Lawrence. 1997. "The Alarmed Vision: Social Suffering and Holocaust Atrocity." In *Social Suffering,* edited by A. Kleinman, V. Das, and M. Lock. Berkeley: University of California Press.

Lara, Patricia. 1982. *Siembra vientos y recogerás tempestades.* 2d ed. Bogotá: Editorial Punto de Partida.

———. 2000. *Las mujeres en la guerra.* Bogotá: Planeta.

LaRosa, Michael. 2000. *De la derecha a la izquierda: La iglesia católica en la Colombia contemporánea.* Translated by J. P. Lombana. Bogotá: Planeta.

Lawyers Committee for Human Rights. 1995. *Improvising History: A Critical Evaluation of the United Nations Observer Mission in El Salvador.* New York: LCHR.

Leal Buitrago, Francisco. 1989. *Estado y política en Colombia.* 2d rev. ed. Bogotá: CEREC/Siglo XXI.

———. 1994. *El oficio de la guerra: La seguridad nacional en Colombia.* Bogotá: Tercer Mundo/Instituto de Estudios Políticos y Relaciones Internacionales de la Universidad Nacional.

———. 1995. *En busca de la estabilidad perdida: Actores políticos y sociales en los años noventa.* Bogotá: IEPRI/Tercer Mundo.

Leal Buitrago, Francisco, and Marc W. Chernick. 1999. *Los laberintos de la guerra: Utopías e incertidumbres sobre la paz.* Bogotá: TM Editores.

Leal Buitrago, Francisco, and Juan Gabriel Tokatlian, eds. 1994. *Orden mundial y seguridad.* Bogotá: Tercer Mundo.

Leal Buitrago, Francisco, and Leon Zamosc. 1990. *Al filo del caos: Crisis política en la Colombia de los años 80.* Bogotá: Tercer Mundo/Universidad Nacional de Colombia.

LeGrand, Catherine. 1986. *Frontier Expansion and Peasant Protest in Colombia, 1850–1936.* Albuquerque: University of New Mexico Press.

———. 1998. *Living in Macondo: Economy and Culture in a United Fruit Com-*

pany Banana Enclave in Colombia, edited by G. M. Joseph, C. LeGrand, and R. Salvatore. Durham, NC: Duke University Press.

León Atehortúa, Adolfo, and Humberto Vélez. 1994. *Estado y fuerzas armadas en Colombia (1886–1953).* Bogotá: Tercer Mundo.

Lernoux, Penny. 1982. *Cry of the People.* New York: Penguin Books.

———. 1989. *People of God: The Struggle for World Catholicism.* New York: Viking.

Levine, Daniel. 1992. *Popular Voices in Latin American Catholicism.* Princeton, NJ: Princeton University Press.

Levitt, Peggy, and Sally Engle Merry. 2006. "Introduction." Paper presented at the conference "Localization of Global Discourses on Women's Rights," Wellesley College, Wellesley, MA.

Levy, Charmain. 2000. "CEBs in Crisis: Leadership Structures in the São Paulo Area." In *The Church at the Grassroots in Latin America: Perspectives on Thirty Years of Activism,* edited by J. Burdick and W. E. Hewitt. London: Praeger.

Lohse, Russel. 2000. "Reconciling Freedom with the Rights of Property: Slave Emancipation in Colombia, 1821–1852, with a Special Reference to La Plata." *Journal of Negro History* 86 (3): 203–27.

López de la Roche, Fabio. 1994. *Izquierdas y cultura política: Oposición alternativa?* Bogotá: CINEP.

Lorentzen, Robin. 1991. *Women in the Sanctuary Movement.* Philadelphia: Temple University Press.

Loveman, Mara. 1998. "High-Risk Collective Action: Defending Human Rights in Chile, Uruguay, and Argentina." *American Journal of Sociology* 104 (2): 477–525.

Lutz, Catherine, and Geoffrey White. 1986. "The Anthropology of Emotions." *Annual Review of Anthropology* 15: 405–36.

Mahony, Liam. 2001. "Military Intervention in Human Rights Crises: Responses and Dilemmas for the Human Rights Movement." Paper presented at the meeting on Military Intervention and Human Rights, International Council on Human Rights Policy, Geneva. www.ichrp.org/paper_files/115_w_ol.pdf.

Mahony, Laim, and Luis Enrique Eguern. 1997. *Unarmed Bodyguards: Case Studies in Protective International Accompaniment.* West Hartford, CT: Kumarian Press.

Manz, Beatriz. 2004. *Paradise in Ashes: A Guatemalan Journey of Courage, Terror, and Hope.* Berkeley: University of California Press.

Marcus, George. 1995. "Ethnography in/of the World System: The Emergence of Multi-Sited Ethnography." *Annual Review of Anthropology* 24: 95–117.

———. 1997. "The Uses of Complicity in the Changing Mise-en-Scène of Anthropological Fieldwork." *Representations* 59: 85–108.

———. 1998. *Ethnography through Thick and Thin.* Princeton, NJ: Princeton University Press.

Markowitz, Lisa, and Karen Tice. 2002. "Paradoxes of Professionalization: Parallel Dilemmas in Women's Organizations in the Americas." *Gender & Society* 16 (6): 941–58.

Marks, Thomas. 2001. *Colombian Army Adaptation to the FARC Insurgency.* Carlisle, PA: Strategic Studies Institute of the U.S. Army War College.

Martinez, Samuel. 1996. "Indifference within Indignation: Anthropology, Human Rights and the Haitian Bracero." *American Anthropologist* 98 (1): 17–25.

Mason, Ann. 2000. "The Colombian Security Crisis: International Causes and Consequences of a Failing State." Paper presented at the conference "Civil Conflicts in Colombia: The Challenges for Peacemaking and Reconciliation," Princeton University, Princeton, NJ.

McClintock, Cynthia. 2000. "Globalization, Political Parties and Communities: U.S. Policy and Peru's 2000 Elections." Paper presented at the annual meeting of the Latin American Studies Association, Miami, FL.

McClintock, Michael. 1992. *Instruments of Statecraft: U.S. Guerilla Warfare, Counterinsurgency, and Counterterrorism, 1940–1990.* New York: Pantheon.

McLagan, Meg. 2000a. "Music, Moshing, and Message: Tibetan Freedom Concerts and the Performance of Human Rights Activism." Paper presented at the Joint Center for International Studies, University of Wisconsin, Milwaukee.

———. 2000b. "Signs of Trauma, Signs of Truth: Tibetan Bodies, Testimonial, and Contemporary Human Rights Activism." Paper presented at the Department of Anthropology Colloquium, New York University.

Medina Gallego, Carlos. 1990. *Autodefensas, paramilitares y narcotráfico en Colombia: Origen, desarrollo y consolidación. El caso "Puerto Boyacá."* Bogotá: Editorial Documentos Periodísticos.

———. 1996. *ELN: Una historia contada a dos voces.* Bogotá: Rodríguez Quinto Editores.

———. 2001. *Ejército de Liberación Nacional: Una historia de los origenes.* Bogotá: Rodríguez Quinto Editores.

Medina Gallego, Carlos, and Mireya Téllez Ardila. 1994. *La violencia parainstitucional, paramilitar y parapolicial en Colombia.* Bogotá: Rodríguez Quinto Editores.

Melucci, Alberto. 1989. *Nomads of the Present: Social Movements and Individual Needs in Contemporary Society.* Philadelphia: Temple University Press.

Melville, Thomas, and Marjorie Melville. 1971. *Whose Heaven? Whose Earth?* New York: Alfred A. Knopf.

Menchú, Rigoberta. 1983. *I, Rigoberta Menchú: An Indian Woman in Guatemala.* Edited by E. Burgos. London: Verso.

Méndez, Juan E., and Human Rights Watch. 1990. *The "Drug War" in Colombia: The Neglected Tragedy of Political Violence. An Americas Watch Report.* New York: Human Rights Watch.

Merry, Sally Engle. 1992. "Anthropology, Law and Transnational Process." *Annual Review of Anthropology* 21: 357–79.

———. 2005. *Human Rights and Gender Violence: Translating International Law into Local Justice.* Chicago: University of Chicago Press.

Messer, Ellen. 1993. "Anthropology and Human Rights." *Annual Review of Anthropology* 22: 221–49.

———. 1995. "Anthropology and Human Rights in Latin America." *Journal of Latin American Anthropology* 1 (1): 48–97.

Meyer, Carrie. 2000. *The Economics and Politics of NGOs in Latin America*. Westport, CT: Praeger.

Meyer, David, and Suzanne Staggenborg. 1996. "Movements, Countermovements, and the Structure of Political Opportunity." *American Journal of Sociology* 101 (6): 1628–60.

Meyer, David, and Nancy Whittier. 1994. "Social Movement Spill-over." *Social Problems* 41 (2): 277–98.

Mignolo, Walter. 2000. *Local Histories/Global Designs: Coloniality, Subaltern Knowledges and Border Thinking*. Princeton, NJ: Princeton University Press.

Mingst, Karen, and Margaret Karns. 1999. *The United Nations in the Post–Cold War Era*. Boulder, CO: Westview Press.

Minkoff, Debra. 1997. "The Sequencing of Social Movements." *American Sociological Review* 62: 779–99.

Mintz, Sidney. 1998. "The Localization of Anthropological Practice: From Area Studies to Transnationalism." *Critique of Anthropology* 18 (2): 117–33.

Molano, Alfredo. 1987. *Selva adentro: Una historia de la colonización del Guaviare*. Bogotá: El Ancora Editores.

———. 1989. *Siguiendo el corte: Relatos de guerras y de tierras*. Bogotá: El Ancora Editores.

———. 1994. *Trochas y fusiles*. Bogotá: IEPRI/El Ancora Editores.

Moore, Sally Falk. 1978. *Law as Process: An Anthropological Approach*. London: Routledge and Kegan Paul.

Morris, Hollman. 2002. *La ballena azul*. Bogotá: Planeta.

Muñera, Alfonso. 1998. *El fracaso de la nación: Región, clase y raza en el Caribe colombiano, 1717–1810*. Bogotá: El Ancora Editores.

Nader, Laura. 1969. "Up the Anthropologist—Perspectives Gained from Studying Up." In *Reinventing Anthropology*, edited by D. Hymes. New York: Vintage Books.

———. 1997. "Controlling Processes: Tracing the Dynamic of Power." *Current Anthropology* 38 (5): 711–38.

Nagengast, C. 1994. "Violence, Terror, and the Crisis of the State." *Annual Review of Anthropology* 23: 109–36.

Nagle, Robin. 1997. *Claiming the Virgin: The Broken Promise of Liberation Theology in Brazil*. New York: Routledge.

Nationaal Centrum voor Ontwikkelingssamenwerking (National Center for Development Cooperation). 1992. *El terrorismo de estado en Colombia*. Brussels: Ediciones NCOS.

———. 1995. *Tras los pasos perdidos de la Guerra Sucia*. Brussels: Ediciones NCOS.

Neier, Aryeh. 1998. *War Crimes: Brutality, Genocide, Terror and the Struggle for Justice*. New York: Times Books.

Nelson, Diane. 2000. *A Finger in the Wound: Body Politics in Quincentennial Guatemala*. Berkeley: University of California Press.

———. 2001. "Indian Giver or Nobel Savage: Duping, Assumptions of Identity, and Other Double Entendres in Rigoberta Menchú Tum's Stoll/en Past." *American Ethnologist* 28 (2): 303–31.

Nordstrom, Carolyn. 1997. *A Different Kind of War Story.* Philadelphia: University of Pennsylvania Press.

Nordstrom, Carolyn, and Antonius Robben, eds. 1995. *Fieldwork under Fire.* Berkeley: University of California Press.

Ochoa, Ana Maria. 1996. "Plotting Musical Territories: Three Studies in Processes of Recontextualization of Musical Folklore in the Andean Region of Colombia." Ph.D. dissertation, Indiana University, Bloomington.

———. 2000. "CREA and the Agendas of Peace." Manuscript.

Office of the High Commissioner for Human Rights in Colombia. 2000. *Report of the High Commissioner for Human Rights on the Situation of Human Rights in Colombia.* Geneva: U.N. Human Rights Commission.

Olson, Elizabeth. 1998. "A Challenge to Immunity of Lobbyists at the U.N." *New York Times,* August 8.

Ong, Aihwa. 1998. *Flexible Citizenship: The Cultural Logics of Transnationality.* Durham, NC: Duke University Press.

Oquist, Paul. 1980. *Violence, Conflict, and Politics in Colombia.* New York: Academic Press.

Osiel, Mark. 2000. *Mass Atrocity, Collective Memory and the Law.* New Brunswick, NJ: Transaction.

Pagnucco, Ron. 1997. "The Transnational Strategies of the Service for Peace and Justice in Latin America." In *Transnational Social Movements and Global Politics: Solidarity beyond the State,* edited by J. Smith, C. Charfield, and R. Pagnucco. Syracuse, NY: Syracuse University Press.

Palacios, Marco. 1995. *Entre la legitimidad y la violencia: Colombia, 1875–1994.* Bogotá: Grupo Editorial Norma.

———. 1999. *Parábola de liberalismo.* Bogotá: Grupo Editorial Norma.

Pardo Rueda, Rafael. 1996. *De primera mano: Colombia 1986–1994: Entre conflictos y esperanzas.* Bogotá: CEREC/Grupo Editorial Norma.

Park, James. 1985. *Rafael Nunez and the Politics of Colombian Regionalism, 1863–1886.* Baton Rouge: Louisiana State University Press.

Partnoy, Alice. 1986. *The Little School: Tales of Disappearance and Survival in Argentina.* Pittsburgh: Cleis Press.

Pécaut, Daniel. 1987. *Orden y violencia en Colombia: 1930–1954.* Bogotá: Siglo XXI.

———. 1989. *Crónica de dos décadas de política colombiana, 1968–1988.* Bogotá: Siglo XXI.

———. 1992. "Guerrillas and Violence." In *Violence in Colombia: The Contemporary Crisis in Historical Perspective,* edited by C. W. Bergquist, R. Peñaranda, and G. Sánchez. Wilmington, DE: Scholastic Resources.

———. 2001. *Guerra contra la sociedad.* Bogotá: Planeta.

Pedelty, Mark. 1995. *War Stories: The Culture of Foreign Correspondents.* New York: Routledge.

Perea, Carlos Mario. 1996. *Porque la sangre es espiritu: Imaginario y discurso político en las elites capitalinas, 1942–1949.* Bogota: IEPRI.

Pérez, Diego. 1998. "En defensa de los derechos humanos." In *Una opción y muchas busquedas,* edited by F. Gonzalez. Bogotá: CINEP.

Peterson, Anna. 1997. *Martyrdom and the Politics of Religion: Progressive Catholicism in El Salvador's Civil War.* Albany: State University of New York Press.

Pinheiro, Paulo Sergio, and David Carlos Baluarte. 2000. "National Strategies: Human Rights Commissions, Ombudsmen, and National Action Plans: The Role of National Human Rights Institutions in State Strategies." In *Human Development Report 2000.* Background Paper. New York: United Nations.

Pizarro Leongómez, Eduardo. 1991. *Las FARC 1949–1966: De la autodefensa a la combinación de todas las formas de lucha.* Bogotá: Tercer Mundo.

———. 1992. "Revolutionary Guerrilla Groups in Colombia." In *Violence in Colombia: The Contemporary Crisis in Historical Perspective,* edited by C. W. Bergquist, R. Peñaranda, and G. Sánchez. Wilmington, DE: Scholastic Resources.

———. 1996. *Insurgencia sin revolución: La guerrilla en Colombia en una perspectiva comparada, académica.* Bogotá: Tercer Mundo/IEPRI.

Pizarro Leongómez, Eduardo, Alvaro Villarraga S., and Francisco Gutiérrez Sanín. 1996. *La oposición política en Colombia: Debate político.* Bogotá: Fundación Friedrich Ebert de Colombia/Universidad Nacional de Colombia, Instituto de Estudios Políticos y Relaciones Internacionales.

Poe, Steven C., Sabine C. Carey, and Tanya C. Vazquez. 2001. "How Are These Pictures Different? A Quantitative Comparison of the U.S. State Department and Amnesty International Human Rights Reports, 1976–1995." *Human Rights Quarterly* 23: 650–77.

Poole, Deborah, and Gerardo Renique. 2000. "Popular Movements, the Legacy of the Left, and the Fall of Fujimori." Manuscript.

Porter, Bruce. 2001. *Blow: How a Small-Town Boy Made $100 Million with the Medellín Cocaine Cartel and Lost It All.* New York: St. Martin's Griffin.

Posada Carbó, Eduardo. 1998. *Colombia: The Politics of Reforming the State.* Institute of Latin American Studies series. Basingstoke: Macmillan in association with Institute of Latin American Studies, University of London.

Power, Jonathon. 2001. *Like Water on Stone: The Story of Amnesty International.* Chicago: Northeastern Press.

Power, Samatha. 2003. *A Problem from Hell: America and the Age of Genocide.* New York: Basic Books.

Preis, Ann-Belinda. 1996. "Human Rights as Cultural Practice: An Anthropological Critique." *Human Rights Quarterly* 18 (2): 286–315.

Premo, Daniel L. 1982. "The Colombian Armed Forces in Search of a Mission." In *New Military Politics in Latin America,* edited by R. G. Wesson. New York: Praeger.

Prieto, Jaime. 1999. "Documento final del proceso de evaluación interna, Coordinación Colombia-Europa de organizaciones no gubernamentales de derechos humanos." Manuscript.

Rabben, Linda. 2002. *Fierce Legion of Friends: A History of Human Rights Campaigns and Campaigners.* Hyattsville: Quixote Center.

Radcliffe, Sarah, and Sallie Westwood, eds. 1993. *Viva: Women and Popular Protest in Latin America.* New York: Routledge.

Ramírez, María Clemencia. 2001. *Entre el estado y la guerrilla: Identidad y ciudadanía en el movimiento de los campesinos cocaleros del Putumayo.* Bogotá: Colciencias–Insituto Colombiano de Antropología e Historia.

Rangel Suárez, Alfredo. 1998. *Colombia: Guerra en el fin de siglo.* Bogotá: TM Editores/Universidad de los Andes.

Rappaport, Joanne. 1994. *Cumbe Reborn: An Andean Ethnography of History.* Chicago: University of Chicago Press.

———. 1998. *The Politics of Memory: Native Historical Interpretation in the Colombian Andes.* Durham, NC: Duke University Press.

———. 2005. *Intercultural Utopias: Public Intellectuals, Cultural Experimentation, and Ethnic Pluralism in Colombia.* Durham, NC: Duke University Press.

Rausch, Jane. 1989. *A Tropical Plains Frontier: The Llanos of Colombia, 1575–1831.* Gainesville: University of Florida Press.

———. 1999. *Colombia: Territorial Rule and the Llanos.* Gainesville: University of Florida Press.

Razack, Sherene. 2000. "From the 'Clean Snows of Petawana': The Violence of Canadian Peacekeepers in Somalia." *Cultural Anthropology* 15 (1): 127–63.

Reif, Linda. 2000. "Building Democratic Institutions: The Role of National Human Rights Institutions in Good Governance and Human Rights Protection." *Harvard Human Rights Journal* 13: 1–69.

Rempe, Dennis M. 2002. *The Past as Prologue? A History of U.S. Counterinsurgency Policy in Colombia, 1958–66.* Carlisle, PA: Strategic Studies Institute of the U.S. Army War College.

Restrepo, Javier. 1995. *La revolución de las Sotanas: Golconda 25 años despues.* Bogotá: Planeta.

Restrepo, Luis Alberto. 2001. "The Equivocal Dimensions of Human Rights in Colombia." In *Violence in Colombia, 1990–2000: Waging War and Negotiating Peace,* edited by C. W. Bergquist, R. Peñaranda, and G. Sánchez. Wilmington, DE: Scholastic Resources.

Reyes, Alejandro, and Ana Lucía Gómez. 1997. "Compra de tierras por narcotraficantes." In *Drogas ilícitas en Colombia: Su impacto económico, político y social.* Bogotá: PNUD/DNE/Ariel Ciencia Política.

Richani, Nazih. 2002. *Systems of Violence: The Political Economy of War and Peace in Colombia.* Albany: State University of New York Press.

Rieff, David. 2002. *A Bed for the Night: Humanitarianism in Crisis.* New York: Simon and Schuster.

Righter, Rosemary. 1995. *Utopia Lost: The United Nations and World Order.* New York: Century Foundation Press.

Riles, Annelise. 1998. "Infinity within the Brackets." *American Ethnologist* 25 (3): 378–98.

Risse, Thomas, Stephen Ropp, and Kathryn Sikkink, eds. 1999. *The Power of Human Rights: International Norms and Domestic Change.* Cambridge: Cambridge University Press.

Robben, Antonius. 1995. "The Politics of Truth and Emotion among Victims and Perpetrators of Violence." In *Fieldwork under Fire*, edited by C. Nordstrom and A. Robben. Berkeley: University of California Press.

Roberts, Kenneth. 1998. *Deepening Democracy? The Modern Left and Social Movements in Chile and Peru*. Berkeley: University of California Press.

Rojas, Fernando. 1984. "Derechos humanos y crítica social en America Latina: Desencuentro y reencuentro. Es imperativa una nueva declaración de los derechos del hombre y de la sociedad." Paper presented at Ciencia, Cultura y Derechos Humanos en la Región Andina, Quito.

Rojas Rodriguez, Jorge. 2004. "Political Peacebuilding: A Challenge for Civil Society." In *Alternatives to War: Colombia's Peace Processes*. Accord Issue 14. London: Conciliation Resources.

Roldán, Mary. 2002. *Blood and Fire: La Violence in Antioquia, Colombia, 1946–1953*. Durham, NC: Duke University Press.

Romero, Amanda. 1992. "Una experiencia de educación popular en derechos humanos: Teoría y practica de los derechos humanos en Colombia." Master's thesis, Centro Internacional de Educación y Desarrollo Humanos "CINDE," Bogotá.

Romero, Flor. 2001. "El movimiemto de derechos humanos en Colombia." In *Movimientos sociales: Estado y democracia en Colombia*, edited by M. Archila and M. Pardo. Bogotá: ICANH.

Ruhl, J. Mark. 1980. *Colombia: Armed Forces and Society, Foreign and Comparative Studies*. Latin American series, 1. Syracuse, NY: Maxwell School of Citizenship and Public Affairs, Syracuse University.

Ruiz Novoa, Alberto. 1956. *El batallón colombia en Korea*. Bogotá: Imprenta Nacional de Publicaciones.

———. 1965. *El gran desafío*. Bogotá: Tercer Mundo.

Safford, Frank, and Marco Palacios. 2001. *Colombia: Fragmented Land, Divided Society*. New York: Oxford University Press.

Salazar, Alonso, and Nick Caistor. 1992. *Born to Die in Medellín*. London: Latin America Bureau.

Sánchez, Gonzalo. 1991. *Guerra y política en la sociedad colombiana*. Bogotá: El Ancora Editores.

———. 1992. "The Violence: An Interpretive Synthesis." In *Violence in Colombia: The Contemporary Crisis in Historical Perspective*, edited by C. W. Bergquist, R. Peñaranda, and G. Sánchez. Wilmington, DE: Scholastic Resources.

———, and Donny Meertens. 2001. *Bandits, Peasants, and Politics: The Case of "La Violencia" in Colombia*. Translated by A. Hynds. Austin: University of Texas Press.

Sassen, Saskia. 2006. *Territory, Authority, Rights: From Medieval to Global Assemblages*. Princeton, NJ: Princeton University Press.

Scarry, Elaine. 1985. *The Body in Pain: The Making and Unmaking of the World*. New York: Oxford University Press.

Scheper-Hughes, Nancy. 1995. "Primacy of the Ethical: Propositions for a Militant Anthropology." *Current Anthropology* 36 (3): 409–40.

Schirmer, Jennifer. 1993. "The Seeking of Truth and the Gendering of Consciousness: The Comadres of El Salvador and the CONAVIGUA Widows of

Political Violence in Guatemala." In *Viva! Women and Popular Protest in Latin America,* edited by S. Radcliffe and S. Westwood. London: Routledge.

———. 1997. "Universal and Sustainable Human Rights? Special Tribunals in Guatemala." In *Human Rights, Culture and Context: Anthropological Perspectives,* edited by R. Wilson. London: Pluto Press.

———. 1998. "Interviewing Military Officers: A Woman Researcher's Perspective." *ReVista: Harvard Review of Latin America* (Winter). www.drdas.fas .harvard.edu/revista/articles/view/388.

_____. 2000. *A Violence Called Democracy: The Guatemalan Military Project, 1982–1992.* Philadelphia: University of Pennsylvania Press.

Schoultz, Lars. 1985. *Human Rights and United States Policy toward Latin America.* New York: Verso.

———. 1998. *Beneath the United States: A History of U.S. Policy toward Latin America.* Cambridge, MA: Harvard University Press.

Scott, James. 1985. *Weapons of the Weak: Everyday Forms of Peasant Resistance.* New Haven, CT: Yale University Press.

———. 1992. *Domination and the Arts of Resistance: Hidden Transcripts.* New Haven, CT: Yale University Press.

———. 1998. *Seeing Like the State.* New Haven, CT: Yale University Press.

Skocpol, Theda. 1985. "Bringing the State Back In: Strategies of Analysis in Current Research." In *Bringing the State Back In,* edited by P. Evans, D. Rueschemeyer, and T. Skocpol. Cambridge: Cambridge University Press.

Silber, Irena. 2000. "A Spectral Reconciliation: Rebuilding Post-War El Salvador." Ph.D. dissertation, New York University.

Silverstein, Ken. 2000. *Private Warriors.* New York: Verso.

Simmons, P. J. 1998. "Learning to Live with NGOs." *Foreign Policy* (Fall): 82–96.

Slatta, Richard W. 1991. "Bandits and Rural Social History: A Comment on Joseph." *Latin American Research Review* 26 (1): 145–51.

Slaughter, Ann-Marie. 2004. *A New World Order.* Princeton, NJ: Princeton University Press.

Smith, Christian. 1996. *Resisting Reagan: The U.S. Central America Peace Movement.* Chicago: University of Chicago Press.

Smith, Jackie. 1997. "Characteristics of the Modern Transnational Social Movement Sector." In *Transnational Social Movements and Global Politics: Solidarity beyond the State,* edited by J. Smith, C. Charfield, and R. Pagnucco. Syracuse, NY: Syracuse University Press.

Snow, David, E. Burke Rochford Jr., Steven Worden, and Robert Benford. 1986. "Frame Alignment Processes, Micromobilization and Movement Participation." *American Sociological Review* 51 (4): 464–81.

Speed, Shannon, and Jane Collier. 2000. "Limiting Indigenous Autonomy in Chiapas, Mexico: The State Government's Use of Human Rights." *Human Rights Quarterly* 22: 877–905.

Speed, Shannon, and María Teresa Sierra. 2005. "Introduction: Critical Perspectives on Human Rights and Multiculturalism in Neoliberal Latin America." *POLAR: Political and Legal Anthropology Review* 28 (1): 1–10.

Spivak, Gayatri. 1988. "Can the Subaltern Speak?" In *Marxism and the Inter-*

pretation of Culture, edited by C. Nelson and L. Greenburg. Bloomington: Indiana University Press.

———. 2004. "Righting Wrongs." *South Atlantic Quarterly* 103 (2–3): 523–81.

Stammers, Neil. 1999. "Social Movements and the Social Construction of Human Rights." *Human Rights Quarterly* 21 (4): 980–1008.

Starn, Orin. 1991. "Missing the Revolution: Anthropologists and the War in Peru." *Cultural Anthropology* 6 (1): 63–91.

———. 1994. "Rethinking the Politics of Anthropology: The Case of the Andes." *Current Anthropology* 35: 45–75.

———. 1999. *Nightwatch: The Politics of Protest in the Andes.* Durham, NC: Duke University.

Stephen, Lynn. 1995. "Women's Rights Are Human Rights: The Merging of Feminine and Feminist Interests among El Salvador's Mothers of the Disappeared (CO-MADRES)." *American Ethnologist* 22 (4): 807–27.

———. 2001. "Gender, Citizenship, and the Politics of Identity." *Latin American Perspectives* 28 (6): 54–69.

Stern, Steve. 2004. *Remembering Pinochet's Chile: On the Eve of London, 1998.* Durham, NC: Duke University Press.

Stoll, David. 1993. *Between Two Armies in the Ixil Towns of Guatemala.* New York: Columbia University Press.

———. 2000. *Rigoberta Menchú and the Story of All Poor Guatemalans.* Boulder, CO: Westview Press.

Strange, Susan. 1996. *The Retreat of the State: The Diffusion of Power in the World Economy.* Cambridge: Cambridge University Press.

Tarrow, Sidney. 1994. *Power in Movement: Social Movements, Collective Action, and the Mass Politics in the Modern State.* Cambridge: Cambridge University Press.

Tate, Winifred. 1997. *Losing Ground: Human Rights Defenders under Attack.* Washington, DC: Washington Office on Latin America.

———. 2003. "The Wrong Road: Colombian National Security Policy." Latin American Working Group, Washington, DC.

———. Forthcoming. "From Greed to Grievance: The Shifting Political Profile of Colombian Paramilitary Groups." In *Colombia: Building Peace in a Time of War,* ed. V. Bouvier. Washington, DC: U.S. Institute for Peace.

Taussig, Michael. 1987. *Shamanism, Colonialism, and the Wild Man: A Study in Terror and Healing.* Chicago: University of Chicago Press.

———. 1992. *The Nervous System.* London: Routledge.

———. 1999. *Defacement: Public Secrecy and the Labor of the Negative.* Stanford: Stanford University Press.

———. 2004. *Law in a Lawless Land: Diary of a Limpieza in Colombia.* New York: New Press.

Taylor, Diana. 1997. *Disappearing Acts: Spectacles of Gender and Nationalism in Argentina's "Dirty War."* Durham, NC: Duke University Press.

Tilly, Charles. 1978. *From Mobilization to Revolution.* Reading, MA: Addison-Wesley.

Time. 1995. "Milestones/Dismissed. Alvaro Velandia Hurtado." *Time* 146 (13), September 25.

Timerman, Jacobo. 1981. *Prisoner without a Name, Cell without a Number*. New York: Alfred A. Knopf.

Tovar, Alvaro Valencia, and Jairo Sandoval Franky. 2001. *Colombia en la Guerra de Corea: La historia secreta*. Bogotá: Planeta.

Tribunal Permanente de los Pueblos. 1991. *Proceso a la impunidad de crímenes de lesa humanidad en America Latina, 1989–1991*. Bogotá: Tribunal Permanente de los Pueblos.

Tsing, Ana. 2000. "The Global Situation." *Cultural Anthropology* 15 (3): 327–60.

———. 2005. *Friction: An Ethnography of Global Connection*. Princeton, NJ: Princeton University Press.

Turner, Terence. 1996. "Human Rights, Human Difference, and Anthropology's Contribution to an Emancipatory Cultural Politics." Manuscript.

United Nations. 1995. *National Human Rights Institutions: A Handbook on the Establishment and Strengthening of National Institutions for the Promotion and Protection of Human Rights*. Geneva: U.N. Centre for Human Rights.

Uribe, María Victoria. 1990. *Matar, rematar y contramatar: Las masacres de la violencia en el Tolima, 1948–1964*. Vol. 159–60. Bogotá: CINEP.

Valencia Tovar, Alvaro. 1970. *Armas e historia*. Bucaramanga, Colombia: Impr. del Departamento.

———. 1974. *General de división José María Córdoba*. Bogotá: Impr. y Litografía de las Fuerzas Militares.

———. 1976. *El final de Camilo*. Colección Andina. Bogotá: Tercer Mundo.

———. 1980. *Uisheda: Violencia en el llano*. Medellín: Bedout.

———. 1992. *Testimonio de una época*. Bogotá: Planeta.

———. 1997. *Inseguridad y violencia en Colombia*. Bogotá: Universidad Sergio Arboleda.

Valencia Tovar, Alvaro, and José Manuel Villalobos Barradas. 1993. *Historia de las fuerzas militares de Colombia*. Bogotá: Planeta.

Van Ness, Peter, and Nikhil Aziz. 1999. *Debating Human Rights: Critical Essays from the United States and Asia*. New York: Routledge.

Vargas M., Ricardo. 1999. *Drogas, máscaras y juegos: Narcotráfico y conflicto armado en Colombia*. Colección Académica. Bogotá: TM Editores/Acción Andina/Transnational Institute.

Vargas Velásquez, Alejo. 1992. *Colonización y conflicto armado*. Bogotá: CINEP.

———. 2002. *Las fuerzas armadas en el conflicto colombiano: Antecedentes y perspectivas*. Bogotá: Intermedio.

Varon, Jeremy. 2004. *Bringing the War Home: The Weather Underground, the Red Army Faction, and Revolutionary Violence in the Sixties and Seventies*. Berkeley: University of California Press.

Vásquez Perdomo, María. 2000. *Escrito para no morir: Bitácora de una militancia*. Bogotá: Ministerio de Cultura.

Vickers, George. 2000. "Human Rights and Military Conduct." *Joint Forces Quarterly* (Autumn): 51–57.

Villamarín Pulido, Luis Alberto. 1996. *El cartel de las FARC.* n.p.: Ediciones El Faraón.

———. 1997. *La selva roja.* Bogotá: Ediciones L. A. Villamarín Pulido.

Villamizar, Darío. 1995. *Aquel 19 será, una historia de M-19.* Bogotá: Planeta.

Villar, Rodrigo, and Confederación Colombiana de ONGs. 1998. "Defining the Nonprofit Sector: Colombia." *Working Papers of the Johns Hopkins Comparative Nonprofit Sector,* no. 29, edited by L. M. Salamon and H. K. Anheier. Baltimore, MD: Johns Hopkins Institute for Policy Studies.

Villarraga, Alvaro S., and Nelson Plazas. 1994. *Para reconstruir los sueños: Una historia del EPL.* Bogotá: Progresar/Fundación Cultura Democrática.

Villaveces, Santiago. 1998. "Violentologists and Magistrates: Questions of Justice and Responses to Violence in Contemporary Colombia." Ph.D. dissertation, Rice University.

Visweswaran, Kamala. 1994. *Fictions of Feminist Ethnography.* Minneapolis: University of Minnesota Press.

Wade, Peter. 1993. *Blackness and Race Mixture: The Dynamics of Racial Identity in Colombia.* Baltimore, MD: Johns Hopkins University Press.

———. 2000. *Music, Race, and Nation: Música Tropical in Colombia.* Chicago: University of Chicago Press.

———. 2002. "The Colombian Pacific in Perspective." *Journal of Latin American Anthropology* 7 (2): 2–33.

———, ed. 1997. *Race and Ethnicity in Latin America.* Chicago: Pluto Press.

Walzer, Michael. 2000. *Just and Unjust Wars: A Moral Argument with Historical Illustrations.* New York: Basic Books.

Warren, Kay. 1993. "Interpreting La Violencia in Guatemala: Shapes of Mayan Resistance and Silence." In *The Violence Within: Cultural and Political Opposition in Divided Nations,* edited by K. Warren. Boulder, CO: Westview Press.

———. 1998. *Indigenous Movements and Their Critics: Pan-Mayan Activism in Guatemala.* Princeton, NJ: Princeton University Press.

Webb, Jason. 2002. "U.S. Strips Visa from Colombian General over Drugs." Reuters, November 20.

Welch, Claude E., Jr., ed. 2001. *NGOs and Human Rights: Promise and Performance.* Philadelphia: University of Pennsylvania Press.

White, Richard. 2004. *Breaking Silence: The Case That Changed the Face of Human Rights.* Washington, DC: Georgetown University Press.

Whitfield, Teresa. 1995. *Paying the Price: Ignacio Ellacuría and the Murdered Jesuits of El Salvador.* Philadelphia: Temple University Press.

Wickham-Crowley, Timothy. 1992. *Guerrillas and Revolution in Latin America.* Princeton, NJ: Princeton University Press.

Willetts, Peter, ed. 1996. *"The Conscience of the World"—The Influence of Non-governmental Organizations in the U.N. System.* Washington, DC: Brookings Institute.

Wilson, Richard, ed. 1997. *Human Rights, Culture, and Context: Anthropological Perspectives.* Chicago: Pluto Press.

———. 2000. "Reconciliation and Revenge in Post-Apartheid South Africa: Rethinking Legal Pluralism and Human Rights." *Current Anthropology* 41 (1): 75–98.

Wilson, Scott. 2002. "True Confessions of a Political Assassin." *Washington Post*, February 9, C1.

Wolf, Eric. 1999. *Envisioning Power: Ideologies of Dominance and Crisis.* Berkeley: University of California Press.

Wood, Elisabeth Jean. 2003. *Insurgent Collective Action and Civil War in El Salvador.* Cambridge: Cambridge University Press.

Yoon, Diana, and Mihaela Serban. 2006. "'Bringing Coals to Newcastle'? Human Rights Discourses and Social Change in New York City." Paper presented at the Localization of Global Women's Rights Discourses Workshop, Wellesley College, Wellesley, MA.

Youngers, Coletta. 2003. "The History of the Human Rights Coordinadora in Peru." Manuscript.

Zamosc, Leon. 1989. "Peasant Struggles of the 1970s in Colombia." In *Power and Popular Protest: Latin American Social Movements,* edited by S. Eckstein. Berkeley: University of California Press.

Index

5th Brigade, 138, 241, 280–81, 285
17th Brigade, 254, 265–66
1886 Constitution, 36, 86, 313n6
1991 Constitution, 60–61, 67, 88, 108–9, 123, 226, 232, 274, 284, 295; activist participation in writing of, 129–131

AAA (American Anti-communist Alliance), 51
Abad Gómez, Hector, 128, 138, 167, 224
activist identity, 88, 148, 159, 204
advocacy: critiques of, 153–54, 210–13; international, 183–84, 187, 201–10, 213, 322n45; for Law 288, 63; at the United Nations, 136, 150, 199–209; in Washington, 121–22, 186, 188; during writing of the 1991 Constitution, 129–31
AFL-CIO Solidarity Center, 187
Afro-Colombian population, 33–35, 54, 113, 222, 321n39
Algiers Declaration, 103
Allen, Lori, 301
Alliance for Progress, 85
Alliance of Like-Minded Social Organizations for International Assistance for Peace and Democracy in Colombia (Alianza), 133–34
Alvarado, Elsa, 156
Amnesty International, 9, 17, 90, 176, 179, 181, 183–84, 229, 263, 305, 335; history, 80–81, 189–90, 308n2; reporting on defenders, 160–61; reporting on persecution of gays and lesbians, 169–70; reporting on women, 54; and the U.N., 194
ANAPO (National Popular Alliance), 40, 43
Apuleyo, Plinio, 112, 323n2, 326n4
Arcila, Daniel, 59, 60, 296, 320n34
armed option, 42, 96, 98–101; rejection of, 114
ASFADDES (Association of Relatives of the Detained and Disappeared), 89, 142, 154, 185, 204, 206–7, 267, 335n23
assassinations, 58, 73, 142, 156, 158–61, 168; by drug traffickers, 51, 105; by the FARC, 40; during La Violencia, 48; of local leaders, 94, 155
Atehortúa, Adolfo, 57, 317n30
AUC (United Self-Defense Forces of Colombia), 33, 52–53, 142, 234, 238, 240, 252, 282. See also paramilitary groups

Ballantyne, Edith, 196
Barco, President Virgilio, 51, 129, 249; human rights initiatives, 223–24
Barnett, Michael, 180
Bauer, Jan, 197, 200
Bautista case, 268
Bedoya, Harold, 273
Bejarano, Ana Maria, 40
Bell, Gustavo, 229
Betancur, Belisario, 57
El Bogotazo, 37–39

Bolivia, 48–50
Bonnett Locarno, José Manual, 271–73, 278
Braun, Herbert, 39
Bush (George W.) administration, 188

Calderón, Mario, 156
Cali Cartel, 48, 57–58, 62, 273, 315n20
Camelo, José Arturo, 269
Camilista Movement, 99
Canadian National Human Rights Commission, 220
Cardenas, Sonia, 216, 220, 222
Carranza, Victor, 52
Carter administration, 101–2, 311n6
Castañeda, Jorge, 85, 96
Castaño, Carlos, 299
Castaño, Fidel, 52
Castells, Manuel, 183
Castro Caicedo, José Fernando, 231
Catholic Church, 34, 36, 45, 56, 59, 66, 68–70, 75, 85, 265, 329n5; condemnation of homosexuality, 168; international institutional links of, 89; liberation theology, 77–78, 86, 115, 148, 204, 306, 323n4; Office on Human Migration, 66; sponsorship of projects, 111; suffering and martyrdom, 157–59; work of priests and nuns, 91; work with local organizations, 115, 116
Catholic Conference of Bishops, 115
Catholic Social Welfare Agency, 245
CCJ (Colombian Commission of Jurists), 1, 14, 33, 94; history of, 114, 118–19, 130, 132, 150, 153, 185; at the U.N., 199, 200–213
CEBs (Christian base communities), 78, 99, 157
Center for International Policy, 189, 263
Chengue massacre, 233–36, 248, 339n14
Children's Mandate for Peace and Rights, 69
Chile, 10, 78, 84, 86, 87, 194, 202
Christian Aid, 67, 249
CINEP (Center for Grassroots Education and Research), 14, 17, 74; history of, 89–91, 94, 101, 114–15, 119, 156, 168, 290
Citizen's Mandate for Peace, Life, and Liberty (1997), 69
Clavijo, Adolfo, 267, 270
Clinton, President William, 188, 263
coca cultivation, 45, 49–50
cocaine. See drug trafficking
CODHES (Council on Human Rights and Displacement), 33, 117, 132
Cohen, William, 262

cold war, 7, 193; post–cold war era, 41, 61, 182, 219, 262, 304, 325n1
collective rights, 101–2
Collier, Jane, 219
Colombia-Europe Coordination, 111, 123–24, 135–36, 164, 185, 201, 208
Colombian Armed Forces, 20, 47, 224–25, 235, 238, 270. See also military
Colombian government. See individual agency entries
Colombian League for the Rights and Freedom of the Pueblos, 90
Colombian NGO Confederation, 111
Colombian Supreme Court, 51
Colombia Steering Committee, 121
Commission 1290, 227
Commission 1533, 227, 338n9
Commission for Historical Clarification in Guatemala (CEH), 302
communism: Communist Party, 37, 41–43, 73–74, 81–82, 84, 96–97, 148, 187, 191, 212, 262, 280; Communist Youth, 43; condemnation of homosexuality, 168–69; international travels, 182; Marxist-Leninist Communist Party, 43; military views of, 266; publications, 82; valorization of suffering, 157
Conference of Religious Superiors of Colombia, 115
CONGO (Conference of Nongovernmental Organizations in Consultative Relationship with the United Nations), 195–97
Congress (Colombian), 80, 131, 166, 223, 226, 232, 236
consciousness-raising, 86–90; with the military, 64. See also human rights: workshops
Conservative Party, 34, 36–39, 45–46, 56, 77–78, 129
Constitutional Assembly, 60, 129, 226
Convivir, 51
corruption, of government officials, 127; within NGOs, 154
counterinsurgency warfare, 45, 47, 166, 258, 261–62. See also psychological operations
CREDHOS (Regional Human Rights Corporation), 91–93, 127, 212, 242, 324n14
criminalization, 241
CRS (Socialist Renovation Current), 44, 69, 227
CSPP (Committee in Solidarity with Political Prisoners), 72, 74, 77, 79, 80, 86, 88, 89, 90, 91, 102, 113–14, 116, 152,

154, 156, 162; history of international work, 189–91

Cuba, 100, 211–12; Bautista dictatorship, 104; Cuban Revolution, influence of, 43, 95, 182

culture: Colombian national identity, 21–22, 31, 35, 45; cultural production, 75, 87–88, 92, 116, 324n12; in exile community, 191; in human rights work, 107, 301; knowledge production, 9, 134–37, 290–91; in Mexico, 219; of peace, 67–68; of terror, 22; in transnational advocacy, 182, 204

CUT (Central Unitaria de Trabajadores), 139

death squads: in La Violencia, 48; paramilitary, 51, 62

Debray, Regis, 42

Decree 0372 of 1996, 228

Defense Ministry, 15, 16, 17, 226, 230, 272, 278, 285–86

Defense Ministry's Judge Advocate General's Office, 269

Defensoria del Pueblo. *See* National Human Rights Ombudsman's Office

democracy: Colombia as Latin America's oldest, 199; limits to, 36–37, 39–41, 49, 81, 149; state human rights agencies as democratization, 229. *See also* electoral reforms

denuncias, 5, 91, 94–95, 102, 122, 128, 138, 155, 172, 240, 249, 269, 274, 282; at the U.N., 191

Department of Planning, 230

disappearances, 58, 81, 89, 161, 238, 266, 324n9; U.N. Working Group on Enforced or Involuntary Disappearances, 194

displacement, 33, 41, 54, 66–67, 92, 94, 117, 141, 168, 246–47, 299–300, 321n39

Doctors without Borders, 67

drug trafficking, 42, 44, 47–52, 100, 224; and Colombia's image abroad, 199; as national security threat, 262–63; role of, in La Gabarra massacre, 239–41; during the Samper administration, 62; in Trujillo, 56; views of human rights groups on, 105

Dudley, Steve, 97, 156

due obedience, 130

Early Warning System, 229, 248, 288–89

economic rights, 101

ECOSOC (United Nations Economic and Social Council), 194–95, 197

Ecuador, 188–89

electoral reforms, 36, 40, 126–28, 224

ELN (National Liberation Army), 33, 158, 227, 239–40, 252, 275, 276, 281, 320n32; history of, 41, 43–44, 77–80, 91, 99, 112; peace talks with, 70; in Trujillo, 56–58, 60

El Salvador, 68, 293–94; insurgent identity, 147; martyrdom in, 157; ombudsman's office, 222

embedded ethnography, 10–13, 17–19, 24–26

emotions: and activism, 23, 146–48, 156–57, 159, 304; at the U.N., 204–5; connection to victims, 150–52, 162–63, 167–68; in state officials, 225, 250. *See also* fear

EPL (Popular Liberation Army), 43, 129, 239, 252

Equipo Nizkor, 234

Escobar, Pablo, 48, 52, 105, 315n20

European Parliament, 184

European Union, 117, 212, 230, 284

FARC (Revolutionary Armed Forces of Colombia), 33; Bojaya attack, 287–88; female members of, 54; history, 41–42; peace talks with, 68, 91–92, 100, 112, 125, 131, 133, 137, 139, 141, 164, 235, 237–39, 252, 262, 264, 270, 273–74, 276, 279, 281–82, 287; relationship with Patriotic Union, 40, 127; resources, 44–45; taxing of coca crops, 50, 100; at the U.N., 199

fear, 22–23, 151–52, 154, 230, 245

Fedefam, 206

Ferguson, James, 144

Fernandez Mafla, Father Tiberio de, 56–60

Filo Gringo, 239

Fiscalía (Attorney General), 61, 218, 226, 232, 234, 247, 265, 282, 284; Human Rights Unit of, 112, 230, 337n7

Fisher, William, 110

Flórez, Gloria, 27, 75, 85–86, 88–89, 101, 116–17, 127–29, 132, 149, 155, 159, 188; at the UN, 191–92

foco theory of guerrilla warfare, 42

Ford Foundation, 59, 118–19, 153, 201, 219, 327n7

Foreign Ministry (Cancellería), 17, 226, 230

Freedom House, 198

Freire, Paulo, 90

Frente Luis Carlos Cardenas Arbelaez, 56

fumigation, 50, 188–89

funding: of NGOs, 59, 117, 144, 152,
    162, 192; of state agencies, 215, 225,
    229, 231–33, 252; U.S. government,
    123, 188
Funprocep, 94

La Gabarra massacre, 238–41, 281
Gaitán, Jorge Eliécer, 37, 39, 91, 313n8
Gaitán, Pilar, 272
Galeano, Eduardo, 87
Gallón, Gustavo, 28, 83–84, 114, 118,
    201, 205, 208
Garcia, Fr. Omar, 156–57
García Márquez, Gabriel, 81, 189, 240,
    290
Garcia Peña, Daniel, 171
Garzón, Lucho, 129
Gaviria, Cesar, 62
gay and lesbian rights activism, 167–72
General Administrative Special Direc-
    torate for Human Rights, (Dirección
    General Unidad Administrativa Espe-
    cial para los Derechos Humanos), 228
Geneva conventions, 6, 65, 165
genocide: expansion of definition of, 128;
    military views of, 287–88
Ghosh, Amitov, 180
Gill, Lesley, 301
Giraldo, Fr. Javier, 28, 59, 112, 115
Giraldo, Josué, 155–56
global imaginaries, 177–79, 182,
    185–86
globalization, folk understandings of,
    178, 182
Golconda, 77–78, 149
Gómez, Jorge (radical lawyer), 93–94
Gómez, Laureano, 37, 46
Gómez, Rafael, 93–94
Gómez Hurtado, Àlvaro, 129
Goodwin, Jeff, 147
Grabe, Vera, 54
Grandin, Greg, 302
Guatemala, research on, 23; peace pro-
    cess, 26, 68, 302, 343n2
guerrilla forces, 42, 53, 96–241, 265,
    266, 268; critiques of, 163–64; illicit
    drugs, 262; Quintín Lame indigenous
    guerrilla movement, 129, 312n4; in
    Trujillo, 56. See also ELN; EPL; FARC
Guevara, Che, 42, 86–87, 96, 153, 251
Gupta, Akhil, 217
Gutierrez, Gustavo, 77

habeas corpus, 88
Hague Conventions, 164
Haymarket Rebellion, 87
Hector Abad Permanent Committee for
    the Defense of Human Rights in
    Medellín, 139, 156, 224
humanitarian crisis, 66–67, 321n39; dis-
    cussed at the U.N., 205; missions as
    part of human rights work, 92–93,
    249; role of the military, 262
humanitarian dialogues, 140–41, 331n13
human rights: activists, as victims, 23–24,
    155–56, 160–61; critiques of, 8, 101–
    2, 300–303; documentation, 120–21,
    135–37, 144, 243–44; economic and
    cultural rights, 101; histories and frame-
    works, 3–4, 6–10, 10–103, 219, 221,
    307n1, 309nn3–5; local committees,
    1–3, 89–91, 94–95; narrative produc-
    tion, 19–20, 121–22, 140, 142–44,
    171; workshops, 86, 88, 90–91, 101,
    108, 113, 122, 125–27, 134–44, 162–
    63, 232. See also military; NGO human
    rights activism; state human rights
    agencies
Human Rights Internet, 197
Human Rights Observatory, 229
Human Rights Watch (HRW), 11, 17,
    112, 130, 156, 160, 170, 177, 179,
    181, 218, 230, 250, 263, 267, 332n6;
    relationship with CCJ, 119
Hunt, Lynn, 7

ICRC (International Committee of the
    Red Cross), 7, 16, 65, 70, 231, 269,
    283, 299, 322n40
IHL (international humanitarian law), 6–
    7, 153, 162–67, 182, 246, 299, 329n8,
    330n9
illegal armed groups, 20. See also AUC;
    ELN; EPL; FARC; guerrilla forces;
    paramilitary groups
impunity, 216–17, 230, 247, 255, 266
independent republics, 42
indigenous communities, 34, 54, 129;
    activism at the U.N., 211; in Mexico,
    219
Institute for Grassroots Training (ICP),
    114
InterAmerican Human Rights Commis-
    sion, 55, 60–61, 63, 112, 115, 117,
    119, 128, 131, 189, 190, 224
InterAmerican Human Rights Court, 117
Inter-American Institute of Human Rights
    in Costa Rica, 122, 130
Intercongregational Commission for Jus-
    tice and Peace. See Justice and Peace
international activism, 144–45, 177–82,
    183; alternative visions, 187–89; cri-
    tiques of, 210–13, 300–303; history
    of, 189–92; at the U.N., 192–214, 305

International Bill of Human Rights, 193
international community, 175–76, 185
International Covenant on Civil and
  Political Rights, 193
International Covenant on Economic,
  Social, and Cultural Rights, 193
International Declaration of Human
  Rights, 179
International League for Liberation and
  the Rights of Peoples, 103
International Service for Human Rights,
  201
International Working Group, 208
Internet, 87, 196–97, 274–75

Jackson, Stephen, 12
José Alvéar Restrepo Lawyer's Collective,
  116–17, 153–54, 185, 201
Justice and Peace, 17, 59, 60, 63, 64, 112,
  115, 116, 155

Keck, Margaret, 10, 124, 183
kidnapping, 33, 44, 51, 69, 100, 164
Kirk, Robin, 156
knowledge, production of, 9, 143, 150,
  294, 301
Korean War, 46, 260

Lara Bonilla, Rodrigo, 51, 105
Latin American Council of Bishops, 78
Latin American Working Group, 263
law: CINEP legal strategy, 89; Colombian,
  88; international, 5, 83, 107–8, 118
Law 11 of 1986, 126. See also electoral
  reforms
Law 48, 51
Law 199 of 1995, 228
Law 288, 17, 63, 117, 131
Leahy Amendment, 266, 273, 299
Ledher, Carlos, 48
the Left, 68, 73, 86–88, 103–4, 108,
  124, 148–51, 267, 323n3; armed left,
  95–101; coming to power, 126; parties
  of, 75–76, 81, 100, 126, 128
Leninism, 92, 97
Levitt, Peggy, 8
Liberal Party, 36–39, 41–42, 45–46, 56,
  76, 129, 167, 313n8
liberation theology, 34, 56, 77–78, 157,
  323n4. See also Golconda
Loaiza, Henry "The Scorpion," 57, 60, 62
Londoño, José Santacruz, 48
López Trujillo, Msgr. Alfonso, 78
Lovemen, Mara, 147

M-19: April 19 Guerrilla Movement, 40,
  43–44, 57, 60, 82–83, 89, 100, 129,
131, 191, 198, 266, 272, 314n14;
M-19 Democratic Movement, 44,
  69; at the U.N., 226
Magdalena Valley: human rights activism
  in, 91, 228, 257, 302; paramilitary
  activity in, 51, 52, 85
Manuel Cepeda Foundation, 204
Manz, Beatriz, 23
Mao Zedong, 280
Mapiripán massacre, 53, 239, 316n27
Marcowitz, Lisa, 110
marijuana trade, 48
Marks, Thomas, 15
martyrdom, 157–58, 160, 162, 328n2
Marxism, 41, 43, 78, 81, 92, 101, 267.
  See also communism
MAS, 156
Masaraza, Almudena, 210
massacres, 73, 161, 218, 240, 291, 299;
  Buga, 285; Chengue, 233–36, 239,
  339n14; of FARC dissidents, 100;
  La Gabarra, 238, 281; Mapiripán,
  53, 239, 316n27; Trujillo, 32, 55,
  294; in Urabá, 227
McClintock, Cynthia, 175
Medellín Cartel, 48–49, 69, 224; and
  paramilitary groups, 51, 105
media coverage of Colombia, 263; Alternativa, 17, 86, 224; CNN, 200; Los
  Angeles Times, 263; New York Times,
  11, 198, 263; El Tiempo, 69–70, 80,
  112, 230, 280, 281; Time magazine,
  266; Wall Street Journal, 112; Washington Post, 112, 233, 263
Mejía, Vicente, 77
Menchú, Rigoberta, 23, 203
Méndez, Juan, 130, 250
Mercado Pelufo, Rodrigo Antiono
  ("cadena"), 234
Merry, Sally Engle, 8, 110, 188, 300–
  301, 313n5
militancia, 72, 75–76, 81, 92, 96, 98,
  148, 101, 151
military: abuse of conscripts, 279, 284;
  employment in, 259–60, 262; and
  human rights, 253–54, 256–58, 271,
  269, 286, 287, 298; human rights reporting, 284–88; institutional history,
  45–47; letter about the Chenge massacre, 235; participation in human rights
  commission, 243–45; participation in
  Trujillo Commission, 63–64, 297; public relations, 286–87; relationship with
  paramilitary forces, 264–65; relationship with U.S. doctrine and ideology,
  258, 260–62, 273; relation to civilian
  government, 47–48; relation to society,

military *(continued)*
259–60; research with, 14–16, 19, 20; rights in the 1991 Constitution, 130; role in counternarcotics, 262, 263; role in the Palace of Justice, 44; training offered by, 279–84; as victim, 258, 270–73. *See also* Colombian Armed Forces
military academy, 45, 112
military court system, 82, 88
military dictatorship: in Colombia, 38, 46; in Southern Cone, 10, 86, 104, 199–200, 309n3
Million Friends Network, 271
MINGA (Association for Alternative Social Education), 116, 153, 155, 159, 185, 188–89
Ministry of Culture, 68
Ministry of the Interior, 17, 66, 228, 230, 247, 252
mística, 148, 150–51
mobilizing shame, 9, 187, 292
Montoya, Omaira, 81
MORENA (National Renovation Movement), 52
Mothers of the Plaza de Mayo, 89, 203, 206, 310n3
Movement for Homosexual Liberation, 168

National Committee of Victims of the Guerrillas (VIDA), 111
National Front, 38, 39, 46, 81, 98, 126, 199
National Human Rights Ombudsman's Office (Defensoria del Pueblo), 17, 60–61, 64, 93, 130, 215–16, 218, 226–27, 230–31, 236, 242–45, 248–49, 251–52, 254, 283, 288, 295
National Security Doctrine, 261
National Security Statute, 82
Navarro Wolff, Antonio (M-19), 129
Nelson, Diane, 25
networks, 11; information flow, 120–21; in NGO activism, 88, 103, 119, 183–84; nodes in, 179, 181, 183–84; of state human rights agencies, 228, 248
NGO human rights activism: attitude toward guerrillas, 99–101, 150, 154, 163, 165–68; Catholic and Communist influence, 106, 148, 157–59; discourse, 152; production of credible information, 118, 134–38, 143–44, 169–70; professionalization of 107–9, 113–14, 135, 146, 149–50, 152–53, 204–5, 213; relationship to peace activism, 71, 82–83, 131–34; role in Trujillo Com-

mission, 59, 116; as state of emergency, 23, 65, 160; at the U.N., 205–6, 208–9, 300; U.S. NGOs, 188, 263, 304, 307n11; World Forum for Human Rights in Vienna, 112. *See also* human rights
NGOs (non-governmental organizations), 110–11
North-South Foundation, 198
Norwegian Refugee Council, 67

OAS, 184, 229, 232, 267, 269, 284; rights mechanisms, 10, 61, 189
Ochoa, Ana Maria, 68
Office of the Presidential Adviser for Human Rights, 236
O'Grady, Mary A., 112
OIDHACO (International Office of Human Rights Action on Colombia), 120
Oquist, Paul, 39
Ospina Ovalle, Carlos, 270
Oxfam, 67, 152, 205

País Libre (Free Country), 69, 322n45
Palacé Battalion, 62, 285–86
Palace of Justice, 232; 1985 takeover, 57, 100
Palacios, Marco, 35, 39
Panama Canal, 37, 313n7
paramilitary groups: ACCU, 142; connections to state, 241, 265, 275; history, 47, 50–53, 70, 92, 139–41, 155, 224–27, 239, 242, 249, 251, 284, 287, 298–300; and illicit drug operations, 49–51, 105, 239–40; legal basis of, 51, 165; new forms of violence, 63, 298–300; public relations campaign, 53
paramilitary leaders, 52; Carlos Castaño, 299; Henry "The Scorpion" Loaiza, 57, 60, 62; Rodrigo Antiono Mercado Pelufo ("cadena"), 234
Pastrana, Andres, 68, 70, 71, 131, 164, 189, 228, 237, 281
Paternina, Yolanda, 236
Patrice Lumumba Peoples' Friendship University of Russia, 182
Pax Christi, 201
Paz Colombia, 132, 133
peace: body as the first territory of, 172; negotiations, 68, 69, 131–32, 237; political peacemaking, 132–34
Peace Brigades International, 156, 173, 234
Peace Community, 264–65
Pécaut, Daniel, 39
Peña, Manuel Vicente, 112
people's tribunals, 102–3

PEPES (People Persecuted by Pablo Escobar), 49, 315n20
Perez, Diego, 168
Perez, Henry, 52
Permanent Assembly of Civil Society for Peace, 70, 132
Permanent Committee for the Defense of Human Rights, 82, 84, 88–89, 93, 114, 128, 154, 158, 190; Alvaro Tirado's membership in, 223–24
personeros, 125–26, 128, 140–43, 226, 235, 248, 288; letter about the Chengue massacre, 235
Peru, 48–50, 66, 118–19, 330n4
Pinzón, Hector, 158
Pizarro, Carlos, 83
Pizarro, Eduardo, 40, 83
Plan Colombia, 123, 132, 188, 263
Planeta Paz, 171–72
Planning Department, 229, 231
police, 46, 142, 154, 166, 230, 262, 273, 278
political peacemaking, 132
political prisoners, 86. See also CSPP
Polo Democrático de Izquierda, 128
Popular Feminine Organization, 242
poverty, 32, 78, 165–66, 312n1; identification with, 157–58, 161–63; military views of, 261
Presidential Special Adviser for Human Rights (Consejeria Presidencial), 223, 225–37, 232, 248
Pressure and Follow-Up Committee (Comité de Seguimiento y Impulse), 227, 238
Prieto, Jaime, 124, 185–87
Procuraduría (Inspector General), 61, 226, 232, 234, 236, 250, 274, 281, 284–85
Project Counseling Services, 67
psychological operations, 261, 275–78, 340n9, 341nn11–12
public secret, 292–94
public transcript, 292–95, 297–98
Push into Southern Colombia, 264
Putumayo, 9, 57, 264–65

Quiñonoz, Rodrigo, 233–34, 236
Quintín Lame (indigenous guerrilla movement), 129
Quiroga, Jahel, 28, 92, 127, 128, 185

Reagan, Ronald, 293
Red Cross. See ICRC
Redepaz, 69, 322n45
Reiniciar, 128
Rendon Group, 286–87, 342n17
reverse agrarian reform, 49

Revolutionary Socialist Union (URS), 81–82
Revolutionary Workers' Party, 129
Ricardo Franco Front, 100
right to intimacy, 168
right to rebellion and collective defense, 73, 99, 104
right-wing NGOs, 111–12
Robert F. Kennedy Memorial Human Rights Prize, 149
Rodriguez, Carlos, 75, 81, 83–84, 114, 190–91; at the U.N., 200–203
Rodriguez, Rogelio, 57
Rojas Pinilla, Gustavo, 38, 40, 46, 315n19
Rojas Rodriguez, Jorge, 117, 132–33
Roldan, Mary, 45
Romero, Amanda, 89, 102, 104
Romero, Flor Alba, 74
Roosevelt, Franklin, 101
Russell Tribunal, 103

sacrifice, celebration of, 160
Samper, Ernesto, 59, 61–63, 66, 68, 227, 231, 266–67, 272–73
Sánchez, Gonzalo, 39
Santos, Enrique, 80
Santos, Francisco, 69, 322n44
Save the Children, 67, 249
Schirmer, Jennifer, 19
School of the Americas, 277
Scott, James, 292
Search Committee for Peace (Comité de Búsqueda de la Paz), 70
security, 245, 258
Seeds of Freedom Corporation (Corporación Semillas de Libertad), 185
self defense, agrarian, 98
self-defense groups. See paramilitary groups
September 11 (2001), 198, 304
Serpa, Horacio, 129
Serrano, Jose Rosso, 262, 273
Shifter, Michael, 118, 119
Shining Path, 23, 330n8
Sikkink, Kathryn, 10, 124, 183
silence: in accounts of violence, 23–24; when confronted with violence, 173–74; denial, 295
Silva Bravo, General Alberto, 238, 241, 281
Slaughter, Ann-Marie, 221
social cleansing campaigns, 170
social movements, 75, 79, 88, 152, 325n18; relating to armed movements, 97; identity, 147
Social Science Research Council, 13

Social Solidarity Network, 66
solidarity, 73, 78–79, 86; committees,
    115; groups, 107; international soli-
    darity, 177, 187, 190, 213; political
    solidarity, 157; transition to profes-
    sional human rights NGOs, 149
Soviet Union, 7, 224
Spanish Republican War, 87
Speed, Shannon, 219
Stalinism, 92
Starn, Orin, 23
state: as enemy, 104; as ideal, 5; repres-
    sive nature of, 166–67; theorizing
    bureaucracy, 216–17
state human rights agencies: in Canada,
    220; in Mexico, 219; and production
    of impunity, 216–19; relationship
    with NGOs, 125–28; in Trujillo, 60–
    61, 63–64; in the United States, 221,
    337n5. See also individual agency
    entries
state of siege decrees, 40, 104, 130
statistics, 33; production of, 118; on vio-
    lence against gays and lesbians, 169
Stoll, David, 23
student movement, 42, 85–86
Supreme Court (Colombian), 88

Taussig, Michael, 22, 292, 294
Taylor, Francis, 304
testimonio, 171–72, 190, 317n30
Tice, Karen, 110
Tirado, Alvaro, 223–28, 298
Tirofijo (FARC commander), 112
Torres, Camilo, 43, 77, 79, 86, 96, 115,
    148–49, 158, 167
torture, 31, 38, 55, 89, 142, 161, 189,
    304
transgovernmental activism, 216, 220,
    221, 231
Trujillo: Commission, 28, 30, 32, 55,
    59, 60–64, 116, 294–98; history of
    region, 317–20n31
Tsing, Ana, 177–78
Turbay, Julio César, 81–82, 190, 224,
    324n9

Umaña, Eduardo, 114, 116, 156, 326n5
UNDP (United Nations Development
    Program), 70, 224
UNHCHR (United Nations High Com-
    missioner for Human Rights), 169,
    198–99, 204, 209–11; office in
    Colombia, 199, 209–10, 249, 335n24
U.N. Human Rights Commission, 14,
    16, 29, 120, 136, 179–81; Colombian
    lobbying at, 199–209, 300, 305, 306;

history of, 191–95; NGO participa-
    tion in, 195–213
UNICEF, 11, 153
unions, 42, 81, 83, 86–87, 97, 187; case
    discussed at workshop, 138–43; doc-
    tors', 79; oil workers', 91, 93; and gay
    rights, 169
UNIR (National Revolutionary Leftist
    Union), 37
United Front (Frente Unido), 77, 79, 82
United Nations, 10, 61, 150, 184, 187,
    213, 229, 236, 269; conference in
    Durban, 198, 334n16; Council on
    Human Rights, 192; Human Rights
    Center, 200; Human Rights Commit-
    tee, 117, 131, 190; missions in Central
    America, 68; research at, 180
United Nations High Commissioner for
    Refugees, 67
universities, public, 74, 85
University Solidarity Committee, 85–86
U.N. special rapporteurs, 194, 332n7;
    travel to Colombia, 200; for women,
    206
U.N. Working Groups, 120, 194, 206
UP (Patriotic Union), 40, 84, 92, 97,
    127–29, 156–57, 167, 204
Ureña Jaramillo, Major Alirio Antonio,
    62
Uribe, President Alvaro, 51, 112, 164,
    229, 236, 249, 305
USAID (U.S. Agency for International
    Development), 123, 188, 229, 233,
    236, 238, 248, 252
U.S. Congress, 11, 18, 20, 121, 181,
    188, 230, 300, 321n37; decertification
    of Colombia, 62; delegation to Colom-
    bia, 263–66; four freedoms speech to,
    101; military human rights forum at,
    269; and the public secret, 293–94;
    relationship with Serrano, 273
U.S. Labor Education Project, 187
U.S. labor movement, 87
U.S. military assistance and training,
    260–63, 270, 273, 277–78, 286–87,
    304–5
USO (Unión Sindical Obrera, oil
    workers' union), 91, 93
U.S. State Department, 31, 180, 263,
    267, 269; as a human rights agency,
    337n5; human rights certification, 188

Valle, Jesus, 128, 138, 156, 167
Vanguardia Liberal, 245
Vargas, Fernando, 111
Vargas Velásquez, Alejo, 104
Vasquez, Maria Eugenia, 54

Vázquez Carrizosa, Alfredo, 84, 130, 158
Velandia Hurtado, Alvaro, 266–68
verification missions, 249
Vice President's Human Rights Program, 233–34, 236–38, 248–49
Vietnam War, 87, 103, 268
violence, 291; classifying, 4, 53, 138, 172–74, 299, 304, 329n7; in Colombian history, 32–33; counterinsurgency, 45–47; drug trafficking, 47–50; insurgent, 41–45; national narratives of, 21–23; new forms of, 63, 298–300; partisan, 35–41, 72; production of knowledge about, 4, 145, 301–2; statistics, 33
La Violencia, 36–38, 46, 76, 96, 167, 260, 319n31
Vivanco, José Miguel, 112

War of a Thousand Days, 36–37
war on terror, 61, 304–5

Washington Office on Latin America (WOLA), 11, 14, 16, 18, 121, 160, 177, 263–66
Western Hemisphere Institute for Security Cooperation, 277
Whitfield, Teresa, 293
Wilson, Scott, 233
witnessing, as transformative experience, 9, 290–91
witness protection, 228, 232
women, 54, 317n28; women's rights, 7, 110, 222
Wood, Elizabeth, 147
World Food Program, 249
World Organization against Torture, 191, 234
World Trade Organization, protests against, 198
World Vision, 205

Zuleta, León, 168–96

CALIFORNIA SERIES IN PUBLIC ANTHROPOLOGY

The California Series in Public Anthropology emphasizes the anthropologist's role as an engaged intellectual. It continues anthropology's commitment to being an ethnographic witness, to describing, in human terms, how life is lived beyond the borders of many readers' experiences. But it also adds a commitment, through ethnography, to reframing the terms of public debate — transforming received, accepted understandings of social issues with new insights, new framings.

Series Editor: Robert Borofsky (Hawaii Pacific University)

Contributing Editors: Philippe Bourgois (University of Pennsylvania), Paul Farmer (Partners in Health), Alex Hinton (Rutgers University), Carolyn Nordstrom (University of Notre Dame), and Nancy Scheper-Hughes (U.C. Berkeley)

University of California Press Editor: Naomi Schneider

1. *Twice Dead: Organ Transplants and the Reinvention of Death,* by Margaret Lock

2. *Birthing the Nation: Strategies of Palestinian Women in Israel,* by Rhoda Ann Kanaaneh (with a foreword by Hanan Ashrawi)

3. *Annihilating Difference: The Anthropology of Genocide,* edited by Alexander Laban Hinton (with a foreword by Kenneth Roth)

4. *Pathologies of Power: Health, Human Rights, and the New War on the Poor,* by Paul Farmer (with a foreword by Amartya Sen)

5. *Buddha Is Hiding: Refugees, Citizenship, the New America,* by Aihwa Ong

6. *Chechnya: Life in a War-Torn Society,* by Valery Tishkov (with a foreword by Mikhail S. Gorbachev)

7. *Total Confinement: Madness and Reason in the Maximum Security Prison,* by Lorna A. Rhodes

8. *Paradise in Ashes: A Guatemalan Journey of Courage, Terror, and Hope,* by Beatriz Manz (with a foreword by Aryeh Neier)

9. *Laughter Out of Place: Race, Class, Violence, and Sexuality in a Rio Shantytown,* by Donna M. Goldstein

10. *Shadows of War: Violence, Power, and International Profiteering in the Twenty-First Century,* by Carolyn Nordstrom

11. *Why Did They Kill? Cambodia in the Shadow of Genocide,* by Alexander Laban Hinton (with a foreword by Robert Jay Lifton)

12. *Yanomami: The Fierce Controversy and What We Can Learn from It,* by Robert Borofsky

13. *Why America's Top Pundits Are Wrong: Anthropologists Talk Back,* edited by Catherine Besteman and Hugh Gusterson

14. *Prisoners of Freedom: Human Rights and the African Poor,* by Harri Englund

15. *When Bodies Remember: Experiences and Politics of AIDS in South Africa,* by Didier Fassin

16. *Global Outlaws: Crime, Money, and Power in the Contemporary World,* by Carolyn Nordstrom

17. *Archaeology as Political Action,* by Randall H. McGuire

18. *Counting the Dead: The Culture and Politics of Human Rights Activism in Colombia,* by Winifred Tate

Display: Sabon
Compositor: BookMatters, Berkeley
Cartographer: Bill Nelson
Printer and binder: Sheridan Books, Inc.